RALLYCOURSE

The World's Leading Rally Annual

HAZLETON PUBLISHING

Publisher
Richard Poulter

Editor
David Williams

Executive Publisher
Elizabeth Le Breton

Art Editor
Julian Bigg

Production Manager
George Greenfield

Production Controller
Peter Lovering

Advertising Co-ordinator
Nigel Bellwood

Results and Statistics
Paul Haines

Chief Photographer
Reinhard Klein

Rallycourse

Published *by*
Hazleton Publishing
3 Richmond Hill, Richmond
Surrey TW10 6RE

Typeset *by*
Bigg Sense Design
25 Calvin Street, Spitalfields
London E1 6NW
on Apple Macintosh™

Colour Reproduction *by*
Adroit Photo Litho Ltd
Birmingham

Printed in England *by*
Ebenezer Baylis & Son Ltd
Worcester

ISBN: 1 874557 25 X

Distributors

United Kingdom
Bookpoint Ltd
39 Milton Park
Abingdon
Oxfordshire OX14 4TD

North America
Motorbooks International
PO Box 1
729 Prospect Avenue
Osceola
Wisconsin 54020, USA

Australia
Technical Book & Magazine Co. Pty
289-299 Swanston Street
Melbourne
Victoria 3000

New Zealand
David Bateman Ltd
'Golden Heights'
32–34 View Road
Glenfield
Auckland 10

South Africa
Motorbooks
341 Jan Smuts Avenue
Craighall Park
Johannesburg

Contents

Toyota and Juha Kankkunen made an irresistible combination in 1993, rounding off the year with victory on the RAC (title page). Subaru was always in the hunt, Ari Vatanen taking second place on the Rally Australia.

Acknowledgements

Photographs appearing in *Rallycourse 1993-94* have been contributed by: Reinhard Klein (Chief Photographer), Hugh Bishop, Pascal Huit, LAT Photographic, Gavin Lodge, Les Kolczak and Colin Taylor Productions. Maps supplied by Castrol.

The Editor of *Rallycourse* wishes to thank the following for their energy, support and good nature during the compilation of the 1993-94 edition: Julian Bigg, Hugh Bishop, Andrzej Borowczyk, Liz Le Breton, Amanda Campbell, David Campbell, Kay Edge, Paul Evans, Mike Greasley, George Greenfield, Malcolm Griffiths, Paul Haines, Pascal Huit, Terry Kaby, Reinhard Klein, Gavin Lodge, Peter Lovering, Martin Sharp, Steve Small and Jerry Williams

GGK EMOTION
MOËT
BRUT IMPÉRIAL
MOËT
BRUT IMPÉRIAL
MOËT
MOËT & CHANDON
250ème Anniversaire
1743 ★ 1993

FOREWORD

by Juha Kankkunen

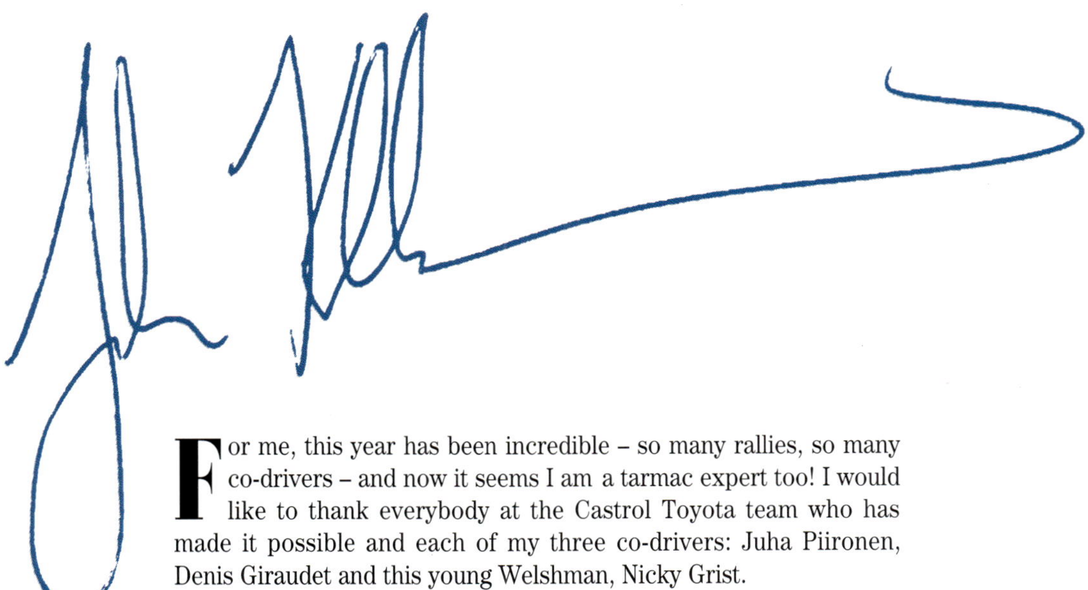

For me, this year has been incredible – so many rallies, so many co-drivers – and now it seems I am a tarmac expert too! I would like to thank everybody at the Castrol Toyota team who has made it possible and each of my three co-drivers: Juha Piironen, Denis Giraudet and this young Welshman, Nicky Grist.

So much has happened and it will be nice to look back at the year in *Rallycourse*. I think this time Mr Editor Williams will have to write something good about me!

AERODY

In designing the new Toyota Supra, we took on the heavyweights in the world of the supercar.

The Italians would describe that sweeping bodywork as super leggera. Because aluminium and newly formulated plastics lightened the car by 220 pounds.

For the Germans, the engine has Wagnerian overtones. It's got 24 valves, six cylinders and twin turbos that work in sequence. Linked to a 6-speed manual or 4-speed automatic gearbox, it delivers a stirring 326 bhp from just three litres.

To put this in perspective, the new Supra can reac 60mph from zero in 4.9 seconds. In other words, it's th car in front of the Ferrari 348 and the Porsche 911 Turbo

Slip into the leather seats. Seal yourself into th thermostatically air-conditioned cabin. And reassure you self that this is also the car in front on safety features.

They go far beyond the driver and passenger air bag and side-impact bars.

Take the Supra's electronic traction control system. I

* SOURCE: 'WHAT CAR?' JULY 1993. MODEL ILLUSTRATED SUPRA TURBO, £37,500 INCLUDING VAT BUT EXCLUSIVE OF DELIVERY CHARGE OF £370 (INC. VAT), NUMBER PLATES AND ROAD FUND LICENC

NAMITE.

never feeds the wheels more power than they can handle.

There's the new 4-channel ABS system, too, with spirally ventilated discs. It lets you brake from 60 mph to standstill in 120 feet. In a straight line, even in the wet.

And that rear wing heightens your control. With the speed-activated front spoiler, it harnesses air to push the Supra squarely against the tarmac.

At every stage of its development, the new Supra was track tested by racing drivers across the world. That's why every inch of this car makes you feel at one with it.

At £37,500, it comes with Toyota's comprehensive warranty, three years or 60,000 miles, and 3 years' RAC membership.

Only a few Supras are available this year from selected Toyota dealers. For your nearest, call 0800 777555 free.

Obviously, these cars will go very quickly.

THE NEW Supra

CALL 0737 768585 FOR TAX-FREE AND EXPORT SALES. THE TOYOTA INFORMATION SERVICE IS OPERATED ON BEHALF OF TOYOTA (GB) LIMITED. SEE DEALER FOR DETAILS OF OUR 3-YEAR/60,000-MILE WARRANTY.

THE CAR IN FRONT IS A TOYOTA

Editor's Introduction

THE GREAT DEBATE

There are precious few conclusions to draw beyond the fact that rallying is in a state of flux. The usual pleas for stability have been drowned by a mounting clamour for change since, above all, the past season has been distinguished by a hypnotic fascination with the bottom line. Money talks and what money is saying at the moment is that, unless television coverage improves, money is going elsewhere.

The prospect of hanging has concentrated minds wonderfully. After years of drift, the sport is on the verge of institutional reform that could safeguard its survival into the next century. The fiercest rivals have found that they have all kinds of things in common and speculation as to the future shape of the World Rally Championship and rally cars has been intense; indeed, discussion of the sport's future has at times obscured what is happening in the present. While the reformers insist to a man that rallies must be shorter and more compact – farewell to the waiting game and to nights out of bed – the London – Sydney Marathon was revived for historic cars and ran so smoothly that plans were instantly announced for another logistical nightmare, also for old cars, to commemorate the 25th anniversary of the London – Mexico Marathon. Competitors and the press generally liked this atavistic celebration of endurance, adventure and all the things that the Rally Australia is not. In its eagerness to please the television moguls, the rule makers and opinion formers need to remember that covering great distances through rugged landscape is an essential part of its appeal – otherwise rallycross would be one of the great television sports. Rallying is now a well-established, if somewhat neglected sport with traditions that are often worth preserving. There is plenty of room for improvement, but it doesn't follow that it needs to re-invent itself. That said, the success of the London – Sydney was further proof that it is becoming a highly specialised, even

Photo Hugh Bishop

compartmentalised sport: once, it might have been divided solely into road and stage rally followers, whereas now it is possible even to categorise historic supporters and Nick Brittan, the man behind the London – Sydney, maintained that modern techniques and costs would make it quite impractical to run such a long distance event for contemporary vehicles. It was a thoroughly practical remark, but one might infer that modern rallying is in danger of losing some of its magic.

In spite of the climate of uncertainty, it has been a good, even a heartening year. Aside from the new enthusiasm for co-operation off the stages, there have been unforgettable individual performances on them: one thinks of Juha Kankkunen's fourth world title, and the burgeoning talents of François Delecour and Colin McRae, properly rewarded at last.

We have examined some of these concerns in the pages ahead. Jerry Williams, rallying's doughtiest supporter in Fleet Street, has squarely tackled the television issue in a provocative, wide-ranging article that exposes some uncomfortable truths. Continuing the debate on the sport's shape and purpose, David Campbell takes a dispassionate look at rally raids, and the cold war between Citroën and Mitsubishi; there is no British writer better qualified to examine this specialised offshoot of stage rallying.

Meanwhile, Martin Sharp reflects on the spectacular resurgence at Ford, dissecting the ultimate homologation special, the Escort Cosworth, with the man who brought it into being – John Wheeler. We also take a closer look at one of the key players in the Ford revival, Miki Biasion.

Rallying has become a multi-faceted sport and Amanda Campbell delves into one of the areas developing at the greatest speed: medical and physical care for rally drivers. She uncovers the astonishing neglect of key figures in a multi-million pound activity and the growing influence of the team doctor. David Campbell and Paul Evans provide authoritative comment on the state of the major British Championships, the international series and the Mintex-backed national contest.

There is one final, indispensable ingredient – the remarkable work of *Rallycourse's* Chief Photographer, Reinhard Klein.

Rallying has a rich history and needs to preserve its contrasts. Could any other sport encompass Les Johnson's London – Sydney Mustang (top left), Armin Schwarz's Lancer in the snows of a ferociously demanding RAC (lower right) and a close encounter for one of Toyota's drivers with the wildlife of Africa?

Shell
ULTIMATE PROTECTION FOR PERFORMANCE MOTORING
Shell HELIX
ULTRA 5W-40
FULLY SYNTHETIC MOTOR OIL
SUPERIOR PROTECTION FOR THE MODERN ENGINE
Shell HELIX
PLUS 10W-40
PREMIUM MOTOR OIL
DEPENDABLE PROTECTION FOR EVERYDAY MOTORING
Shell HELIX
STANDARD 15W-50
MOTOR OIL

Photo Pascal Huit

There was so much to celebrate in 1993 that it is hard to know where to start. There were new faces on the winners' rostrum, a restoration of the sort of white-hot competitiveness that typified 1990 and '91, which the 'Deltona' largely eradicated in 1992 and, above all, a long-awaited triumph at World Championship level for a British driver, Colin McRae. Yet the season was also characterised by a pervasive air of gloom. To look at, never mind listen to Ove Andersson, one wouldn't have guessed that Toyota Team Europe led the title race for much of the season and finally became the first Japanese firm to win the World Championship for Manufacturers. Other team managers were equally pessimistic. The economic imperative that disrupted the free-spending party in 1992 became stronger still. Soberly, they warned that rallying must change or die – or if not die, cease to be an international sport of any significance.

The sport's apparent health was no more than skin-deep in any case. There aren't very many people left at the party now and the trouble that a driver of Carlos Sainz's stature experienced in finding a new team for 1994 was the most eloquent proof of the team managers' case.

In such a climate, there was as much talk of the future as of the present. New rules or procedures were advocated for almost every facet of the sport, from the technical regulations to servicing, television coverage, reconnaissance and the formats of the rallies themselves. The sense of unease was not confined to team management, since there were also renewed signs of rebelliousness from the works drivers and co-drivers at the insane pressure exerted by a 13-round World Championship and ceaseless practising and testing. This wasn't simply a playboy lament at being made to work hard: there are drivers who welcome the idea of compact rallies that incorporate a press day, and shorter, more manageable routes that might be easier to televise.

The widespread sense of disquiet reflected a belief that some of the proposed changes were heading in entirely the wrong direction, not merely that the pace of change was far too slow. The technical regulations were a case in point. The FIA went back on its stated promise to announce new rules in the autumn, which simultaneously emphasised the depth of division and fanned the flames of uncertainty.

At times, it was possible to detect the whiff of vested interest rather than disinterested pleading. The manufacturer representatives who insisted that front-wheel drive Formula 2 cars would cost just as much as the current breed of turbocharged, four-wheel drive projectiles were apt to sound like small children who, on being told that they cannot have trifle, retort that jelly will also make them sick. Nevertheless, the alarm was real enough. At last, the major teams were prepared to contemplate a drastic transformation that may change the face of the sport entirely. Despite the emollient language that accompanied its launch, the formation of the World Rally Teams Association was a clear sign that they meant business. There were signs of change in Paris too, such as the appointment of Cesar Torres, the presiding genius of the Rally of Portugal, as the FIA's rally supremo, and the merging of the technical and manufacturers' committees. Whether anyone at the FIA is prepared to behave in a genuinely imaginative manner, or whether this more gentlemanly brand of motor sport will be riven by the sort of conflict that seems inseparable from Formula One are two of the most fascinating questions that the sport now faces.

In a sense, 1993 was the calm before the storm. There was a good deal of talk of change and a handful of key developments that lead in that direction, but little in the way of progress – or regression

Review of the Year

A SUMMER OF DISCONTENT

by David Williams

come to that – which can be held up for all to see. Yet there is a clear sense that rallying is on the brink of metamorphosis.

The obsession with the future was all the more pronounced, since there was more than enough going on in the present to occupy the most inquisitive mind. 1993 was a memorable and momentous season, not least because it marked the final overthrow of Lancia. In a sense, that alone proved that Group A has come of age. The fact that the Turin manufacturer failed to retain the makes' title for a seventh year was perhaps less extraordinary, but the speed and extent of its fall from grace was quite stunning. Remarkably, the team that had swept all before it in 1992 failed to win a single round of the World Championship – a fact that surprised the Jolly Club's rivals quite as much as the Italians themselves.

Even though Lancia had not so much entrusted its competition programme to the Milan-based Jolly Club as washed its hands of the sport, it is not easy to account for such a dramatic decline in the firm's fortunes. Development moves at a rapid pace in World Championship rallying but, as an engineer in a British team observed, not so rapidly as to turn a dominant car into junk overnight. Claudio Bortoletto, the Jolly Club Team Manager, suggested that a season that starts badly is likely to go on in the same vein. Perhaps he is right. Certainly, it took Sainz a while to get the measure of the Integrale and he had had three major accidents (including one in testing) by the middle of March. New parts, notably a higher-ratio steering rack, had to be made to adapt the car to his style; some of his rivals suggested that he never did master the Integrale, which is a much more nervous machine than the Celica, even in its ultimate form.

Much of the problem may have been simple bad luck. It was no fault of the team that both drivers crashed on the Monte, nor that Sainz did so again in Portugal and Australia. In other circumstances, the Spaniard might easily have won in Greece or New Zealand. For

Ford and Subaru pressed Toyota hard in 1993, the former collecting a string of successes with the new Escort, while Subaru readied a new car of its own. Meanwhile, Ari Vatanen took the old one to second in Perth (below).

whatever reason though, possibly a lack of funds, unreliability began to dog the Integrales, mysterious suspension breakages occurring in Corsica, Greece and Argentina. They would have been inconceivable in the old Abarth days.

Moreover, a lack of development did not help and contrasted sharply with the usual policy when Abarth held the reins. Lancia's success was built on being a step ahead of its rivals, whereas the Jolly Club pinned its hopes on the assumption that the car that had swept all before it in 1992 would certainly be no worse than anything else the following season. Once this proved to be some way from the truth, the effect on morale may have been just as important as any loss of performance. From an early stage, Sainz was convinced that the lack of new ideas and parts was a handicap, and he was casting around for something else to drive in 1994 long before the end of the season. Under the circumstances, it seems fair to ask whether he had his mind entirely on the job in hand. The absence of progress prompted Abarth's chief mechanic, Rino Buschiazzo, to depart for Astra and RAS in mid-season. When staff of his calibre begin to leave, the end is clearly at hand.

By the time Lamborghini Engineering was enlisted to redress the balance, it was too late. A battery of engine changes was introduced for Sanremo, whereupon Lancia endured the supreme humiliation – defeat at the hands of a privateer, Franco Cunico. If the car retained a future on gravel, it was plain that time had finally caught up with it on tarmac, in part because the 1993 rules, enforcing a higher weight limit and narrower tyres, affected the Integrale more than any other car. Ultimately, Bortoletto could not continue the run of success without factory support. He can hardly be blamed for the failure; quite simply, the Jolly Club isn't equipped to develop as well as run cars against full factory teams, especially when an organisation like Toyota Team Europe is said to be running through £50 million per year.

The natural beneficiary of Lancia's fall should have been TTE and, sure enough, 20 years after it came into being in a shed on a farm in Sweden, it confirmed its position as the colossus of rallying by taking its first clean sweep of manufacturers' and drivers' championships. It was by no means a straightforward success, however, for although the makes' title was clinched in Australia, with three rallies in hand, and even the drivers' series didn't go down to the wire for the first time since 1989, TTE had a good deal of trouble in beating Ford, since the purpose-built Escort Cosworth was without doubt the rally car of the year. The fact that Ford, which had initially regarded 1993 as a learning season rather than a full-scale championship assault, came so close to felling a well-established force may account for some of the minor criticism to which TTE was subjected. Andersson might have dismissed the charge out of hand, but there was a belief in some quarters that TTE would not have won had Lancia been seriously interested in the World Championship. According to this theory, it won the title with a comparatively unsophisticated car and a positively unadventurous transmission. Certainly, there was little sign that it always had an

What Britain's top rally drivers drive home.

The 4WD Subaru Legacy Saloon.

The full-time four wheel drive saloon they've driven home to win the British Rally Championship in 1991, 1992 and again in 1993.

And with stunning success in the Rally of New Zealand.

When Colin McRae powered his 555 Subaru Legacy to victory, becoming the first Briton ever to win a World Championship Rally overseas.

A car you can drive in a road-going version (2.0 MPFi, 2.2 MPFi or 2.0 Turbo).

Safe in the knowledge that its strength, reliability and surefootedness have all been proven on the world's toughest rallies.

The 4WD Subaru Legacy. The car Britain's best drive home.

For more information write to the address below or call 0753 696200.

SUBARU

THE WORLD'S FAVOURITE FOUR WHEEL DRIVE

2.0 MPFi GL FROM £13,149, 2.2 MPFi GX FROM £16,199, 2.0 4 CAM TURBO £18,499. PRICES CORRECT AT TIME OF GOING TO PRESS, EXCLUDE DELIVERY CHARGE TO DEALER PREMISES OF £330.00 (INC. VAT) (UK MAINLAND ONLY) NUMBER PLATES AND ROAD FUND LICENCE. SUBARU (UK) LTD., RYDER STREET, WEST BROMWICH, WEST MIDLANDS B70 0EJ. A SUBSIDIARY OF I.M. GROUP LTD.

extra ace up its sleeve, as Lancia usually did. Strange as it may seem, there was an element of nostalgia for the style with which Abarth ran rings round the opposition, even among those who used to be on the receiving end of Italian cunning.

Such criticism of TTE is bound to be unfair, because it cannot be proved, but it cannot be accused of letting the grass grow under its feet in any case. When the Sierra Cosworth 4x4 first appeared, Andersson commented that, on paper, it was the best rally car; the Escort is without doubt a major step forward. Given that Subaru enjoyed growing success with another longitudinally engined car, TTE faced a mounting problem in winning rallies with a transverse-engined coupé with an unfavourable weight distribution. The fact that it triumphed despite this theoretical disadvantage was the fruit of all kinds of labours, but a ceaseless quest to refine the Celica bulked large among them. Perhaps TTE didn't display Lancia's facility for moving the goalposts, turning the tables and generally outsmarting its rivals, but arguably it faced a harder task in beating cars that should have been superior the moment they left the drawing board.

Take the Catalonia Rally as a case in point. Ford conducted a massive asphalt test before the start of the season and the two works Escorts that turned up in Lloret de Mar were to all intents and purposes in Monte Carlo trim. In contrast, TTE arrived with a heavily modified engine management system, new brake-cooling scoops and a new, kevlar fan cowling that not only improved cooling and saved weight, but shifted mass towards the rear wheels. It denied that it was using traction control, but that had already been evaluated on a third car entered for Hannu Mikkola on the 1000 Lakes. Behind the scenes, it was hard at work on a sequential gearbox and, apparently, active suspension.

Ford won in Catalonia nevertheless, but the Celicas were good enough to beat Miki Biasion and thus ensure that Juha Kankkunen seized the drivers' crown. Faced with a superior car, TTE had done everything possible to refine its own (there was never much doubt that the Celica had more power than any of its rivals) and made the most of the traditional virtues of teamwork: it had a better all-round driving team than Ford, its tactical awareness was superior and it could call on a good deal more experience. Whereas the Köln squad knew every rally inside out, Ford tackled three rallies either for the first time or for the first time in a decade. TTE also possessed strength in depth. Apart from certain key staff, it could afford to rest a good proportion of its service crews at regular intervals. There was no guarantee that the same old faces would always crop up at service points, yet this wasn't a sign of weakness.

Toyota's success thus followed a traditional pattern: you don't need the best car if you've got everything else right. The strangest aspect of its championship victory was that it owed so much to Juha Kankkunen and so little to Didier Auriol, a combination who, between them, can justly claim to be masters of every event in the World Championship. 1993 was expected to be Auriol's year. It was manifestly unjust that he failed to win the 1992 World Championship and he had dominated Kankkunen to such a degree that one expected him to carry on in a similar vein in a new car and a new team. A spectacular, not to say controversial Monte Carlo victory suggested that only the colours and the car had changed, but he struggled to adapt to the Toyota thereafter and fell prey to a mixture of bad luck, and perhaps to trying too hard. There were a number of occasions when the sumpguard was smashed or ripped off the French Celica – the Acropolis, the 1000 Lakes and Australia spring to mind – and that never happened to the laid-back Kankkunen.

The tall Finn underwent the most extraordinary season. He should have been knocked sideways by the dreadful illness that struck down his long-time co-driver, Juha Piironen, while practising in Argentina. Despite Piironen's injunction to find another co-driver and get on with the job in hand, stitching together 11th-hour partnerships with Nicky Grist for two events and Denis Giraudet for the 1000 Lakes (when the Welshman dutifully returned to Armin Schwarz and Mitsubishi) looked like nothing more than a better alternative to doing the rallies alone. Yet Kankkunen thrived on adversity and, who knows, the shock of the new, winning Argentina and the 1000 Lakes convincingly. Teamed with the young, ambitious Grist on a permanent basis, the 1993 World Champion can only be described as a new man. Everyone at TTE remarked on the change, on the renewed competitive spirit and the thirst for success. Kankkunen and Grist not only enjoyed one another's company, but Kankkunen was even moved to remark that his English had improved no end!

Finland and Australia were crucial victories on events where Ford was weak or absent, but the most extraordinary performance came in Spain. Predictably, the French held the upper hand, François Delecour beating Auriol by precisely a minute. Kankkunen, however, was a revelation. Spurred on by Grist, he set fastest stage times, steamed back into the fray after a tyre blew out, looked set to overhaul a down-on-power Biasion even before the Escort's wastegate failed and expressed genuine enthusiasm for dry tarmac. Third place clinched his record-breaking fourth championship, but it also signalled a new development. Rejuvenated and highly motivated, it seems that there is nothing that Kankkunen cannot do and is not prepared to try in a rally car – which is all the more remarkable considering that he is the most experienced works driver and ought by rights to be the most jaded.

Losing both titles was ultimately a disappointment to Ford, yet this was Boreham's best season since it last used Escorts more than a decade ago and it far exceeded the team's wildest expectations at the begining of the year. It not only finished second in the manufacturers' series and got both its drivers into the championship lead at one point or another, but won five events – more in 12 months than in the previous 12 years. By the end of the season, the Escort was generally acknowledged as the tarmac car to beat. This was a remarkable performance. Certainly the Escort Cosworth owes a good deal to the Sierra and has been under development in its own right since 1990, but it was a new car, the team had not been to an event outside Europe since 1987 and, above all, it is still shackled by the constraints of operating within a big company, which vastly increase bureaucracy and costs. The last works team in the traditional sense of the term, Boreham proved that structures laid down in the 1950s and '60s can still work, which isn't to say that they are the best way of doing things.

The car was the star. The willingness to part with money and take on new events stemmed from the Escort Cosworth's instant success. Most of Ford's failings were the result of inexperience. The most demoralising and mystifying came in Australia, when the cars were drastically off the pace for no obvious reason, although reliability enabled Delecour to pick up third place nonetheless. No doubt the drivers' corresponding ignorance of the terrain played its part, but then McRae had never set foot in the country either and he held second for most of the rally. The difference was that Subaru had been prepared to go to the event before, even when it didn't stand a particularly good chance of winning the rally and none whatsoever of taking the World Championship. If Ford has an abiding weakness, it is a reluctance to commit itself whole heartedly. There is still a belief that rallying is first and foremost a useful marketing exercise and that coming second will just about do. When the drivers' championship was in the balance, Delecour felt that his chances of winning were minuscule, because he had contested the RAC only once before; Ford hadn't sent him in 1992. At the same time, Biasion expressed the wish that he could tackle the RAC in place of Catalonia, because

Lancia and Andrea Aghini (below) had a dreadfully disappointing year, whereas François Delecour had a pretty good one, even if the expression suggests otherwise.

Motorsport
Ford
Mobil
1
Mobil 1
K746 GOO

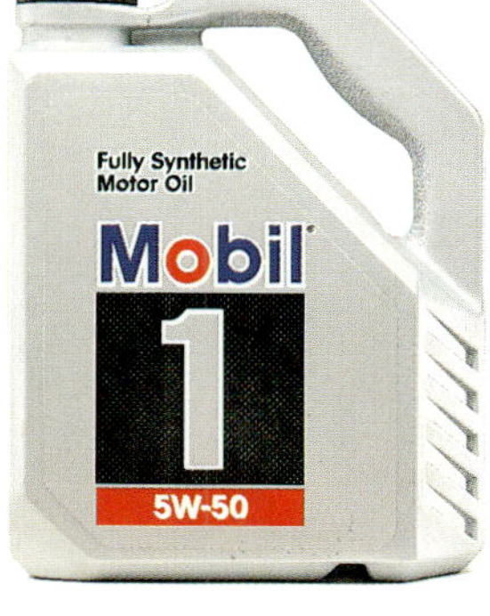
Fully Synthetic
Motor Oil
Mobil
1
5W-50

Blowing hot and cold: Ford put its faith in Mikael Ericsson in Sweden, while Subaru relied on the tiny Vivio for the Safari, on which Patrick Njiru finished 12th (inset).

Photos Pascal Huit

the RAC is part of the 1994 World Championship and the Spanish event is not. Bearing in mind that neither of the two is an RAC expert, these considerations matter. Unfortunately, they seem to escape Ford management's notice until it is far too late.

Missing the 1000 Lakes may also come to haunt Boreham, since it is an event that neither Biasion nor Delecour knows well. Together, they make one of the strongest driving teams in the World Championship and Delecour in particular possesses a blinding turn of speed on a growing range of events, but they don't possess the all-round knowledge of the Toyota duo. That, rather than a lack of ability, played its part in TTE's triumph.

There were several instances of Ford's tactical clumsiness. Nominating semi-works cars to score points on the Swedish was a somewhat hasty move, especially when it meant that the factory itself could not score points on the RAC, while the decision to go to Argentina was taken so late that all the available sponsorship that would have paid for the trip had been snapped up by other teams. The team management seemed torn between aiming for the 1993 title and laying the groundwork for 1994. Missing the 1000 Lakes and the Safari made plenty of short-term sense, but none in the long term – and, as manufacturers never tire of pointing out, a Group A rally car is a long-term investment.

No doubt a few mistakes were to be expected in Ford's first true World Championship season since 1979, but there was no doubting the progress made. In TTE's hour of triumph, in Australia, one of its mechanics suggested that it was a good thing it had won the title in 1993, because it would never stand as good a chance again. Ford personnel should take that as a compliment.

Historically, World Championship rallying is a game for two players. It is most unusual to find three teams sharing victories evenly between them, yet there is now a distinct possibility that this will indeed be the case in 1994. While Ford and Toyota became the main protagonists in 1993, Subaru was coming up fast on the rails. Including an all-Japanese effort with Vivios on the Safari, it took part in nine of the permitted ten World Championship events and, knowing that this was not enough to win the series, Prodrive concentrated on plugging the gaps in its knowledge for 1994 and on developing the Legacy's replacement, the Impreza.

Arguably, the Legacy was the best car of the lot on gravel and Prodrive's main handicaps were the driving team (McRae was still contesting a number of events for the first time, while Ari Vatanen, despite his latest resurgence, is no longer at the zenith of his career) and the lack of recent development on tarmac. In more favourable circumstances, Subarus might have won up to half a dozen World Championship rounds: the Legacys were quickest on the loose surface stages in Portugal, they held first and second on the Acropolis, and Vatanen only just failed to beat Kankkunen on the 1000 Lakes; if it hadn't been for a couple of minor but crucial mechanical problems, notably a collapsed wheel bearing, McRae might easily have won the Swedish. Any team can cry into its beer about the near-misses and the outrageous doings of fate, but Prodrive conveys the impression that it learns from its mistakes. The speed of Piero Liatti's semi-works Legacy at Sanremo hinted that Subarus can no longer be written off on tarmac.

The New Zealand victory was easily the team's most significant result, indicating to the Japanese that the project was worthwhile and settling doubts over McRae's temperament. The 25-year-old Scot proved at various times that he has still to conquer an agonising capacity to make unnecessary mistakes, notably in Greece and Australia, but he also reaffirmed his ability to adapt instantly to strange territory and, by winning in New Zealand, that he can withstand the most intense pressure. If he keeps going at the present rate, the national press will begin to take rallying seriously.

Elsewhere, the chilly economic climate ensured that few teams prospered. Prior to a marked resurgence on the RAC, Mitsubishi stood still in 1993. In spite of having a new, more compact homologation special, the toe-in-the-water approach continued to be the third Japanese team's undoing. It wasn't until autumn 1993 that some of the testing that should have been done a year earlier took place and things came to such a pass after a dismal 1000 Lakes showing that the team management resorted to blaming the drivers.

Above all, Mitsubishi's World Championship programme is badly compromised by easy success in cross-country events. It might be better if it concentrated on off-road competition rather than draining resources from Ralliart Europe, which invariably makes do with fewer service vans, fewer engineers and less testing than any of its counterparts. It is a shame, because the RAC result suggested that the Lancer has real promise and a 'second evolution' car is due in 1994. Typically, while other teams reckon that cost savings achieved by the WRTA might allow them to enter more cars, Ralliart believes that they are its one realistic hope of augmenting its current programme.

The World Championship gained a new award in 1993, for naturally aspirated front-wheel drive cars. The FIA's official title was just as cumbersome and nothing like as informative, but the new category was known to the world as Formula 2. It stimulated a fierce discussion at all levels, but the impact on entries and on stages was a trifle disappointing. Perhaps that was to be expected. On the other hand, it was a surprise that Renault hardly supported the category at all outside France, considering that Patrick Landon has been a tireless campaigner for two-wheel drive. The Clios demolished the opposition in Corsica and the team later ran a semi-automatic gearbox on home soil, which was ample proof that Landon is itching to join the fray. Paradoxically, his team's absence may rebound to Formula 2's advantage; no one can accuse it of being a publicity vehicle for Renault alone. While Renault poured francs into Formula One, the field was left clear for Opel Belgium (Germany has set its face against rallying with a vengeance) and Skoda. Given the disparity in engine size and Bruno Thiry's sparkling talent, a comfortable win for Opel was to be expected, but it was rough luck on Thiry that no one had had the imagination to offer a drivers' award as well.

While manufacturer support was conspicuous by its absence, there were more drivers pursuing the Group N title, yet the tide had unmistakeably turned in favour of the new category. Firms such as Nissan and Peugeot are preparing Formula 2 cars for the future and there were some notably impressive performances from importers' teams in Europe during the autumn, whereas Group N is still handicapped by its traditional failings: if the car is good in Group N, it makes sense for the factory to run it in Group A and most turbocharged Group N cars remain catastrophically fragile. A sponsor is much more likely to see a return on its investment in a Formula 2 car than a Group N machine.

Whatever the manufacturers think, the economic evidence in favour of Formula 2 is mounting. Thiry reckoned that he would have been able to afford only one World Championship event if the Belgian team had chosen a four-wheel drive Calibra Turbo, while two of Britain's better-known Ford teams shared a seven-speed Group A gearbox, because they couldn't afford a spare each; three years ago, they were bitter rivals. While the factories can perhaps sustain seven-speed expense, even the wealthiest importers and privateers vehemently protest that they are living in a five-speed world.

Colin McRae (below) joined the select club of British drivers to win a World Championship rally. There is little that Toyota's mechanics will not attempt in the field, even changing a cylinder head on the Safari (left).

The year was marked by tragedy, as well as controversy and excitement. The deaths of Rodger Freeth and Marian Bublewicz, both after collisions with trees, might have been expected to attract more comment, as both were leading competitors with international reputations and such deaths have been extremely rare since Group B was banned seven years ago. Unfortunately, sorrow was mingled with helplessness. There is only so much that can be done to root out the element of danger.

Would it be going too far to describe the new BMW M3 as the understatement of the year? BMW think not.

There is little in its appearance to hint that, yet again, BMW has totally redefined the sports car. Spoilers are nowhere to be seen. (As with the legendary Z1, they're underneath the car.)

Here is a machine launched, some might imagine, in the shadow of the most successful sports car ever built.

The previous M3 notched up 1500 victories on the track, one for almost every day of its life.

Yet the performance of the new M3, with 286 bhp, eclipses its forerunner. At idle speed, it delivers virtually the same torque as its predecessor achieved at full revs.

This was made possible by BMW Motorsport's revolutionary continuously variable valve timing system.

Thus for the new M3, there is no such thing as a torque curve. From idle, the torque climbs to 236 ft.lbs at 3600rpm. From there, it's a straight line all the way to 6500 rpm.

As a result, power is available in any situation, even when 5th gear is engaged at 1000 revs.

0-62 takes 6 seconds. 62-0 a mere 2.8.

CARS FEATURED: BMW M3. PRICE £32,450, EXCLUDES METALLIC PAINT SHOWN, AT A COST OF £405. PRICE, CORRECT AT TIME OF GOING TO PRESS, INCLUDES VAT, EXCLUDES ROAD FUND LICENCE AND, AT AN ESTIMATED COST OF £470, DELIVERY AND NUMBER PLA
THE CAR. FOR MORE INFORMATION ON BMW CARS AND BMW FINANCE WRITE TO BMW INFORMAT

WCRS

Yet to BMW, what makes the M3 revolutionary is not merely its exceptional responsiveness and performance but something more down to earth.

This is the first sports car to put fuel efficiency top on the agenda with performance. Its normally aspirated 24 valve, 3 litre engine is more fuel efficient than many a production 2 litre engine. And it exceeds the world's toughest emission regulations by 50%.

Two quotes sum up the new M3's achievements.

'Point to point, this is probably the fastest car BMW has built.' Autocar & Motor, 9th December 1992.

And 'Considering the strength of its performance, the M3's average fuel consumption of 30.9mpg is sensationally low.' Car, January 1993.

In other words, in the BMW M3, response and responsibility go together. But then, that's BMW.

THE ULTIMATE DRIVING MACHINE

RFORMANCE FIGURES, MANUFACTURER'S DATA. MANUFACTURER'S FUEL CONSUMPTION DATA: 21.7MPG AT URBAN, 43.5MPG AT 56MPH, 35.8MPG AT 75MPH. ALL NEW BMW's COME WITH BMW EMERGENCY SERVICE. THIS IS VALID THROUGHOUT FIRST OWNERSHIP OF
ERVICE, P.O. BOX 161, CROYDON, SURREY, CR9 1QB OR FREEPHONE 0800 325600.

Profile: Miki Biasion

THE MOUSE THAT ROARED

by David Williams

Appearances are often deceptive, but Miki Biasion positively scatters misleading signals at the stranger. He doesn't even look Italian, far less conform to the national stereotype – why, he even likes beer with a meal. Pale skinned, softly spoken and undemonstrative, he exudes a placid charm. No wonder people assume that his co-driver, Tiziano Siviero, is not merely the spokesman, but the driving force behind the partnership and that Biasion is fully in charge only when he drops the clutch at a stage start. He leaves the service area histrionics to others. With a smile, he says that life is 'too nice' to be angry for long; in practice, few have ever seen him angry at all. A little man who looks in physical danger when engulfed by enthusiastic hordes of Italian or Portuguese well-wishers, he has surely prospered through being an Italian in an Italian team during an extraordinarily successful period in its history. Four years of sensational triumphs with Lancia, between 1987 and 1990, brought two world titles, established an enduring reputation and led to a £3 million contract with Ford.

Probe a little deeper and the image changes. Biasion may not raise his voice much, but he has a knack of getting his own way. Eight years in the snakepit of Lancia politics made him an accomplished operator and the outward charm hides a steely resolve. Boreham sources gladly acknowledge the good manners and the punctuality – no superstar cussedness here – but remark on the ability to bend others to his way of thinking. Persuading Ford to send him to Argentina last July, long after the team had turned away the cheap deals and local sponsorship, was a case in point. He waged a campaign for weeks until his wish was granted. Biasion is a tireless, methodical worker who needs and demands that every detail should be perfect. He has never been the sort of instinctive driver who takes a car by the scruff of the neck and hurls it through a stage no matter what. He has a knack of getting first-class treatment and it is no accident that he is rarely let down by his machinery.

He has a well-earned reputation for being shrewd. At the time, his decision to sign for Ford seemed extraordinary. Boreham was struggling to sort out the Sierra Cosworth 4x4 (indeed, the Fords were slower at Sanremo in October 1991 than they had been a year previously) and Lancia was on course for another clean sweep of the makes' and drivers' titles. However, Biasion knew that there were no plans for a successor to the Integrale and, reasoning that Lancia would shortly lose interest in supporting an outdated model, he cast around for a new team. He wanted a new car and since he believes that it takes three years to bring a new design to peak competitiveness, he was prepared to go to a team that wasn't necessarily winning at that precise moment; besides, a new car implied at least a medium-term commitment. Ford and the Escort Cosworth fitted the bill. If Lancia's official withdrawal that Christmas came as a bombshell to some, it had merely happened a little faster than expected, in his eyes. He had made the move away from Turin not through the rallying equivalent of insider dealing, but by assessing information that was also available to his team-mates. He had been shrewd rather than visionary.

Even the close relationship with Siviero is not what it appears. In the early days, Ford mechanics used to grumble that Miki was alright, but Tiziano – well, he had ideas above his station. Who was this co-driver marching round telling them which tyres to fit, without so much as consulting the driver? How come he was needed at every test session? No wonder he earned the nickname 'Ingegnere Siviero'. Press Biasion on the subject and a different slant emerges. They work as a team and, to use the driver's words, 'He is like my secretary.' During a test session, Siviero notes down Biasion's impressions of every technical change, no matter how small. During the recce, they will discuss tyres and make a wet and dry choice for each stage. Siviero writes that down as well. Once the rally is under way, Biasion is free to concentrate on his driving, without the distractions of yelling tyre choices or anti-roll bar settings across crowded service points. His co-driver is better at that in any case and Miki no doubt recognises someone with a greater gift for noisy confrontation.

Siviero as secretary doesn't make such a dramatic impression as Siviero as puppet master, yet he is entrusted with an extraordinary level of responsibility for a co-driver, even one who was also a childhood friend. Biasion values him for his precision – quite a compliment from someone with his own eye for detail – and says that occasionally even he grows tired of it. There are drawbacks to Siviero as a co-driver, albeit not serious ones: his quiet, gravelly tones don't travel well over the intercom and he uses a special microphone to amplify his voice. Mischievously, Biasion observes that he has won each of the three rallies he has contested with other people, including his maiden victory.

Signing Biasion was a tremendous fillip for Ford, for if there is anyone who can claim to have created the modern rally driver, it is he. When he joined Lancia, top drivers practised as much or as little as they pleased and were happy to turn up before the start, give the car a quick run and drive it in competition.

Testing could be left largely to test drivers. Biasion was told he was mad to practise so much and some of the Finns argued that he was only quick for that reason. At the same time, he had shouldered chief responsibility for Lancia testing during the last months of the Group B Delta S4: he knew how he wanted the car to perform and it would be prepared accordingly for each rally, not as Giorgio Pianta or Lele Pinto (Lancia's test drivers) deemed appropriate.

The technique has served him well. It has brought him 17 victories on World Championship rallies as well as two titles, and it has transformed both the role and methods of the works driver. The drivers who retorted that they were paid day-rate, not night-rate when it came to practising are now unemployed or confined to raids and everyone has been sucked into a constant round of testing. Australia was new to Biasion and he covered more than 4000 miles in eight days of reconnaissance; since New Zealand, he had tested in Australia, Italy and Spain. His cars invariably have completely different transmission and suspension settings to François Delecour's.

The methods have become near-universal, for Biasion's speed and thoroughness shattered the old Nordic supremacy. When Cesare Fiorio coined the phrase the 'Latin revolution', he didn't name names, but he could only have had Biasion in mind. Others, notably Didier Auriol and Carlos Sainz, followed the Lancia star through the breach and they have now won more than 40 World Championship rallies between the three of them. Biasion points out, without arrogance or even emotion, that he was responsible for most of these changes. Ask him if he's proud of it and he shrugs. So far as he is concerned, it is a matter of fact, an achievement of a kind, but hardly the reason for climbing into a rally car in the first place.

The professionalism isn't confined to driving or preparing the car. He speaks good English and French, not to mention a smattering of Spanish, and he is as deft at handling a collection of Australian journalists and Mobil dealers whom he has never met in his life as specialist journalists he has known for years.

Biasion's arrival at Ford was accompanied by a transformation in its fortunes. It didn't change overnight and he had to endure an exasperating Monte Carlo Rally, dogged by brake and power steering problems, before setting a number of fastest times and finishing second in Portugal. In his view, Boreham was 'turned over 100 per cent. In a matter of months, the Sierra that was 1.5 seconds per kilometre off the pace at Sanremo had developed into a car capable of beating Sainz and the new Toyota. Detailed work on the suspension and transmission had paid off handsomely, and it was no flash in the pan either. Biasion is proud of the fact that he had finished every rally he had started in a Cosworth until the 1993 Rally of New Zealand. It's tempting to assume that the labours of a highly experienced crew from Lancia brought about this remarkable switch in Ford fortunes more or less single handed, but Biasion doesn't see it like that. He points out that most of the personnel at Boreham were there before he joined and he feels that the turning of Ford from an also-ran into a major World Championship force has been a team effort. If there has been a striking change in the way the team goes about doing things, it is in the raising of morale.

Biasion has been one of the most influential figures in his chosen sport for nearly a decade. Driving for Ford – he is pictured in Australia – has not so far yielded the kind of results he enjoyed in a breathtakingly successful stint at Lancia, during which he became World Champion twice.

Biasion went to Ford with two specific purposes, beyond winning rallies. He wanted to prove that he could succeed in a non-Italian car and he wanted to create a winning team, 'like Sainz at Toyota'. The second aim might be viewed as applying the Lancia technique elsewhere – getting the team on his side and working as he wanted – but the first reveals a rare trace of insecurity. Biasion is proud that he has won against some of the strongest team-mates imaginable, including Markku Alén, Auriol and Juha Kankkunen, and resents the implication that he did so because he was the favoured local boy who got better equipment than his colleagues. Winning for a team based in faraway Essex would nail that suggestion once and for all.

Accordingly, victory on the 1993 Acropolis was much more than the ending of a drought that had lasted nearly three years. In fact, Biasion scored plenty of good results between his last victory in Argentina and his third in Greece, but he had spent an uncomfortably long

THEY BOTH WENT TO AUSTRA

(But by slightl

The Unipart sponsored Sasol Jordan Hart 193s went to Australia the long way – with a journey via Japan.

The journey began at Jordan Grand Prix's Silverstone Headquarters with the packing of the cars by FOCA handlers for their 6,200 mile trip from Heathrow to Tokyo.

This entailed placing both cars on to a specially built frame (weighing some 1600 kilos when loaded) and fitting them front and back with, appropriately enough, Kangaroo Bars.

Over 13 hours later, the Jordan Formula 1 cars were returned to FOCA for unloading for the drive from Tokyo Airport to the Suzuka circuit, where the extensive preparation for the Japanese Grand Prix was to begin, incorporating the fitting of Unipart products, including Unipart Spark Plugs.

These preparations paid dividends and resulted in a 5th place from Rubens Barrichello and that memorable 6th place position from debut boy Eddie Irvine.

After the celebrations and buoyed by their success, the Jordan Grand Prix team took to the air again for their trip to Australia.

Having completed their pre-flight preparations (once again courtesy of FOCA) the Jordans took their places along with 18 other Formula 1 cars on 10 pallets in the hold of a Boeing 747-200 Freighter, in addition to the 19 other pallets of Formula 1 equipment making up the total load of 105 tonnes.

One fuel stop, 12 hours and almost 5000 miles later, Jordan Grand Prix reached the final leg of their journey of the 1993 season – the 190 mile race over the gruelling Adelaide street circuit for the Australian Grand Prix.

IA ACCOMPANIED BY UNIPART

different routes)

The Unipart sponsored and equipped Lotus Cortina went to Australia in 1993 the hard way – as a participant in the London/Sydney classic rally, leaving London in April and covering the entire 11,500 miles.

Over the two month journey, much of it on the dirt track roads, the car crossed Europe, India and Australia and provided an exacting test for the 80 plus Unipart products used.

Ice, mountains, deserts, heat, potholes, rivers, mud and even kangaroos had to be negotiated by the team on their journey.

The Lotus Cortina made it all the way – which came as no big surprise to Unipart! In fact, the performance of the Unipart products was a significant factor in the car being dubbed the 'most reliable in the rally'.

Unipart Supreme Oil was changed a mere three times and the oil filter (it's a bit more inconvenient) just twice!

The Lotus Cortina ran the whole journey on one set of Unipart spark plugs (admittedly they were cleaned in Perth just to be on the safe side)!

Finally, after the participating cars arrived back in the UK after a 7 week journey by sea, the Unipart Lotus Cortina started under its own battery – not surprisingly, a Unipart Samson.

Whether it's a trip to Australia or even just to the local shops, for reliability fit Unipart products.

Part of your life.

UNIPART

time away from the winner's rostrum for a driver of his eminence and price tag. He had proved that a Lancia had not been the magic ingredient and that Ford could win against any opposition in the most arduous conditions. It suggested that the Escort has acquired all the virtues one used to associate with the Delta.

Biasion argues that Ford has started winning again a good deal more quickly than TTE did when Sainz joined the team, but there has been a complicating factor in the process of re-creating Ford in his own image: Delecour. Previous team-mates may have succumbed to Biasion's grasp of strategy and appetite for hard work, but Delecour has not and isn't the easiest man to get along with either; when he has a problem, he expects to be pushed out of stages by his colleague and there are no rallies on which he has obvious weaknesses – or none at least on which Biasion is superior.

Biasion handles the Delecour Question with characteristic tact. 'François has a special character and in ten years I don't think he will change,' is a polite way of saying that the Frenchman is impulsive, often selfish, and capable of driving his mechanics to distraction, although Biasion will touch on those same points at slightly greater length without much prompting. Miki admits that Delecour is faster under certain circumstances – quite an admission for a top driver – and pays him an enormous compliment by describing him as the most highly motivated driver he has ever met. In his opinion, their contrasting approaches make a good combination. A team needs one driver who is constantly on the limit and demanding the utmost from the machinery and one with a little more experience, able to drive with something in reserve. He feels the subtle method can still produce results and, after all, the Acropolis was a triumph for guile rather than brute force. Only plain bad luck prevented him from profiting in the same manner in Australia and at Sanremo. If his failure to overshadow Delecour has been a disappointment to him, he is not about to admit it, however.

From Biasion's point of view, Delecour might be regarded as an unwelcome intrusion – the flaw in the master plan – but his own motivation has been called into question in any case. His detractors would argue that the man from Bassano del Grappa is no longer the force that won consecutive World Championships, in 1988 and 1989. Some have even suggested that three-year contracts and being paid thousands of pounds per day have been counter-productive. However, in maintaining that his powers have declined, they overlook Biasion's cool assessment of his own driving. Whereas a Markku Alén or a François Delecour refuses to believe that anyone else is physically capable of driving a stage faster, Biasion has long held an unusually modest view of his own ability. He used to complain that he was far too highly placed in *Rallycourse's* assessment of the top ten drivers, that his advantage over other Italian drivers was consistency, not speed, and he describes the late 1980s – when in a phenomenal three-year period, he won 75 per cent of the events he took part in – as a 'period of high motivation for me and the team', almost as though he were riding a lucky streak. If others think he has gone to seed since then, he does not. Indeed, he describes the 1993 Monte as one of his outstanding drives and a better performance than his victory in 1989, even though he finished third behind two Frenchmen, including his team-mate. To his way of thinking, he can't do much better than that on their territory. To an extent, he has become a victim of his own success: by the end of 1989, journalists were running out of ways of describing a Biasion victory in a Lancia and the only way was down.

Tarmac may be the Escort's strong suit, but Ford's Italian recruit is at his happiest on loose surfaces, scoring a decisive victory on the Acropolis (top right). Biasion still harbours an ambition to return to the Safari, an event he won twice running for Lancia.

Yet he is also candid enough to admit that, having won two world titles, the thirst for personal glory is no longer the same. Carlos Sainz may have retained his appetite for winning rallies after becoming World Champion twice, but Biasion describes turning the Escort Cosworth into a championship-winning car as his new challenge. With his usual precision, he describes it as around 70 per cent developed and says that Ford will need to make advances in electronics and transmission design. He claims not to mind whether he is champion again and he was prepared to accept team orders in the latter part of 1993 if that aided

Delecour's quest for the title. One can find echoes of this elsewhere. Kankkunen was less than ecstatic on winning his third World Championship – it had been a long, exhausting season and he had done enough driving to last a lifetime – and publicly declared last summer that his main aim was to make Toyota World Champion; it didn't make any odds if he was champion himself three or four times.

That may be so, but Kankkunen is winning a good deal more frequently than his erstwhile team-mate and thriving on swapping co-drivers. Biasion has off-key rallies, including two particularly unremarkable drives in Corsica in the past two years, an event on which he has finished second in the past. While he insists that he enjoys driving on tarmac, he admits that it has never been a priority. He has always regarded rallying as a loose surface sport and, although a friend ran a racing team, the teenage Biasion chose not to exploit the contact and to go rallying instead. He has never driven a single-seater and shows no sign of feeling deprived. In expressing a preference for gravel, he again refuses to conform to the stereotype of the Italian rally driver.

Despite his record, Biasion doesn't have as broad a range of experience to draw on as most of his rivals. Fiorio was inclined to protect his Italian star as he rocketed to prominence and he was well established before he contested events such as the RAC and the 1000 Lakes, to which the likes of Auriol and Sainz were introduced at a significantly earlier stage in their careers. He has stated a desire to win what he calls the 'specialist rallies', such as the RAC, but there is no doubt that he remains strongest on the rallies he knows best, such as Portugal and the Acropolis. Records and backgrounds can be compared in microscopic detail; ultimately, it isn't possible to measure motivation in mathematical terms.

At the age of 35, Biasion has no thoughts of retirement and is as fascinated by his job as ever, speaking willingly of future prospects. He sees his Ford contract as a three-year process and has the patience to realise that success may not come overnight. While others may be quick to judge him, he can afford to wait; he is still younger than Hannu Mikkola was when he won the 1983 World Championship.

Like all factory drivers he complains about the workload though, arguing that there should be two clear weeks between the end of one World Championship rally and the start of the recce for the next. Granted that he has played his part in adding to this expanding burden, he believes that the FIA is to blame for not grasping the nettle and lopping the calendar down to size, and for failing to appreciate the scale of a modern driver's commitments. After ten full seasons, he admits that he is tired and suggests that two to three more years of uninterrupted competition will burn out the top drivers. He grumbles that his daughter is growing up as a stranger.

It is a state of affairs that he will have to accept, at least for the time being. His chances of winning the 1993 championship may have faded in late summer, but Biasion is still in mid-chapter. He retains one of the plum drives and his fortunes are irrevocably bound up with Ford's. The strength of the car and the team are the old bugbears that have let drivers down since the dawn of motorsport, but they are precisely the aspects that Biasion is so good at turning to his advantage.

Ford
Motorsport
Mobil 1
Mobil 1
MICHELIN
Motorsport
Coca-Cola
PORTO WINE
5
SG Gigante SG
BILSTEIN
GEMINI
index
K748 GOO

Winning On All Fronts

ALLY OF PORTUGAL | TOUR OF CORSICA | ACROPOLIS RALLY | RALLY SANREMO | CATALUNYA RALLY

"Motorsport is a highly charged, extremely competitive sport, attended and watched on television by almost two billion people every year. It provides Ford with an emotional focus for intense product loyalty and fan support, while allowing the company to compete head-to-head with other auto manufacturers around the globe. Even more importantly, though, the lessons learned in motorsport can be translated directly into improvements for roadgoing Ford products."

Ford had one of its best-ever years in motorsport in 1993. It is the only major manufacturer to be involved in what are generally regarded as the world's top four motorsport disciplines: the Formula One World Championship, the World Rally Championship, the PPG Indy Car World Series and the NASCAR Winston Cup stock car championship. Ford-powered cars scored major victories in every one of these series during 1993. But Ford's commitment is not just at the very top levels of motorsport. It extends right down to the "grassroots" with enduring support for such categories as Formula Ford and the Fiesta Challenge, as well as a wide range of national championships around the world. Nor is the company's involvement just on a short-term basis. Ford's commitment to motorsport dates back to the early 1900s, when Henry Ford decided to compete in a vehicle of his own construction in order to publicise his fledgling company.

Publicity remains a very valid reason for Ford's continued involvement in motorsport, providing a high-profile shop window for the company to display its latest wares. More importantly, though, it now provides the most rigorous "test bench" imaginable for developing future products.

In the past, the links between the technology developed for use in the top levels of motorsport and that used in road cars were not particularly obvious. That is no longer the case. Much of what goes on under the skin of the current generation of cars competing in such disciplines as Formula One, the World Rally Championship, Indy Car and NASCAR racing are of direct relevance to the ordinary motorist.

Some excellent examples of just what is achievable can be seen in Ford's involvement in the Formula One arena. Working in concert with its partners, Benetton Formula and Cosworth Engineering, Ford has been at the forefront of developing a number of dynamic vehicle systems which have contributed directly to the competitiveness of the Benetton-Fords of Michael Schumacher and Riccardo Patrese this season.

The systems include active suspension, traction control, anti-lock braking, four-wheel steering and telemetry. Significantly, all are either currently in use on Ford production vehicles, or will have direct application to them in the near future. Formula One racing was specifically chosen as the arena in which to conduct this programme since it was felt to offer the most demanding real-world challenge currently in existence when it comes to the development of automotive components.

There are several other specific examples of the technology transfer from Formula One to production vehicles resulting from Ford's involvement in Grand Prix racing.

In 1989, for instance, the Ford Taurus SHO model was introduced fitted with a high-performance three litre V6 engine. The rev rate of this power unit was so fast that a standard rev limiter simply would not work with it. The rev limiter used by Ford on its Formula One engines, however, which can achieve transient rev rates of 30,000 rpm/second in the racing environment, was applied directly to the SHO Taurus with success.

The portable calibration tools developed to support Ford technicians in Formula One have also proven extremely useful in the course of powertrain development for production vehicles. They are estimated to have saved several thousand hours of time, and associated expenditure, by allowing engineers to change the computer calibration of powertrains quickly and accurately via a laptop computer.

There are many other areas of direct benefit which also deserve a place on the list, including the development of fuel consumption algorithms, electronic data storage and processing, connector and air charge temperature sensor designs.

The same is true of Ford's involvement in the World Rally Championship. The lessons learned from the Sierra Cosworth and, most recently, Escort Cosworth programmes have added to the company's collective store of knowledge on such areas as suspension and differential design, four-wheel drive systems, including viscous coupling technology, and transmission design.

Nor is the "technology transfer" all one way. In a number of instances, Ford engineers have been able to apply lessons learned in the course of road car development to solve problems encountered in various motorsport arenas. The worth of this two-way flow of information is clearly reflected in the impressive results which Ford notched up in top-level motorsport during 1993.

In Formula One, Benetton-Ford drivers Michael Schumacher and Riccardo Patrese, and McLaren-Ford's Ayrton Senna, Michael Andretti and Mika Hakkinen led Ford's efforts in the global 16-race series. By the end of the season, the tally for Ford-engined cars was six victories with at least one Ford-powered driver finishing in the top three of every Grand Prix of 1993.

Wins in three of the last four events of the year also confirmed the competitiveness of the latest version of the Ford HB V8 engine. Senna's dominant victory in the final Grand Prix of the year, in Adelaide, was particularly significant. It locked up second place in the World Drivers' Championship for the Brazilian and also provided McLaren with its 104th win in Formula One competition, making the team the most successful in Grand Prix history.

Schumacher's victory in Portugal, and his scintillating performances elsewhere have served to secure the young German's reputation as one of the rising stars of Formula One. "I've been very fortunate to have Ford power throughout my Formula One career," he commented after the win in Estoril. "Having the power and reliability of the HB V8 behind me meant I was able to score several podium finishes early on this season. Next year, I have no doubt we will be battling for the World Championship".

Ford currently has 12 Formula One World Championships and 166 Grand Prix wins to its credit, significantly more than any other manufacturer.

On the rally front, too, Ford has had a superb year. The sleek Escort Cosworth made its World Rally Championship debut on the traditional curtain-raiser for the season, the Monte Carlo Rally, and from the opening stage of that event proved to be the most competitive car in the 1993 Championship. Francois Delecour and the Mobil 1-backed Escort Cosworth led for the first 19 stages, only to be denied a dream win by Didier Auriol's Toyota, the Frenchman putting in an astonishingly fast run on the final night to grab victory. Nonetheless, Delecour's fine second place served notice of intent on the other competitors.

Two months later, in Portugal, Delecour confirmed the Escort Cosworth's promise by scoring a maiden World Rally Championship win for both himself and the car. Adding to the Boreham team's joy, Miki Biasion finished a close second in the sister car, the two drivers between them setting 27 fastest stage times.

Delecour followed up this performance with a dominant win on the tortuous roads of Corsica, while Biasion took a beautifully calculated victory on the gruelling Acropolis Rally in Greece. The diminutive Italian collected more valuable points with second place on the Rally Argentina while Delecour responded with second in New Zealand.

At this point, Ford shared the lead in the Manufacturers' title race, but Delecour's third-place finish on the next event, the Rally Australia, saw the title go to Toyota. Franco Cunico, Ford Italy's entry in the Sanremo Rally, demonstrated the

superiority of the Escort Cosworth by taking a surprise win in the Italian round of the World Rally Championship ahead of many factory drivers and teams.
Delecour then stormed back with a win on the Catalunya Rally in Spain, but Biasion's fourth-place finish meant the Ford Motorsport team could do nothing further to prevent Toyota's Juha Kankkunen from taking his fourth Driver's title. Nonetheless, five World Championship victories for the Escort Cosworth in its first year of competition has to augur well for the future.
Ford will be back in the World Rally Championship in 1994, aiming to win nothing less than both the Manufacturers' and Drivers' titles.
In 1992, after a 21-year hiatus, Ford returned to the Indy Car circuit in a joint effort with long-time partner, Cosworth Engineering. The Ford-Cosworth XB engine immediately demonstrated its potential by winning five races in its first season of competition.
Powering as many as 10 cars in 1993, the XB V8 was victorious in six events, including the penultimate round, at Nazareth, Pennsylvania, where Nigel Mansell locked up the 1993 PPG Indy Car World Series title at his first attempt. Confounding the pundits who had expected him to show strongly on the road circuits but struggle on the ovals, Mansell won at four of the five oval tracks on which he competed (he missed Phoenix after a heavy crash in testing) and also took victory on the Surfer's Paradise street course in Australia en route to the Championship. For one brief week in early October, the Englishman had the unique distinction of being both the reigning Formula One World Champion and the Indy Car Champion.
Nor was Mansell the only Ford-powered driver to do well in Indy Car racing in 1993. Twelve of 16 pole positions were claimed by Ford drivers, including Mario Andretti, Raul Boesel, Arie Luyendyk, Scott Goodyear and, of course, Mansell. Luyendyk also led a three-strong Ford-Cosworth front-row sweep in qualifying for the Indianapolis 500, while Mario Andretti's 234 mph run on the daunting Michigan oval was the fastest in racing history.
Ford and Cosworth's efforts have now resulted in 252 Indy Car victories, including 16 Indianapolis 500 wins (six for Ford, 10 for Cosworth), while the six wins in 1993 means Ford's tally in Indy Car competition has now risen to 99.

After a marathon 30-race season, the ultra-competitive NASCAR Winston Cup Manufacturers' Championship came down to a straight fight between long-time rivals Ford and Chevrolet at the final round in Atlanta, Georgia, in November. In the end, victory went to Rusty Wallace and his Pontiac with Earnhardt's 10th-place finish enough to win him his sixth Winston Cup Championship. Ricky Rudd's second place gave Chevrolet the Manufacturers' crown by one point from Ford.

Heading up Ford's NASCAR Winston Cup program in 1993 were drivers Mark Martin, Ernie Irvan, Bill Elliott and Geoff Bodine. Martin, driving the Valvoline Ford Thunderbird of Roush Racing, was the sensation of the season. He scored a NASCAR-record four consecutive Winston Cup wins and finished the season in third place, behind Earnhardt and Wallace. Irvan, a former Chevrolet Lumina driver, switched to a Ford Thunderbird in September, replacing the late Davey Allison, and promptly tallied two victories in his first six races with the Robert Yates team.

Elliott left his family-run team in 1992 to drive the Budweiser Thunderbird of the famous Junior Johnson team. He has 39 career victories to his credit, all scored in Ford products, and was the 1988 Winston Cup Champion. He also has the distinction of being NASCAR's fastest-ever qualifier with a lap of 212.809 mph set at Talladega in 1987. Bodine began the 1993 season driving the Motorcraft Thunderbird for Bud Moore's team and scored a win at Sears Point in mid-May. He was also instrumental in helping Ford to seal its first NASCAR Manufacturers' Championship in 1992.

On the other side of the Atlantic Ocean, Ford's newly-launched Mondeo proved to be the car to beat in the British Touring Car Championship. Despite only making their first appearance at the eighth round of the Championship after spending the first part of the season under development, the two litre, V6-engined Mondeos of Andy Rouse and Paul Radisich were immediately on the pace. They amassed three wins and seven podium finishes by the end of the season and New Zealander Radisich then went on to impress motorsport fans the world over by winning the inaugural FIA World Touring Car Challenge in Monza, Italy. Underlining their competitiveness, Radisich and his Mondeo captured pole position and led every lap of both Challenge races on their way to the overall victory.

As mentioned earlier, though, there is far more to Ford's involvement in motorsport than the "glitter and bright lights" of the world's top championships. Many current and former Formula One and Indy Car drivers began their careers in the highly competitive arena of Formula Ford, the only true global series for aspiring young racers. Lotus-Ford driver, Johnny Herbert, has observed on more than one occasion that Formula Ford was instrumental in developing his career as a racing driver, while McLaren's new Finnish recruit, Mika Hakkinen, has a similar view. "Formula Ford was the perfect series to teach me the basics of open-wheel racing," he says emphatically.

In 1993, the British Open Formula Ford Championship witnessed the introduction of the 1.8 litre Zetec engine. The 16-valve, double overhead camshaft power unit, which is used in Ford Escort and Mondeo models, provided a useful performance increase when compared with the older 1.6 litre, Kent-engined cars and also has the benefit of being fitted with a catalytic converter to reduce exhaust pollutants.

The winner of the 1993 Open Formula Championship was Russell Ingall. Quite simply, the experienced Australian dominated the series and now adds his name to a list of competitors which reads like the "Who's Who" of modern motor racing. It includes Nigel Mansell, Ayrton Senna, Johnny Herbert, Michael Schumacher, Paul Tracy, Emerson Fittipaldi and Mika Hakkinen, to name but a few.

In closed-wheel cars, former rallycross ace, Trevor Reeves, turned his hand to circuit racing with good effect, winning the ever-popular Fiesta Challenge for identical XR2i models, while Ian Gwynne took his second title on the trot in the multi-disciplinary Ford Escort RS 2000 Rallye Sport Championship.

Back in North America, Ford has been a long-time supporter of both IMSA's GTS (formerly GTO) and SCCA's Trans-Am road racing championships. Roush Racing, with drivers Robby Gordon, Wally Dallenbach Jr, Tommy Kendall, Mark Martin and Robbie Buhl kicked off the 1993 IMSA season by scoring its ninth consecutive GTS class win in the Daytona Rolex 24-hour endurance race. Kendall, who rebounded from a serious crash in 1991, went on to win the IMSA Exxon Supreme GTS Championship at the wheel of his Ford Mustang Cobra. It marked his seventh career racing title and his first for Ford.

In the SCCA Trans-Am category, Ford was in the hunt for its first title since 1989, with driver Ron Fellows leading the way. The Canadian won three of Ford's Trans-Am victories this year and finished second in the Championship standings.

In the Pro Stock drag racing class, the vastly experienced Bob Glidden pilots the rocket-like Motorcraft Ford Probe down the quarter-mile straightaways of the National Hot Rod Association circuit. Glidden is the premier drag racer of all time, having collected 84 NHRA Pro Stock career wins – two of those in 1993 – which is almost double the number of his nearest rival. He won five consecutive Pro Stock Championships between 1985-1989, his career total currently standing at an NHRA-record 10. Glidden has at least one victory in each of the last 21 seasons.

The drivers in Ford's Rough Rider off-road racing programme have plenty to boast about with six championships scored during their first season of competition, in 1990. The Simon brothers, Paul and Dave, headed up an eight-truck, desert assault party in 1993, having won four consecutive Class 7S off-road titles before switching to the "high-tech" Class 1/2 series with a new F150 in 1992. John Swift returned to defend his 1992 Class 6 title with his Ford Explorer while Dave Ashley stayed with his Class 4 Ford F150.

Ford trucks scored a total of 28 class victories (more than triple the nearest competitor) on their way to winning a total of seven off-road championships in 1992. They currently have 29 class victories to their credit in 1993, and have the chance to notch up seven more championships with one event remaining – the famous Baja 1000.

These results, and many others, justify Ford's wide-ranging commitment to motorsport. The final word on the subject, however, must go to Mike Kranefuss, the recently retired head of Ford's worldwide Motorsport programme.

"Motorsport is a highly charged, extremely competitive sport, attended and watched on television by almost two billion people every year," he says. "It provides Ford with an emotional focus for intense product loyalty and fan support, while allowing the company to compete head-to-head with other auto manufacturers around the globe.

"Even more importantly, though, the lessons learned from motorsport can be translated directly into improvements for current and future roadgoing Ford products."

Ford Mondeo:
Three wins from eight events in The British Touring Car Championships and winner of the FIA World Touring Car Challenge

Ford Escort Cosworth:
Winner of the Rally of Portugal, Tour of Corsica, Acropolis Rally, Rally of Sanremo and The Catalunya Rally

Benetton - Ford B193B:
Winner of The Portuguese Grand Prix

Technical Review

LONG FUSE

by Martin Sharp, Deputy Editor Cars and Car Conversions

'If the Escort Cosworth does or doesn't win next year, it won't be down to the car that they homologated, it'll be how well Ford Motorsport exploits it,' was a gauntlet thrown down by a rival team engineer in late 1993.

The Escort RS Cosworth certainly entered its debut World Rally Championship season with a bang. Victory in three out of its first seven world events, with four second and two third places was an immediate demonstration of on-the-pace potential. It was encouraging stuff for the Boreham-based Ford Motorsport team, which had been able to grab a healthy slice of that most important ingredient, time, in preparation for these impressive first results.

Group A rules meant that Ford had to consider the Escort Cosworth project as a full production procedure, rather than develop it exclusively for motor sport purposes. By definition, this alone is a complex and time-consuming exercise, never mind the effort required to develop the resulting car for motor sport. Ford Motorsport was fortunate in having an existing combination of drive-train and vehicles from which to build its new weapon. It had a production car with a component configuration providing opportunities for advantageous weight distribution, favourable aerodynamic performance, cooling airflow and transmission layout. Power-train accessibility is superior to that of a transverse engine configuration, together with many other potentially useful feature details for a rally car – a resulting rally car which embodies a conceptual layout deriving from what is effectively the first true Group A homologation special road car.

The Escort Cosworth is certainly no Lancia Stratos, yet it is the only current production car, named as part of a manufacturer's model range, which has a unique drive-train layout, the first such vehicle to appear since Group B was banned. Not surprisingly the Escort Cosworth has turned out to be a very good rally car, but its impact on world rallying has not been to introduce an altogether new level of performance, simply to demonstrate that the moment it started rallying, it had the measure of the opposition.

However, the new Ford's introduction does illustrate that the current Group A regulations – in principle – allow even more super rally supercars which could change the close level of competition we have between today's World Championship cars. Whether revised regulations, or indeed even more super supercars, are desirable is beyond the scope of this article. Suffice to say that, had circumstances – economic or otherwise – been different, who's to say that a Group A homologation special, perhaps more radical than the Escort Cosworth, could not now dominate as the Delta did? Or begin to do so in the future?

Ford Motorsport's Chief Engineer, John Wheeler, is not just charged with making sure the works Escorts are capable of winning World Championship rallies, it was also his task to co-ordinate the many and varied corporate strands in developing the Escort RS Cosworth into a production road car.

It is history now that Wheeler's professional abilities saw this through to fruition, but there's no doubting it was his fundamental motor sporting motivation that drove him. Whenever his duties as Chief Engineer for the works Escorts free him, John's enthusiasm will take him to soak up the atmosphere at motor sport events, from the smallest club event upwards. Provided, that is, they don't clash with his son Scott's kart racing. And not only does Scott have dad on his side when he goes racing, very frequently another inveterate motor sport enthusiast will join the team to help out: 1984 World Rally Champion, Stig Blomqvist.

While motor sport courses through John Wheeler's veins, it is pumped by an engineer's heart. The Escort Cosworth probably would not have happened if

John hadn't spend evenings and weekends thinking deeply through the details; the same goes for the Group B RS200. Today, while heavily involved in the Escort Cosworth rally programme, Wheeler somehow still finds time to continue building at home a personal motor sport project car with a very exciting specification. As ever, his agile mind has already devised future projects – and prototypes – for Ford Motorsport.

Once Escort Cosworth production viability and approval were achieved, in the knowledge that the car concept is good, Wheeler turned his attentions to its *raison d'être*: winning world-status rallies: 'We had to see the proof of it in reality, which is by no means simple, because even the best concept in the world can lie dormant for years if you don't do the application work properly for rallying'.

Ford Motorsport decided on a concentrated development programme for the Escort Cosworth's first-ever World Championship event, the 1993 Monte Carlo Rally. The plan included establishing two completely separate test teams, each with a test car, to develop a technical specification for the rally independently with each of its two drivers.

As Wheeler explains: 'In the south of France, we were testing in two different venues and then the test teams would come together in the evening, compare notes and exchange specifications. So it's not the closed shop that you sometimes get in Formula One teams, where one driver doesn't know what the other driver's using. It's a complete interchange of information, but just working by day in different directions with the driver's preference – the following day probably trying the other driver's spec.

'I think it was particularly successful when we worked with it. And it enabled us to see the potential of the car early in the season, whereas any fundamental errors we might have made in the development could have disheartened us at the beginning of the season and led us to doubting the specification of the car. Then all sorts of other factors come into it.'

Ford Motorsport spent August 1992 at Château-Lastours in southern France establishing a gravel specification for the Escort Cosworth. This work was aimed essentially at the Acropolis Rally, and Motorsport's satisfaction with the resulting specification bore fruit with Miki Biasion's victory by 73 seconds in Greece in 1993.

Happy with the gravel specification, in mid-September 1992 the Boreham team began its twin-test team concentration on optimising the tarmac specification of the Escort Cosworth. Achieving this entailed taking manpower resources from its World Championship team, but this way Ford was soon able to see the potential in its car.

The word got round: people were hearing that the Escort Cosworth was right, 'straight out of the box', and that its concept was so good there was little chance of beating it. Here, Wheeler adds perspective: 'I think that it was probably a combination of some small advantages the Escort had in its layout, balance and serviceability, and so on. A combination of that and doing some very thorough rally development preparation work which maybe other people, because of the programmes they were involved in, hadn't been able to do. But it wasn't a car that came out all of a sudden – a fresh car that was suddenly better than everybody else; it wasn't as simple as that: if there were advantages, they were small.'

Later developments in the 1993 World Rally Championship tended to support Wheeler's comment. The arrival on the championship scene of the Escort Cosworth certainly 'raised the game' forcing opponents to react; but later in the season there was evidence of elimination of that initial gap. In conceptual terms a longitudinally arranged engine, such as that in the Escort, carries significant advantages for a rally car. With today's higher Group A minimum weight limits, weight distribution becomes more critical; this is easier to optimise in a car with a 'north – south' engine location. Accessibility, cooling and transmission design can also be better optimised in such an arrangement.

Toyota's transversely engined Celica is certainly optimised; early in the season it was never far from the Escort Cosworths, and in the final reckoning its world-class performance forced the pace enough for Toyota to take the manufacturers' title in 1993. It is worth noting, indeed perhaps significant, that the car which arguably closed its gap to the Escort quickest through the year, the Subaru – in Legacy and Impreza form – also has a longitudinal engine.

Despite the knowledge that the years of development had paid off with a competitive rally car, Ford's initial aspirations for the 1993 World Rally Championship were conservative. Although the company wanted to be involved in tack-

The Escort Cosworth left an indelible mark on the international scene the moment it was homologated. It has been at its most formidable on asphalt, François Delecour crushing the opposition on the Tour of Corsica (above), while Bernard Béguin took his second French title in a row.

ling the manufacturers' championship, initially that was not a clear objective, Boreham taking the realistic view that the aim for the first year of the Escort Cosworth was to try and win a few World Championship rallies 'and see how it went along'.

Within that brief, the Rally of Portugal wasn't even seriously on the 1993 Ford Motorsport calendar until it was certain that all the objectives for the Monte Carlo Rally had been met. The scheme of things in World Championship rallying means that the time at which the Monte specification is finalised and that rally is just about to begin is coincident with when test teams should be in Portugal. Ford didn't even send an engineer to its Portugal test – they were all involved in preparing for Monte Carlo. In the second week of January just a car, a driver and two mechanics went to Portugal for testing.

John Wheeler is the presiding genius behind the Escort Cosworth (below) – but he is easily overlooked, lurking in the background with his laptop. Delecour (right, tackling the sinuous roads of Corsica) regards the Ford's chassis as well-nigh perfect.

The potential shown in Monte Carlo spurred Ford on to establish where the cars stood competitively for Portugal. Wheeler explained, 'We did actually go down and do another quick test, but we weren't particularly optimistic that we'd prepared well for the gravel.' Ford dominated the 1993 Rally of Portugal, leading from start to finish, with 26 fastest stage times and François Delecour took the Escort Cosworth to its maiden World Rally Championship victory. Biasion's Escort was a strong second.

Understandably delighted and encouraged by this result, after analysis of the results from Portugal, Ford Motorsport concluded, however, that the rally was essentially won on the tarmac stages and that the Escort Cosworth did not exhibit any advantages over the opposition on gravel.

Boreham's testing philosophy had been to establish specifications for the two extremes, tarmac, and Acropolis-type gravel, with the faster gravel specification sitting 'somewhere in the middle'. A great deal was learned about front and rear suspension geometry during the tarmac testing. A significant improvement in the balance of the car was found through trying different roll centres, a process which Wheeler admits 'was going quite a long way away from theory to some extent'.

Ford Motorsport's drivers have significantly different tarmac driving techniques, and therefore car specification preferences. The result is that each works Escort Cosworth has a unique chassis set-up on tarmac. Indeed, in the next round, the Tour of Corsica, Ford ran its cars with different torque splits, extremes of differential stiffness settings and different spring rates.

Wheeler provides an insight to the reasons why: 'François seems to be a driver who lets the car into the corner at very high speed, and then is quite happy just to balance it round with very little throttle and come out with a fast exit speed; whereas Miki wants his braking and turning-in point to be precise and secure and then power it through. So, right from when he's turned in, he's using a lot of power.

'All I can say from riding in the car with them is that they both seem right – neither method seems to be wrong. But they are so totally different in the way in which they operate. Both of these methods are efficient, but they are still poles apart in the way that they are executed.'

Delecour took the Escort Cosworth to its second World Championship victory in Corsica, while Biasion came seventh after losing 11 minutes, thanks to a penalty for late arrival at a time control, following a problem re-aligning the clutch after a gearbox change.

Initially, Ford Motorsport went through the same development process on gravel as for tarmac, with both drivers setting off in different car specification directions, but each finally settling on almost identical gravel specifications to that of Biasion's original.

Certainly, in car specification terms, there are advantages to be gained on gravel from maximised traction at the front and rear axles, together with a centre differential which is free enough to allow the car to be manoeuvred. Wheeler commented: 'I think the confidence factor is different on tarmac – I think both our drivers have got the same level of feel and car control on gravel to be able to play with the car, whereas on tarmac it needs a special level of confidence to be able to go into the corners at speeds which seem too high. I think that's where you see the difference.'

The initial priorities of reliability and strength for the gravel specification Escort Cosworth meant that the car became considerably overweight. By late 1993, knowing the basics of the gravel specification, Ford was confident that it wasn't taking undue risks by embarking on an urgent and hefty re-design to reduce the car's weight. 'Really you have to treat them separately; you have to think in one direction for reliability and another direction for minimum weight,' observed Wheeler.

He is the first to admit that during 1993, Ford Motorsport has been very conservative in its attitude to the Group A Cosworth specifications: 'We haven't come up with any great innovations during the year; we've just been learning as we go along'. He also makes the point that the team has been fairly stretched throughout the year just in running the programme and building cars. It was stretched further when it became apparent that Ford could be in the running for the manufacturers' championship and a single entry for Biasion on the Rally of Argentina was crammed in at short notice.

'So, we spent the first half of the season getting all the different specifications sorted out, including Acropolis. That is a mountainous amount of work; to effec-

tively win on the tarmac and win Acropolis you've covered an awful lot of ground. We were very pleased with that. Then, slotting in an extra car for Argentina went well.

'Then we had to ask ourselves the question, "OK, we've done that job well, but where is the development work in the second half of the season for next year?" And the answer was, it wasn't there; we'd committed all the resources to just getting that far, and the "B" team that would be bringing along the future stuff didn't exist.'

While facing the need to re-group the engineering development side of Ford Motorsport and find ways to commit resources to advanced developments, Wheeler concedes that Motor-sport's conservatism in its first year, despite the results, could threaten its competitiveness in the future. Semi-active and active control technology for the Escort Cosworth transmission and suspension exists. It went through early tests and was then shelved, before test resurrection in the latter part of 1993. With the knowledge gained from success in the 1993 World Championship, might it have been advantageous to have employed such technology during the Escort Cosworth's debut championship year? After the Rally Australia, Wheeler responded: 'I think the big problem with that is that if you have too many elements of the car which are unknown, you can work round in circles without actually getting anywhere.

'Now there are examples of people who have brought it together successfully and very quickly – Prodrive are obviously the prime example of that – but our argument in favour of the way in which we've approached it is that we took the time which we could have spent on advancing our technology into making sure that we were competitive at the beginning of this season. I still think, at the moment, that it's the right decision that we took; although we could, fairly soon, be overhauled if we don't now make some catching-up moves.

'The trouble is that you get involved in some of these systems, you take the engineers off the basic job. And, if that means that you're then turning out on rallies with some fundamental things that are unreliable, or some basic incorrect setting-up, because you haven't been out and done any tarmac testing, then you could argue that you've done it the wrong way round.'

A large part of the competitiveness of a rally car is, of course, its driver. There are very few superstar drivers who are sufficiently talented – and determined – to be able to extract the utmost from today's top Group A cars. Although dedicated professionals, these drivers will still have their off-days. It's human nature that if things aren't going swimmingly a driver can lose confidence and problems become amplified; stage times increase. Equally, it is human nature that if a driver is winning a rally and in full swing, even if the car's suspension suffers damage, he could be in the frame of mind still to achieve amazing stage times, even with wheels pointing at the wrong angles.

When Toyota clinched the 1993 World Manufacturers' Championship in Australia, although Delecour came third, for the first time the Fords were evidently not on the pace. After the rally, Boreham conducted a deep investigation into possible technical reasons why, but Wheeler didn't discount the fact that Ford's drivers are human beings. 'That's still a huge factor; even the handful of superdrivers can have a really black week where they're just not performing, maybe because they'd been up practising too much. One of the things we're aware of possibly with Australia is that we were concerned that our drivers had overworked themselves – we're busy chasing all of our technical deficiencies, but maybe there's nothing there at all. When you start trying to analyse this lot it's quite a difficult equation.'

After the Rally Australia, Ford Motorsport realised that its honeymoon period was probably over. 'We're now stepping up our testing and development. We've got a lot of work to do on engine electronics; we're going to now advance our transmission development – differentials and controlled differentials. It's difficult to predict how many months before we see it come to fruition, but we've got a programme which aims to see some elements working for, I hope, Monte Carlo '94 and others for slightly later in the year. But, once again, we're going to have to do it step by step, so we don't actually introduce factors which make us unreliable. We're working on electronic control of the diffs, but I don't think that will be for Monte Carlo because I don't think we have a necessity. It's not an issue for Monte Carlo, for tarmac – unless there's snow.

'The way I see it is that unless you do a parallel conventional development you never have a clue whether your special componentry is giving you an advantage or a disadvantage...unless you have total faith in something, in which case you can just concentrate on that and take it for what it is. But that's certainly not the way that we would be prepared to work. We're only prepared to work on continuing to advance the conventional set-up, while trying to bring along the more advanced stuff in parallel.'

While a big Boreham priority is capitalising on 'free' performance improvements in braking, acceleration and cornering on gravel by bringing the gravel specification Escort nearer the weight limit, judging by the performance of its competitors in the latter half of the 1993 season, Ford acknowledges that engine development is also a pressing necessity. Wheeler commented: 'Theoretically nobody's going to get any more power, but I think the name of the game is to get optimum engine performance all the time, and the biggest issue there is knowing how to handle the restrictor, because it is a very sensitive balance between the turbo and the air going through the restrictor – by sucking too hard you can actually destroy the amount of air that goes through the restrictor. Optimisation of the engine performances is a real issue – which is power under certain conditions. That's where we've got to work very hard.'

Ford Motorsport's traditionally cautious approach to development is without doubt time-consuming, but it has provided the team with proven, fundamentally competitive components. The team now has a good grasp of what it needs to do, and what is needed to get there.

Other World Championship teams also know what they have to do. Each may adapt alternative technical solutions in challenging for future World Rally Championship victory, but all could be spurred by heeding the attributed words of John Fitzgerald Kennedy: 'Victory has a thousand fathers, but defeat is an orphan'.

Plan form

The Ford Escort RS Cosworth 4X4 is a direct result of a European-wide market survey. This was conducted in 1987, the year that World Championship rallying adopted Group A, to help Ford establish the marketing priorities of motor sport disciplines in relation to other sports and the levels of public interest in each sphere of motor sport.

Formula One racing came first, but rallying held a firm second place, exhibiting overwhelmingly that, together with touring car racing, it has the strongest perceived technical links for the ordinary motorist.

Armed with these survey results, Ford Motorsport established a rally plan, steered by its Chief Engineer, John Wheeler. In 1987 Lancia was ready to start winning Group A and overall honours with its Delta HF 4x4. In those early days of Group A, Ford knew that Toyota was preparing a significant assault, and that Mazda and Mitsubishi were well placed with turbocharged, four-wheel drive, Group A-homologated cars in their ranges. Ford had a competitive tarmac rally car in the three-door, two-wheel drive Sierra Cosworth, with that car's hardware scheduled to go into a four-door Sapphire bodyshell, which was to become four-wheel drive in mid-1990.

Insiders were aware, though, that the four-wheel drive Sapphire would be roughly on a par with the Lancias and Toyotas of the 1989 period. A four-wheel drive version of the CE14 Escort (then only a prototype), fitted with a transversely located Cosworth engine was planned, but CE14 volume production requirements meant that that car would not go on the market until around 1993 and Wheeler knew that it would be a car nearly identical in concept to the 1989 Lancia.

Back at the drawing board, the new Fiesta was discounted as too tight a package in which to cram rally-winning equipment. By then Ford Motorsport had useful, recent experience with the Sierra Cosworth, a car with a favourable weight distribution and long wheelbase, giving good stability at high speed and over bumps, but a car that was essentially too long and rather heavy.

Logical reasoning led to Ford Motorsport adapting the Sierra Cosworth 4X4's north – south power-train for use in its new CE14 Escort bodyshell. By August 1988 Boreham had completed a concept car, based on the previous Escort bodyshell, which, by demonstrating the mix of high road performance and sophistication planned into the concept, was a significant help in convincing Ford top brass. 'Absolutely mind-boggling' is how Wheeler describes the complexity of steering this Escort RS Cosworth concept through Ford corporate committees to final approval for production. Once pre-programme approval was gained, Wheeler was seconded to Ford's Special Vehicle Engineering department to see the vehicle through into production and 'Treat it as any other vehicle...obviously with some licence, because some of the motor sporting requirements were carrying a bit more weight than some of the production requirements.'

Motorsport started building the first Group A rally Escort RS Cosworth in May 1990. By March 1991 the road car's engineering design was complete and by May of that year the rally car was tested over the tarmac roads of Corsica. Engineering sign-off for the road car came by August, and production got under way at Karmann in Germany. In January 1992 Malcolm Wilson put the rally car through its paces on the stages of the Monte Carlo Rally, and by March Mia Bardolet had taken the car to victory on its second event, the Mijas Rally in Spain, where unhomologated cars are allowed to contest its gravel rally championship.

Early in 1992, Wheeler explained how he envisaged future technical developments for the Group A Escort Cosworth. This encompassed four-wheel steering, adaptive damping, active roll control, seven-speed semi-automatic shift transmission, different engines, different suspensions: 'Not all of these by any means will see the light of day, but they are the sort of areas that we have to be actively working in'. Although he was very keen to speed such developments and see early benefits, they were not pursued with much energy in the Escort's first World Championship year.

Ford Motorsport tested Escort Cosworths with initial developments of such advanced technical systems in the rally car's early days, but these systems had to be put back on the shelf while the team put all its efforts into running 'conventional' cars in the 1993 World Championship. Wheeler won't be drawn on the future, however: 'Wait and see what we do actually come up with'.

7

Photo Les Kolczak

Doctors in Rallying

DOCTOR ON THE LOOSE

by Amanda Campbell

Richard Gordon did for doctors in the '50s what James Herriott proceeded to do for vets in the '70s. Immortalised on film by Dirk Bogarde, the dashing young docs that peppered Gordon's pages got up to all sorts of high jinks in the pursuit of their profession and the early experience of Subaru doctor, David Williams, could have come straight from one of Gordon's scripts. 'It was my very first event with Subaru,' he recalled, 'the 1989 RAC, and my first call-out was at three a.m., to a member of the press. Stumbling from my room I knocked on the hotel door and as I went in there were these two rather attractive ladies in bed while my patient was waiting for me. I can remember thinking, "Hello, if this is rallying, this is the life!"'

Pity the poor doctor, four years on and still knocking on patients' doors expectantly. Even so, it was as good a starting point as any in a discipline still finding its way in the sport, for Williams and his contemporaries are breaking new ground in rallying.

The stresses and strains on a modern rally driver are at an all-time high, from nurturing his employer's multi-million pound investment to victory, via a virtually non-stop travel schedule, to the 3G-forces constantly pounding his neck as he takes each corner. They all take their mental and physical toll and the team doctor, naturally enough, is charged with fixing each symptom.

Inevitably, Lancia was the first team to have a seconded doctor travelling around the world and other manufacturers followed suit in due course, even if they weren't always clear what to do with the extra member of the team when they had him. 'I think when I first started at Prodrive no one really knew what to do with me, so I wrote my own brief. Rally drivers have been a completely neglected set of people and I was totally amazed at how unprofessional a lot of them were in terms of fitness – it's still hamburgers and pints in a lot of cases – so it was a case of concentrating on three main areas: fitness, nutrition and mental preparation,' said Williams.

Giving advice on safe sex to a couple of dozen young, free and single lads let loose in a foreign country, acting as a sounding post for over-wrought drivers, checking injuries, monitoring calorie intakes and preparing to deal with a serious accident are just some of the roles that land neatly into a team doctor's lap, quite apart from the normal day-to-day injuries and ailments which would ordinarily befall a group of people travelling for something in the region of 200 days a year. 'Mechanics, for instance, are always burning themselves changing turbos, brakes or whatever and although in itself the burn could be pretty harmless, because the risk of infection can be high in some foreign countries, everything has to be looked at,' explained Williams. He has the perfect c.v. for the job, progressing from motor bikes to chief medical officer with the BRSCC, before being snapped up by Prodrive.

Ford's doctor, Mark Porter (who coincidentally went to the same medical school as his opposite number at Subaru) is quick to acknowledge the work Williams is doing in winning recognition for the importance of fitness and general preparation at World Championship level. 'I think teams are only just coming to realise that time and money should be spent on preparing the driver as well as the car, and David is addressing the problem in great depth. If you look at 40 minutes in a rally car as being the equivalent of playing a game of squash, then you begin to realise that some kind of fitness is called for.'

Williams concurred. 'A lot of drivers are a long way from being as fit as they could be and so are also not driving as well as they could be. If you're fit it's easier to concentrate, and in temperatures of up to 40 degrees for three to four days, no way can you afford to be unfit, because by the end of the event you'll be in no shape at all. Rallying has nothing to do with strength. It's all based on endurance and stamina.'

TTE has the services of Dr Kjell Gustavsson, who feels that modern drivers are aware of the need for physical discipline. 'Nowadays they go to bed early, train hard and are careful with drink; it is much different from when I was competing in the '60s!' Fortunately it isn't all work and no play for the Toyota drivers, as they still seem to know how to celebrate after a rally.

With Ari Vatanen and Colin McRae to concentrate on, Williams has met with a mixed reception, particularly as far as diet is concerned. 'I use the same technique that long-distance runners use, since rallying is all about stamina and endurance, so carbohydrate loading with things like pasta, potatoes and cereal products is essential. Ari has been very good and takes the whole thing fairly seriously, but I think Colin still feels that he's young enough to be able to get away with it!'

At 41, Vatanen is certainly enjoying the pay-off with impressive showings, which Porter directly relates to his pre-event training: 'Ari's return to driving on the Acropolis is a testimony to his fitness. He admits he's never been as fit and it shows in his performance.' He also feels that drivers these days strive for fitness as a whole. 'Take François (Delecour) – he takes it all very seriously. We had a test session in Italy last year and he turned up on his mountain bike!' The previous year, Malcolm Wilson had been dispatched to the National Sports Centre at Lilleshall for a racing driver assessment, running through a series of tests to reveal any areas which needed work.

While a crew's physical needs are looked after by concentrating on fitness and nutrition, their mental preparation is also seen by Williams as an important factor. 'We work on mental imagery, whereby you go through a process of "driving" through a stage corner by corner, from start to finish, and imagining driving that stage faster than anybody else, and we would do this every evening on an event so that a driver really knows how it's going to feel.'

Photos of drivers in near trance-like states during a rally have caused much speculation as to the cause of the intense, fixed-eye stare, particularly of Carlos Sainz. Has he been hypnotised/drugged/under too much strain? Williams laughs. 'I think it's a case of the story being written around the photo really, but we do encourage our drivers to focus just before a stage, to have complete time to themselves to concentrate on the job in hand. A minute or two before the stage starts, they will put their helmets on, not talk to anyone, not sign autographs, just wind their window up and have complete focus for the next five to 20 minutes, without any distractions.'

The role of the sports psychologist will, he believes, come into its own as the sport continues to progress. 'I think it's a much undervalued role but, like a lot of things, it will take time to get into the mainstream.'

Ford's doctor took a rather more sanguine approach to his drivers: 'I don't really like the idea of mucking around with anyone's psyche,' he said. 'I feel that if drivers have reached this level then they already have the edge, the confidence in themselves and the approach needed to win that sets them apart from other drivers, and I wouldn't want to change that.' Delecour, however, is well known for his highly strung nature. Doesn't this merit some kind of psyching-down? 'The important thing for François is just to absorb him and it's the job of the whole team; I'll talk to him and try to calm him down if he's under a lot of stress, but so do the engineers and Colin Dobinson. It's very much a team effort. Everyone remains calm, as there'd be nothing worse for a driver if everyone was rushing around like headless chickens when he was worried himself.'

Heat is the biggest hazard on events and poses a particular problem on the Safari and in Greece. On the latter, for example, a driver will need between ten and 15 litres of water a day, while a mechanic requires between five and ten litres to keep his body well served. Sometimes even the best medical attention can't prevent mishaps, as with 'Possum' Bourne, whose body's temperature control system just shot out of control in the heat: the only way to cool him down was to pack him in ice, which the team promptly did, only to watch in amazement as steam rose from the ice. According to Gustavsson, a two per cent loss of body water is equivalent to losing 20 per cent of physical and brain activity and so, on an event like the Safari, it is particularly important that the right balance of salts and water is maintained but, as Williams pointed out, the important thing is to make sure all the team has water freely available and not just the drivers. Porter had cause to see the problem rather differently, as he joined the Ford team for his first World Championship rally in Sanremo in 1989. 'There I was, I'd never been on a rally before, so I had no idea what to expect. We were running Malcolm at the time, and when he came into service after five or six stages, he got out and I leant over on his seat to pass something out, and my knee was completely wet! All I could think of was that Malcolm had had a narrow squeak at a corner or else was completely incontinent, so I didn't say anything. It took me a couple of days to realise that it was sweat, and what a relief that was!'

It is to combat this dehydration problem that the special potions are brought out. No self-respecting modern rally team is without its endless supply of 'magic drinks', which are dispensed at regular intervals throughout an event, turning tired and sweaty rally drivers into fresh-faced and zestful chargers once more ready to do battle. The reality is that they often consist of nothing other than commercially available brands, depending on a driver's individual preference, or occasionally they will be made up by the team to a formula. 'They are high in carbohydrates and contain long-chain carbohydrates, the simple sugars such as you would put in tea. They serve two functions, firstly as fuel for the body – glycogen is immediately absorbed into muscles – and secondly they take water with them, so they are basically rehydration solutions, but which are freely available to anyone,' explained Williams.

It all seems another world to the days when Andrew Cowan was contesting the Monte Carlo Rally and he used to load up a case of Lucozade as a precaution. 'People used to think I was a mad Scot, but doing Monte and not eating for 24 hours and then taking a drink of Lucozade, you could feel the bubbles coming through. It was a tremendous pick-me-up!'

Although what were widely known as 'wakey-wakey pills' were commonly used by co-drivers in the 1960s on long-distance events such as the Liège, drug abuse is not seen as a problem in rallying, which is lucky since dope testing is random and, as Subaru found out, on occasions hit-and-miss. 'My team has only been drug tested in Corsica, and it was such a complete fiasco that a complaint was lodged to FISA. The samples that were taken weren't sealed, the whole procedure was carried out incorrectly and in the end samples weren't labelled correctly, so if there had been a problem no one would have known who it was anyway! I was just glad I was there and felt very sorry for FISA that they had employed the wrong people,' said Williams. Dr Gustavsson, who works on the FISA dope testing list, although he wasn't involved in Corsica, feels it is unlikely that a drug could be found to have the sustained effect necessary to benefit a driver. Yes, certain drugs could give a quick burst of improved performance, but not over the length of a rally. 'I think that motor sport has less doping than any other sport and there's none at all in rallying, I am 100 per cent sure.' Williams agreed that there is not the same kind of pressure for performance as there is with track athletes and that there are enough legal drugs available to cope with any requirements. 'Drivers know that their whole careers could be at risk if they tried to continue with an injury; on the whole they are sensible. I've never come across a problem in all the time that I've been involved in motor sport.'

Richard Castellani (left) and David Williams (below) are at the sharp end of the sport, providing constant moral and physical support for the most expensive commodities of all – drivers such as Carlos Sainz and Colin McRae.

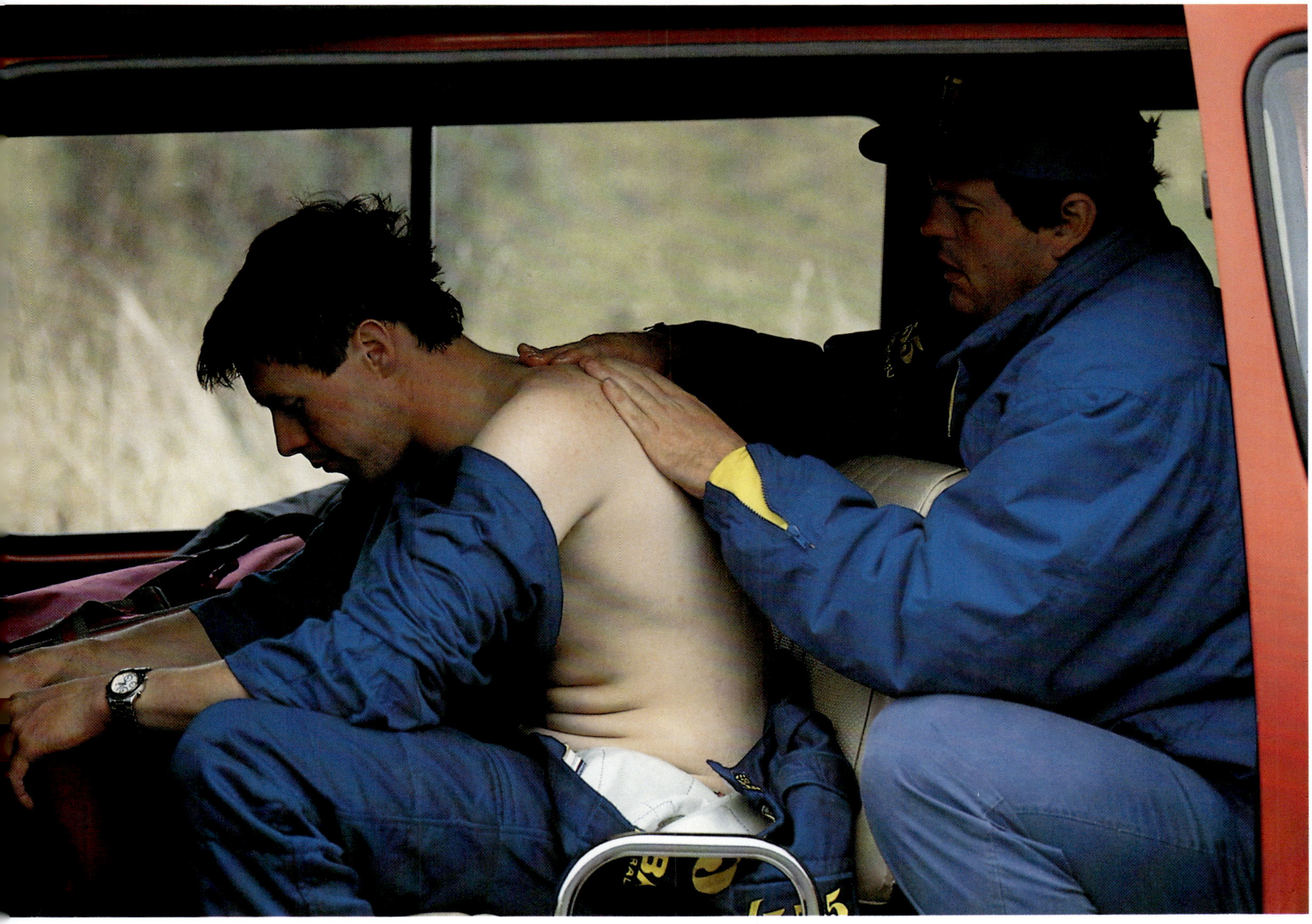

Historically, rallying has trotted after Formula One racing in many respects, from technical specifications to safety, and medical and drug-testing facilities should soon follow, thinks Williams. 'I'd like to see a rallying equivalent of Professor Sid Watkins who, as an independent observer, travels to all the circuits inspecting all the medical facilities. If they're not up to scratch the race doesn't happen and he also has the power to say that a driver is fit to race. As a neutral third party he is also useful as the drivers are able to go to him with their problems.'

Lugging 80 kilos of medical equipment around the world – and by mid-October, Williams had circumnavigated it six times this year – is a necessity when he has not only the drivers and co-drivers in his care, but also management and a full complement of mechanics. 'As well as the actual rallies I always attend all the tests. It's worth doing, because testing can be several hours away from medical care and it is the team's most vulnerable time. When you're miles away from anywhere, you are literally the difference between life and death.'

Carrying 'all the drugs a GP would dispense', he also carries a rucksack designed for the Gulf War paramedics. Known as a 'Thomas Pack' the bag contains enough plasma substitutes and drips to stabilise a patient as well as all the equipment necessary to look after respiratory functions until more permanent arrangements can be made. A separate 'crew bag' contains the two different kinds of splints required to remove patients from a car.

Ideally, he feels, every World Championship team should travel with a three-piece medical team: a medical officer, a sports physiotherapist and a sports psychologist, 'but I know that everything costs money and in an already expensive sport it would just be prohibitive. The simple reason that I get the job over the other two is that I can dispense drugs to cover anything from a cough or cold to meningitis.'

A rally crew's most common workplace injuries come as a result of the forces in motion and the constant changes in direction. Imagine, if you will, being shaken by the shoulders with two and a half large bags of potatoes firmly attached to your head and you will begin to realise why most drivers suffer from neck problems sooner or later. The straight line acceleration isn't a problem, but laterally, a helmeted head can hit 3G any number of times in one stage. That and a similar number of jolts to the back is why many teams also employ masseurs to keep the crew supple during an event and also why the number of drivers who choose to wear back supports is ever increasing. 'It's movement that causes injury, so we must work closely with seat manufacturers, as it's absolutely vital that a driver gets as much support from his seat as possible,' stated Williams.

An important part of their job description is the 'feel-good factor'. As Porter observed, 'I'm essentially there as an insurance policy. I can talk my job up, but that's what you're basically there for.' However, when this translates into being a familiar face in a hospital thousands of miles away, it can seem like a policy worth having.

'Obviously, the local facilities can vary a great deal when you're abroad,' explained Williams diplomatically. 'We were testing in Portugal when one of the Michelin tyre technicians hurt his arm and I thought it might have been broken. We took him to the local hospital where they produced the most antiquated X-ray machine I'd ever seen and even after developing the film all they had was a bare light bulb to view it with, so there we all were trying to puzzle out whether this fuzzy image had a broken bone or not – it was lucky it wasn't anything too bad!'

Most of the doctors combine their rallying duties with a 'day job'; Williams has established his own sports clinic where he looks after the England netball team and Lennox Lewis, among others, while Porter combines 20 hours a week of general practice with a television 'Doc-Spot', a combination which, although hectic, he feels lucky to have. 'General practice can get very repetitive if you're doing it all the time and, although I'm not a full-time employee, I do very much feel part of the team. I think you must regard yourself as such, as often you are privy to all sorts of conversations which could be sensitive and it's nice to know that people don't start ending conversations when I'm around.'

The time hasn't yet come when the positions become full time, although Williams does get involved beyond testing and event duties. 'If we're going somewhere which calls for vaccinations, I'll give them in-house, because it makes economic sense; if everyone has to take a morning off to go to see their doctor, you lose a lot of hours, whereas if I go down to Prodrive everyone can be done in half an hour.'

As a lobbyist for more specialised treatment for rally crews, Williams sees these as exciting times. 'We're just beginning to exploit the information and statistics available from other athletes, and young drivers will undoubtedly benefit from this. OK, in the NHS if you go into general practice you have a very well-paid job for life. As it is, I earn a third of what I could get, but I'm five times as happy. I have a tremendous life!'

His career as a rally doctor was almost over before it got started. Shortly after his bedroom call-out, on that very first RAC, he was standing in a cold and wet North Wales service area in the small hours. The team at the time was led by Markku Alén and Ilkka Kivimäki. 'I only knew Markku by his fearsome reputation, and I'd been sent to get some water. I could only get the fizzy kind, so I thought, "Oh well," and handed it to him. Markku drank some, spat it out and then threw the glass at me, roaring, "I don't drink this water, I only drink Evian!" Well, Kivimäki had asked for a can of Coca-Cola, but I could only get Pepsi, but I thought he'd never notice, poured it into a glass and handed it to him. Sure enough, he took some of it, spat it out and threw the glass at me, shouting, "I tell you doctor, I only drink Coca-Cola, not Pepsi-Cola". At five a.m., feeling shivery and cold in the middle of Wales, I thought maybe I'd made a wrong choice in joining Subaru and then Kivimäki laughed and it became apparent that Kivimäki's reputation as a joker was as strong as Alén's for being difficult!'

Richard Gordon would have loved it!

No self-respecting professional rally team would venture afield without its doctor now: Peugeot even took one to the Pike's Peak hillclimb (above); Andrea Zanussi receives attention (above). Janne Jönsson (left, with Björn Waldegård) was a familiar presence at TTE across the globe.

P. KUUKKALA
K. SHINOZUKA
YOKOHAMA
三菱石油
KYB
RALLIART

4
三菱石油

The Future of Cross-Country Rallying

A POCKETFUL OF SAND

by David Campbell, Editor, Top Race and Rally

The senior team member of a leading 'rally raid' outfit edged forward in his seat. The sun was sinking behind him and, while his sponsor and PR man slumped back and sipped their third gins and tonics, gazing vacantly across the impatiently quivering Red Sea, he remained nervous and fidgety.

After a polite five minutes in their company, he stood up briskly. 'It's dark. I'm going to the car,' he said, finished his drink standing, and left. The PR man raised his hand for another G and T; who could blame him – it had been the first time in two weeks he had felt confident enough to have ice in his drink in Egypt. The boy serving him had promised that the ice had been made from bottled water.

Late that night, the door of a rally car clicked open. A furtive figure slipped quietly inside, careful not to make the slightest noise that would attract attention. He pulled his sleeping bag around his shoulders, and for the first time in days, relaxed enough to sleep. He wasn't nervous any more; sleeping in the car meant that it was safe from whatever enemies, imaginary or real, there might be.

That illustrates everything one needs to know about rally raids or, to give the sport its new, less evocative title, cross-country rallying. It tells of the intense rivalry between teams which leads to paranoia in extreme cases, and of the risks of rallying in Africa – not the more mundane possibilities of crashing a car, rather the risks unique to raids, such as dehydration, food poisoning, and all manner of alien creatures inhabiting the local water.

Living in the desert is not easy. The four- and five-star hotels of the World Rally Championship are swapped for tiny one-man tents; crews, mechanics, management and press queue together for food served by mobile caterers who may, or may not serve you food that is going to harm you; and in the evenings, there is little to do except gossip, and worry.

True, there are occasions like that described above where one might chance across a good hotel and a beach bar to while away the evening, but these are extremely rare. Instead, the cold desert nights breed paranoia and fear, as each side gathers in huddles around its plastic plates of re-heated food and tries to second-guess the opposition. At times, accusations fly. Threats of protests are common, but these generally ring hollow and are merely designed to wrong-foot the opposition.

The main protagonists are Mitsubishi and Citroën. The rivalry between these two great teams is more intense than any witnessed in the World Rally Championship. Perhaps it's because the long-distance raids such as the Paris – Dakar or the Pharaohs are cut off from the rest of the world, the circus forming its own microcosm of society. It puts one in mind of William Golding's *Lord of the Flies*: a degeneration of normal social mores occurs and baser instincts rise to the surface.

'It's like a war,' declared Saeed Al Hajri during the Pharaohs Rally. 'I've never seen anything like it. It's not like in normal rallies. Each side doesn't speak to the other.' This war, with the blue Rothmans Mitsubishi team on one side, and the red Total Citroëns on the other, can reach epic proportions.

The battle commences months before each rally. Practice is usually banned, but North African deserts are not easily policed and, if you happened to be walking in the Sahara at certain times of the year, you would be likely to come across the familiar faces of rally drivers and co-drivers, zipping around in the sand dunes looking for short cuts, easier routes and hidden hazards. It's all done in total secret, of course. Said one works co-driver: 'It's crazy, you know. We all do it. Everybody knows we do it. I know they do it, and they know we do it. You book into a hotel in Africa before a rally, and you pull out the register, and there are all the familiar names of the other team

Salvador Servia (left) has tried an Integrale on European cross-country rallies, but Lancia has left the field to the specialists, notably Sonauto, which prepares the official Pajeros.

who have been there a week before you!'

Technological advances play their part too. Thierry Viardot of the Mitsubishi team couldn't wait to see the new Citroëns when they were wheeled out before the Atlas Rally earlier this year. He leapt all over them like an excited school boy and then gleefully announced that he still thought that his Pajeros had the edge. But try looking underneath a Red car with a Blue Team shirt on during an event, and you'll find yourself quickly removed to the other side of the sand dune!

It's the little things that count. Citroën brought along a giant mobile hotel to the Atlas Rally. It was a large truck, with bedrooms, a shower and even toilets for its drivers. The look of envy on the faces of the Mitsubishi die-hards brought big grins to the Citroën team management. Forget the World Cup; scoring points this way brings far more satisfaction!

It is a psychological war. Despite the suspicion, there is no evidence or any record of 'nobbling' another car, but the mere suggestion late at night in the bivouacs can raise worries that soon mushroom out of all proportion. The bivouacs – little tented cities that grow up overnight in the middle of the desert and disappear early the next morning – are rumour mills. At the centre of each bivouac, there is usually a large marquee, or group of large tents, where food is served and where the organisers' and press offices are housed. Surrounding them are the ghettoes, the Mitsubishi and the Citroën camps, generally no-go areas for the other team. Out in the suburbs, the private teams create their own camps, but the amateur drivers behave much like any other enthusiastic rally team, helping each other out with tools, parts and practical support.

Al Hajri undoubtedly fell victim to the psychological conflict that was waged while he was leading the Pharaohs Rally in his Mitsubishi Pajero. With a lead of over two hours and only two days left of the 11-day charge through the Egyptian deserts, the Qatar driver was virtually assured of victory. But before he started the penultimate stage, there was clearly something wrong. Saeed was disturbed. He'd had a restless night's sleep, and the Mitsubishi team doctor Bruno Geoffray was called over to have a word with him. 'He was very tense that morning,' said Bruno. 'I spent 15 minutes with him telling him not to worry and to race as normal.'

But as the team waited anxiously for Saeed's arrival at the Fayoum bivouac, the confidence and smiling faces disappeared when Jean-Louis Schlesser charged into the camp in his Schlesser Original buggy and straight up the massive sand dune to the Mitsubishi base perched on the top. 'Saeed has rolled over. I think he is hurt,' he shouted.

The medical team swung into action as helicopters took off towards the scene of the accident, just two kilometres from the end of the 300-kilometre competitive section. Saeed was helicoptered to Cairo with a suspected spinal injury and Mitsubishi had lost the rally. The car had flipped onto its roof while descending a dune. Few could work out why it happened. Dune driving was Saeed's big strength and, since he was so far in the lead, he could either have driven around it, or driven over it very carefully. Strangely, he was first car on the road: in normal circumstances, with the risk of hidden hazards and navigational errors, it has always been the practice to drop back when so far in the lead and follow other cars.

A study of video footage afterwards revealed that he had charged over the dune at full speed. Only Bruno the doctor knew the real answer: Saeed had been worried by suggestions that Citroën was about to lodge a protest over a route infringement. The Red team had made its intentions clear and, with so much fuss going on, Saeed had become convinced that he would either be disqualified or awarded a massive time penalty. With

While the MT, with it's rugged, self-cleaning tread, has been specially developed
o handle the roughest, toughest, and even the muddiest terrain. And when you're
iding back into town, they'll give a smoother, quieter performance that's hard to beat.
So get down to your local Goodyear Wrangler dealer today for the best
dvice and fitting. He'll never let you down.

R ONE 4X4 TIRE

GOODYEAR WRANGLER 4X4

this playing on his mind, the only answer was to drive as quickly as possible. Of course, there was no real evidence put forward to suggest an infringement. After Al Hajri's crash, there was no need to protest.

Both Mitsubishi and Citroën take the whole business very seriously. However, both sides deny any real interest in the World Cup, a championship set up at the beginning of 1993 with a view to forming a full World Championship. Certainly, for the marketing departments of the two manufacturers, events like the Atlas Rally and the Pharaohs, and especially the cross-country calendar serve only as expensive test sessions and they provide the opportunity for the two heavyweight teams to circle each other before the big fight. It is this that makes winning the lesser events in the series important. For Citroën, beating Mitsubishi on events like the Pharaohs means it can grab a psychological advantage for the Paris – Dakar and it enables the teams to measure up to each other in terms of technological advances. If you find your main rival has a more powerful engine, better suspension, or a transmission improvement, you have time to discover these strengths and weaknesses on the lesser events, and prepare for the Paris – Dakar.

Yet despite its importance and the vast sums of money involved (the cost of running each car can run to over a million pounds per season) to Sonauto Ralliart's boss, Ullrich Brehmer, it is not a matter of sporting life and death. 'For me the rally raid is a holiday. My job is Technical Director of Sonauto, one of Europe's biggest car distribution companies. I enjoy raids very much. Of course, there is rivalry; this is a competition. Everyone is very competitive and wants to win. I want to win – that is very important to me, and the drivers, and the team. But, you know, we must not forget that this is sport.'

For the easy-going Brehmer, cross-country rallies are his method of relaxation. For this reason, it is often the case that he does not stay with the team throughout the rally, appearing only at the start and finish. On the Pharaohs, he did not even make an appearance when his 'day job' required him to be at his desk, but with the very capable Viardot running the team in his absence, he can often direct from a distance. One event he never misses a day of, however, is the Paris – Dakar. 'It is the event where we started. I love to go to Africa; we all do. It is a beautiful place, and many things to see. This is why I do not like normal rallies in the World Championship. They are not for me. That is more like Formula One, with just the racing and nothing else to see.'

Guy Fréquelin's position at Citroën is quite different. Formerly a distinguished competitor in 'normal' rallies, he took over the mantle of Citroën team director when his old co-driver and boss, Jean Todt, moved on to greater things. Running the cross-country team forms part of his day job. He managed the team during the infamous Paris – Cape Town Rally, on which Citroën was defeated thanks to Brehmer's superb tactical manoeuvring. That hurt Fréquelin.

During the long section through the Ténéré desert, the Pajeros pulled out a massive lead quite suddenly. They had found a legal short cut that the Citroën men had failed to spot. Fréquelin, smarting from his defeat, since it was in the Ténéré that Mitsubishi effectively won the event, accused Brehmer of sharp practice and called for a revision of the rules. 'We must make a change that does not allow the recce of the route,' he said at the time. 'It is not how this rally should be won.'

Further humiliation came as the three leading Mitsubishis calmly trundled through the stages, day after day from Chad to South Africa, knowing that any form of overtaking was ruled out on the narrow tracks south of the Equator.

Relations between Citroën and Mitsubishi cooled after that. Fréquelin and Brehmer maintained a dialogue and often came to private agreements to limit practising, but neither openly forgave the other; Fréquelin for Brehmer's Ténéré

Relying heavily on Peugeot's Group B technology, Citroën has become a major force in cross-country rallying. Vast distances and vast horizons are the essence of the sport, crews battling the wilderness unaided (right).

shorter one-day events such as the Spanish Baja, are of little importance. It's the Big One they want to win – the Paris – Dakar. It is this event which captures the imagination above all others, much like the Monte Carlo Rally in the Sixties, before there was a proper World Championship. The other events in the

short-cut, Brehmer for Fréquelin's hostile reaction.

They both agree that the Paris – Dakar is almost the be-all and end-all of their involvement, however. Fréquelin has confirmed: 'The Paris – Dakar is important, because it has the most publicity. We test on other events for the Paris – Dakar.'

He did add that the other events were important to Citroën's plans. After being the Kings of the Desert for so long on the Paris – Dakar, before being ousted by Mitsubishi, the team has taken a greater interest in the new World Cup for Cross-

Country Rallies. Nevertheless, there were some events in 1993 that Citroën refused to attend. Along with Mitsubishi, Fréquelin's team stayed away from the Sardinian round, famed for its poor organisation and legal wrangles. The event has even suffered competitor strikes and protests in recent times, and this year's event suffered once again from terrible organisational errors.

For Fréquelin and Brehmer alike, the World Cup would have to mature considerably before they could take more than a passing interest. As a result, the series suffered in credibility terms for much of

the year, as the Big Guns often kept their powder dry. Mitsubishi delighted in the fact that Jean-Pierre Fontenay led the classification for much of the season in his works-supported T2 Pajero – T2 being the equivalent of Group A, T3 Group B, and the T1 category similar to Group N. The sponsor, Rothmans, began to get excited, and demanded that Fontenay's Pajero should be liveried in its colours before the Pharaohs Rally.

However, even Bruno Musmarra, Fontenay's navigator, was mildly amused by it all. 'I can just imagine: a big party with all the motor racing World Champions. Alain Prost will say: "I am champion and I can offer you a lot of money." And I will say: "I am champion and I can offer you...(at this point he dug deep into the pockets of his dusty overalls) sand!"'

As Fontenay, laughing at his friend's joke, crawled under his Pajero once again to repair an oil leak, the absurdity of the situation became clear. From under his car, the oil-stained Fontenay called out: 'Bruno, does Prost work like this?'

When the FIA World Council agreed that the sport of rally raids could have its own championship, both teams and the hundreds of mainly French enthusiasts became excited. It was unfortunate, perhaps, that it was decided the term 'rally raid' should be converted to the less inspiring label, 'cross-country rally', but a World Championship could bring the sport out of its French shell and into the global arena, perhaps competing for status with the World Rally Championship.

The World Cup for Cross-Country Rallies was supposed to start with the Tunisia Rally, but the arguments began almost immediately. Fréquelin refused to take his team to an event that did not allow reconnaissance. He, like Brehmer, was fed up with the secret practising farce. It not only spoilt relationships between both teams, but they both agree that practising is necessary: firstly, if one doesn't do it, the other certainly will and secondly, the cars are becoming so powerful and the rallies so competitive that both want some idea of the hazards so as to avoid potentially dangerous accidents.

Tunisia also found itself in hot water with the FIA over television rights. These belonged, as with all FIA championships, to the FIA. Television, however, is the only means for cross-country events to present themselves to the public (there are few spectator grandstands in the desert) and therefore obtain revenue from sponsors, and create a saleable package for manufacturers and their sponsors. Tunisia, and all the other rallies, wanted to strike their own deals. FISA cancelled the series, and Tunisia

Mitsubishi has a fine record in the desert, thanks to the likes of Bruno Saby and Saeed Al Hajri (below). If you think the drivers are tough, spare a thought for the hard men of the sport, traversing the desert on two wheels (right).

SUZUKI 93
WORLD 500cc CHAMPION
Kevin Schwantz
For more information on the 1994 range
FREEPHONE
0500 526262

ran as a one-off event.

The French promotions company, Promocourse, which has had a close involvement with such events for many years, tried to institute a rebel championship. A meeting with all the raid organisers was set up, but gentle pressure and persuasion from FISA soon convinced the national sporting authorities that this might not be in their best interests and the idea died.

The Atlas Rally organisers agreed to limited reconnaissance in the meantime, to bring Citroën back into the equation, and FISA managed to come to an arrangement with the organisers of all the events over television rights. Everyone was happy once more and the World Cup was back.

For Citroën, this has turned out to be a blessing. Pierre Lartigue and Timo Salonen found themselves holding the lead jointly after the penultimate round in Egypt, and Citroën announced its entry in the 'final', the Dubai Desert Challenge: the Cup had suddenly become important. Mitsubishi had always intended to go to Dubai, because Rothmans was aware that this was a particularly important market, especially since it was Middle Eastern money that was contributing a sizeable budget for Al Hajri.

But will the Cross-Country Cup develop into a full-blown World Championship to rival the current World Rally Championship? The appeal of such a series would be very strong. The T3 cars are technically innovative, more like the Group B cars that no longer have a place in the 'conventional' World Championship. There are, obviously, no spectator problems with the desert events, and no right-minded environmentalist could argue that the desert is threatened by rally cars. The stages are extremely long, some almost 800 kilometres (although the 1994 Paris – Dakar – Paris organiser 'Fenouil' proposes a 400-kilometre limit for his event) and marathon rallies can offer total stage distances in excess of 4000 kilometres. The stage lengths of most World Championship rallies pale in comparison. Raids bring back the adventure and endurance factors missing from the modern rally scene, and the enthusiasm of many European terrestrial and satellite television stations is surprising. Raids might not be easy to film, but with a helicopter and satellite communication they can make spectacular programmes.

However, the events are very French and, while Italians and Spaniards are warming to the idea, few other countries feel welcome. Britain, for example, is simply not interested and any journalist or competitor on a marathon event without an excellent command of the French language would find even basic survival difficult!

Few British competitors take part and the British media has never considered covering the events since Mark Thatcher got lost on the 1982 Paris – Dakar, aside from the occasional paragraph in a few national newspapers. The Paris – Cape Town became a topical subject in 1991 because it was the first international sporting event to enter South Africa after sanctions were lifted, but even then, coverage was proportionately low for such a historic occasion. Several journalists used the Paris – Cape Town to justify a trip to South Africa to interview South African sports personalities.

If desert motor sport is to thrive, a more international approach must be adopted and consistent organisational standards must be achieved. And, after that, the rally raid fraternity must consider that ASNs will be very keen to keep their rounds of the World Rally Championship both intact and healthy, and any threat from a rival championship could find itself short of votes!

Ever the individualist, Jean-Louis Schlesser has forsaken the circuits for the desert, piloting a two-wheel drive, self-built buggy.

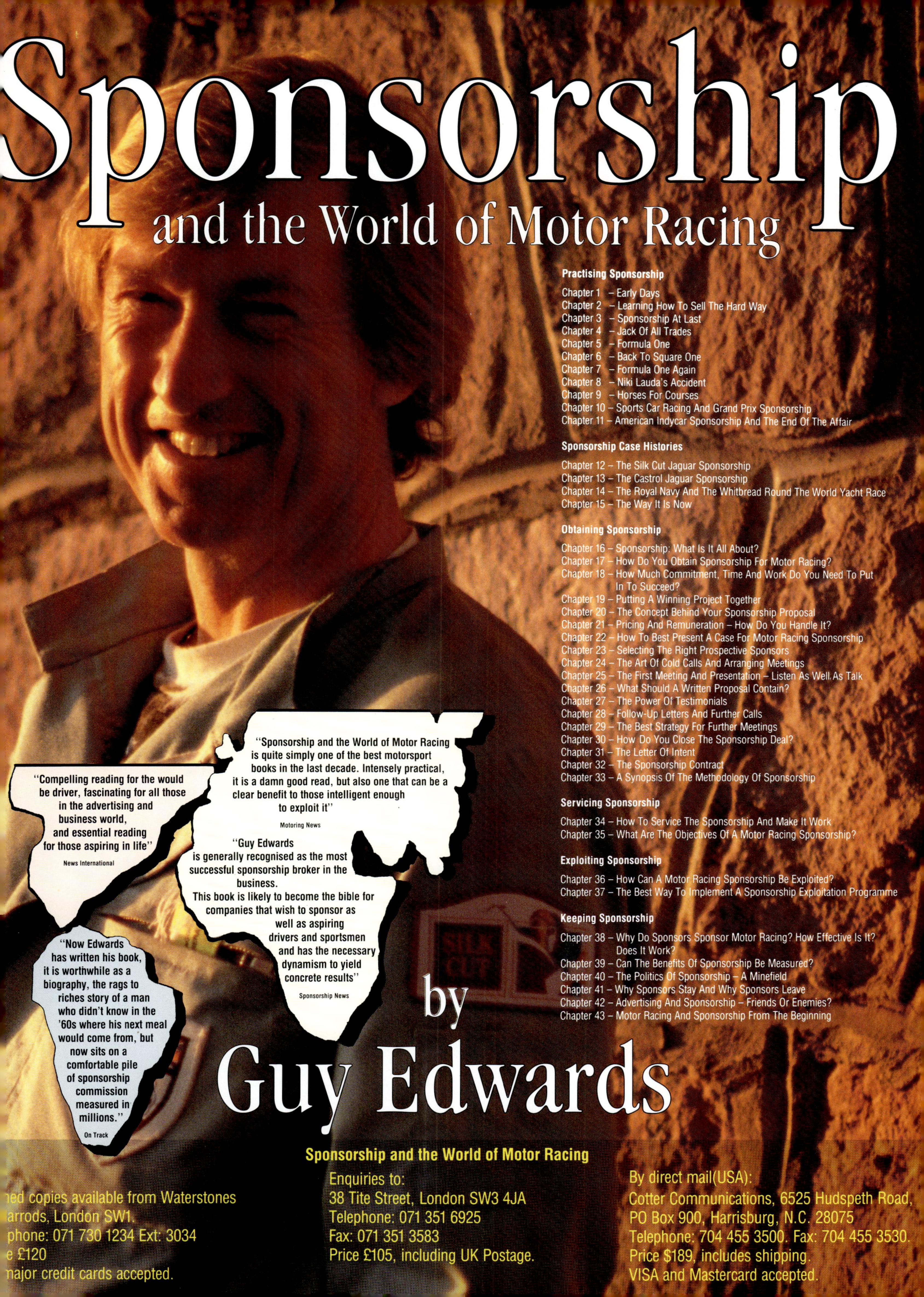

Sponsorship
and the World of Motor Racing
Practising Sponsorship
Chapter 1 – Early Days
Chapter 2 – Learning How To Sell The Hard Way
Chapter 3 – Sponsorship At Last
Chapter 4 – Jack Of All Trades
Chapter 5 – Formula One
Chapter 6 – Back To Square One
Chapter 7 – Formula One Again
Chapter 8 – Niki Lauda's Accident
Chapter 9 – Horses For Courses
Chapter 10 – Sports Car Racing And Grand Prix Sponsorship
Chapter 11 – American Indycar Sponsorship And The End Of The Affair
Sponsorship Case Histories
Chapter 12 – The Silk Cut Jaguar Sponsorship
Chapter 13 – The Castrol Jaguar Sponsorship
Chapter 14 – The Royal Navy And The Whitbread Round The World Yacht Race
Chapter 15 – The Way It Is Now
Obtaining Sponsorship
Chapter 16 – Sponsorship: What Is It All About?
Chapter 17 – How Do You Obtain Sponsorship For Motor Racing?
Chapter 18 – How Much Commitment, Time And Work Do You Need To Put In To Succeed?
Chapter 19 – Putting A Winning Project Together
Chapter 20 – The Concept Behind Your Sponsorship Proposal
Chapter 21 – Pricing And Remuneration – How Do You Handle It?
Chapter 22 – How To Best Present A Case For Motor Racing Sponsorship
Chapter 23 – Selecting The Right Prospective Sponsors
Chapter 24 – The Art Of Cold Calls And Arranging Meetings
Chapter 25 – The First Meeting And Presentation – Listen As Well As Talk
Chapter 26 – What Should A Written Proposal Contain?
Chapter 27 – The Power Of Testimonials
Chapter 28 – Follow-Up Letters And Further Calls
Chapter 29 – The Best Strategy For Further Meetings
Chapter 30 – How Do You Close The Sponsorship Deal?
Chapter 31 – The Letter Of Intent
Chapter 32 – The Sponsorship Contract
Chapter 33 – A Synopsis Of The Methodology Of Sponsorship
Servicing Sponsorship
Chapter 34 – How To Service The Sponsorship And Make It Work
Chapter 35 – What Are The Objectives Of A Motor Racing Sponsorship?
Exploiting Sponsorship
Chapter 36 – How Can A Motor Racing Sponsorship Be Exploited?
Chapter 37 – The Best Way To Implement A Sponsorship Exploitation Programme
Keeping Sponsorship
Chapter 38 – Why Do Sponsors Sponsor Motor Racing? How Effective Is It? Does It Work?
Chapter 39 – Can The Benefits Of Sponsorship Be Measured?
Chapter 40 – The Politics Of Sponsorship – A Minefield
Chapter 41 – Why Sponsors Stay And Why Sponsors Leave
Chapter 42 – Advertising And Sponsorship – Friends Or Enemies?
Chapter 43 – Motor Racing And Sponsorship From The Beginning
"Compelling reading for the would be driver, fascinating for all those in the advertising and business world, and essential reading for those aspiring in life"
News International
"Sponsorship and the World of Motor Racing is quite simply one of the best motorsport books in the last decade. Intensely practical, it is a damn good read, but also one that can be a clear benefit to those intelligent enough to exploit it"
Motoring News
"Guy Edwards is generally recognised as the most successful sponsorship broker in the business. This book is likely to become the bible for companies that wish to sponsor as well as aspiring drivers and sportsmen and has the necessary dynamism to yield concrete results"
Sponsorship News
"Now Edwards has written his book, it is worthwhile as a biography, the rags to riches story of a man who didn't know in the '60s where his next meal would come from, but now sits on a comfortable pile of sponsorship commission measured in millions."
On Track
SILK CUT
by
Guy Edwards
Sponsorship and the World of Motor Racing
ned copies available from Waterstones
arrods, London SW1.
phone: 071 730 1234 Ext: 3034
e £120
major credit cards accepted.
Enquiries to:
38 Tite Street, London SW3 4JA
Telephone: 071 351 6925
Fax: 071 351 3583
Price £105, including UK Postage.
By direct mail(USA):
Cotter Communications, 6525 Hudspeth Road,
PO Box 900, Harrisburg, N.C. 28075
Telephone: 704 455 3500. Fax: 704 455 3530.
Price $189, includes shipping.
VISA and Mastercard accepted.

Rallying as a Television Sport

THE REVOLUTION WILL BE LIVE

by Jerry Williams, Deputy Chief Sub-Editor, Daily Mail

TV or not TV? That is the question looming over rallying. In global terms the answer might not amount to a hill of beans, but it's going to bring a gale of change to this most mysterious branch of motor sport, for the wrong reply could threaten the World Rally Championship's existence. Discontent among rallying's money men at its share of TV has been bubbling under the surface for some years. Now it has come down to this: without a quantum increase in good quality screen time, the big team parent companies will steel themselves to quit the World Championship. That hint has left their own motor sport barons running more than a little scared, so much so that, after years of agreeing about nothing, they have – astonishingly – banded together.

The result is the World Rally Teams Association. Two of the WRTA's main aims are reform of the world series and pursuing the Holy Grail of television. If successful, it could save the World Championship from extinction.

In the manufacturers' boardrooms, rallying has a narrow band of uses, none of which is the sheer thrill of watching God-given talents like Colin McRae or Didier Auriol at work. For empires like Ford, Toyota, Subaru, Castrol, Mitsubishi, British American Tobacco, Renault, Mobil and Repsol, the sport is no more than a tool for PR, image enhancement, corporate hospitality...and shifting the product. If throwing rally cars off mountains became a better sales line than motor sport, you can bet that Escort Cosworths, Imprezas and Celicas would be helicoptered en masse to the top of Mont Blanc.

But the sporting manufacturers worship TV. Nothing beats that moving image in the corner of millions of living rooms, and head office number crunchers have made it crystal clear that their World Championship efforts can no longer be justified without more and better screen time. From where they stand, one can see their point. A five-year championship programme starting from scratch can cost £30-£50 million. Sporting manufacturers aren't charities.

The problem is that at the sharp end – big team management and the sport's international administration – the story has for years been one of disarray, disagreement and in-fighting. Now, they all need each other to achieve their masters' demands.

Prodrive's boss, David Richards, explains the recent history of ineffectual dabbling with television thus: 'Five years ago there was no central control over TV in the World Championship. The manufacturers – our benefactors don't forget – demanded TV. So I began taking Barrie Hinchliffe along and making programmes with a Subaru slant and pumping them out. Toyota, among others, were doing the same with their own film crew. In Britain that sometimes meant you had the ridiculous situation of ITV having one film and the Beeb another. Inevitably both were biased and not a true reflection of the sport. It was repeated elsewhere and it wasn't to anyone's benefit. The TV companies got fed up with the piecemeal coverage. And until you get consistency they're never going to commit to it. What's more, people were spending too much on it, sometimes to the detriment of their team budgets.'

That, according to Richards, was the cue for Bernie Ecclestone to enter, stage right. 'He came along with his International Sports Communicators outfit and FISA behind him, and said, "Let's clean up this act. We'll control all the rights and we'll stop the advertorials and give everyone the same fair film." It was the right idea, but it was all a bit half-hearted. This was the problem. They didn't stop the peripheral filming and there were no quality programmes either. You had the worst of both worlds. Then, 18 months ago, Bernie got heavy handed.

'At a manufacturers' meeting I then argued for a pact with Bernie. I said, "Let's get into bed with him." Last year I was delegated to sort it all out. It's taken a long time but I do believe things are coming together.'

Mr Ecclestone is very much a TV animal and in the past he has made no secret of his distaste at rallying's failure to adapt to the medium. Nevertheless, Richards for one is prepared to give him free rein for a while.

'Yes, I will give Bernie the benefit of the doubt. True, I have been sceptical like others. Bernie knows very little about rallying and most of his negative comments have come about through ignorance, but he does have ideas on how to make the sport more appealing, and we have to listen to them. After all, his product with Grands Prix is superb, so he knows what he is doing with TV and you can't ignore that.

'The first and most important thing to do is get one quality programme. If you get that then teams in the WRC don't mind that there is only the one programme. We have agreed on that basis. The key players put together one TV unit, all working together, and Barrie Hinchliffe produced an end product.'

Film-maker Hinchliffe has been at the forefront of televised rallying for 15 years. He's seen it all, from scratching around for budgets, to the BBC's shameless sacrificing of its coverage to anti-tobacco campaigners. Not surprisingly, he is another with pungent views.

'I do think change is now vital for the survival of the sport. If TV isn't maintained and improved, then they'll all be out. I think absolutely things are that serious. Subaru, for instance, would not have continued without TV and now they want it done better.'

The Rally Australia, arguably the best promoted rally of all, is held up as television's ideal; Ari Vatanen puts on a show for the crowds in his Subaru (above left). Barrie Hinchliffe (left) and TTE's crew (right) have been in the thick of a long-running dispute over television coverage. Sometimes it's best just to ask a local (above).

To Hinchliffe, the Rally Australia is a pointer to the future, with its well-funded promotion, TV stages and tight route.

'That's the road it has to go down. Rallying is a funny world to get over to the general public and it's also a slightly weird sport. Its definition has to be re-written – just like Formula One was – to take account of television.

'I do feel strongly about it. Rallying at world level has become the art of controlling a car at high speed on rough surfaces and it needs to build on this. Like Formula One, it can no longer survive as a live punters' sport. It needs to be aimed at TV and then, maybe, millions will tune in to it.'

Think of TV sport and one visualises boxing, soccer, cricket, rugby, skiing, golf. All have one venue per event and constant conflict. TV can concentrate resources. Everything and everyone is to hand. Now take a TV eye to the World Rally Championship. It has no cohesion. None of the major teams or drivers does all the same events. Each event is far too long and wide-ranging. The classes are confusing. The sport's language is arcane and inward-looking. Few of the top drivers have any skill at presentation. There is no sense of playing to the crowd. Spectators, TV and other media are often seen as a nuisance. A mafia-like code of *omerta* smothers any conflict and disagreement (the stuff of life to all media). As a package, it's pathetic.

Hinchliffe thought it could be summed up by the 1993 Sanremo – a classic example of all that's wrong from the camera's eye. 'Despite reverting to an all-tarmac format, the organisers just couldn't resist a long, drawn-out route. The result was that it was almost impossible to keep up with. Even the service crews and chase cars had a tough time of it, and from my point of view it was patently not designed for TV. It didn't even make a gesture to TV. I suspect Sanremo is a brilliant example of how things shouldn't be done these days. It was a disgrace and I believe Sanremo should lose its WRC status.'

Richards might not go that far, but he would heartily endorse most of Hinchliffe's other comments. DR is firmly of the 'Let's drag rallying kicking and screaming out of its ditch' camp. You can see why. His Prodrive empire is based on rallying as a high-tech, aspirational sport. TV is essential to this image. But love him or loathe him – and not for nothing is he sometimes known as The Ego – Richards is still a passionate aficionado at heart. Most of the world team managers run under the same banner. So what have they got in mind? What is it they want to do to our sport in the name of television? They say there are three options. We can dismiss the whole idea of tailoring rallying to the TV age; we can play brinkmanship and offer as few concessions as possible while simply buying air time; or we can make a clean sweep.

The advantage of the first two options is that the sport stays firmly with what it knows: it retains its traditional nature and independence. The downside is simple. To the small-screen men it is already a troublesome dinosaur and, faced with intransigence, they may just ignore it to the point that it withers and dies.

The WRTA route is to mutate into a different form. After all, its advocates claim, no tablets of stone lay down that

World Championship events have to be organised as club rallies on steroids. What this means is turning the World Championship, and possibly each country's top national series, into a kind of high technology, razzmatazz mixture of televised skiing and forest racing.

I can hear traditionalists snorting in derision, but here's the deal:

1. An eight- to ten-round world series with all works teams and their drivers contesting all events. Without that basic starting point there is no hope of TV projecting it as a real championship.

2. Entry by invitation and restricted to, say, 50 cars.

3. A 100-off silhouette car formula.

4. Each event is compressed into two and a half mid-week days.

5. Each rally has one – at most, two – central hubs, with stages looping in a cloverleaf, none more than 50 miles from the day's hub. The cars return to the centre after each loop where TV and sponsors are at the heart of the action.

Photo Les Kolczak

6. Organisers must use TV super specials at least to open and close each day, with cars going off in pairs as they do on the Rally Australia stages in Perth.

7. Every stage has several timing points with a ski-style clock running on-screen, heightening tension for viewers as the top men fight it out. We could also look at an Indy-type screen display showing how each car is performing.

8. Separate awards for fastest time on key stages and after each loop, giving the chance of regular sound-bite interviews with a point to them.

Does all that sound like the ravings of a mind that has slipped its clutch? If so, prepare for a shock. By the time you read this, something like it could be official policy for the future.

At the end of last October the WRTA held a brainstorming session at Au Jardin des Gourmets in Soho. Present were the major team chiefs, Mike Greasley (the man who formed the WRTA and is delegated to run it), Cesar Torres, representing the FIA, and Ecclestone himself. Many of the above points, or something very close to them, were accepted in principle.

There are no grounds for panic. Nothing is going to be swept away overnight. 'The situation is fluid, it's happening now. But we can't do much about 1994 – the calendar is already settled,' said one of those present at the restaurant meeting.

'For future years there's a lot of work and hard bargaining to be done. We may not get all we want, may have to settle for some kind of halfway house. There are a lot of vested interests to be overcome.'

He's right there. Rallying's hierarchy remains a tower of Babel. The ASNs, event organisers, sponsors, PR people, teams, the FIA and its associates, and TV itself are all still muddying the waters with their own sticks. It's all a bit like the United Nations without simultaneous translation. Cutting through all this to streamline the sport for broadcasting will be a massive task.

October's seminal meeting was, said another of those present, 'An attempt to put cards on the table; see where we go from here.' Some of the rally people went into it with their antennae twitching, extremely wary of Bernie.

But it is understood that they had a pleasant surprise. It seems that Ecclestone was positive and forward-looking. He took to Greasley in a big way. 'We've got to have one person at the centre of things and I want everything funnelled to me through Mike,' he is reported to have told the table.

So the job of shepherding through changes is falling largely on the WRTA man's brush-cut head. He is a deceptive operator – in appearance an amiable Postman Pat lookalike, with the bite of a Norman Tebbit. Greasley has spent his life at the centre of motor sport. He is a good man for the job.

But perhaps the biggest surprise that came out of Soho is that, after years of dismissing rallying as a lost cause, Ecclestone gave the appearance of being on board in a big way. With Bernie, of course, there are always wheels within wheels and it takes a clever operator to spot which cogs his engine is driving at any given moment. It seems that he has been spooked by the increasing success of Indycar racing on worldwide TV. Indy has taken off and one can see why. The presentation is slick, the commentators knowledgeable and informative without being intrusive. The racing is often far more gripping than a Grand Prix.

Ecclestone let it be known that he sees the World Rally Championship as a second string to his television bow, another attraction that could be moulded into a package to enable him to fight off the Indy challenge.

If Ecclestone has been converted, it has been recently. When I eventually spoke to him in October, he was still full of the problems of TV rallying.

'It's an extremely difficult sport to televise, bloody hard in fact, the way the events are run,' he said. 'It isn't organised in such a way as to make TV possible. No one knows where each car is in relation to the others, or what is going on. Television companies are expected to commit to it and I can't tell them which drivers and cars are going to be on each event. I don't know the hell myself. It's ridiculous.

'You've got to try to look at it like skiing. I thought it might be possible if you made a race of each stage. Even then you need four or five cameras per stage. I had the idea of running each event like a wheel. There would be a hub with a stage to each of the four spokes – short ones, with the cars going up and down.'

Ecclestone admitted that he probably didn't know as much about the sport as he should. But he smarted at the commonest criticism, that he and ISC have done a poor job so far of marketing the championship.

'I think with all the problems we've had with people sticking their noses in and interfering we've handled TV as well as we could this year. Viewing figures are up. Remember that for TV it's a case of quality, not quantity. To get top quality broadcasters you've got to have quality programmes. Only rubbish broadcasters take rubbish film.'

One can see that some of the disapproval has got to him. But there remains the question of whether he should make TV stations pay for the coverage. Rallying is a weak sport and needs every boost it can get. There is an oft-told story that Austrian TV recently approached ISC for world rally programmes, only to be told it would have to take five years of Formula One on the back of it. Surely the deal should be reversed, with rallying given a televisual lift on Grand Prix shoulders? I didn't get the chance to take this up with him. There was a more important call waiting.

But, as one observer who should know put it: 'There's nothing free with Bernie. However, I would suggest he has so far made it too difficult to get rallying on screen. Hopefully, this is where the WRTA will come into play. To establish the sport it has to be given to broadcasters, and this is where Bernie is wrong. I think he's absolutely wrong to make them pay. It's no good because they ain't going to do it.' Ecclestone would no doubt say that if you can make people pay for something, they will take more care of it than if it is buckshee.

We also have to address the question of what sort of TV we want. Something like Top Gear? A slot in Grandstand? The sport's own dedicated programme? Satellite?

I doubt the Top Gear option will appeal. I'm not even sure it has done much service to British rallying in the last two years, beyond imparting a warm feeling in the Mobil boardroom. The problem with TG is that it is light entertainment: a magazine programme – which involves short attention spans, jump-shot sound-bites and intrusive commentators.

It's also expensive. The days are long gone when Greasley thought up the Open Championship media fund and persuaded each of the then six manufacturers to put in £7000. Off that, he ran all Hinchliffe's TV films, and also courted national and regional papers. Now, as best I can understand the maze, all TV rights have gone to BBC Enterprises, which in turn sub-contracts filming and placement of the programmes to Top Gear. This year, Mobil, the money sponsor, put in just under £100,000 and all but a fraction of that flowed straight out to the BBC. It seems that the Beeb also sold a record 16,000 compilation videos of the 1992 series – and Mobil and the MSA saw, reputedly, 59p each per video. Enterprises also pulls in money from syndication and this year several countries have taken a full 25-minute version. Malcolm Wilson and Richard Burns are heroes in Portugal.

So: a Grandstand-type slot? One former motor sport journalist and now leading PR person had some surprising views on that. Grandstands the world over, he said vehemently, are for slobs who stumble out of the bar to slump in front of the box with glazed eyes. 'Your As and Bs and C1s are the people rallying should focus on. And what are they doing on Saturday afternoon? They're in Sainsbury's or Carrefour, gardening or taking the children out, possibly spending an hour reading their ever-heftier Saturday paper.

'Sunday is when they take their lunchtime drinks and Sunday afternoon TV sport is when they sit down, relax and tune in. That's where rallying should aim at if it wants such a slot.'

Most people I've questioned agree that rallying really needs terrestrial TV, and its own dedicated programme – something like the evening Grand Prix slot. But this, of course, begs the question of whether it could reap the ratings to justify such screen time. There are no guarantees. French TV has taken very little World Championship footage this year, despite possessing national heroes in François Delecour and Didier Auriol.

Satellite lovers point to its gigantic audience 'footprints'. All this really means is that the eye-in-the-sky beams down over a wide area of potential viewers. True, no TV audience is captive in the modern age, but satellite viewers are always more elusive (and in any one target area smaller) than those of terrestrial programmes.

An ideal solution would be for 15 minutes on each championship round to be tacked on to the appropriate Grand Prix slot for 1994, giving rallying a leg up to a point where it could think of sustaining its own programme the following year.

Whatever, it means big changes and risks. Among the doubters are those worried that, even if Ecclestone is on the level, he and the manufacturers will turn rallying into a TV special with a life-span of perhaps five years, and let it go to the dogs after that. They point to the sport's painful lack of depth at the highest level and to snooker as an example of how television can destroy a sport. Fifteen years ago you couldn't switch on the box without seeing the green baize warriors. But snooker, with as many as 50 world-class performers on its books, has collapsed inwards under the glare of constant TV. World rallying has fewer than a dozen real stars at present.

Such fears are to be respected, but perhaps they are illusory. After all, the World Rally Championship is never going to get the level of screen attention snooker was subjected to during the late 1970s and '80s.

Hinchliffe for one is scornful. 'If we do get five good years, then who cares what happens after that? We'll worry later. To look so far ahead and get scared is amazing. We have to look to the immediate future. Five years ahead can take care of itself. Now is the crunch time. Greasley's initiative with the WRTA has given us one more year's grace with the big teams to get something moving.'

Far from the madding studio, film crews work to get their footage in often unfavourable conditions. They play a large part in conveying the atmosphere of a sport that ventures into remote countryside.

So there you have it. I suspect that in the coming months we will be promised yet another sequel, Rallying's Golden Era IV. It's a familiar enough scenario. The question is, will it be a great motor sport serial or death by a thousand TV cuts?

I'm as much a traditionalist as any *Motoring News* reader. But you can't go on replicating the past for ever. The world today is an altogether tougher place than the era into which special stage rallying was born and to which it still clings, the 1960s.

The warning signs should by now be plain enough for even the dimmest FIA official. Today you have to be fit and hard to survive and, if our paymasters decree that means rallying is transformed into a TV spectacular, then so be it, but doubts over Ecclestone's commitment linger. Conceivably, his endgame is to drive the manufacturers into his fiefdom, Formula One, and their new alliance remains fragile; it will certainly be tested by sunspot temperatures. Yet without patrons, we have no rallying summit, no World Championship. Sports grow upwards; they die downwards.

1992-1993

OBITUARIES

Marian Bublewicz

One of the most frustrating aspects of motor sport is that the most talented people don't necessarily have the money to succeed. Yet, if the odds seem daunting in western Europe, consider how they must appear in the east. Marian Bublewicz was special not merely because of his talent behind the wheel, but because he had the determination to reach a position in which he could demonstrate it.

Born in the town of Olsztyn in northern Poland, he became a successful motor cyclist, finishing as

Marian Bublewicz

runner-up in the national championship before a road accident ended his career and prompted the move to cars. Even with a competition background, changing sports wasn't easy. He took part in his first rally in a Polski 125, which he borrowed from his parents without their knowledge. He later used a rear-wheel drive Kadett GT/E, before joining the works FSO team. That gave him his first taste of western motor sport, when he took the ungainly Polonez to the Condroz Rally in Belgium, and set top five stage times when it grew foggy and driving skill mattered more than power to weight ratio.

He recognised that east European machinery was a handicap and transferred to a Mazda 323. His record had already made him Poland's leading driver. He won the Polish Championship six times, claiming a host of class and group wins besides.

It took a change to Ford to make him an international name, though. Hiring Sierra Cosworths from the Belgian tuner, RAS, he finished second in the 1992 European Championship. Characteristically, he celebrated his success quietly – he hardly drank – and laid ambitious plans for 1993. He had visited Boreham, arranged to drive a Group A Escort Cosworth and was aiming for the European crown.

He took part in the Winter Rally on 21 February, intended to be his last event in a Sierra, purely as a loosener for the new season; he was very much at home on snow and ice, and had already won the event seven times. Tragically, he crashed into a tree at high speed and died some hours later from his injuries. Aged 42, he was without doubt Poland's best driver since Sobieslaw Zasada.

Bob Freeborough

If Bob Freeborough had been a soldier, he would have been a quartermaster, for there was nothing that he could neither find nor fix. He knew how to handle authority too, whether it was marshalling a bunch of mechanics or reporting to senior management. If efficiency is a knack, Bob had it in spades. Once, during a national bread strike, he hired a lorry, drove it to France, filled it with loaves and drove it back to Towcester; as the owner of the most successful local dairy, he already had the distribution network in place. The story epitomises his energy, generosity and down-to-earth refusal to be daunted by any obstacle. On the contrary, he thrived on tackling overwhelming odds.

Perhaps that is what made him such a good rallyman, in every sense of the word. In the '60s, his skilful handling of a Cooper S made him what amounted to a semi-works driver – although he rallied in the furthest-flung parts of Europe without a service crew – but he was also an able navigator and, latterly, he earned a formidable reputation as a service co-ordinator with Nissan and Mike Little.

Although he started rallying in the early 1950s when still in his teens, he made his reputation a decade later in Minis, sharing cars with the likes of Paul Easter, Terry Harryman and the Reverend Rupert Jones. Offered a short-stroke 999 cc engine by the factory, he took class wins on events as different as the RAC and the Geneva Rally. Subsequently, he turned his hand to autocross and rallycross, and also finished an excellent ninth overall on the 1970 World Cup Rally in an 1800. Minis remained his first love, though, and he kept two of them long after he had retired from active competition.

He adored France and could be persuaded to reminisce happily for hours about the old days. He was plainly concerned that the French Alps were being over-rallied by the early 1990s. Yet nostalgia never clouded his judgement, or blinded him to the appeal of modern rallying. He first made contact with Nissan while making ice notes on the 1981 Monte and, sensing that the future lay with Japanese manufacturers, he became a priceless asset to the company on its forays into European motor sport. It didn't matter how many changes of management took place, or whether the event in question was the Acropolis or the Le Mans 24 Hours: Bob played a vital role in planning it. His attention to detail and innate shrewdness enabled him to turn this into a second career, long after he had sold the dairy.

His name will always be linked with Terry Kaby's but, through his work as a team manager, he also helped other young drivers such as Mark Lovell. He was modest about his achievements, though, and his distaste for the limelight was genuine.

To anyone who had witnessed his bustling energy on a rally, it was hard to imagine that he had much time for anything else. However, he was a family man with three children and also a pillar of the community. Apart from the dairy in Towcester, he was always in the thick of sorting out a natural disaster such as a flood and he was a keen rugby player, helping found the town's rugby club. Indeed, he was described as the best-known figure in the district.

Born in Nottingham on 4 March 1933, he died after a short, unexpected illness on 22 October. He lived a full and active life, yet there seemed to be as much stretching in front of him as there was behind: when he died, he had just returned from Nissan's assault on the Monza touring car race and was drawing up a service plan for the Minis tackling the 1994 Monte.

Dave Metcalfe

Rodger Freeth

Rodger Freeth could never be too serious for long. The business of having his photograph taken seemed altogether too solemn, so he explained that a friend of his – a keen mountaineer – had told him that, if he had had a nose like that on the back of his head as well, he would have made a great icepick.

In fact, he seemed very good at everything, with the possible exception of being an icepick. To see him in party mood, the life and soul of a pre- or post-rally celebration, it was impossible to picture him as a university lecturer, introducing his students to the finer points of astrophysics, the subject in which he took his doctorate. Perhaps the idea of him in a rally car or on a racing motor bike seemed just as outlandish to them. Part of the difficulty in reconciling these conflicting images stemmed from the sheer breadth of his talents, but part equally from a modest nature and the kind of self-deprecating humour one associates with New Zealanders. There wasn't a trace of pomposity or pride in him.

Many of his friends in rallying may not have appreciated that 'Possum' Bourne's co-driver had achieved notable success in many different forms of motor sport. He had started racing motor bikes as a student and went on to take 14 New Zealand titles, winning the Arai 500 at Bathurst twice into the bargain; he was the only non-Australian to do so. He was a thoughtful as well as a successful bike racer, experimenting with aerofoils independently of Yamaha shortly before they were banned. Sadly, his bike racing career came to an end following the 1986 Olympus Rally, when Neil Allport left the road in his Mazda. Neither of the crew was injured and their Mazda wasn't badly damaged, but Rodger tore some tendons in one of his hands while lifting the car back onto the road.

Rodger Freeth

Unabashed, he turned his hand to racing cars during the New Zealand summer, developing a highly successful Toyota Starlet fitted with a large V8. He won national titles in that as well. Perhaps his most daring exploit was in a single seater, though: he obtained a Lola Indy car and, having closed off a bumpy North Island back road, he raised the New Zealand Land Speed Record to 194 mph in February 1992.

He had started rallying in 1973 as a co-driver and was considered good enough to navigate Pentti Airikkala when the Finn appeared in New Zealand in 1978. His international career took off when he teamed up with Bourne six years ago, the two competing on the Safari, in Argentina and on the RAC (finishing 13th on the latter at their first attempt in the underpowered RX Turbo), while establishing themselves as an integral part of Subaru's competition activities.

Auckland University awarded Rodger a Blue for his motor sport achievements before he left in 1991 to concentrate on co-driving. He won the New Zealand and Australian Championships and, at the time of his death in Western Australia on 18 September 1993, he was leading both the Asia–Pacific and Australian series. He was 39, married with two small sons. His death seemed unusually wasteful.

Bob Freeborough

Dave Metcalfe

Months after his death, writing this summons painful memories, as fresh as they were at the time – the sense of shock on hearing that Dave Metcalfe had been killed in a road accident, the grim, disbelieving faces at the funeral on a raw December day in Cumbria. Few people in British rallying could have generated such a widespread sense of loss, for he was not only a popular and well-liked man among the insiders who make their living from the sport, but a hero to countless fans. For all his success as a professional, he always seemed like a clubman made good and the mourners included members of local motor clubs as well as the works teams.

Most factory drivers occasionally sound tired or jaded, but Dave's enthusiasm was infectious and he sounded genuinely as interested in what other people were doing as he did in his own exploits. He was willing to drive anything and, even when he was on the fringes of the works Vauxhall team, he was persuaded to drive a Talbot Samba on a night event. His only reservation was that this might not be an adroit move politically; while he was aware of the politics inseparable from professional rallying, he never displayed the slightest interest in them. A very capable mechanic, he retained a mechanic's interest in every detail of his car and a corresponding lack of airs and graces. He was a generous competitor too: he would point out for instance that Phil Sandham not only navigated, but provided his builder's Bedford CF for servicing.

His manner scarcely matched his results. He was without doubt one of Britain's top drivers, a fact universally acknowledged in spite of the fact that he never drove a truly competitive car. Instead, he made his name as the underdog, the man who could wring more out of an underpowered car than anyone else, whether it was a 1600 Escort in the BTRDA Championship or a works Nova GSi on a British international. He won his championship class in the Escort in 1983 and effortlessly moved up to international competition in one bound, making a good impression the following year in a Group A Manta; on the Manx, he even beat Hannu Mikkola's works Quattro going down Tholt-y-Will in the fog.

By then, GM was much more interested in the Astra than the Manta and he was told that he could only expect support in 1985 if he transferred to the new model. Although he had achieved all his previous results in a motley selection of Cortinas (which he had used on road events) and Escorts, he made the swap to front-wheel drive without hesitation and taught himself left-foot braking within a matter of months. Indeed, he won the two-litre class on the Ulster that year by handling the car a little more sympathetically than the works drivers.

Having joined the works team in 1988, he was transferred from Astras to the Nova in 1989. Rather than grumble at the loss of 50-odd brake horsepower, he seized the 1.6-litre machine by the scruff of the neck and took the fight to much faster machinery. He was fourth overall three times on the Manx International – which ought to have been next to impossible on such a fast, bumpy rally – and twice finished inside the top 15 on the RAC, beating every other two-wheel drive car both times. It is fair to say that he was never outdriven in a comparable car.

In his early days, his refusal to accept defeat sometimes turned to impetuosity; there were some big accidents, particularly on the Isle of Man, but they were partly the consequence of running against works machinery on a low budget. By the time the latest Astra made its appearance late in 1992, he had established an enduring reputation in the Nova and Vauxhall had no need even to consider another driver. Tragically, a terrible accident near Selside robbed him of the chance to achieve the kind of overall results he deserved. He was 35 and in his prime.

WORLD CHAMPIONSHIP RALLIES

1993

The list of times at the end of the Couillole told its own story (top right). A demoralised François Delecour (right) was overwhelmed by Didier Auriol's last gasp charge; it was the third Monte victory for the Millau star and Toyota's second (above). Ford made an enormous impact nevertheless, the likes of Dionisio making the running in Group N.

WORLD RALLY CHAMPIONSHIP ROUND 1

MONTE CARLO RALLY

Questions were superfluous. Body language proclaimed who was winning and who was losing. While François Delecour slumped in the front seat of a Transit like a rag doll, all resistance beaten out of him by the explosive power of Didier Auriol's assault, Bernard Occelli strolled jauntily round the Toyota service point without a jacket, fuelled – like his driver – by pure adrenalin. With a glance at his watch, he sprinted towards the car, vaulted the tape, clapped his hands and cried, 'Tyres!' Were the Toyota crew having fun yet? You bet.

At that moment, on the northern slopes of the Col de Bleine, Delecour and Ford still led the Monte by 20 seconds, but no one, from the Radio Monte Carlo commentators proclaiming that the leader was demoralised to the man himself was in any doubt that the lead was on the point of changing hands. Confronted with the evidence that the Celica had abruptly turned into an irresistible force and that the three days when he had stamped his authority on the event counted for nothing now, Delecour had surrendered to despair.

It was easy to sympathise, impossible to argue. For most of the event, the Celicas had been capable of matching the Escorts at best, despite the gravel specification engines and the slight misfires that should have hampered the latter on bone dry asphalt. Ford's relentless testing had paid off handsomely, the cars handled superbly, and complaints of poor tyre choice, or ill-adapted suspension and transmissions were confined to Toyota, Lancia, and Mitsubishi drivers.

The first stage of the last night had given no inkling of what was to come, for Delecour was quickest over the Col de Turini and had broken his own stage record, whereas his fellow countryman had suffered a minor brake problem and gained only a second from Miki Biasion. Since then, Auriol had reeled in the Escorts hand over fist, gaining a second per kilometre and, if unofficial Ford and Mitsubishi timing was to be believed, double that on uphill sections. A deficit of more than 70 seconds had been slashed to 20 seconds in just two stages and, with two remaining, Auriol had as good as won. Sure enough, he swept into the lead on the Col de Bleine and extended it to 15 seconds on the final stage, Delecour vainly struggling to get anywhere close, while Biasion pointedly eased off and settled for third. The margin didn't even hint at what a crushing win this was.

After the victory came the analysis. Auriol's capacity to rise to the occasion is unrivalled and his last gasp charges on the Monte have already passed into legend. However, they have often been accompanied by controversy and this was no exception. As Ove Andersson praised his new signing's victory with an almost Latin extravagance, veiled accusations burst into the open. The startling increase in performance, notably uphill, prompted suggestions that TTE had found something extra under the bonnet and the implication was that fuel additives were a factor. There was no evidence to back it, despite exhaustive scrutineering – on FISA's part – that had extended to taking fluid samples from windscreen washer bottles.

Yet there could be no question that Auriol had given his utmost and Occelli proudly pointed to the small dent in the rear wing to prove it. It merely emphasised their invulnerability.

rallycourse

MONTE CARLO RALLY

Miki Biasion put in one of his best Monte performances in his own eyes to come third (above), although he was rarely a match for his team-mate, Delecour (below left). Over and out: Andrea Aghini successfully negotiated this slimy hairpin (far left), but crashed his Integrale on a patch of ice later on, whereas Bruno Thiry got away with rolling his two-wheeling Astra to give Opel maximum two-wheel drive points.

WORLD RALLY CHAMPIONSHIP ROUND 2

SWEDISH RALLY

Mats Jonsson has never been one to make a drama out of a crisis. Perhaps his passive nature has been his undoing: an incredible feat for another driver is all in a day's work for Mats, whose manner practically invites people to underestimate him.

The Swedish Rally had reached its decisive moment, at last, and TTE certainly wasn't taking Jonsson for granted – not that he was being demanding: here was the leader, his face pink with cold, standing outside the motorhome chatting to some friends almost as though this was a test session. Asked to assess the position, he laughed apologetically. There was only one, 12-mile stage to run, Colin McRae was 13 seconds in arrears, Juha Kankkunen 17, and Jonsson had his home rally in the palm of his hand for the second year running – provided there were no more twists of fate in an event that had been too fiercely fought to develop a pattern.

Jonsson could have been forgiven for despairing three times at least. He had been hot on the heels of Didier Auriol and McRae in the first leg, only to clip a stone on the sixth stage and puncture a tyre. It cost him 45 seconds, at a time when Nordic supremacy was not so much under fire as in full retreat. The following morning, another puncture pitched him back into the Toyota scrum, virtually level with Auriol and Kankkunen, and then, as the second leg neared Karlstad and the stages he knows best, the engine had begun to overheat severely. As he finished the last stage that night, the windscreen was smeared ominously with coolant.

TTE's superb organisation was equal to a head gasket change and he re-started the following morning second, five seconds behind Kankkunen, but only 15 seconds ahead of McRae and 23 ahead of Auriol. There was no knowing whether the engine had been saved, but a certainty that the 'southerners' (who had been generally quickest so far) would be in full cry.

Yet the cards fell Jonsson's way. Within a stage, Auriol's Celica had developed a crippling – and controversial – oil leak. The Frenchman's machine was out of contention long before TTE decided to withdraw it, allegedly because it was leaking petrol. Kankkunen should have been the most dangerous opponent in this war of nerves, but the weather changed at the crucial moment: after two days of patchy ice and gravel, it began to snow – not much, but enough to hamstring the first car on the road. Helpless, the Finn was obliged to plough the roads for his opponents. It took only three stages for first to become third.

McRae had surmounted a broken driveshaft when leading by a handsome margin and an electronic problem that cost the Subaru 50 bhp for four critical stages during the second leg, only to find that the original gearbox, repaired and re-fitted for the final showdown, had lost fourth gear after all. Prodrive could only turn up the boost, re-map the electronics, and hope. The handicap wasn't apparent from his stage times, for the Scot drove magnificently, but it was all in vain. Jonsson had been given the glimpse of an opportunity and he had felt secure enough to ease off a fraction on the narrow, twisty stretch of the penultimate stage, fearing the consequences of a third puncture. While McRae survived a sixth gear spin on the final test, dropping him to third, and Kankkunen set a defiant fastest time, Jonsson's nerve, along with the head gasket, had held.

Nordic pride had been saved, by a whisker. Nonetheless, McRae and Auriol had indicated that it would not be long before the most specialised rally in the World Championship also falls to an outsider.

Toyota was present in force, but the works drivers had to give best to Mats Jonsson and Lars Bäckman (far left) in the Toyota Sweden car. Either Didier Auriol (above) or Juha Kankkunen might have won an enthralling event that had onlookers on tenterhooks.

555
SUBARU
555
THE INTERNATIONAL
SWEDISH RALLY
2
BILSTEIN
NGK
555
MICHELIN
555
prodrive

rallycourse

SWEDISH RALLY

As servicing was frequently restricted, the works drivers, Colin McRae included (top) changed their own tyres where necessary. The Scot was in superb form and unlucky to be restricted to third in the Legacy (left). Malcolm Wilson was in the lead when he crashed his Escort (above). Stud patterns are supposed to be the black art in the snow, but its absence led to tread-cutting.

François Delecour (far right top) broke his duck at last – and in some style. Miki Biasion settled for second (below), while Colin McRae was generally quickest on the loose in his Legacy (bottom), but lost far too much time on the asphalt. Kenneth Eriksson salvaged a respectable result for Mitsubishi after a troubled run in his Lancer (far right bottom). Servicing limitations have become an integral part of World Championship competition; since turbo changes were restricted to one per day, the seal (right) identifies each unit as well as ensuring that it has a restrictor.

RALLY OF PORTUGAL

In retrospect, the pattern had been cast on the tarmac – a most unusual state of affairs in Portugal, even though the first leg contains more stage mileage than any other. As expected, the works Escorts had been quickest on the asphalt, but no one – least of all Ford's engineers – had thought that the lead established then would be more than sufficient to repel the Lancias on the loose surface stages subsequently. In the event, only the Subarus were capable of outrunning the Fords and they had suffered so badly on the asphalt, both Markku Alén and Colin McRae being hampered by brake and driveshaft problems, that they were too far behind to constitute a real threat. It was of purely academic interest that Alén was quickest overall on the last three legs of the rally and that McRae might have been quicker still but for a roll in Arganil. No, once Carlos Sainz destroyed his Jolly Club Delta near Fafe early in the third leg, Ford was more or less safe. The moment its star driver had retired, the Jolly Club men were always likely to settle for third and some points, and Andrea Aghini wasn't a real match for the Cosworth-powered machines on gravel in any case.

Understandably, François Delecour hadn't seen it quite that way. There had been the small matter of Arganil to negotiate and the constant danger that he might be overhauled by his team-mate, that renowned Portuguese expert, Miki Biasion. So long as Aghini was within a minute of the Escorts and running strongly, Ford management had dared not impose team orders and Biasion was free to go onto the attack – purely in the interests of keeping Aghini at bay.

Delecour had been quite capable of holding his own on tarmac of course, but he had previously completed only one loose surface stage in Portugal and there had been ominous signs that Biasion could pick his moment like a cat toying with a mouse. He had clipped nine seconds from his French colleague on Aboboreira, midway between Povoa and Viseu during the third leg, and no more than 36 seconds divided the two at the overnight halt. Ford had duly imposed team orders that evening, since Aghini had fallen almost two minutes behind, but Delecour clearly didn't believe that these would necessarily apply.

In practice, Biasion had been in no real state to threaten his colleague since the very first gravel stage at the Lousada rallycross circuit. He had yumped his Escort much too violently and the impact had not only smashed the radiator, but injured his back. It turned out that he had damaged his sacro-iliac joint, where the backbone joins the pelvis; it was nothing serious, but it was painful. The car didn't make an instant recovery either. The water temperature soared to 110 degrees and, even though the mechanics took the head off later that day, it continued to run so hot that the crew carried a water container in the cockpit for the rest of the rally. By the time Biasion reached Arganil, the wiring had been modified to run the fans permanently and, whatever designs on the lead he might have entertained earlier in the rally, he was now concentrating firmly on finishing.

Delecour had watched certain victories slither through his fingers before and he attacked Arganil as though no orders had been given. Easily fastest on the first stage of the last leg, he ran wide and knocked down a spectator on the second. Then the alternator light came on and, with no time to replace the generator itself, he soberly completed the stages to Pampilhosa da Serra and safety. Meanwhile, Biasion had needed an emergency fuel pump change, a task his service crew completed in six minutes. It had been a nerve-wracking few hours for the whole of the Ford team.

Once he had completed Arganil, even Delecour was prepared to concede that he was almost in the clear, although he continued to pace the service point with nervous excitement. Reason told him that nothing could deny him this time, but a nagging doubt remained. His joy at a long overdue first victory that evening was tempered by relief – relief that none of the niggling problems had turned into full scale disasters, but above all, that the nagging doubt had been laid to rest.

SAFARI RALLY

TTE began playing safe before the rally had even started. If there had been any real prospect of a fight, the Celicas' old Xtrac centre differentials would have been replaced by the viscous couplings used everywhere else, but the Xtrac unit is well-proven, the winner of two previous Safaris, and the main risk from TTE's point of view was of falling flat on its face: nothing less than absolute domination would do.

Accordingly, the event took on the nature of a cycling race in which the last lap never came. None of the Toyota drivers took any risks, each of them conserving their cars as though they were their own property. Predictably, Juha Kankkunen struck the best compromise between looking after his car and doing just enough to stamp his authority on the event. The hot, tiresome drive to and from the coast didn't prove much, yet he pulled far enough ahead to ensure that Markku Alén would have to overtake him on the road to grab the lead on the longer, tougher sections to the north and west – and no one was under any illusions that fighting a way past through the dust would be no easy matter.

After two legs, it was still possible to believe that the rally might conceivably come to life, for Kenjiro Shinozuka was fourth – albeit nearly 40 minutes behind Ian Duncan – and theoretically capable of profiting from a Toyota catastrophe. Once the lone Mitsubishi succumbed to a blown engine just before dawn in the third leg, Toyota's drivers barely kept up the pretence. When Kankkunen broke a rear shock absorber near Sabatia, Alén dutifully pulled up rather than seize his chance. Duncan, meanwhile, was cruising along in third place with a badly warped cylinder head following an emergency gasket change, yet lost no further ground to his colleagues between Nairobi and Eldoret until the head itself was replaced just before the end of the leg.

The following morning, the tempo slackened further. Equipped with a new head, Duncan gained in reliability rather than speed, setting much the same times as Guy Jack's one-litre Daihatsu. Sure enough, the four works-built Celicas swept the first four places, Alén and Duncan taking their best Safari results in the process. It was a demonstration of TTE's African might but, against such meagre opposition, it carried uncomfortable echoes of its past domination of the Ivory Coast, rather than the jewel in the World Championship crown, the Safari. It wasn't so much a victory earned through blood, sweat and tears, as 20 points methodically collected like tokens on the back of a cereal packet.

There had been fine individual performances, ranging from Kankkunen's professionalism to Jack's remarkable fifth in the top Daihatsu, or Hasmat Shamji's Group N win on his first attempt at the rally, but no escaping the fact that this was the lowest-key Safari in decades. Beside discussions of the event's future, Kankkunen's triumph paled into insignificance.

The rally car as hippopotamus: Juha Kankkunen lapped up everything the Safari could throw at him to take his first victory of the season (above). Toyota's one realistic challenger was Kenjiro Shinozuka (below left), but the Japanese retired when his Lancer blew its engine. No one took the Vivios too seriously, but Patrick Njiru somehow coaxed his to the finish in 12th place.

rallycourse

SAFARI RALLY

The Safari is a photogenic feast, but sadly it wasn't much more than that in 1993. Ian Duncan steers clear of a plain of mud on his way to a a solid third (previous page). Mud and dust were all the same to the TTE parade. Colin McRae dragged his Vivio into the top six fleetingly, but the 660 cc micro-car was unequal to the strain; this was only the first front suspension breakage (above) and no amount of pushing would get the protesting machine beyond Mombasa.

WORLD RALLY CHAMPIONSHIP ROUND 5

TOUR OF CORSICA

François Delecour hesitated, sensing that this was something Ford would rather he did not say, and then said it anyway. Yes, there was more at stake than winning the rally. The finish was almost in sight and, barring an unforeseen disaster, it would be the first time he had beaten Didier Auriol. In a sense, he was exorcising a personal demon, but he was also settling a score: winning in Corsica would be revenge for his controversial 11th hour defeat in Monte Carlo.

He hadn't won yet. Pacing up and down, ignoring the handful of autograph hunters, he discussed the tyre choices anxiously with the Michelin men, as though Auriol might yet spring a last minute ambush; he admitted that he was 'not calm' – in any case, winning had by no means lost its novelty value. Ford left nothing to chance. There were team members taking split times on every junction of the last 25-mile test and passing the results to the next junction by radio; 'pit signals' then informed Delecour whether he was gaining or dropping time. There were no last minute surprises. The north Frenchman took soft slicks and paced himself perfectly to beat his southern rival by six seconds on the stage and 62 seconds overall, re-taking the World Championship lead in the process, but he wasn't going to let the Monte Carlo business drop. As the runner-up explained to a packed press conference that Ford's success clearly owed something to improved engines, Delecour leaned back in his chair and theatrically shook his head, as if to say, 'No change!'

Auriol was gracious in defeat. TTE could do nothing but put a brave face on the situation – indeed, it had been doing so since the re-group in Calvi, midway through the final leg. By then, Auriol had done everything he could to erase the effects of an indifferent start. Curiously off-colour himself, he had dropped time on two vital stages in the first leg when a problem with the ECU sapped the motor's torque and, while François Chatriot was making a good impression on his first event in a Toyota, neither he nor TTE's third recruit, Yves Loubet, could do anything to bring down Delecour.

Once the engine was cured, Auriol had been able to match and occasionally beat the flying Escort, especially when the leader ran into engine trouble of his own during the second leg. It had been a glimmer of hope rather than a turning of the tide. After a broken sparking plug and a lethargic turbo had been replaced, Delecour stemmed Auriol's charge with blistering times at the end of the afternoon, as the well-balanced Cosworth preserved its front tyres better on long stages than the transverse-engined Celica. There had been signs of a repeat performance early in the morning of the third leg: the Toyota's front Michelins were wilting in the heat and the long, ceaselessly winding stages along the coast would offer no respite. As TTE feared, dry roads and Mediterranean warmth tilted the odds decisively towards Delecour. Auriol held his own for two long stages, but no service was permitted before the short, scenic stage at Porto, and the Ford man gained seven seconds in only six miles.

While Toyota made do with second and third, and Carlos Sainz recorded his first finish in a Lancia – a disconsolate fourth – Boreham could reflect that it had beaten all-comers, and that it had done so through technical superiority.

There was no holding François Delecour in Corsica, the Lille driver romping home to his second win of the season. The heat was too much for the Celicas, the front tyres going off on the longer stages. François Chatriot gave Didier Auriol stout support nonetheless (top left). Colin McRae stayed out of trouble on this occasion, bringing the lone Legacy home in a spectacular fifth.

DELECOUR
AURIOL
SAINZ
AGHINI
MAC RAE

rallycourse

TOUR OF CORSICA

There is nothing to rival the enthusiasm of a Mediterranean crowd, the banners proclaiming allegiance to the heroes of 1993. Andrea Aghini was certainly one of them, the curly-haired Italian outrunning Carlos Sainz until his Delta's suspension broke and pitched the car into the trees.

ACROPOLIS RALLY

Miki Biasion often seems preoccupied, but never flustered. As he climbed from his Ford at the service point before stage 31, he appeared more than usually lost in thought, commencing an earnest discussion with Philip Dunabin while mechanics swarmed over the back of the car. The morning heat was sweltering and he politely requested some water. As he doused his face, he explained that the Escort had just caught fire. A secure lead and his first victory in nearly three years now depended on half a dozen men working furiously in the hatchback.

It was a rally that either Lancia or Subaru might have won: Carlos Sainz completed it in a good second place, having set more fastest stage times than anyone else, while the Legacys had left the rest of the field gasping in their wake; Ari Vatanen in particular had looked very much in command, despite a fierce assault from François Delecour, until he launched his car into the trees midway through the second leg on Dipotamia. Sainz lost more than three minutes when his front suspension broke on the same test. Biasion's win had owed something to luck then, but a great deal to judgement. Escort number seven led the shattered survivors back to Athens without a mark on it: scarcely anyone knew about the fire and the victor had blended speed and restraint to such good effect that a host of other problems had paled into insignificance.

Biasion had badly needed to win and had increased the pressure a fraction by admitting as much before the start. His rally hadn't begun promisingly either, as the Subarus and Toyotas charged off into the distance, a relaxed Delecour stuck to his tail and the first signs of overheating made their presence felt. At first, the second day was no better, since his team-mate passed him and began to pull away. Just before Dipotamia, two minutes covered the first six crews and the Italian was a struggling third, beset by overheating and poor handling; rocks had torn off the rear anti-roll bar mountings, leading to pronounced understeer and there would be no chance to replace them until the evening.

It took the patience of a sage to turn down the turbocharger and ease off on uphill sections to preserve the engine as his team-mate pulled clear, only for Ford's abiding weakness, the fuel system, to strike down Delecour just before it began to affect his own car. While Delecour crawled through the final stage of the leg at a snail's pace, Biasion escaped with just one fuel pump working. He was two minutes and 32 seconds in the lead that night, there had been time to carry out an exhaustive rebuild and he was under no immediate pressure – but more than a third of the rally lay ahead.

Sure enough, the overheating returned with a vengeance as the sun climbed. Both Sainz and Armin Schwarz knew they stood no real chance of catching the Escort, but merely coaxing the Cosworth through the stages was a constant struggle: the coolant temperature accelerated to almost 120 degrees and the inlet charge temperature to 100, which meant that turbo boost was virtually non-existent. Far from being a parade, this was a battle for survival.

And the fire? The cause turned out to be relatively trivial – the wiring to an uprated water injection pump – but Biasion had no way of knowing that in mid-stage as the cockpit filled with smoke and he studied the flames in the mirror. All he knew for certain was that the fuel tank had been replaced the night before.

RALLI ART

Mobil
1
Mobil 1
7
index
Motorsport
Ford
BILSTEIN
TAT

rallycourse

ACROPOLIS RALLY

David Richards had plenty of reasons to frown in Greece, both his drivers crashing when the Subarus were the class of the field; François Delecour drove his heart out, but ultimately his Escort let him down when another victory looked a distinct possibility (previous page). The winner was therefore the canny Miki Biasion (far left) in the sister Escort. Armin Schwarz gave Mitsubishi a heartening third place, having held second for a time (above), while Juha Piironen lets it all hang out in the heat.

555
SUBARU
BILSTEIN
NGK
10

REPSOL

For a while, it seemed that Ari Vatanen would end a drought that dates back to 1985 at World Championship level, only for the Finn to roll his Subaru violently during the second leg (left). For once, Lancia reliability wasn't a telling factor on the destructive back roads of central Greece. Andrea Aghini took a solid finish, whereas Jorge Recalde's Integrale succumbed to the incessant battering when a Group N victory looked on the cards.

WORLD RALLY CHAMPIONSHIP ROUND 7

RALLY OF ARGENTINA

'Pray for wind!' said one of the Ford men cheerily, but so far as Miki Biasion was concerned, his chances of victory had passed beyond the power of prayer. Unusually still conditions at the beginning of the second leg had wrecked his hopes as surely as a puncture or broken suspension. Dust hovered in the air for minutes on end and it had been so bad on the second stage that morning that he had been forced to stop at one point. Try as he might, he could do no more than pick his way through Juha Kankkunen's wake as the canny Finn dictated the pace to his pursuers as surely as on the driest Safari. Undemonstrative as ever, there was no concealing Biasion's dejection as he sat in the Ford motorhome in Villa Cura Brochero and quietly summarised his predicament. He had not merely lost a rally, but his best chance of winning a third World Championship.

He had pinned a good deal on Argentina. The setting for his first World Championship rally win in 1986, it has long been one of his favourite events, although it had taken a good deal of persistence and ingenuity to persuade Ford that it was worth including in his programme. Few doubted that Biasion could add a fourth victory to his South American tally, but the first day had not gone according to plan, a slight misfire costing him a few seconds to Kankkunen, before Didier Auriol's gearbox problems played into the Finn's hands with a vengeance. Biasion was running next on the road, following Carlos Sainz's retirement with a blown engine and he was furious that the Frenchman had not pulled over when plainly in difficulty, despite allegedly getting a clear view of the pursuing Escort at a hairpin.

While the first leg had been long enough to knock Sainz and Auriol out of the running, there had been everything to play for as the first two headed into the mountains west of Cordoba at dawn the next day, 37 seconds splitting Toyota and Ford. If there had been so much as a breath of wind, perhaps Biasion would have been able to turn the tables. In his own mind, he was sure that he could, but he was just as certain that two impenetrably dusty stages had ensured that he could not; the sporadic fastest times later on were mere gestures of defiance and even voluntarily incurring road penalties at the beginning of the final leg to secure a bigger gap made no difference. Kankkunen had been presented with a gift.

A nightmare for Biasion had become a dream for the winner, the more so because the outlook had been so poor a week previously. His co-driver of six years' standing, Juha Piironen, had collapsed one evening during the recce and lay in a hospital bed in Cordoba recovering from brain surgery. As a stop-gap measure, with Piironen's full approval, Nicky Grist had been summoned from Wales in his place. There was time for the shotgun partnership to carry out the most cursory recce and barely time for Grist to re-write the pace notes. It was hardly an auspicious start and yet the new pairing was an instant success. It was plain that the two were working hard to build up a satisfactory relationship, but naturally, as their opponents ran into trouble one by one, their confidence soared. While Biasion and Auriol made the best of a bad job, the latter cutting his way through the field to salvage third after serious clutch and gearbox maladies, quite apart from baulking while running in the dust of slower cars, the winners relished the satisfaction not just of a good job well done, but of seeing a long shot hit the target.

RALLY OF ARGENTINA

It was a rocky ride for Didier Auriol, as on so many other events, the Frenchman forced to give best to his team-mate (previous page). It was Juha Kankkunen's week, the Finn instantly settling in with his new co-driver, Nicky Grist (below); Argentine spectators pack the hillsides and they have healthy appetites (centre). Ford tasted mixed fortunes, Miki Biasion making do with second on an event he dearly wanted to win, Mohammed Bin Sulayem taking a long-awaited Group N success in his MLP Escort.

Marlboro
Mobil
PIAA
MLP
K744 GOO

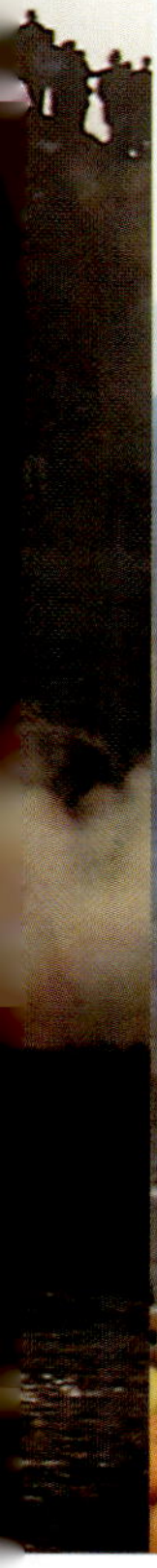

MICHELIN
BILSTEIN
OMP
WHEELS

The agony gave way to ecstasy. Although Ari Vatanen (overleaf) broke his Legacy's front suspension when in the lead, Colin McRae did everything Prodrive could have wished, the Scot curbing his sideways style – much of the time anyway – to score a tremendous victory. Poor Biasion's trip to the far side of the world was less fruitful; he crashed his Escort on the first long stage.

WORLD RALLY CHAMPIONSHIP ROUND 8

RALLY OF NEW ZEALAND

It took Carlos Sainz and Luis Moya to inject a trace of Latin drama into the occasion. They parked their Delta at Subaru's service point, walked across to Colin McRae and Derek Ringer, and gave each of them an extravagant hug, Moya hoisting McRae off his feet as he offered his congratulations. It was a small indication of the esteem in which the Scottish crew are held.

Until then, it had been hard to believe that the first victory on a round of the World Championship for the team or crew was a special moment at all. There had been smiles and handshakes, the epitome of British reserve, but no sign of elation. It was almost as though McRae was bemused by his success. He certainly wasn't sure what had gone so differently this time. Without question, it had not been a victory in the McRae style, even if the Prodrive mechanics were methodically replacing the most crumpled panels – the result of a brush with a post on the first day of the event. Instead of trying to murder the opposition with paralysing times on each stage, he had concentrated on staying in touch, keeping abreast of François Delecour and Didier Auriol. He had made a conscious effort to drive neatly, curbing his natural inclination to let the tail hang out. Yes, two previous attempts at the rally had helped; no, he didn't feel that New Zealand forests were like those in Britain. He had tried '101 per cent', but driven more quickly in the past.

Above all, he had kept his head throughout an epic, four-day battle, in which the top three were rarely more than 20 seconds apart. This time, the cool exterior had reflected an inner calm. Even when Delecour had lopped eight seconds from his lead on Kiwitahi during the final leg, the Subaru driver had kept his head. He acknowledged that the surface gravel on the next stage would probably favour the cars running behind him again. Perhaps the next downpour came to his rescue, perhaps it was Delecour's turn to be too cautious but, as soon as he gained four seconds, McRae knew he still had a chance. A stage later, he was 25 seconds in front and the rally was as good as settled.

For much of the event the outcome had been too close to call and no one could be said to have enjoyed a real measure of superiority. Each of the first three could point to crucial moments at which the event was won and lost. Delecour could reflect on the 20 seconds of road penalties voluntarily sacrificed at the end of the first leg, when Ford had feared the possibility of ice in the forests east of Rotorua and decided to let someone else run first on the road, or to the wrong tyre choice for the Motu Road, when McRae had catapulted from fifth to first. The winner had had his narrowest escape midway through the third leg, when a bolt fell out of a cam cover and emptied the sump. Miraculously, the flat four was undamaged. Auriol's defeat had been sealed when TTE decided to leave his car alone at the end of the second day, rather than replace the rear differential.

Delecour had some grounds for feeling hard done by, but he had exceeded expectations nonetheless. His neat, economical style had worked superbly on the twisty North Island stages and he had developed an instant affinity for this new challenge. While he had fallen to McRae in the end, he had beaten Toyota on an event which ought to have suited the Japanese team – all the more so after an intensive test there in June.

Indeed, Toyota's championship aspirations had suffered a major reverse. Rear differential problems for both Auriol and Juha Kankkunen had ensured that neither could capitalise on his considerable experience of the terrain. An epic contest had gone to the newcomers.

SUBARU

Rothmans
RALLY NEW ZEALAND
4
A
555
BILSTEIN
NGK

555

François Delecour produced a stunning drive, almost winning the rally at his first attempt; Didier Auriol might also have won for France (near right), if TTE's rear differential problem hadn't struck at the crucial moment, while Sepp Haider flew the Audi flag until the gear linkage failed. The spectators overcome obstacles every bit as severe as the drivers'!

SMS S2
Revo
SMS
BILSTEIN
SMS 1
BILSTEIN

TOYOTA
Castrol
MICHELIN

WORLD RALLY CHAMPIONSHIP ROUND 9

1000 LAKES RALLY

Nothing – even the new, semi-automatic Subaru – could stop Juha Kankkunen in Finland, the local boy scoring a decisive victory for Toyota (left). Malcolm Wilson was impressively quick, but two enormous accidents sidelined the Mobil Escort (below). Beforehand, the Impreza and its steering wheel-mounted gearchange attracted most of the attention.

Someone remarked, with a certain relish, that he didn't fancy being Denis Giraudet at the moment. Giraudet himself didn't appear to be enjoying the experience much either. The 1000 Lakes Rally was 25 stages old and Juha Kankkunen's stand-in co-driver not only had the drawn features of a condemned man, but firmly believed that things were now getting out of hand.

Despite yet another change of partner, Kankkunen had been in dazzling form. Driving largely on a mixture of memory and instinct, he had led from the first stage, pushing his luck, but unable to shake off the relentless pursuit from Ari Vatanen's new Impreza and his team-mate, Didier Auriol. The 30-minute re-group at Jämsä towards the end of the third leg gave time to take stock and the general belief was that the rally had now reached its decisive phase. Two long stages, totalling more than 50 kilometres, had preceded the re-group and Vatanen had emerged in markedly better shape than the Toyotas. On a sprint event such as this, Auriol was now out of contention. The diminutive Frenchman hadn't been over-pleased with his driving from the start, but he had been in with a chance nevertheless until he vaulted far too fast over a double yump on Päijälä. The impact ripped off the sumpguard, smashed the oil cooler, and deranged the suspension. The geometry was still out of line for the next stage, Hassi, and he slumped 40 seconds in arrears.

Kankkunen had been flirting with disaster all day. On paper, the rock-hard, ultra-fast stages round Tampere – the 'runways' as Vatanen graphically described them – might have offered the Toyota a minute advantage. In the event, he had never been able to put more than 12 seconds between himself and his opponents and, but for Michelin's miraculous ATS tyres, he would have had three separate punctures as a result of leaving the road. Two of these had occurred on Hassi – hence Giraudet's palpable air of disquiet – and the front struts had seized for good measure. Vatanen had narrowed the divide to just eight seconds. Even Kankkunen was coming round to the idea that the Impreza might be too much for him. It was too stable on yumps, too easy to drive, too kind to its front tyres; Vatanen promised that he was driving down the middle of the road, taking no chances. The pre-event hype had been justified.

Yet Kankkunen never gave up, even when his adversary forged into the lead with a stunning time on the following stage, Vaheri. Just when it seemed that the new Subaru would take a decisive victory on its first event, Vatanen was tripped by the most freakish obstacle: the twin auxiliary lamp pods switched the aerodynamics in one crucial respect, drawing air out of the intercooler scoop on the bonnet and thus depositing its cooling spray on the windscreen. Combined with a sudden deluge, the onset of nightfall, and the difficulty in activating the de-mister and the screen heater in a strange car, he lost 15 seconds peering through a misted screen. Kankkunen completed the leg with a relatively comfortable 17-second lead.

In retrospect, it was decisive. Vatanen badly needed to turn the tables at once, the following morning. However, the leader gained three seconds on the morning's second stage and Ari clattered the Impreza into a ditch briefly on the third; he decided the game was no longer worth the candle. Toyota's delight was mingled with relief. There was no denying that this had been a personal triumph – testimony to Kankkunen's courage and obduracy in the face of daunting odds. In true 1000 Lakes fashion, it had been a victory for the man rather than the machine.

1000 LAKES RALLY

The Impreza more than lived up to its name (right), but it wasn't quite enough to give Ari Vatanen his third 1000 Lakes victory. There were some impressive performances from the younger Finns, notably Tommi Mäkinen, who brought his Delta home in a fine fourth (below) and Sebastian Lindholm, who studies carefully modified pace notes, explaining the latest hazards – who says the locals drive from memory? Neither of the works Lancers landed in a lake (overleaf), but there wasn't much else for Ralliart to celebrate, Armin Schwarz losing to Lasse Lampi's aged Galant.

SUBARU
SUBARU
IMPREZA
MICHELIN
prodrive
L 555 BAT

50 OVT 160
OE + SILTA VK HEITTÄÄ 70

TOYOTA
Castrol
Telecom
TOYOTA TEAM EUROPE
6
Castrol
MICHELIN

WORLD RALLY CHAMPIONSHIP ROUND 10

RALLY AUSTRALIA

Once the rally is over and the press conference is out of the way, Juha Kankkunen generally strolls across the road from the Perth Sheraton to Fenians Pub for a celebratory Guinness. It has become a routine, rather like winning in Australia: his 1993 victory was the fourth in five years.

Yet this victory was somewhat different. His second win with Nicky Grist, it had also ensured that Toyota became the first Japanese car manufacturer to win a World Championship in its own right, crushing a Ford team that was struggling helplessly in unfamiliar conditions. While the hero of the hour sat in the pub with a quiet pint, Japan was buzzing with excitement. Naturally, Juha was pleased. He had led from start to finish and, following the events of the first day of the rally, his task had been comparatively straightforward. Once Carlos Sainz had crashed his Delta on the third stage and Didier Auriol had wrecked his Toyota's sump against a large stone in the middle of the road on the seventh, it had been a question of driving briskly enough to keep the upstart Colin McRae at arm's length rather than exploring the Celica's limits. By the time the Scot slipped off the road and down to sixth place on the final morning, handing second to his teammate, Ari Vatanen, Kankkunen had long since eased off.

Above all, though, the rally had been overshadowed by the death of Rodger Freeth in a savage accident on the third stage. The New Zealand co-driver complained of severe chest pains after 'Possum' Bourne's Legacy careered off a narrow, bumpy straight and into a tree at undiminished speed. Everything possible was done: a helicopter delivered a doctor to the scene within three minutes and a back-up team arrived when requested. As his condition deteriorated, he was airlifted to hospital in Perth. It was to no avail and he succumbed to massive internal injuries in the emergency ward two hours after the accident.

While Subaru's decision to continue had given proceedings a veneer of normality, the last three days of the event had not been disputed with much enthusiasm. McRae had entertained no illusions that Kankkunen might be catchable, but had never sounded interested in the possibility in any case. It was seven years since a top competitor had died on a World Championship rally and it had been tempting to hope that, with the demise of Group B, it might never happen again; the accident had been a sobering reminder that rallying can never be wholly safe. Little known in Europe, Freeth was a popular figure among the works crews and the sense of grief at losing such a remarkable personality was palpable. Hundreds turned up to mourn at a memorial service the day after the rally.

As he sat in Fenians, Kankkunen reluctantly contemplated the possibility of making a speech about Rodger Freeth at prizegiving that night. Plainly, he had no wish to discuss the death of a friend in public; his loss had tainted what might in happier circumstances have been a resounding victory.

SUBARU
555
SUBARU
SUBARU TECNICA INTERNATIONAL
prodrive
MICHELIN

BIASION
sparco

RALLY AUSTRALIA

Re-united with Nicky Grist, Juha Kankkunen rapidly outdistanced the opposition and clinched the manufacturers' crown for Toyota; photos of Carlos Sainz were a rare commodity in Australia, the Spaniard crashing the sole Lancia within hours of the start (previous page). Ari Vatanen finally took second place on a shocking event for Subaru (top left). Ford had a fairly grim time of it in Australia: even François Delecour (below) could only inherit third, while Miki Biasion was driven to despair, a last-minute electronic problem depriving him of any chance of winning the World Championship. Colin McRae drove with remarkable assurance on his first visit to Australia, only for a momentary lapse of concentration to demote him to sixth place on the final day.

SUBARU
555
555
PIAA

SUBARU

SANREMO RALLY

There was no doubting the commitment. Carlos Sainz was pouring with sweat from a 25-minute battle with the Repsol Delta over Monte Ceppo and the Colle Langan, yet there was no sign of the disappointment, even rage one might have anticipated after he had dropped 27 seconds to Franco Cunico's Escort. Rather, there was an overwhelming air of resignation. He had picked the wrong Michelins – again – and the Integrale had been distinctly short of grip on the numerous damp stretches, when he had badly needed to take a large bite from Cunico's lead on the first attempt at the longest stage. Now, the gap had climbed well beyond the two-minute mark and, while almost 90 miles of stages remained the following day, the Jolly Club was reduced to hoping that Cunico would lose the rally, for Sainz could no longer expect to win it. Defeat at Sanremo of all places, on a rally that Lancia had not lost since 1985, was quite definitely in the offing.

The day before, Sainz's mood had swung from depression, to hope, to disillusion in rapid, unpredictable stages. At first, he had picked suspension settings that were far too soft and had found himself trailing private Escorts, as well as the works cars and Piero Liatti's Subaru. Just when it had seemed that François Delecour could win by whatever margin he chose, SS7 came to the Jolly Club's rescue. Technically, Miki Biasion was in the lead after Delecour, Andrea Aghini and Liatti had all left the road for varying lengths of time in vile conditions, but the unfortunate Bassano driver's engine had been cooked when a water pipe failed and Sainz had, to all intents and purposes, vaulted from sixth to first in a single stage.

It was not altogether surprising to find that the Integrale was no longer a match for the works Escorts on asphalt, despite the latest, Lamborghini-inspired improvements, but it seemed fair to assume that the Jolly Club would capitalise on its unexpected good fortune with the Boreham cars out of the way; Group A's old stager would take one last curtain call. Instead, Sainz was knocked sideways by a superb performance in the rain and fog around Carrara from Cunico in his self-run Ford.

Tyre choice had once more played its part and Sainz might reasonably have hoped to redress the balance the following day, especially once the roads began to dry. However, Pirelli's latest R76 slick proved ideal for the mixture of dry and damp conditions and, despite a scare when the fans failed to cut in and the Cosworth overheated on SS15, the man rejected by Lancia and Ford in turn began to pull clear. Unemotionally, Cunico prepared to inflict the ultimate indignity: defeat at the hands of a privateer, on home ground. His handicap wasn't purely a question of car specification or the number of vans at his disposal. He had only one weather note crew and therefore lacked detailed information for several stages – and he freely admitted that he would regard second place as victory of a kind under the circumstances. The Jolly Club had no such excuses.

Of course Cunico was lucky. He had got away with going off the road for a minute on the first stage. Obligingly, others had crashed more seriously and his engine had lasted the distance, even if it was consuming water and petrol in roughly equal quantities by the finish. Despite that and Pirelli's substantial contribution to Cunico's victory, Sainz knew that the result had reflected more than the luck of the draw on tyre choices and weather conditions: there had been little to choose between the two cars even when the roads were bone dry and he was on the right rubber. While Claudio Bortoletto and Franco Antoniazzi made optimistic noises about Catalonia, their driver recognised that the game was up and, as it applied itself to the unaccustomed task of writing headlines about Bassano del Grappa's other rally driver, the rest of the world knew it too.

Franco Cunico (far left) did it his way, with an Escort that differed markedly from works tune. The vanishing point took another step closer for the Delta (below), Carlos Sainz having to make do with second place.

SANREMO RALLY

Foul weather was just what the Formula 2 men had ordered. Bruno Thiry cruises through Baiardo during the last leg on his way to a superb sixth in the Astra (right), while Angelo Medeghini made a name for himself by finishing ninth in a 140 bhp 106.

m. s.l.m. 910

Photo Pascal Huit

Any number of drivers might have won: Patrick Snijers was ahead of Cunico after all when the Belgian's Escort (left) ran into turbo trouble. Piero Liatti was in fine form in Subaru Italy's Legacy, but spent too much time off the road to improve on fifth.

TOYOTA
Castrol
MICHELIN
REPSOL
K-AM 5951

ADESITAL
MICHELIN
Ford
Motorsport
RACC
5
A
DIESEL JEANS
REPSOL
Bradi
BILSTEIN
sparco
TAT
TECFRIGO

WORLD RALLY CHAMPIONSHIP ROUND 12

CATALONIA RALLY

To François Delecour's way of thinking, it had been his finest victory to date. Toyota had sent no cars to Portugal and the Tour of Corsica had been a straightforward matter of driving flat out from start to finish, whereas this had demanded tactical skills; it had been a meticulously planned triumph. Changeable weather had made it impossible to drive on the limit throughout and, in any case, he had badly needed a finish if he was to retain any chance of winning the World Championship, having squandered a secure lead by crashing at Sanremo. It had therefore been vital to pick his moment, making sure that he won with the least possible risk.

By the beginning of the final leg, the Lille man had stretched his lead over Didier Auriol to 35 seconds, matching the Celica's every move. His mechanics were in no doubt that he had something in hand. Since only 130-odd kilometres of stages remained, Toyota management was resigned to defeat but, as the rain returned, Delecour still needed to convince Auriol that further resistance was hopeless. A helter-skelter charge at the first stage, soon after dawn, gained 15 seconds at a stroke. It was a masterly display of controlled aggression, but it didn't give him the freedom to relax. Two stages later, he was caught on pure slicks when the clouds opened, knowing full well that Auriol was on hand-cut tyres and should therefore have the upper hand; driving as fast as he dared, trying to get ahead of the rain, he lost only five seconds.

Having scared himself twice, Auriol recognised the inevitable and Delecour eventually won by exactly a minute. Aside from the ill-advised choice of hard compound slicks for La Riba, the longest stage of the rally, it had been a flawless performance. He had done everything that Ford had asked of him.

It had not been enough. An admirable victory had been overshadowed by a still more remarkable showing from Juha Kankkunen, who had vanquished Miki Biasion (aided somewhat by a Ford wastegate failure that cost the Italian three minutes on the last stage of the second leg) and taken the third place he needed to clinch a record-breaking fourth world title. It was an astonishing exploit, for the Finn had not only made up a minute after a tyre blew out on SS14, but had the temerity to beat the French stars on an occasional basis too. Given Kankkunen's past exploits on dry asphalt, it was akin to watching a lumbering full back dribbling round half a dozen defenders and chipping the ball calmly into an empty net.

It was all very well for Delecour to insist that, if there was any justice in the world, Auriol would have been the 1992 World Champion and that, with due respect to Kankkunen, there would be no true World Championship until everyone contested every rally. For once, the press displayed no more than a passing interest in the Frenchman's addiction to controversy and the crowd was thickest round the Toyota driver. Delecour might just as well have come second.

Ford won its duel with Toyota, despite Didier Auriol's best efforts (top left), but Miki Biasion couldn't overhaul Juha Kankkunen. Every face tells a story: Kankkunen (bottom) looks like a man on his way to the title: François Delecour, Auriol, Miki Biasion and Alex Fiorio fight their own battles.

Photo Pascal Huit

7

rallycourse

CATALONIA RALLY

François Delecour collected his third-ever outright victory as though he had been winning rallies for years (top right). Gustavo Trelles salvaged sixth on the Jolly Club's last sortie with the Delta (above) and Bruno Thiry floored the Spaniards with a brilliant drive in his Astra.

ADESITAL
MICHELIN
Ford
Motorsport
DIESEL JEANS
RACC
3
A
REPSOL
TECFRIGO
Bradi
BILSTEIN
sparco
TAT
DANIEL GRATALOUP
FRANCOIS DELECOUR
Mobil
MICHELIN

OPEL
Lloret prestige
RACC
8
Marlboro
MICHELIN
Mobil 1
CAE·167

WORLD RALLY CHAMPIONSHIP ROUND 13

RAC RALLY

Nothing – certainly not a tyre failure in Wales – could come between Juha Kankkunen and his fifth victory of the year (top right), although Kenneth Eriksson tried his utmost, restoring Mitsubishi's morale in the process (right). There were mixed fortunes for the home contingent: Colin McRae (top) led convincingly, but it was left to Malcolm Wilson to soldier home to a fine third in his Escort. At least they get some sleep in a warm hotel room, unlike some of their fans.

Juha Kankkunen's audience was spellbound. In the enthusiastic tones that someone else might reserve for gardening or stamp collecting, he was describing different types of accident. There had been no sense in trying to avoid crashing altogether on the RAC – in such unpredictable conditions, driving at competitive speeds had positively required going off the road from time to time. The trick had been to minimise the after-effects. Above all else, Kankkunen explained, the crucial need was to avoid hitting anything solid with the vulnerable front wheels; if the worst came to the worst, the mechanics could rebuild the back of the car a good deal more easily than the front. Better still was hitting the scenery amidships, well away from the front and rear axles. That obviously explained the post in Cropton that morning, which had shattered Nicky Grist's window, bending the door and the sill. Suppose it had been a tree suggested someone jokingly. Kankkunen turned solemn. 'I would not do that to him,' he answered.

In fact, the Cropton excursion had come close to costing him the rally nonetheless, for the Celica had all but rolled and it wouldn't have taken much of a delay to hand the lead to the relentless Kenneth Eriksson. It had been the narrowest escape in a week of narrow escapes, during which the pre-event favourite had never had a moment's respite.

In the end, it was a triumphant conclusion to a dazzling year, but it was scarcely what Kankkunen and Grist had imagined when they confidently discussed the event following the Rally Australia. Run on a mixture of snow and ice that turned each forest into a booby trap, it was the sort of rally that wilfully refused to conform to anybody's plans for it. Every corner was a potential accident and, more than once, Kankkunen admitted that he was exhausted.

At first, it had gone swimmingly. Colin McRae had started slowly, Kankkunen elbowed his way past Armin Schwarz's bravely driven Lancer towards the end of the first leg and then he had been handed a generous 45-second lead after the first 'real' stage in Dyfnant, when his opponents were too cautious or strayed too close to the edge of the road. As McRae got into his stride, that advantage was hacked away so quickly that some of the Finn's rivals wondered if he was aware of the Scotsman's times.

As usual, the north was McRae's undoing. He overcame his Grizedale bane, only to hole the Impreza's radiator after hitting something solid – perhaps a branch or a log – in Kershope. The engine was cooked by the time he reached the stage finish and the air of disappointment was palpable, nationwide. As a result, Kankkunen was sitting pretty, two and a half minutes ahead of Eriksson. Kielder changed all that, as Eriksson had suspected it would. The snow was deep enough to demand snow tyres, yet not so plentiful as to eliminate the risks of using them. As they lacked Michelin's ATS system, the sensible course was to drive on the icy crown of the road, avoiding the rocks and Kielder's quicksand ditches, yet the only way to slow down was often to seek grip at the edge of the track. While Malcolm Wilson set the bulk of the fastest times, the main protagonists freely confessed to misjudging the conditions. To his intense annoyance, Eriksson picked up a front puncture and then drove too cautiously on the following stage. The words were barely out of his mouth before Kankkunen hobbled into service with two punctures. As the Finn pulled himself together, Eriksson pressed home the attack. The difference between them plunged to 32 seconds.

Kankkunen's response was breathtaking. Driving with complete abandon, he added 49 seconds to his lead on the final stage of the leg while his adversary steered away from trouble. Of course he had been lucky – just as he was in Cropton the following morning – and poor Eriksson had been able neither to banish the memory of his two punctures in Dyfnant, nor to throw caution to the winds when Ralliart badly needed a good result, but, listening to Kankkunen that night, one realised that there is a skill that transcends luck.

TOYOTA
TOYOTA
TEAM EUROPE
K AM 828

RAC RALLY

Smiling all the way to the rostrum, Juha Kankkunen emerges from the winning Toyota (above). Robbie Head (right) became Kielder's most illustrious victim, whereas Gwyndaf Evans (below right) was in a class of his own in Group N at the wheel of the Shell Escort. Armin Schwarz fought back from 77th to eighth after leaving the road in Wales.

22
Pilot

RALLY SCHOLARSHIP
Shell
COSWORTH
K6 SBG
30
DUNLOP

Monte Carlo Rally, 21-27 January, FIA World Rally Championship Round 1

Leading Entries

1	Carlos Sainz/ Luis Moya	Lancia Delta HF Integrale	Gr A
2	Miki Biasion/ Tiziano Siviero	Ford Escort Cosworth	Gr A
3	Didier Auriol/ Bernard Occelli	Toyota Celica Turbo 4WD	Gr A
4	Armin Schwarz/ Nicky Grist	Mitsubishi Lancer RS-E	Gr A
5	Andrea Aghini/ Sauro Farnocchia	Lancia Delta HF Integrale	Gr A
6	François Delecour/ Daniel Grataloup	Ford Escort Cosworth	Gr A
7	Juha Kankkunen/ Juha Piironen	Toyota Celica Turbo 4WD	Gr A
8	Kenneth Eriksson/ Staffan Parmander	Mitsubishi Lancer RS-E	Gr A
9	Pavel Sibera/ Petr Gross	Skoda Favorit 136L	Gr A
10	Bruno Thiry/ Gilles Favier	Opel Astra GSI	Gr A
11	Emil Triner/ Jiri Klima	Skoda Favorit 136L	Gr A
14	Isolde Holderied/ Tina Thörner	Mitsubishi Galant	Gr N
15	Olivier Burri/ Christophe Hoffman	Ford Sierra Cosworth 4x4	Gr A
16	Christophe Spiliotis/ Hervé Thibaud	Lancia Delta HF Integrale	Gr N
19	Christine Driano/ Marie-Christine Lallement	Citroën AX GT	Gr A
20	Pierre Bos/ Michel Rousseau	Ford Sierra Cosworth 4x4	Gr A
21	Pierre-Manuel Jenot/ 'Slo'	Ford Escort Cosworth	Gr N
22	Jean-Pierre Ballet/ Pierre Dupont	Peugeot 309 GTI 16v	Gr A
23	Christian Dorche/ Thierry Barjou	Nissan Sunny GTI-R	Gr N

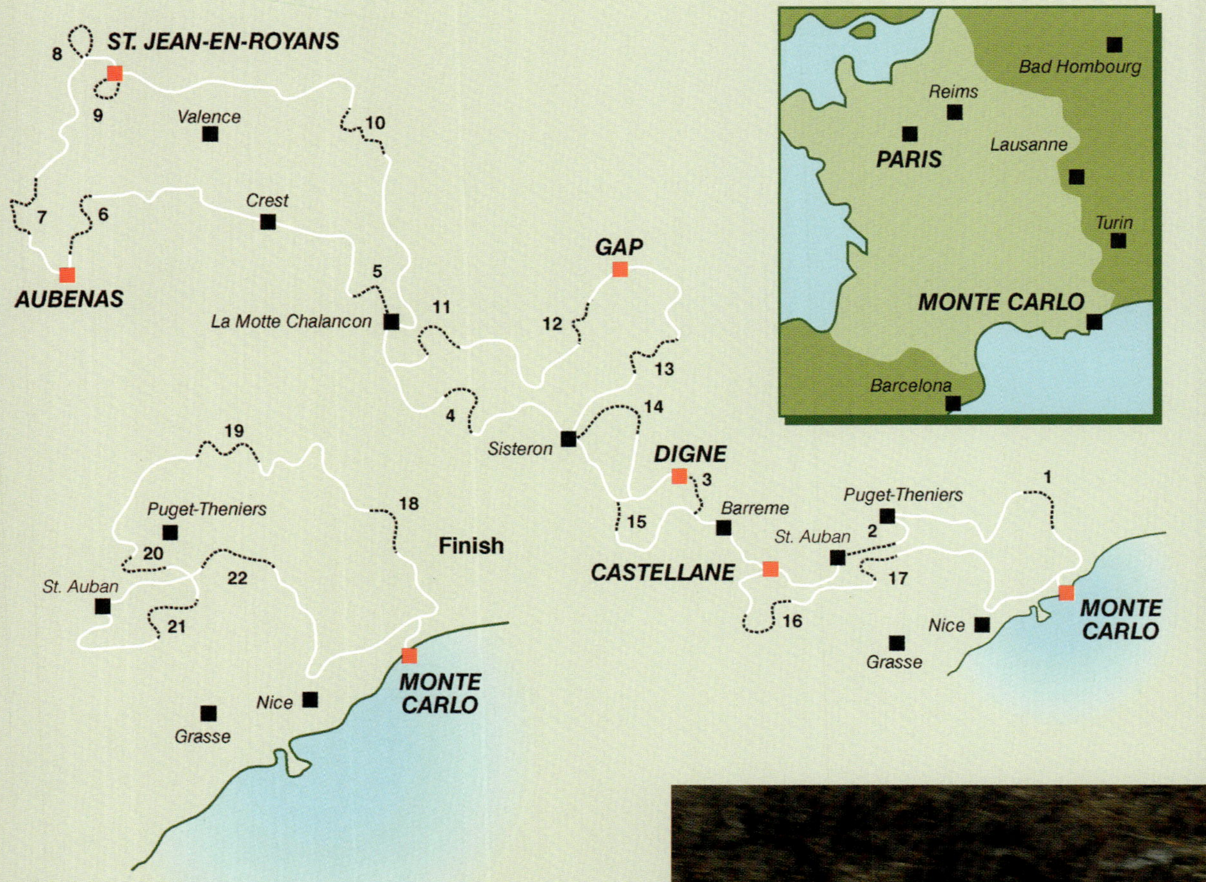

Special Stage Times

SS1 Col de Turini 1 (22.21 km)
1 A.Aghini/S.Farnocchia (Lancia Delta HF Integrale) 15m 50s; **2** F.Delecour/D.Grataloup (Ford Escort Cosworth) 15m 51s; **3** M.Biasion/T.Siviero (Ford Escort Cosworth) 16m 00s; **4** A.Schwarz/N.Grist (Mitsubishi Lancer RS-E) 16m 07s; **5** J.Kankkunen/ J.Piironen (Toyota Celica Turbo) 16m 22s; **6** C.Sainz/L.Moya (Lancia Delta HF Integrale) 16m 32s

SS2 Pont des Miolans-St. Auban (22.72 km)
1 Delecour/Grataloup (Ford) 13m 47s; **2** Aghini/ Farnocchia (Lancia) 14m 05s; **3** Kankkunen/ Piironen (Toyota) 14m 13s; **4** Sainz/Moya (Lancia) 14m 14s; **5** Biasion/Siviero (Ford) 14m 20s; **6** Kenneth Eriksson/ Staffan Parmander (Mitsubishi Lancer RS-E) 16m 32s

SS3 Col de Corobin (19.60 km)
1 Delecour/Grataloup (Ford) 12m 56s; **2** Didier Auriol/Bernard Occelli (Toyota Celica Turbo) 12m 59s; **3** Biasion/Siviero (Ford) 13m 03s; **4** Sainz/Moya (Lancia) 13m 09s; **5** Schwarz/Grist (Mitsubishi) 13m 11s; **6** Aghini/Farnocchia (Lancia) 13m 12s

SS4 Col du Perty (27.37 km)
1 Biasion/Siviero (Ford) 16m 18s; **2** Delecour/ Grataloup (Ford) 16m 19s; **3** Auriol/Occelli (Toyota) 16m 23s; **4** Sainz/Moya (Lancia) 16m 30s; **5** Aghini/ Farnocchia (Lancia) 16m 33s; **6** Schwarz/Grist (Mitsubishi) 16m 37s

SS5 La Motte Chalancon (23.39 km)
1 Auriol/Occelli (Toyota) 14m 23s; **2** Delecour/ Grataloup (Ford) 14m 24s; **3** Schwarz/Grist 14m 33s; **4** Sainz/Moya (Lancia) 14m 36s; **5** Aghini/Farnocchia (Lancia) 14m 38s; **6** Biasion/Siviero (Ford) 14m 41s

SS6 Pierreville-Antraigues (35.97 km)
1 Delecour/Grataloup (Ford) 21m 59s; **2** Auriol/ Occelli (Toyota) 22m 12s; **3** Sainz/Moya (Lancia) 22m 23s; **4** Aghini/Farnocchia (Lancia) 22m 28s; **5** Biasion/Siviero (Ford) 22m 29s; **6** Kankkunen/ Piironen (Toyota) 16m 40s

Miki Biasion was third in the end and reckoned he had produced one of his finest Monte drives.

SS7 Burzet (41.41 km)
1 Biasion/Siviero (Ford), Sainz/Moya (Lancia) 24m 40s; **3** Aghini/Farnocchia (Lancia), Delecour/ Grataloup (Ford) 24m 47s; **5** Schwarz/Grist (Mitsubishi) 24m 56s; **6** Kankkunen/Piironen (Toyota) 25m 04s

SS8 St. Bonnet le Froid (25.74 km)
1 Delecour/Grataloup (Ford) 13m 27s; **2** Auriol/ Occelli (Toyota) 13m 32s; **3** Biasion/Siviero (Ford) 13m 35s; **4** Aghini/Farnocchia (Lancia) 13m 37s; **5** Sainz/Moya (Lancia) 13m 38s; **6** Kankkunen/Piironen (Toyota) 13m 40s

SS9 Lalouvsec (32.76 km)
1 Biasion/Siviero (Ford) 19m 52s; **2** Sainz/Moya (Lancia) 19m 56s; **3** Auriol/Occelli (Toyota) 20m 09s; **4** Aghini/Farnocchia (Lancia), Delecour/Grataloup (Ford) 20m 14s; **6** Kankkunen/Piironen (Toyota) 20m 30s

SS10 St. Jean-en-Royans (25.44 km)
1 Delecour/Grataloup (Ford) 12m 52s; **2** Aghini/ Farnocchia (Lancia) 13m 00s; **3** Biasion/Siviero (Ford) 13m 01s; **4** Sainz/Moya (Lancia) 13m 04s; **5** Schwarz/Grist (Mitsubishi) 13m 08s; **6** Auriol/Occelli (Toyota) 13m 09s

SS11 Rosans-Col de la Saulce (30.38 km)
1 Auriol/Occelli (Toyota) 18m 29s; **2** Sainz/Moya (Lancia) 18m 33s; **3** Biasion/Siviero (Ford) 18m 42s; **4** Delecour/Grataloup (Ford) 18m 44s; **5** Kankkunen/ Piironen (Toyota) 19m 01s; **6** Eriksson/Parmander (Mitsubishi) 19m 21s

SS12 Plans de Vitrolles-Sigoyer (18.86 km)
1 Auriol/Occelli (Toyota) 11m 26s; **2** Delecour/ Grataloup (Ford) 11m 41s; **3** Biasion/Siviero (Ford) 11m 49s; **4** Kankkunen/Piironen (Toyota) 11m 54s; **5** Eriksson/Parmander (Mitsubishi) 12m 24s; **6** Schwarz/Grist (Mitsubishi) 12m 43s

SS13 Col des Garcinets (22.78 km)
1 Sainz/Moya (Lancia) 14m 37s; **2** Auriol/Occelli (Toyota) 14m 45s; **3** Schwarz/Grist (Mitsubishi) 14m 55s; **4** Biasion/Siviero (Ford) 15m 06s; **5** Delecour/ Grataloup (Ford) 15m 11s; **6** Kankkunen/ Piironen (Toyota) 15m 18s

SS14 Sisteron-Thoard (36.87 km)
1 Sainz/Moya (Lancia) 23m 22s; **2** Delecour/ Grataloup (Ford) 23m 28s, Auriol/Occelli (Toyota) 23m 28s; **4** Biasion/Siviero (Ford) 23m 29s; **5** Schwarz/Grist 23m 38s; **6** Kankkunen/Piironen (Toyota) 23m 47s

SS15 Malijai-Puimichel (12.32 km)
1 Biasion/Siviero (Ford) 7m 46s; **2** Auriol/Occelli (Toyota) 7m 49s; **3** Sainz/Moya (Lancia) 7m 51s; **4** Delecour/Grataloup (Ford) 7m 52s; **5** Kankkunen/ Piironen (Toyota) 7m 53s; **6** Eriksson/Parmander (Mitsubishi) 8m 05s

SS16 Trigance-Chateauvieux (27.57 km)
1 Auriol/Occelli (Toyota) 15m 08s; **2** Sainz/Moya (Lancia) 15m 12s; **3** Biasion/Siviero (Ford) 15m 14s; **4** Delecour/Grataloup (Ford) 15m 22s; **5** Kankkunen/ Piironen (Toyota) 15m 23s; **6** Eriksson/Parmander (Mitsubishi) 15m 50s

SS17 Col de Bleine 1 (33.52 km)
1 Auriol/Occelli (Toyota) 22m 50s; **2** Sainz/Moya (Lancia) 22m 56s; **3** Biasion/Siviero (Ford) 23m 05s; **4** Delecour/Grataloup (Ford), Kankkunen/Piironen (Toyota) 23m 13s; **6** Eriksson/Parmander (Mitsubishi) 24m 06s

SS18 Col de Turini 2 (22.21 km)
1 Delecour/Grataloup (Ford) 15m 37s; **2** Auriol/ Occelli (Toyota) 15m 42s; **3** Sainz/Moya (Lancia), Biasion/Siviero (Ford) 15m 43s; **5** Schwarz/Grist 16m 14s; **6** Kankkunen/Piironen (Toyota) 16m 21s

SS19 Col de la Couillole (22.15 km)
1 Auriol/Occelli (Toyota) 13m 37s; **2** Sainz/Moya (Lancia) 13m 50s; **3** Biasion/Siviero (Ford) 14m 00s; **4** Delecour/Grataloup (Ford) 14m 02s; **5** Kankkunen/ Piironen (Toyota) 14m 20s; **6** Schwarz/Grist (Mitsubishi) 14m 22s

SS20 Entrevaux (30.57 km)
1 Auriol/Occelli (Toyota) 20m 01s; **2** Sainz/Moya (Lancia) 20m 06s; **3** Biasion/Siviero (Ford) 20m 31s; **4** Delecour/Grataloup (Ford) 20m 32s; **5** Schwarz/ Grist (Mitsubishi) 21m 03s; **6** Eriksson/Parmander (Mitsubishi) 21m 38s

SS21 Col de Bleine 2 (33.52 km)
1 Auriol/Occelli (Toyota) 22m 33s; **2** Delecour/ Grataloup (Ford) 22m 55s; **3** Sainz/Moya (Lancia) 23m 07s; **4** Biasion/Siviero (Ford) 23m 21s; **5** Kankkunen/Piironen (Toyota) 23m 37s; **6** Schwarz/ Grist (Mitsubishi) 23m 47s

SS22 St Antonin-Tourette (26.26 km)
1 Auriol/Occelli (Toyota) 18m 32s; **2** Delecour/ Grataloup (Ford) 18m 45s; **3** Sainz/Moya (Lancia) 18m 52s; **4** Kankkunen/Piironen (Toyota) 19m 09s; **5** Schwarz/Grist (Mitsubishi) 19m 38s; **6** Eriksson/ Parmander (Mitsubishi) 19m 47s

Major Retirements

5 Aghini/Farnocchia	Lancia Delta HF Integrale	
Accident	SS12	Gr A
21 Jenot/Slo	Ford Escort Cosworth	
Accident	SS19	Gr N

FIA Class Winners

A7 Over 2000 cc	Auriol/Occelli Toyota Celica Turbo 4WD
A6 1300-2000 cc	Thiry/Favier Opel Astra GSi
A5 Up to 1300 cc	Sibera/Gross Skoda Favorit 136L
N4 Over 2000 cc	Spiliotis/Thibaud Lancia Delta HF Integrale
N3 1600-2000 cc	Rubiolo/Pascal Renault Clio 16s
N2 1300-1600 cc	Le Cozanet/Lacroix Peugeot 205 GTI-1.6
N1 Up to 1300 cc	Soureillat/Derreumaux Citroën AX Sport

Rally Leaders

SS1 Aghini; **SS2-20** Delecour; **SS21-22** Auriol

World Championship Points

Drivers
1 Auriol 20; **2** Delecour 15; **3** Biasion 12; **4** Eriksson 10; **5** Kankkunen 8; **6** Schwarz 6; **7** Burri 4; **8** Thiry 3; **9** Spiliotis 2; **10** Serpaggi 1

Manufacturers
1 Toyota 20; **2** Ford 17; **3** Mitsubishi 12

FIA Cup for Production Car Drivers
1 Spiliotis 13; **2** Serpaggi 10; **3** Holderied 7; **4** Dionisio 5, etc.

FIA Cup for Manufacturers
1 GME 10; **2** Peugeot 8; **3** Citroën 6; **4** Skoda 5, etc.

Route Details
Leg 1 Concentration Run
Thursday, 21 January - Friday, 22 January: five starting towns (Bad Homburg, Barcelona, Lausanne, Reims, and Turin)
Leg 2 Classification Run
Saturday, 23 January. 6 stages (151.26 km) in a total route of 584.32 km
Leg 3 Common Run
Sunday, 24 January-Monday, 25 January. 11 stages (308.65 km) in a total route of 944.24 km
Leg 4
Tuesday, 26 January-Wednesday, 27 January. 5 stages (134.81 km) in a total route of 413.48 km

Weather

Mainly dry with some ice

Special Stage Analysis

	1	2	3	4	5	6
Auriol (Toyota)	9	7	2	-	-	1
Delecour (Ford)	6	7	1	7	1	-
Biasion (Ford)	4	-	1	3	2	1
Sainz (Lancia)	3	6	5	5	1	1
Aghini (Lancia)	1	2	1	3	2	1
Schwarz (Mitsubishi)	-	-	2	1	7	4
Kankkunen (Toyota)	-	-	1	3	6	7
Eriksson (Mitsubishi)	-	-	-	-	1	7

Finish Lines

The Jolly Club had a dreadful rally, both **Carlos Sainz** and **Andrea Aghini** rolling on icy patches on SS12. Aghini demolished a bridge parapet and retired on the spot, whereas Sainz struggled home in 14th place in a car that was an inch shorter on one side than the other... Transmission frailty dogged the works **Lancers** on their first World Championship appearance, but **Kenneth Eriksson** soldiered on to finish fourth, despite completing the Common Run with a badly slipping centre differential and a brake problem that led to road penalties...**Juha Kankkunen** clipped a rock and broke a bolt in his **Toyota**'s rear suspension three stages from the finish. It cost him ten minutes and narrowly deprived him of fourth...**Armin Schwarz** was sixth on his first event with **Mitsubishi** or with English pace notes... **Bruno Thiry** won the Touring Car Cup (two-wheel drive) category in his **Opel Belgium Astra**, surviving a roll on the flying finish of SS11 without much loss of time...**Christophe Spiliotis** transferred from Ford to Lancia, but still won **Group N**, the Monegasque grabbing the lead when **Pierre-Manuel Jenot** crashed his **Escort Cosworth** on the last night.

Results

1	Didier Auriol/ Bernard Occelli	Toyota Celica Turbo 4WD 6h 13m 43s	Gr A
2	François Delecour/ Daniel Grataloup	Ford Escort Cosworth 6h 13m 58s	Gr A
3	Miki Biasion/ Tiziano Siviero	Ford Escort Cosworth 6h 16m 59s	Gr A
4	Kenneth Eriksson/ Staffan Parmander	Mitsubishi Lancer RS-E 6h 31m 30s	Gr A
5	Juha Kankkunen/ Juha Piironen	Toyota Celica Turbo 4WD 6h 32m 43s	Gr A
6	Armin Schwarz/ Nicky Grist	Mitsubishi Lancer RS-E 6h 39m 45s	Gr A
7	Olivier Burri/ Christophe Hoffman	Ford Sierra Cosworth 4x4 6h 51m 03s	Gr A
8	Bruno Thiry/ Gilles Favier	Opel Astra GSI 6h 54m 08s	Gr A
9	Christophe Spiliotis/ Hervé Thibaud	Lancia Delta HF Integrale 6h 56m 24s	Gr N
10	Jean-Baptiste Serpaggi/ Francis Serpaggi	Ford Escort Cosworth 6h 57m 58s	Gr N
14	Carlos Sainz/ Luis Moya	Lancia Delta HF Integrale 7h 09m 07s	Gr A

170 starters, 86 finishers

Previous Winners (since 1960)

1960	Walter Schock/Rolf Moll	Mercedes-Benz 220SE
1961	Maurice Martin/Robert Bateau	Panhard
1962	Eric Carlsson/Gunnar Haggbom	Saab 96
1963	Eric Carlsson/Gunnar Palm	Saab 96
1964	Paddy Hopkirk/Henry Liddon	Mini-Cooper S
1965	Timo Mäkinen/Paul Easter	Mini-Cooper S
1966	Pauli Toivonen/Ensio Mikander	Citroën DS21
1967	Rauno Aaltonen/Henry Liddon	Mini-Cooper S
1968	Vic Elford/David Stone	Porsche 911T
1969	Björn Waldegård/Lars Helmer	Porsche 911
1970	Björn Waldegård/Lars Helmer	Porsche 911T
1971	Ove Andersson/David Stone	Alpine Renault A110
1972	Sandro Munari/Mario Mannucci	Lancia Fulvia
1973	Jean-Claude Andruet/'Biche'	Alpine Renault A110
1975	Sandro Munari/Mario Mannucci	Lancia Stratos
1976	Sandro Munari/Silvio Maiga	Lancia Stratos
1977	Sandro Munari/Silvio Maiga	Lancia Stratos
1978	Jean-Pierre Nicolas/Vincent Laverne	Porsche 911 Carrera
1979	Bernard Darniche/Alain Mahé	Lancia Stratos
1980	Walter Röhrl/Christian Geistdörfer	Fiat 131 Abarth
1981	Jean Ragnotti/Jean-Marc Andrié	Renault 5 Turbo
1982	Walter Röhrl/Christian Geistdörfer	Opel Ascona 400
1983	Walter Röhrl/Christian Geistdörfer	Lancia Rally 037
1984	Walter Röhrl/Christian Geistdörfer	Audi Quattro A2
1985	Ari Vatanen/Terry Harryman	Peugeot 205 Turbo 16
1986	Henri Toivonen/Sergio Cresto	Lancia Delta S4
1987	Massimo Biasion/Tiziano Siviero	Lancia Delta HF 4x4
1988	Bruno Saby/Jean-François Fauchille	Lancia Delta HF 4x4
1989	Miki Biasion/Tiziano Siviero	Lancia Delta HF Integrale
1990	Didier Auriol/Bernard Occelli	Lancia Delta HF Integrale
1991	Carlos Sainz/Luis Moya	Toyota Celica GT4
1992	Didier Auriol/Bernard Occelli	Lancia Delta HF Integrale

SWEDISH RALLY/Statistics

Swedish International Rally, 12-14 February, FIA World Rally Championship Round 2

Leading Entries

1	Mats Jonsson/ Lars Bäckman	Toyota Celica Turbo 4WD	Gr A
2	Colin McRae/ Derek Ringer	Subaru Legacy RS	Gr A
3	Juha Kankkunen/ Juha Piironen	Toyota Celica Turbo 4WD	Gr A
4	Stig Blomqvist/ Benny Melander	Opel Calibra Turbo	Gr A
5	Hannu Mikkola/ Bruno Berglund	Subaru Legacy RS	Gr A
6	Didier Auriol/ Bernard Occelli	Toyota Celica Turbo 4WD	Gr A
7	Mikael Ericsson/ Tina Thörner	Ford Escort Cosworth	Gr A
8	Sebastian Lindholm/ Timo Hantunen	Ford Escort Cosworth	Gr A
9	Tommi Mäkinen/ Seppo Harjanne	Lancia Delta HF Integrale	Gr A
10	Per Eklund/ Johnny Johansson	Subaru Legacy RS	Gr A
11	Malcolm Wilson/ Bryan Thomas	Ford Escort Cosworth	Gr A
12	Sepp Haider/ Klaus Wendel	Audi Coupé S2	Gr A
13	Jarmo Kytölehto/ Arto Kapanen	Mitsubishi Galant VR-4	Gr N
14	Alister McRae/ David Senior	Ford Sierra Cosworth 4x4	Gr N
15	Mohammed Bin Sulayem/ Ronan Morgan	Ford Escort Cosworth	Gr N
16	Tomas Jansson/ Ingemar Algerstedt	Toyota Celica GT4	Gr A
17	Björn Johansson/ Anders Olsson	Mazda 323 GT-R	Gr A
18	Håkan Eriksson/ Jan Svanstrom	Mazda 323 GT-R	Gr A
19	Stig-Olof Walfridsson/ Gunnar Barth	Mitsubishi Galant VR-4	Gr N
20	Kjell Olofsson/ Jorgen Skallman	Nissan Sunny GTI-R	Gr N

Special Stage Times

SS1 Kalvholmen (2.0 km)
1 M.Jonsson/L.Bäckman (Toyota Celica Turbo), C.McRae/D.Ringer (Subaru Legacy RS), J.Kankkunen/J.Piironen (Toyota Celica Turbo), D.Auriol/B.Occelli (Toyota Celica Turbo), P.Eklund/J.Johansson (Subaru Legacy RS), M.Wilson/B.Thomas (Ford Escort Cosworth) 1m 52s

SS2 Alvsbacka (10.90 km)
1 Wilson/Thomas (Ford) 5m 50s; **2** B.Johansson/A.Olsson (Mazda 323 GT-R) 5m 51s; **3** Jonsson/Bäckman (Toyota) 5m 52s; **4** Auriol/Occelli (Toyota) 5m 55s; **5** McRae/Ringer (Subaru) 5m 56s; **6** H.Mikkola/B.Berglund (Subaru) 5m 59s

SS3 Backa (29.35 km)
1 Auriol/Occelli (Toyota) 16m 11s; **2** McRae/Ringer (Subaru) 16m 15s; **3** Kankkunen/Piironen (Toyota) 16m 20s; **4** Jonsson/Bäckman (Toyota) 16m 27s; **5** S.Lindholm/T.Hantunen (Ford Escort Cosworth) 16m 28s; **6** Mikkola/Berglund (Subaru) 16m 41s

SS4 Uddeholmshyttan (23.68 km)
1 Auriol/Occelli (Toyota) 12m 46s; **2** Jonsson/Bäckman (Toyota), McRae/Ringer (Subaru) 12m 48s; **4** Kankkunen/Piironen (Toyota) 12m 56s; **5** T.Mäkinen/S.Harjanne (Lancia Delta HF Integrale) 12m 58s; **6** Johansson/Olsson (Mazda) 13m 00s

SS5 Sågen (14.82 km)
1 Jonsson/Bäckman (Toyota) 8m 22s; **2** McRae/Ringer (Subaru) 8m 25s; **3** Auriol/Occelli (Toyota) 8m 26s; **4** Lindholm/Hantunen (Ford) 8m 28s; **5** Kankkunen/Piironen (Toyota) 8m 29s; **6** Johansson/Olsson (Mazda) 8m 32s

SS6 Laxtjam (27.97 km)
1 Kankkunen/Piironen (Toyota) 14m 51s; **2** McRae/Ringer (Subaru), Auriol/Occelli (Toyota), Johansson/Olsson (Mazda) 14m 56s; **5** Mäkinen/Harjanne (Lancia) 15m 11s; **6** Eklund/Johansson (Subaru) 15m 20s

SS7 Telningsberg (10.84 km)
1 Auriol/Occelli (Toyota) 6m 05s; **2** Jonsson/Bäckman (Toyota), McRae/Ringer (Subaru) 6m 07s; **4** Kankkunen/Piironen (Toyota) 6m 10s; **5** Mäkinen/Harjanne (Lancia) 6m 11s; **6** Mikkola/ Berglund (Subaru) 6m 15s

SS8 Nyhammar (24.53 km)
1 McRae/Ringer (Subaru) 13m 01s; **2** Auriol/Occelli (Toyota) 13m 06s; **3** Jonsson/Bäckman (Toyota) 13m 12s; **4** Kankkunen/Piironen (Toyota) 13m 13s; **5** Mikkola/Berglund (Subaru) 13m 27s; **6** Mäkinen/Harjanne (Lancia) 13m 28s

SS9 Vibberbo (27.05 km)
1 Kankkunen/Piironen (Toyota) 16m 00s; **2** McRae/Ringer (Subaru) 16m 13s; **3** Jonsson/Bäckman (Toyota) 16m 14s; **4** Johansson/Olsson (Mazda) 16m 22s; **5** Lindholm/Hantunen (Ford) 16m 25s; **6** Mäkinen/Harjanne (Lancia) 16m 44s

SS10 Nisshyttan (28.92 km)
1 McRae/Ringer (Subaru) 17m 01s; **2** Kankkunen/Piironen (Toyota) 17m 04s; **3** Jonsson/Bäckman (Toyota), Auriol/Occelli (Toyota) 17m 06s; **5** Mäkinen/Harjanne (Lancia) 17m 18s; **6** Johansson/Olsson (Mazda) 17m 19s

SS11 I13 (10.85 km)
1 Kankkunen/Piironen (Toyota) 6m 22s; **2** Jonsson/Bäckman (Toyota), Auriol/Occelli (Toyota) 6m 24s; **4** McRae/Ringer (Subaru) 6m 26s; **5** Johansson/Olsson (Mazda) 6m 31s; **6** Eklund/Johansson (Subaru) 6m 34s

SS12 Grycksbo (14.45 km)
1 Auriol/Occelli (Toyota) 8m 22s; **2** McRae/Ringer (Subaru) 8m 25s; **3** Lindholm/Hantunen (Ford) 8m 27s; **4** Mikkola/Berglund (Subaru) 8m 29s; **5** Johansson/Olsson (Mazda) 8m 31s; **6** Eklund/Johansson (Subaru) 8m 40s

SS13 Djura (23.15 km)
1 Auriol/Occelli (Toyota) 12m 12s; **2** Johansson/Olsson (Mazda) 12m 17s; **3** Jonsson/Bäckman (Toyota), Lindholm/Hantunen (Ford) 12m 19s; **5** Mikkola/Berglund (Subaru) 12m 24s; **6** Kankkunen/Piironen (Toyota), Mäkinen/Harjanne (Lancia) 12m 27s

SS14 Skalo (26.58 km)
1 Auriol/Occelli (Toyota) 13m 42s; **2** McRae/Ringer (Subaru) 13m 47s; **3** Lindholm/Hantunen (Ford), Johansson/Olsson (Mazda) 13m 55s; **5** Mäkinen/Harjanne (Lancia), Kankkunen/Piironen (Toyota) 13m 56s

SS15 Likenäs (42.81 km)
1 McRae/Ringer (Subaru) 20m 32s; **2** Auriol/Occelli (Toyota) 20m 36s; **3** Kankkunen/Piironen (Toyota) 20m 38s; **4** Jonsson/Bäckman (Toyota) 20m 44s; **5** Johansson/Olsson (Mazda) 20m 46s; **6** Lindholm/Hantunen (Ford) 20m 52s

SS16 Branas (3.0 km)
1 Jonsson/Bäckman (Toyota), Lindholm/Hantunen (Ford) 1m 05s; **3** Kankkunen/Piironen (Toyota), Auriol/Occelli (Toyota), Eklund/Johansson (Subaru) 1m 06s; **6** McRae/Ringer (Subaru) 1m 07s

SS17 Ho Chi Min Road (14.99 km)
1 Auriol/Occelli (Toyota) 8m 22s; **2** Jonsson/Bäckman, Kankkunen/Piironen (Toyota) 8m 28s; **4** McRae/Ringer (Subaru) 8m 30s; **5** Mäkinen/Harjanne (Lancia) 8m 32s; **6** Lindholm/Hantunen (Ford) 8m 39s

SS18 Mitandersfors (12.64 km)
1 Jonsson/Bäckman (Toyota) 8m 06s; **2** Mäkinen/Harjanne (Lancia) 8m 18s; **3** McRae/Ringer (Subaru), Kankkunen/Piironen (Toyota) 8m 19s; **5** Mikkola Berglund (Subaru) 8m 20s; **6** S.Blomqvist/B.Melander (Opel Calibra Turbo) 8m 34s

SS19 Mangen (22.09 km)
1 McRae/Ringer (Subaru) 13m 05s; **2** Auriol/Occelli (Toyota) 13m 06s; **3** Kankkunen/Piironen (Toyota) 13m 07s; **4** Jonsson/Bäckman (Toyota) 13m 11s; **5** Mäkinen/Harjanne (Lancia) 13m 16s; **6** Johansson/Olsson (Mazda) 13m 28s

SS20 Tobyn (10.19 km)
1 Kankkunen/Piironen (Toyota) 5m 20s; **2** Jonsson/Bäckman (Toyota), Auriol/Occelli (Toyota) 5m 22s; **4** McRae/Ringer (Subaru) 5m 24s; **5** Mäkinen/Harjanne (Lancia) 5m 26s; **6** Mikkola/Berglund (Subaru), Johansson/Olsson (Mazda) 5m 33s

SS21 Henstad (8.03 km)
1 Auriol/Occelli (Toyota) 4m 59s; **2** Jonsson/Bäckman (Toyota) 5m 00s; **3** Kankkunen/Piironen (Toyota) 5m 01s; **4** McRae/Ringer (Subaru), Mäkinen/Harjanne (Lancia) 5m 02s; **6** Mikkola/Berglund 5m 03s

Audi made a low-key, unofficial return with the adaptable Austrian, Sepp Haider.

SS22 Molnbacka (14.72 km)
1 McRae/Ringer (Subaru) 7m 46s; **2** Kankkunen/Piironen (Toyota) 7m 47s; **3** Auriol/Occelli (Toyota) 7m 49s; **4** Jonsson/Bäckman (Toyota) 7m 50s; **5** Mäkinen/Harjanne (Lancia) 7m 55s; **6** Johansson/Olsson (Mazda) 8m 02s

SS23 Godåsen (26.24 km)
1 Jonsson/Bäckman (Toyota), Kankkunen/Piironen (Toyota) 13m 19s; **3** McRae/Ringer (Subaru) 13m 29s; **4** Johansson/Olsson (Mazda) 13m 31s; **5** Mäkinen/Harjanne (Lancia) 13m 37s; **6** Mikkola/Berglund (Subaru) 13m 42s

SS24 Malta (11.88 km)
1 Jonsson/Bäckman (Toyota) 6m 06s; **2** McRae/Ringer (Subaru) 6m 09s; **3** Kankkunen/Piironen (Toyota) 6m 15s; **4** Mäkinen/Harjanne (Lancia) 6m 16s; **5** Johansson/Olsson (Mazda) 6m 23s; **6** Auriol/Occelli (Toyota) 6m 27s

SS25 Vargåsen (18.10 km)
1 McRae/Ringer (Subaru) 11m 44s; **2** Jonsson/Bäckman (Toyota) 11m 49s; **3** Kankkunen/Piironen (Toyota) 11m 56s; **4** Mäkinen/Harjanne (Lancia) 11m 57s; **5** Johansson/Olsson (Mazda) 12m 04s; **6** Eklund/Johansson (Subaru) 12m 13s

SS26 Bjälverud (21.58 km)
1 Jonsson/Bäckman (Toyota) 11m 23s; **2** McRae/Ringer (Subaru) 11m 25s; **3** Kankkunen/Piironen (Toyota) 11m 30s; **4** Johansson/Olsson (Mazda) 11m 39s; **5** Mäkinen/Harjanne (Lancia) 11m 45s; **6** Auriol/Occelli (Toyota) 11m 49s

SS27 Lonnhojden (19.83 km)
1 McRae/Ringer (Subaru) 10m 53s; **2** Jonsson/Bäckman (Toyota) 11m 01s; **3** Kankkunen/Piironen (Toyota) 11m 03s; **4** Mäkinen/Harjanne (Lancia) 11m 11s; **5** Eklund/Johansson (Subaru) 11m 34s; **6** Johansson/Olsson (Mazda) 11m 37s

SS28 Långjohanstorp (19.44 km)
1 Kankkunen/Piironen (Toyota) 9m 58s; **2** Jonsson/Bäckman (Toyota) 10m 02s; **3** McRae/Ringer (Subaru), Mäkinen/Harjanne (Lancia) 10m 17s; **5** Eklund/Johansson (Subaru) 10m 34s; **6** A.Radstrom/K.Engstrom (Audi 90 Quattro) 10m 49s

Major Retirements

4	Blomqvist/Melander Engine	Opel Calibra Turbo SS21	Gr A
5	Mikkola/Berglund Engine	Subaru Legacy RS SS23	Gr A
6	Auriol/Occelli Excluded	Toyota Celica Turbo 4WD SS26	Gr A
7	Ericsson/Thörner Gearbox	Ford Escort Cosworth SS4	Gr A
8	Lindholm/Hantunen Engine	Ford Escort Cosworth SS18	Gr A
11	Wilson/Thomas Accident	Ford Escort Cosworth SS2	Gr A
14	McRae/Senior Excluded	Ford Sierra Cosworth 4x4 SS6	Gr N
15	Bin Sulayem/Morgan Gearbox	Ford Escort Cosworth SS4	Gr N
16	Jansson/Algerstadt Electrics	Toyota Celica GT4 SS5	Gr A
18	Eriksson/Svanstrom Mechanical	Mazda 323 Turbo GT-R SS12	Gr A
20	Olofsson/Skallman Accident	Nissan Sunny GTI-R SS20	Gr N

FIA Class Winners

A8 Over 2000 cc	Jonsson/Bäckman Toyota Celica Turbo 4WD
A7 1600-2000 cc	Svan/Olsson Opel Astra GSI
A6 1300-1600 cc	Hult/Fredriksson Peugeot 205 GTI 1.6
A5 Up to 1300 cc	Sibera/Gross Skoda Favorit 136L
N4 Over 2000 cc	Bäcklund/Andersson Mitsubishi Galant VR-4
N3 1600-2000 cc	Levin/Cervin Peugeot 309 GTI
N2 1300-1600 cc	Andersson/Wann Opel Corsa GSI
N1 Up to 1300 cc	Bergea/Murray Suzuki Swift GTI

Rally Leaders

SS1 Jonsson, Auriol, McRae, Kankkunen, Eklund, Wilson; **SS2** Wilson; **SS3-8** Auriol; **SS9-12** McRae; **SS13-17** Auriol; **SS18** Jonsson, Kankkunen; **SS19-23** Kankkunen; **SS24-28** Jonsson

World Championship Points

Drivers
1 Kankkunen 23; **2** Auriol, Jonsson 20; **4** Delecour 15; **5** Biasion, McRae 12; **7** Eriksson, Mäkinen 10; **9** Johansson 8; **10** Schwarz, Eklund 6, etc.

Manufacturers
1 Toyota 40; **2** Mitsubishi 23; **3** Ford 17; **4** Subaru 14

FIA Cup for Production Car Drivers
1 Spiliotis, Bäcklund 13; **3** Serpaggi, Kytölehto 10; **5** Holderied, Walfridsson 7, etc.

FIA Cup for Manufacturers
1 GME 20; **2** Citroën 14; **3** Peugeot, Skoda 11; **5** VW 4; **6** Nissan 2

Route Details

Leg 1
Friday, 12 February. 11 stages (210.91 km) in a total route of 519.85 km
Leg 2
Saturday, 13 February. 10 stages (176.93 km) in a total route of 528.50 km
Leg 3
Sunday, 14 February. 7 stages (131.79 km) in a total route of 382.97 km

Weather

Mainly cold with some snow

Special Stage Analysis

	1	2	3	4	5	6
Auriol (Toyota)	9	6	4	1	-	2
McRae (Subaru)	8	9	4	4	1	1
Jonsson (Toyota)	7	9	5	4	1	-
Kankkunen (Toyota)	7	3	10	3	2	1
Wilson (Ford)	2	-	-	-	-	-
Lindholm (Ford)	1	-	3	1	2	2
Eklund (Subaru)	1	-	1	-	2	4
Johansson (Mazda)	-	3	1	3	5	7
Mäkinen (Lancia)	-	1	1	4	11	3
Mikkola (Subaru)	-	-	-	1	3	6
Blomqvist (Opel)	-	-	-	-	-	1
Radstrom (Audi)	-	-	-	-	-	1

Finish Lines

Tommi Mäkinen was the top privateer, finishing fourth in an **Astra Team Delta** despite brake trouble, but scoring no World Championship points for Lancia, as he wasn't an officially nominated driver...**Didier Auriol** was excluded for accepting illegal service (an oil can given to him by the 1980 Swedish winner, Anders Kullang) between the 22nd and 23rd stages. FISA subsequently fined TTE $300,000...**'Nalle' Johansson** recorded startling stage times in the latest **Mazda 323 GT-R** and took fifth overall...**Audi** made a discreet return to rallying with a Konrad Schmidt-prepared Quattro S2. **Sepp Haider** survived a last-minute excursion to finish an impressive seventh...**Kenneth Bäcklund** was a convincing **Group N** winner in his **Mitsubishi Sweden Galant VR-4**...**Opel** scored maximum Touring Car Cup ('Formula 2') points again, thanks to Per Svan, who brought his **Astra** home in tenth place...the MotorSport Developments **Calibra 4x4** was less impressive, **Stig Blomqvist** hampered by a faulty centre differential before the head gasket blew...**Ford** had a dreadful Swedish: **Malcolm Wilson** crashed on the third stage, when leading, **Mikael Ericsson** retired with a broken clutch, and **Sebastian Lindholm** blew his engine.

Results

1	Mats Jonsson/ Lars Bäckman	Toyota Celica Turbo 4WD 4h 49m 05s	 Gr A
2	Juha Kankkunen/ Juha Piironen	Toyota Celica Turbo 4WD 4h 49m 18s	 Gr A
3	Colin McRae/ Derek Ringer	Subaru Legacy RS 4h 49m 33s	 Gr A
4	Tommi Mäkinen/ Seppo Harjanne	Lancia Delta HF Integrale 4h 52m 51s	 Gr A
5	Björn Johansson/ Anders Olsson	Mazda 323 Turbo GT-R 4h 57m 35s	 Gr A
6	Per Eklund/ Johnny Johansson	Subaru Legacy RS 4h 58m 35s	 Gr A
7	Sepp Haider/ Klaus Wendel	Audi Coupé S2 5h 05m 46s	 Gr A
8	Kenneth Bäcklund/ Tord Andersson	Mitsubishi Galant VR-4 5h 07m 30s	 Gr N
9	Jarmo Kytölehto/ Arto Kapanen	Mitsubishi Galant VR-4 5h 08m 24s	 Gr N
10	Per Svan/ Johan Olsson	Opel Astra GSI 5h 12m 05s	 Gr A

109 starters, 52 finishers

Previous Winners

1960	Carl Magnus Skogh/Rolf Skogh	Saab 96
1961	Carl Magnus Skogh/Rolf Skogh	Saab 96
1962	Bengt Söderström/Rune Olsson	Mini-Cooper
1963	Berndt Jansson/Erik Petterson	Porsche S90
1964	Tom Trana/Gunnar Thermenius	Volvo 544
1965	Tom Trana/Gunnar Thermenius	Volvo 544
1966	Ake Andersson/Sven-Olof Svedberg	Saab 96
1967	Bengt Söderström/Gunnar Palm	Ford Lotus Cortina
1968	Björn Waldegård/Lars Helmer	Porsche 911T
1969	Björn Waldegård/Lars Helmer	Porsche 911S
1970	Björn Waldegård/Lars Helmer	Porsche 911S
1971	Stig Blomqvist/Arne Hertz	Saab 96 V4
1972	Stig Blomqvist/Arne Hertz	Saab 96 V4
1973	Stig Blomqvist/Arne Hertz	Saab 96 V4
1975	Björn Waldegård/Hans Thorszelius	Lancia Stratos
1976	Per Eklund/Björn Cederberg	Saab 96 V4
1977	Stig Blomqvist/Hans Sylvan	Saab 99 EMS
1978	Björn Waldegård/Hans Thorszelius	Ford Escort RS
1979	Stig Blomqvist/Björn Cederberg	Saab 99 Turbo
1980	Anders Kullang/Bruno Berglund	Opel Ascona 400
1981	Hannu Mikkola/Arne Hertz	Audi Quattro
1982	Stig Blomqvist/Björn Cederberg	Audi Quattro A1
1983	Hannu Mikkola/Arne Hertz	Audi Quattro A1
1984	Stig Blomqvist/Björn Cederberg	Audi Quattro A2
1985	Ari Vatanen/Terry Harryman	Peugeot 205 Turbo 16
1986	Juha Kankkunen/Juha Piironen	Peugeot 205 Turbo 16
1987	Timo Salonen/Seppo Harjanne	Mazda 323 Turbo
1988	Markku Alén/Ilkka Kivimäki	Lancia Delta HF Turbo
1989	Ingvar Carlsson/Per Carlsson	Mazda 323 Turbo
1991	Kenneth Eriksson/Staffan Parmander	Mitsubishi Galant VR-4
1992	Mats Jonsson/Lars Bäckman	Toyota Celica GT4

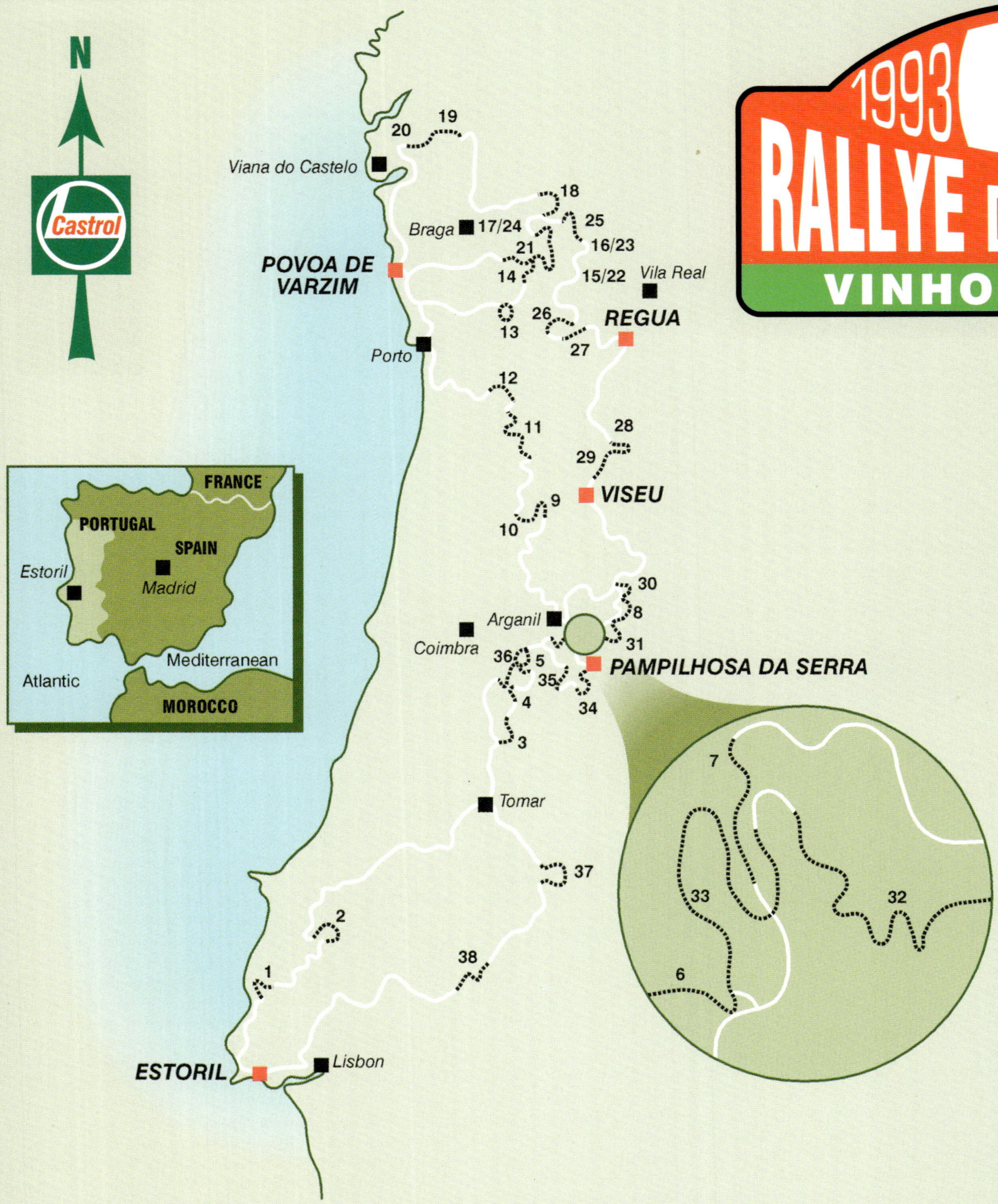

Rally of Portugal, 3-6 March, FIA World Rally Championship Round 3

Leading Entries

1	Carlos Sainz/ Luis Moya	Lancia Delta HF Integrale Gr A
2	Miki Biasion/ Tiziano Siviero	Ford Escort Cosworth Gr A
3	Kenneth Eriksson/ Staffan Parmander	Mitsubishi Lancer RS-E Gr A
4	Colin McRae/ Derek Ringer	Subaru Legacy RS Gr A
5	François Delecour/ Daniel Grataloup	Ford Escort Cosworth Gr A
6	Andrea Aghini/ Sauro Farnocchia	Lancia Delta HF Integrale Gr A
7	Armin Schwarz/ Nicky Grist	Mitsubishi Lancer RS-E Gr A
8	Markku Alén/ Ilkka Kivimäki	Subaru Legacy RS Gr A
9	Fernando Peres/ Ricardo Caldeira	Ford Escort Cosworth Gr A
10	Bruno Thiry/ Stéphane Prévot	Opel Astra GSi Gr A
11	Emil Triner/ Jiri Klima	Skoda Favorit 136L Gr A
12	Alessandro Fiorio/ Vittorio Brambilla	Lancia Delta HF Integrale Gr A
14	Pavel Sibera/ Petr Gross	Skoda Favorit 136L Gr A
15	Jorge Recalde/ Martin Christie	Lancia Delta HF Integrale Gr A
16	Jorge Bica/ Joaquim Capelo	Lancia Delta HF Integrale Gr A
17	Christine Driano/ Marie-Christine Lallement	Citroën AX Sport Gr A
18	Carlos Menem Jnr/ Victor Zucchini	Lancia Delta HF Integrale Gr N
19	Mohammed Bin Sulayem/ Ronan Morgan	Ford Escort Cosworth Gr A
20	Hiroshi Nishiyama/ Rocky Sugura	Nissan Sunny GTI-R Gr N
21	Alessandro Fassina/ Luigi Pirollo	Mazda 323 GT-R Gr N

Special Stage Times

SS1 Gradil (9.02 km)
1 F.Delecour/D.Grataloup (Ford Escort Cosworth) 5m 01s; **2** M.Biasion/T.Siviero (Ford Escort Cosworth) 5m 03s; **3** A.Aghini/S.Farnocchia (Lancia Delta HF Integrale) 5m 04s; **4** C.Sainz/L.Moya (Lancia Delta HF Integrale) 5m 05s; **5** A.Fiorio/V.Brambilla (Lancia Delta HF Integrale) 5m 10s; **6** A.Schwarz/N.Grist (Mitsubishi Lancer RS-E) 5m 12s

SS2 Montejunto (9.57 km)
1 Delecour/Grataloup (Ford), Biasion/Siviero (Ford) 4m 57s; **3** Aghini/Farnocchia (Lancia) 5m 01s; **4** Sainz/Moya (Lancia) 5m 02s; **5** M.Alén/I.Kivimäki (Subaru Legacy RS) 5m 04s; **6** K.Eriksson/S.Parmander (Mitsubishi Lancer RS-E), Fiorio/Brambilla (Lancia) 5m 05s

SS3 Figueiro dos Vinhos (20.45 km)
1 Sainz/Moya (Lancia), Delecour/Grataloup (Ford) 12m 20s; **3** Biasion/Siviero (Ford) 12m 25s; **4** Aghini/Farnocchia (Lancia) 12m 26s; **5** Alén/Kivimäki (Subaru) 12m 30s; **6** Eriksson/Parmander (Mitsubishi), Fiorio/Brambilla (Lancia) 12m 32s

SS4 Campelo (10.35 km)
1 Biasion/Siviero (Ford) 6m 52s; **2** Sainz/Moya (Lancia) 6m 57s; **3** Aghini/Farnocchia (Lancia), Schwarz/Grist (Mitsubishi), Alén/Kivimäki (Subaru) 6m 58s; **6** Eriksson/Parmander (Mitsubishi) 7m 01s

SS5 Serra da Lousa (24.90 km)
1 Delecour/Grataloup (Ford) 14m 41s; **2** Biasion/Siviero (Ford) 14m 51s; **3** Sainz/Moya (Lancia), Schwarz/Grist (Mitsubishi), Aghini/Farnocchia (Lancia) 14m 57s; **6** Eriksson/Parmander (Mitsubishi) 14m 59s

SS6 Gois (17.98 km)
1 Delecour/Grataloup (Ford) 10m 46s; **2** Sainz/Moya (Lancia) 10m 48s; **3** Aghini/Farnocchia (Lancia) 10m 50s; **4** Biasion/Siviero (Ford) 10m 51s; **5** Fiorio/Brambilla (Lancia) 10m 52s; **6** Alén/Kivimäki (Subaru) 10m 54s

SS7 Arganil (12.60 km)
1 Delecour/Grataloup (Ford), Aghini/Farnocchia (Lancia) 8m 02s; **3** Sainz/Moya (Lancia), Biasion/Siviero (Ford) 8m 06s; **5** Fiorio/Brambilla (Lancia) 8m 09s; **6** Schwarz/Grist (Mitsubishi) 8m 10s

SS8 Piodao (18.33 km)
1 Delecour/Grataloup (Ford) 12m 18s; **2** Aghini/Farnocchia (Lancia) 12m 23s; **3** Biasion/Siviero (Ford) 12m 24s; **4** Sainz/Moya (Lancia) 12m 25s; **5** Schwarz/ Grist (Mitsubishi) 12m 27s; **6** Fiorio/Brambilla (Lancia) 12m 28s

SS9 Muna (9.27 km)
1 Sainz/Moya (Lancia) 5m 55s; **2** Schwarz/Grist (Mitsubishi) 5m 58s; **3** Biasion/Siviero (Ford) 6m 04s; **4** Delecour/Grataloup(Ford), Aghini/Farnocchia (Lancia) 6m 05s; **6** Eriksson/Parmander (Mitsubishi) 6m 09s

SS10 Caramulo (14.08 km)
Cancelled

SS11 Freita (24.10 km)
1 Delecour/Grataloup (Ford), Aghini/Farnocchia (Lancia) 14m 22s; **3** Sainz/Moya (Lancia) 14m 27s; **4** Biasion/Siviero (Ford) 14m 34s; **5** Schwarz/Grist (Mitsubishi) 14m 36s; **6** Fiorio/Brambilla (Lancia) 14m 44s

SS12 Arouca (22.21 km)
1 Delecour/Grataloup (Ford) 13m 28s; **2** Aghini/Farnocchia (Lancia) 13m 32s; **3** Biasion/Siviero (Ford) 13m 38s; **4** Sainz/Moya (Lancia) 13m 40s; **5** C.McRae/D.Ringer (Subaru Legacy RS) 13m 51s; **6** Schwarz/Grist (Mitsubishi) 13m 54s

SS13 Lousada (3.00 km)
1 McRae/Ringer (Subaru), Delecour/Grataloup (Ford), Aghini/Farnocchia (Lancia) 2m 45s; **4** Eriksson/Parmander (Mitsubishi), Sainz/Moya (Lancia) 2m 46s; **6** Biasion/Siviero (Ford), Alén/Kivimäki (Subaru) 2m 47s

SS14 Santa Quiteria (8.84 km)
1 Delecour/Grataloup (Ford) 6m 22s; **2** Alén/Kivimäki (Subaru) 6m 27s; **3** Biasion/Siviero (Ford) 6m 28s; **4** Aghini/Farnocchia (Lancia) 6m 30s; **5** Fiorio/Brambilla (Lancia) 6m 32s; **6** Sainz/Moya (Lancia) 6m 37s

SS15 Montim 1 (5.00 km)
1 McRae/Ringer (Subaru) 3m 56s; **2** Biasion/Siviero (Ford) 3m 57s; **3** Alén/Kivimäki (Subaru) 3m 59s; **4** Sainz/Moya (Lancia), Fiorio/Brambilla (Lancia) 4m 00s; **6** Delecour/Grataloup (Ford), Eriksson/Parmander (Mitsubishi) 4m 01s

SS16 Lameirinha 1 (10.04 km)
1 Biasion/Siviero (Ford) 6m 42s; **2** McRae/Ringer (Subaru) 6m 43s; **3** Sainz/Moya (Lancia) 6m 44s; **4** Alén/Kivimäki (Subaru) 6m 46s; **5** Delecour/Grataloup (Ford) 6m 47s; **6** Fiorio/Brambilla (Lancia) 6m 48s

SS17 Luilhas 1 (13.08 km)
1 McRae/Ringer (Subaru) 9m 42s; **2** Sainz/Moya (Lancia) 9m 46s; **3** Biasion/Siviero (Ford) 9m 47s; **4** Alén/Kivimäki (Subaru) 9m 48s; **5** Delecour/Grataloup (Ford), Fiorio/Brambilla (Lancia) 9m 53s

SS18 Vieira do Minho (14.48 km)
1 Delecour/Grataloup (Ford) 9m 41s; **2** Sainz/Moya (Lancia), McRae/Ringer (Subaru) 9m 43s; **4** Alén/Kivimäki (Subaru) 9m 48s; **5** Biasion/Siviero (Ford), Aghini/Farnocchia (Lancia) 9m 50s

SS19 Arcos-Portelo (18.57 km)
1 McRae/Ringer (Subaru) 12m 01s; **2** Biasion/Siviero (Ford) 12m 03s; **3** Delecour/Grataloup (Ford) 12m 06s; **4** Alén/Kivimäki (Subaru) 12m 07s; **5** Aghini/Farnocchia (Lancia) 12m 12s; **6** Fiorio/Brambilla (Lancia) 12m 17s

SS20 Ponte de Lima (26.34 km)
1 McRae/Ringer (Subaru) 20m 12s; **2** Deleçour/Grataloup (Ford) 20m 14s; **3** Biasion/Siviero (Ford) 20m 17s; **4** Aghini/Farnocchia (Lancia) 20m 18s; **5** Sainz/Moya (Lancia) 20m 24s; **6** Alén/Kivimäki (Subaru) 20m 39s

SS21 Veiga (5.83 km)
1 Alén/Kivimäki (Subaru) 3m 54s; **2** Sainz/Moya (Lancia) 3m 55s; **3** Delecour/Grataloup (Ford) 3m 56s; **4** McRae/Ringer (Subaru) 3m 57s; **5** Biasion/Siviero (Ford) 3m 58s; **6** Eriksson/Parmander (Mitsubishi), Aghini/Farnocchia (Lancia), Fiorio/Brambilla (Lancia) 3m 59s

SS22 Montim 2 (5.00 km)
1 McRae/Ringer (Subaru), Alén/Kivimäki (Subaru) 3m 56s; **3** Biasion/Siviero (Ford) 3m 58s; **4** Eriksson/Parmander (Mitsubishi), Delecour/Grataloup (Ford) 3m 59s; **6** Fiorio/Brambilla (Lancia) 4m 00s

SS23 Lameirinha 2 (10.04 km)
1 Alén/Kivimäki (Subaru) 6m 39s; **2** Biasion/Siviero (Ford), McRae/Ringer (Subaru), Fiorio/Brambilla (Lancia) 6m 42s; **5** Eriksson/Parmander (Mitsubishi), Delecour/Grataloup (Ford) 6m 44s

SS24 Luilhas 2 (13.08 km)
1 McRae/Ringer (Subaru) 9m 36s; **2** Alén/Kivimäki (Subaru) 9m 43s; **3** Aghini/Farnocchia (Lancia) 9m 45s; **4** Eriksson/Parmander (Mitsubishi) 9m 47s; **5** Biasion/Siviero (Ford), Fiorio/Brambilla (Lancia) 9m 48s

SS25 Cabeceiras de Basto (13.50 km)
1 Alén/Kivimäki (Subaru) 8m 42s; **2** McRae/Ringer (Subaru) 8m 43s; **3** Delecour/Grataloup (Ford) 8m 44s; **4** Biasion/Siviero (Ford) 8m 46s; **5** Fiorio/Brambilla (Lancia), Aghini/Farnocchia (Lancia) 8m 49s

SS26 Carvalho de Rei (10.85 km)
1 Biasion/Siviero (Ford), Delecour/Grataloup (Ford) 7m 40s; **3** McRae/Ringer (Subaru) 7m 41s; **4** Alén/Kivimäki (Subaru) 7m 43s; **5** Aghini/Farnocchia (Lancia) 7m 46s; **6** Fiorio/Brambilla (Lancia) 7m 47s

SS27 Aboboreira (20.84 km)
1 Biasion/Siviero (Ford), McRae/Ringer (Subaru) 14m 33s; **3** Alén/Kivimäki (Subaru) 14m 39s; **4** Eriksson/Parmander (Mitsubishi) 14m 40s; **5** Delecour/Grataloup (Ford) 14m 42s; **6** Fiorio/Brambilla (Lancia) 14m 47s

SS28 Nogueira (7.53 km)
1 Delecour/Grataloup (Ford), Alén/Kivimäki (Subaru) 3m 56s; **3** Biasion/Siviero (Ford), McRae/Ringer (Subaru) 3m 57s; **5** Eriksson/Parmander (Mitsubishi) 4m 00s; **6** Aghini/Farnocchia (Lancia), Fiorio/Brambilla (Lancia) 4m 02s

SS29 Viseu (22.93 km)
1 Biasion/Siviero (Ford) 14m 40s; **2** Delecour/Grataloup (Ford) 14m 41s; **3** Alén/Kivimäki (Subaru) 14m 45s; **4** McRae/Ringer (Subaru) 14m 50s; **5** Aghini/Farnocchia (Lancia) 14m 53s; **6** Eriksson/Parmander (Mitsubishi) 14m 54s

SS30 Alvoco das Varzeas (10.42 km)
1 Delecour/Grataloup (Ford) 8m 39s; **2** Aghini/Farnocchia (Lancia) 8m 50s; **3** Biasion/Siviero (Ford), Eriksson/Parmander (Mitsubishi), Alén/Kivimäki (Subaru) 8m 53s; **6** Fiorio/Brambilla (Lancia) 8m 55s

SS31 Malhada Cha (21.25 km)
1 Delecour/Grataloup (Ford), Aghini/Farnocchia (Lancia) 16m 50s; **3** Fiorio/Brambilla (Lancia) 16m 55s; **4** Eriksson/Parmander (Mitsubishi) 16m 56s; **5** Biasion/Siviero (Ford) 16m 58s; **6** Alén/Kivimäki (Subaru) 17m 06s

SS32 Arganil-Alqueve (25.94 km)
1 Delecour/Grataloup (Ford) 18m 45s; **2** Alén/Kivimäki (Subaru) 18m 52s; **3** Biasion/Siviero (Ford) 18m 56s; **4** Fiorio/Brambilla (Lancia) 18m 57s; **5** Eriksson/Parmander (Mitsubishi) 18m 59s; **6** Aghini/Farnocchia (Lancia) 19m 00s

SS33 Folques (32.84 km)
1 Delecour/Grataloup (Ford) 24m 08s; **2** Eriksson/Parmander (Mitsubishi) 24m 10s; **3** Alén/Kivimäki (Subaru) 24m 12s; **4** Aghini/Farnocchia (Lancia) 24m 13s; **5** Biasion/Siviero (Ford) 24m 19s; **6** McRae/Ringer (Subaru) 24m 23s

SS34 Pampilhosa (12.83 km)
1 Biasion/Siviero (Ford) 11m 03s; **2** Delecour/Grataloup (Ford), Eriksson/Parmander (Mitsubishi) 11m 04s; **4** Alén/Kivimäki (Subaru) 11m 07s; **5** Fiorio/Brambilla (Lancia) 11m 09s; **6** Aghini/Farnocchia (Lancia) 11m 13s

SS35 Amoreira (15.90 km)
1 Alén/Kivimäki (Subaru) 12m 52s; **2** Biasion/Siviero (Ford) 12m 56s; **3** Fiorio/Brambilla (Lancia) 12m 58s; **4** Eriksson/Parmander (Mitsubishi) 12m 59s; **5** Delecour/Grataloup (Ford) 13m 00s; **6** McRae/Ringer (Subaru) 13m 04s

SS36 Lousa (20.37 km)
1 Eriksson/Parmander (Mitsubishi) 14m 37s; **2** Alén/Kivimäki (Subaru) 14m 38s; **3** McRae/Ringer (Subaru) 14m 43s; **4** Biasion/Siviero (Ford) 14m 45s; **5** Fiorio/Brambilla (Lancia) 14m 46s; **6** Delecour/Grataloup (Ford) 14m 47s

SS37 Abrantes (15.25 km)
1 Alén/Kivimäki (Subaru) 8m 14s; **2** Eriksson/Parmander (Mitsubishi) 8m 23s; **3** Fiorio/Brambilla (Lancia) 8m 25s; **4** Biasion/Siviero (Ford) 8m 29s; **5** McRae/Ringer (Subaru), Delecour/Grataloup (Ford) 8m 31s

SS38 Coruche (19.52 km)
1 Biasion/Siviero (Ford) 9m 35s; **2** Alén/Kivimäki (Subaru) 9m 40s; **3** Aghini/Farnocchia (Lancia) 9m 49s; **4** Delecour/Grataloup (Ford) 9m 51s; **5** Eriksson/Parmander (Mitsubishi) 9m 58s; **6** McRae/Ringer (Subaru) 10m 12s

Major Retirements

1	Sainz/Moya Accident	Lancia Delta HF Integrale SS21	Gr A
7	Schwarz/Grist Road accident	Mitsubishi Lancer RS-E SS12	Gr A
9	Peres/Caldeira Accident	Ford Escort Cosworth SS17	Gr A
15	Recalde/Christie Engine	Lancia Delta HF Integrale SS2	Gr A
18	Menem/Zucchini Engine	Lancia Delta HF Integrale SS20	Gr N
19	Bin Sulayem/Morgan Suspension	Ford Escort Cosworth SS5	Gr N

FIA Class Winners

A8 Over 2000 cc	Delecour/Grataloup Ford Escort Cosworth
A7 1600-2000 cc	Thiry/Prévot Opel Astra GSi
A6 1300-1600 cc	Hoshino/Sugimura Toyota Corolla
A5 Up to 1300 cc	Sibera/Gross Skoda Favorit 136L
N4 Over 2000 cc	Fassina/Pirollo Mazda 323 GT-R
N3 1600-2000 cc	Azeredo/Leal Peugeot 309 GTI
N2 1300-1600 cc	No starters
N1 Up to 1300 cc	Sagnard/Muller Peugeot 205 Rallye

Rally Leaders

SS1-3 Delecour; **SS4** Biasion; **SS5-38** Delecour

World Championship Points

Drivers
1 Delecour 35; **2** Biasion 27; **3** Kankkunen 23; **4** Auriol, Jonnsson 20; **6** Eriksson 18; **7** McRae 16; **8** Aghini 12; **9** Mäkinen, Alén 10, etc.

Manufacturers
1 Toyota 40; **2** Ford 37; **3** Mitsubishi 33; **4** Subaru 26; **5** Lancia 14

FIA Cup for Production Car Drivers
1 Spiliotis, Bäcklund, Fassina 13; **4** Serpaggi, Kytölehto, Coutinho 10, etc.

FIA Cup for Manufacturers
1 GME 30; **2** Citroën 20; **3** Skoda 19; **4** Peugeot 16; **5** VW, Toyota 4; **7** Nissan 2

Route Details

Leg 1
Wednesday, 3 March. 11 asphalt stages (1 cancelled)
Leg 2
Thursday, 4 March. 8 gravel stages
Leg 3
Friday, 5 March. 9 gravel stages
Leg 4
Saturday, 6 March. 9 gravel stages

Weather

Special Stage Analysis

	1	2	3	4	5	6
Delecour (Ford)	18	3	3	3	6	2
Biasion (Ford)	8	6	12	5	5	1
McRae (Subaru)	8	4	3	2	2	3
Alén (Subaru)	7	5	6	6	2	4
Aghini (Lancia)	4	3	7	5	5	4
Sainz (Lancia)	2	5	4	6	1	1
Eriksson (Mitsubishi)	1	3	1	6	4	8
Fiorio (Lancia)	-	1	3	2	8	12
Schwarz (Mitsubishi)	-	1	2	-	2	3

Carlos Sainz was well placed to challenge the Fords when he rolled his Integrale heavily near Fafe.

Finish Lines

Alessandro Fassina and **Luigi Pirollo** scored an impressive Group N victory in their **Mazda** Italy 323GT-R, beating Bruno Thiry in the top two-wheel drive car, the Opel Belgium Astra; however, Thiry would have been well ahead if he hadn't suffered 14 minutes of road penalties through electrical problems... Gearbox trouble delayed **Kenneth Eriksson** in the top Lancer during the second leg, but he finally beat **Alex Fiorio**'s Astra Team Integrale, despite hitting a rock four stages from the finish...**Armin Schwarz** broke a wheel on the second stage and retired when his Mitsubishi went out of control and crashed on a road section at the beginning of the second leg...**Colin McRae** was on course for a top six finish until he rolled his Subaru in Arganil and lost a total of nine minutes...**José Carlos Macedo** was holding a comfortable Two-Wheel Drive Cup lead until his **Clio** 16V's gearbox broke...**Mohammed Bin Sulayem** became the first major retirement when the Marlboro Escort **Cosworth** broke its front suspension when he was leading Group N comfortably...**Christine Driano** took her first Ladies' award of the season in her **Citroën AX** Sport.

Results

1	François Delecour/ Daniel Grataloup	Ford Escort Cosworth 6h 20m 37s	Gr A
2	Miki Biasion/ Tiziano Siviero	Ford Escort Cosworth 6h 21m 32s	Gr A
3	Andrea Aghini/ Sauro Farnocchia	Lancia Delta HF Integrale 6h 23m 17s	Gr A
4	Markku Alén/ Ilkka Kivimäki	Subaru Legacy RS 6h 24m 23s	Gr A
5	Kenneth Eriksson/ Staffan Parmander	Mitsubishi Lancer RS-E 6h 25m 28s	Gr A
6	Alessandro Fiorio/ Vittorio Brambilla	Lancia Delta HF Integrale 6h 26m 18s	Gr A
7	Colin McRae/ Derek Ringer	Subaru Legacy RS 6h 37m 25s	Gr A
8	Jorge Bica/ Joaquim Capelo	Lancia Delta HF Integrale 6h 51m 42s	Gr A
9	Alessandro Fassina/ Luigi Pirollo	Mazda 323 Turbo GT-R 7h 11m 46s	Gr N
10	Bruno Thiry/ Stéphane Prévot	Opel Astra GSI 7h 12m 18s	Gr A

84 starters, 32 finishers

Previous Winners

1967	Carpentiro Albino/Silva Pereira	Renault Gordini
1968	Tony Fall/Ron Crellin	Lancia Fulvia HF
1969	Francisco Romaozinho/'Jocames'	Citroën DS21
1970	Simo Lampinen/John Davenport	Lancia Fulvia HF
1971	Jean-Pierre Nicolas/Jean Todt	Alpine Renault A110
1972	Achim Warmbold/John Davenport	BMW 2002ti
1973	Jean-Luc Thérier/Jacques Jaubert	Alpine Renault A110
1974	Rafaelle Pinto/Arnaldo Bernacchini	Fiat 124 Abarth
1975	Markku Alén/Ilkka Kivimäki	Fiat 124 Abarth
1976	Sando Munari/Silvio Maiga	Lancia Stratos
1977	Markku Alén/Ilkka Kivimäki	Fiat 131 Abarth
1978	Markku Alén/Ilkka Kivimäki	Fiat 131 Abarth
1979	Hannu Mikkola/Arne Hertz	Ford Escort RS
1980	Walter Röhrl/Christian Geistdörfer	Fiat 131 Abarth
1981	Markku Alén/Ilkka Kivimäki	Fiat 131 Abarth
1982	Michéle Mouton/Fabrizio Pons	Audi Quattro
1983	Hannu Mikkola/Arne Hertz	Audi Quattro A1
1984	Hannu Mikkola/Arne Hertz	Audi Quattro A2
1985	Timo Salonen/Seppo Harjanne	Peugeot 205 Turbo 16
1986	Joaquim Moutinho/Edgar Fortes	Renault 5 Turbo
1987	Markku Alén/Ilkka Kivimäki	Lancia Delta HF Turbo
1988	Miki Biasion/Tiziano Siviero	Lancia Delta HF Integrale
1989	Miki Biasion/Tiziano Siviero	Lancia Delta HF Integrale
1990	Miki Biasion/Tiziano Siviero	Lancia Delta HF Integrale
1991	Carlos Sainz/Luis Moya	Toyota Celica GT4
1992	Juha Kankkunen/Juha Piironen	Lancia Delta HF Integrale

Guy Jack was in superb form in the leading Daihatsu and scored his best-ever Safari result.

Safari Rally, 8-12 April, FIA World Rally Championship Round 4

Leading Entries

1	Juha Kankkunen/ Juha Piironen	Toyota Celica Turbo 4WD	Gr A
2	Markku Alén/ Ilkka Kivimäki	Toyota Celica Turbo 4WD	Gr A
3	Ian Duncan/ Ian Munro	Toyota Celica Turbo 4WD	Gr A
4	Kenjiro Shinozuka/ Pentii Kuukkala	Mitsubishi Lancer RS-E	Gr A
5	Yasuhiro Iwase/ Sudhir Vinayak	Toyota Celica Turbo 4WD	Gr A
6	Colin McRae/ Derek Ringer	Subaru Vivio	Gr A
7	Patrick Njiru/ Rick Matthews	Subaru Vivio	Gr A
8	Masashi Ishida/ Mohammed Verjee	Subaru Vivio	Gr A
9	Hiroshi Nishiyama/ Rocky Sugura	Nissan Sunny GTI-R	Gr N
11	Rudi Stohl/ Peter Diekmann	Audi Coupé S2	Gr A
12	Marco Brighetti/ Abdul Sidi	Daihatsu Charade GTti	Gr A
14	Jonathan Toroitich/ Ibrahim Choge	Toyota Celica GT4	Gr A
15	Azar Anwar/ Shailen Shah	Subaru Legacy RS Estate	Gr A
16	Manfred Stohl/ Kay Gerlach	Audi 90 Quattro	Gr A
17	Hasmat Shamji/ Peter Stone	Subaru Legacy RS	Gr N
18	Ranjit Chager/ Mahesh Saleh	Subaru RX Turbo	Gr A
19	Guy Jack/ Dez Page-Morris	Daihatsu Charade GTti	Gr A
20	Glen Edmunds/ James Dennis	Mitsubishi Galant VR-4	Gr A
21	Sammy Aslam/ Farakh Yusef	VW Golf GTI-16v	Gr A
22	Ashok Pattni / Zahid Mogul	Daihatsu Charade GTti	Gr A

Finish Lines

Subaru endured a bruising event with its tiny, 660 cc Vivios. **Colin McRae** climbed to fourth briefly before destroying his 555 version's suspension, while **Masashi Ishida** wrecked his engine when it swallowed some water...**Patrick Njiru** coaxed his **Vivio** to the finish, but not before the gearbox, the clutch, and the suspension had all broken, delaying him sufficiently to put him outside the top ten...The well-proven **Daihatsus** fared much better, **Guy Jack** distinguishing himself with an impressive fifth. He dropped no time on service sections throughout the event ...Fuel pump trouble and broken rear door hinges slowed **Ashok Pattni**, but not enough to stop him finishing sixth in his **Charade**...**Rudi Stohl**'s new **Quattro** S2 failed to live up to expectations: both the clutch and sump needed repairs, but the shock absorbers were the main weakness, being far too soft...**Manfred Stohl**, Rudi's son, completed the Safari for the first time, even though his well-used 90 **Quattro** lost all its oil pressure twice during the final leg...**Hiroshi Nishiyama** rolled his Group N **Sunny** GTI-R out of the event during the first leg.

Results

1	Juha Kankkunen/ Juha Piironen	Toyota Celica Turbo 4WD 3h 54m	Gr A
2	Markku Alén/ Ilkka Kivimäki	Toyota Celica Turbo 4WD 4h 03m	Gr A
3	Ian Duncan/ Ian Munro	Toyota Celica Turbo 4WD 5h 24m	Gr A
4	Yasuhiro Iwase/ Sudhir Vinayek	Toyota Celica Turbo 4WD 5h 35m	Gr A
5	Guy Jack/ Dez Page-Morris	Daihatsu Charade GTti 7h 44m	Gr A
6	Ashok Pattni/ Zahid Mogul	Daihatsu Charade GTti 8h 39m	Gr A
7	Marco Brighetti/ Abdul Sidi	Daihatsu Charade GTti 8h 57m	Gr A
8	Rudi Stohl/ Peter Diekmann	Audi Coupé S2 9h 14m	Gr A
9	Hasmat Shamji/ Peter Stone	Subaru Legacy RS 10h 07m	Gr N
10	Manfred Stohl/ Kay Gerlach	Audi 90 Quattro 10h 43m	Gr A

44 starters, 17 finishers

Positions at end of each leg

Leg 1 (TC 16)

1	Kankkunen/Piironen Toyota Celica Turbo 4WD	19m 00s
2	Alén/Kivimäki Toyota Celica Turbo 4WD	22m 00s
3	Duncan/Munro Toyota Celica Turbo 4WD	38m 00s
4	Iwase/Vinayak Toyota Celica Turbo 4WD	1h 06m 00s
5	Shinozuka/Kuukkala Mitsubishi Lancer RS-E	1h 08m 00s
6	Jack/Morris Daihatsu Charade GTti	1h 17m 00s

Leg 2 (TC 28)

1	Kankkunen/Piironen Toyota Celica Turbo 4WD	30m 00s
2	Alén/Kivimäki Toyota Celica Turbo 4WD	41m 00s
3	Duncan/Munro Toyota Celica Turbo 4WD	54m 00s
4	Shinozuka/Kuukkala Mitsubishi Lancer RS-E	1h 32m 00s
5	Iwase/Vinayak Toyota Celica Turbo 4WD	1h 38m 00s
6	Toroitich/Choge Toyota Celica GT4	2h 15m 00s

Leg 3 (TC 54)

1	Kankkunen/Piironen Toyota Celica Turbo 4WD	2h 08m 00s
2	Alén/Kivimäki Toyota Celica Turbo 4WD	2h 17m 00s
3	Duncan/Munro Toyota Celica Turbo 4WD	3h 33m 00s
4	Iwase/Vinayak Toyota Celica Turbo 4WD	3h 36m 00s
5	Jack/Morris Daihatsu Charade GTti	5h 01m 00s
6	Pattni/Mogul Daihatsu Charade GTti	5h 48m 00s

Leg 4 (TC 73)

1	Kankkunen/Piironen Toyota Celica Turbo 4WD	3h 36m 00s
2	Alén/Kivimäki Toyota Celica Turbo 4WD	3h 46m 00s
3	Duncan/Munro Toyota Celica Turbo 4WD	5h 02m 00s
4	Iwase/Vinayak Toyota Celica Turbo 4WD	5h 13m 00s
5	Jack/Morris Daihatsu Charade GTti	7h 07m 00s
6	Pattni/Mogul Daihatsu Charade GTti	8h 06m 00s

Major Retirements

4	Shinozuka/Kuukkala Engine	Mitsubishi Lancer RS-E	SS30	Gr A
6	McRae/Ringer OTL	Subaru Vivio	SS15	Gr A
8	Ishida/Verjee Engine	Subaru Vivio	SS44	Gr A
9	Nishiyama/Sugura Accident	Nissan Sunny GTI-R	SS11	Gr N
14	Toroitich/Choge OTL	Toyota Celica GT4	SS44	Gr A
15	Anwar/Shah	Subaru Legacy RS	SS31	Gr A
20	Edmunds/Dennis Suspension	Mitsubishi Galant VR-4	SS33	Gr A

FIA Class Winners

A8 Over 2000 cc	Kankkunen/Piironen Toyota Celica Turbo 4WD
A7 1600-2000 cc	Jack/Page-Morris Daihatsu Charade GTti
A6 1300-1600 cc	Bailey/Trempeneau Toyota Levin
A5 Up to 1300 cc	Njiru/Matthews Subaru Vivio
N4 Over 2000 cc	Shamji/Stone Subaru Legacy RS
N3 1600-2000 cc	No starters
N2 1300-1600 cc	No finishers
N1 Up to 1300 cc	No finishers

Rally Leaders

TC1-3 Many crews; **TC4-5** Kankkunen, Alén; **TC6-79** Kankkunen

World Championship Points

Drivers
1 Kankkunen 43; **2** Delecour 35; **3** Biasion 27; **4** Alén 25; **5** Auriol, Jonsson 20; **7** Eriksson 18; **8** McRae 16; **9** Aghini, Duncan 12, etc.

Manufacturers
1 Toyota 60; **2** Ford 37; **3** Mitsubishi 33; **4** Subaru 26; **5** Lancia 14

FIA Cup for Production Car Drivers
1 Spiliotis, Bäcklund, Fassina, Shamji 13, etc.

Route Details

Leg 1
Thursday, 8 April, Nairobi-Mombasa, 15 time controls in a route of 825.50 km

Leg 2
Friday, 9 April, Mombasa-Nairobi, 13 time controls in a route of 690.00 km

Leg 3
Saturday, 10 April, Nairobi-Eldoret, 26 time controls in a route of 1094.45 km

Leg 4
Sunday, 11 April, Eldoret-Aberdare, 19 time controls in a route of 867.90 km

Leg 5
Monday, 12 April, Aberdare-Nairobi, 6 time controls in a route of 240.80km

Weather

Hot and dry

Previous Winners

1960	Bill Fritschy/Jack Ellis	Mercedes-Benz 219
1961	Johnny Manuss/Bill Coleridge	Mercedes Benz 220E
1962	Tommy Fjastad/Bernard Schmider	VW1300
1963	Nick Norwicki/Paddy Cliff	Peugeot 404
1964	Peter Hughes/Bill Young	Ford Cortina GT
1965	Joginder Singh/Jaswant Singh	Volvo
1966	Bert Shankland/Chris Rothwell	Peugeot 404
1967	Bert Shankland/Chris Rothwell	Peugeot 404
1968	Nick Norwicki/Paddy Cliff	Peugeot 404
1969	Robin Hillyar/Jock Aird	Ford Taunus
1970	Edgar Herrmann/Hans Schuller	Datsun 160SSS
1971	Edgar Herrmann/Hans Schuller	Datsun 240Z
1972	Hannu Mikkola/Gunnar Palm	Ford Escort RS
1973	Shekhar Mehta/Lofty Drews	Datsun 240Z
1974	Joginder Singh/David Doig	Mitsubishi Colt Lancer
1975	Ove Andersson/Arne Hertz	Peugeot 404
1976	Joginder Singh/David Doig	Mitsubishi Colt Lancer
1977	Björn Waldegård/Hans Thorszelius	Ford Escort RS
1978	Jean-Pierre Nicolas/Jean-Claude Lefebvre	Peugeot 504
1979	Shekhar Mehta/Mike Doughty	Datsun 160J
1980	Shekhar Mehta/Mike Doughty	Datsun 160J
1981	Shekhar Mehta/Mike Doughty	Datsun Violet GT
1982	Shekhar Mehta/Mike Doughty	Datsun Violet GT
1983	Ari Vatanen/Terry Harryman	Opel Ascona 400
1984	Björn Waldegård/Hans Thorszelius	Toyota Celica Turbo
1985	Juha Kankkunen/Fred Gallagher	Toyota Celica Turbo
1986	Björn Waldegård/Fred Gallagher	Toyota Celica Turbo
1987	Hannu Mikkola/Arne Hertz	Audi 200 Quattro
1988	Miki Biasion/Tiziano Siviero	Lancia Delta HF Integrale
1989	Miki Biasion/Tiziano Siviero	Lancia Delta HF Integrale
1990	Björn Waldegård/Fred Gallagher	Toyota Celica GT4
1991	Juha Kankkunen/Juha Piironen	Lancia Delta HF Integrale
1992	Carlos Sainz/Luis Moya	Toyota Celica Turbo 4WD

TOUR OF CORSICA/Statistics

Tour of Corsica, 2-4 May, World Rally Championship Round 5

Leading Entries

1	Didier Auriol/ Bernard Occelli	Toyota Celica Turbo 4WD Gr A
2	Carlos Sainz/ Luis Moya	Lancia Delta HF Integrale Gr A
3	François Delecour/ Daniel Grataloup	Ford Escort Cosworth Gr A
5	François Chatriot/ Denis Giraudet	Toyota Celica Turbo 4WD Gr A
6	Andrea Aghini/ Sauro Farnocchia	Lancia Delta HF Integrale Gr A
7	Miki Biasion/ Tiziano Siviero	Ford Escort Cosworth Gr A
8	Colin McRae/ Derek Ringer	Subaru Legacy RS Gr A
9	Yves Loubet/ Didier Breton	Toyota Celica Turbo 4WD Gr A
11	Bruno Thiry/ Stéphane Prévot	Opel Astra GSi Gr A
12	Christine Driano/ Marie-Christine Lallement	Citroën AX Sport Gr A
14	Giovanni Manfrinato/ Claudio Condotta	Ford Escort Cosworth Gr N
15	Bernard Begun/ Jean-Paul Chiaroni	Ford Escort Cosworth Gr A
16	Alain Oreille/ Jean-Marc Andrié	Renault Clio Williams Gr A
17	Jean Ragnotti/ Gilles Thimonier	Renault Clio Williams Gr A
18	Jean-Marie Santoni/ Marcel Cesarini	Ford Escort Cosworth Gr N
19	Frédéric Dor/ Philippe Viale	Subaru Legacy RS Gr A
21	Serge Jordan/ Jack Boyère	Renault Clio Williams Gr N
22	Gilles Panizzi/ Hervé Panizzi	Peugeot 106 XSi Gr A

1993 5 1993
RALLYE DE FRANCE
37e TOUR DE CORSE

Special Stage Times

SS1 Vignolo-Capo di Feno (2.86 km)
1 F.Delecour/D.Grataloup (Ford Escort Cosworth) 1m 44s; **2** D.Auriol/B.Occelli (Toyota Celica Turbo), F.Chatriot/D.Giraudet (Toyota Celica Turbo) 1m 45s; **4** C.Sainz/L.Moya (Lancia Delta HF Integrale), Y.Loubet/D.Breton (Toyota Celica Turbo) 1m 46s; **6** A.Aghini/S.Farnocchia (Lancia Delta HF Integrale), M.Biasion/T.Siviero (Ford Escort Cosworth) 1m 47s

SS2 Gare de Carbuccia-Tavera (17.18 km)
1 Delecour/Grataloup (Ford) 12m 01s; **2** Aghini/Farnocchia (Lancia), Biasion/Siviero (Ford) 12m 12s; **4** Auriol/Occelli (Toyota) 12m 15s; **5** Chatriot/Giraudet (Toyota) 12m 16s; **6** Loubet/Breton (Toyota) 12m 19s

SS3 Vero-Casaglione (44.27 km)
1 Delecour/Grataloup (Ford), Aghini/Farnocchia (Lancia) 31m 03s; **3** Auriol/Occelli (Toyota) 31m 12s; **4** Loubet/Breton (Toyota) 31m 19s; **5** Sainz/Moya (Lancia) 31m 20s; **6** Biasion/Siviero (Ford) 31m 49s

SS4 Tiuccia-Canelle d'Orcino (14.93 km)
1 Delecour/Grataloup (Ford) 11m 17s; **2** Chatriot/Giraudet (Toyota) 11m 21s; **3** Auriol/Occelli (Toyota) 11m 22s; **4** Sainz/Moya (Lancia) 11m 23s; **5** Loubet/Breton (Toyota), Biasion/Siviero (Ford), C.McRae/D.Ringer (Subaru Legacy RS) 11m 24s

SS5 Eccica Suarella-Col de Marcucciu (25.21 km)
1 Delecour/Grataloup (Ford) 17m 52s; **2** Chatriot/Giraudet (Toyota) 17m 56s; **3** Auriol/Occelli (Toyota) 17m 59s; **4** Sainz/Moya (Lancia), Loubet/Breton (Toyota), Biasion/Siviero (Ford) 18m 00s

SS6 St Marie Sicche-Moca (23.88 km)
1 Delecour/Grataloup (Ford) 17m 02s; **2** Chatriot/Giraudet (Toyota) 17m 05s; **3** Sainz/Moya (Lancia) 17m 06s; **4** Biasion/Siviero (Ford) 17m 08s; **5** Loubet/Breton (Toyota) 17m 11s; **6** Auriol/Occelli (Toyota) 17m 13s

SS7 Bicchisano-Pila Canale (14.47 km)
1 Biasion/Siviero (Ford) 9m 19s; **2** Delecour/Grataloup (Ford) 9m 22s; **3** Chatriot/Giraudet

(Toyota) 9m 23s; **4** Auriol/Occelli (Toyota) 9m 24s; **5** Sainz/Moya (Lancia) 9m 29s; **6** McRae/Ringer (Subaru) 9m 30s

SS8 Cognocoli-Agosta Plage (24.47 km)
1 Delecour/Grataloup (Ford) 15m 40s; **2** Chatriot/Giraudet (Toyota) 15m 51s; **3** Sainz/Moya (Lancia) 15m 53s; **4** Auriol/Occelli (Toyota) 15m 56s; **5** Aghini/Farnocchia (Lancia) 15m 57s; **6** Biasion/Siviero (Ford) 16m 14s

SS9 Verghia-Pietra Rossa (26.55 km)
1 Delecour/Grataloup (Ford) 16m 47s; **2** Auriol/Occelli (Toyota), Loubet/Breton (Toyota) 16m 59s; **4** Chatriot/Giraudet (Toyota) 17m 00s; **5** Aghini/Farnocchia (Lancia) 17m 03s; **6** Sainz/Moya (Lancia) 17m 15s

SS10 Sartène-Radicci (29.26 km)
1 Chatriot/Giraudet (Toyota) 18m 44s; **2** Aghini/Farnocchia (Lancia) 18m 50s; **3** Auriol/Occelli (Toyota) 18m 55s; **4** Sainz/Moya (Lancia) 18m 57s; **5** Loubet/Breton (Toyota) 18m 58s; **6** McRae/Ringer (Subaru) 19m 02s

SS11 Aullene-Zicavo (25.36 km)
1 Aghini/Farnocchia (Lancia) 16m 23s; **2** Auriol/Occelli (Toyota) 16m 27s; **3** Loubet/Breton (Toyota) 16m 28s; **4** Chatriot/Giraudet (Toyota) 16m 31s; **5** Delecour/Grataloup (Ford) 16m 36s; **6** Sainz/Moya (Lancia) 16m 37s

SS12 Tasso-Ghisoni (39.52 km)
1 Auriol/Occelli (Toyota) 26m 45s; **2** Chatriot/Giraudet (Toyota) 27m 01s; **3** Sainz/Moya (Lancia) 27m 05s; **4** Delecour/Grataloup (Ford) 27m 06s; **5** Biasion/Siviero (Ford) 27m 21s; **6** McRae/Ringer (Subaru) 27m 42s

SS13 Muracciole-Les Caselles (21.00 km)
1 Delecour/Grataloup (Ford) 12m 54s; **2** Auriol/Occelli (Toyota), Chatriot/Giraudet (Toyota) 12m 55s; **4** Biasion/Siviero (Ford) 13m 06s; **5** Sainz/Moya (Lancia) 13m 10s; **6** B.Béguin/J.P.Chiaroni (Ford Escort Cosworth) 13m 21s

SS14 Corte-Taverna (26.86 km)
1 Delecour/Grataloup (Ford) 16m 12s; **2** Auriol/Occelli (Toyota) 16m 20s; **3** Chatriot/Giraudet (Toyota) 16m 29s; **4** Sainz/Moya (Lancia) 16m 32s; **5** Biasion/Siviero (Ford) 16m 34s; **6** McRae/Ringer (Subaru) 16m 46s

SS15 Morosaglia-Crocicchia (29.15 km)
1 Delecour/Grataloup (Ford) 18m 55s; **2** Chatriot/Giraudet (Toyota) 19m 07s; **3** Auriol/Occelli (Toyota) 19m 12s; **4** Sainz/Moya (Lancia) 19m 21s; **5** McRae/Ringer (Subaru) 19m 38s; **6** Biasion/Siviero (Ford) 19m 45s

SS16 Barchetta-Borgo (17.18 km)
1 Chatriot/Giraudet (Toyota) 12m 26s; **2** Delecour/Grataloup (Ford) 12m 29s; **3** Auriol/Occelli (Toyota) 12m 30s; **4** Biasion/Siviero (Ford) 12m 36s; **5** Sainz/Moya (Lancia) 12m 39s; **6** McRae/Ringer (Subaru) 12m 47s

SS17 Col San Stefano (14.18 km)
1 Auriol/Occelli (Toyota) 10m 32s; **2** Delecour/Grataloup (Ford) 10m 34s; **3** Sainz/Moya (Lancia) 10m 42s; **4** Chatriot/Giraudet (Toyota) 10m 44s; **5** Biasion/Siviero (Ford) 10m 46s; **6** McRae/Ringer (Subaru) 10m 54s

SS18 Casta-Pietra Monetta (15.74 km)
1 Delecour/Grataloup (Ford), Auriol/Occelli (Toyota) 10m 02s; **3** Chatriot/Giraudet (Toyota) 10m 11s; **4** Biasion/Siviero (Ford) 10m 16s; **5** Sainz/Moya (Lancia) 10m 25s; **6** McRae/Ringer (Subaru) 10m 30s

SS19 Corbara-Montemaggiore (13.58 km)
1 Delecour/Grataloup (Ford), Auriol/Occelli (Toyota) 8m 01s; **3** Chatriot/Giraudet (Toyota) 8m 02s; **4** Sainz/Moya (Lancia) 8m 08s; **5** Biasion/Siviero (Ford) 8m 15s; **6** McRae/Ringer (Subaru), Béguin/Chiaroni (Ford) 8m 16s

SS20 Notre Dame de la Serra-Olmo (27.99 km)
1 Delecour/Grataloup (Ford) 16m 38s; **2** Auriol/Occelli (Toyota) 16m 42s; **3** Chatriot/Giraudet (Toyota) 16m 46s; **4** Sainz/Moya (Lancia) 16m 57s; **5** Béguin/Chiaroni (Ford) 16m 58s; **6** Biasion/Siviero (Ford), McRae/Ringer (Subaru) 17m 09s

SS21 Fango-Partinello (31.48 km)
1 Auriol/Occelli (Toyota) 22m 09s; **2** Delecour/Grataloup (Ford) 22m 11s; **3** Chatriot/Giraudet (Toyota) 22m 14s; **4** Biasion/Siviero (Ford) 22m 16s; **5** Sainz/Moya (Lancia) 22m 22s; **6** McRae/Ringer (Subaru) 22m 24s

SS22 Porto-Piana (9.97 km)
1 Delecour/Grataloup (Ford) 6m 36s; **2** Biasion/Siviero (Ford) 6m 38s; **3** Auriol/Occelli (Toyota) 6m 43s; **4** Sainz/Moya (Lancia), Béguin/Chiaroni (Ford) 6m 44s; **6** Chatriot/Giraudet (Toyota) 6m 45s

SS23 Liamone-Appricciani (18.18 km)
1 Auriol/Occelli (Toyota) 12m 28s; **2** Sainz/Moya (Lancia) 12m 29s; **3** Delecour/Grataloup (Ford), Chatriot/Giraudet (Toyota) 12m 30s; **5** Biasion/Siviero (Ford) 12m 39s; **6** McRae/Ringer (Subaru) 12m 42s

SS24 Vico-Valle Di Mezzano (43.15 km)
1 Sainz/Moya (Lancia) 31m 49s; **2** Delecour/Grataloup (Ford) 31m 51s; **3** Auriol/Occelli (Toyota) 31m 57s; **4** Biasion/Siviero (Ford) 32m 06s; **5** McRae/Ringer (Subaru) 32m 19s; **6** Chatriot/Giraudet (Toyota) 32m 23s

Major Retirements

6	Aghini/Farnocchia	Lancia Delta HF Integrale	
	Accident	SS12	Gr A
9	Loubet/Breton	Toyota Celica Turbo 4WD	
	Accident	SS12	Gr A
11	Thiry/Prévot	Opel Astra GSI	
	Brakes/OTL	SS6	Gr A
12	Driano/Lallement	Citroën AX Sport	
	Accident	SS5	Gr A
19	Dor/Viale	Subaru Legacy RS	
		SS17	Gr A

Peugeot's impressive little 106s were easily quickest in the 1600 Group A class

FIA Class Winners

A7 Over 2000 cc	Delecour/Grataloup Ford Escort Cosworth
A6 1300-2000 cc	Ragnotti/Thimonier Renault Clio Williams
A5 Up to 1300 cc	Papini/Martini Peugeot 205 Rallye
N4 Over 2000 cc	Manfrinato/Condotta Ford Escort Cosworth
N3 1600-2000 cc	Jordan/Boyère Renault Clio Williams
N2 1300-1600 cc	No finishers
N1 Up to 1300 cc	Antonini/Seni Peugeot 205 Rallye

Rally Leaders

SS1-24 Delecour

World Championship points

Drivers
1 Delecour 55; **2** Kankkunen 43; **3** Auriol 35; **4** Biasion 31; **5** Alén 25; **6** McRae 24; **7** Jonsson 20; **8** Eriksson 18; **9** Aghini, Duncan, Chatriot 12, etc.

Manufacturers
1 Toyota 77; **2** Ford 57; **3** Subaru 36; **4** Mitsubishi 33; **5** Lancia 26

FIA Cup for Production Car Drivers
1 Coutinho 14; **2** Spiliotis, Bäcklund, Fassina, Shamji, Manfrinato 13, etc.

FIA Cup For Manufacturers
1 GME 34; **2** Peugeot 22; **3** Citroën 20; **4** Skoda 19; **5** Renault 10, etc.

Weather

Very wet at first, dry later

Special Stage Analysis

	1	2	3	4	5	6
Delecour (Ford)	15	5	1	1	1	-
Auriol (Toyota)	6	6	8	3	-	1
Chatriot (Toyota)	2	8	7	3	1	2
Aghini (Lancia)	2	2	-	-	2	1
Sainz (Lancia)	1	1	4	9	6	2
Biasion (Ford)	1	2	-	7	6	4
Loubet (Toyota)	-	1	1	3	3	1
Béguin (Ford)	-	-	-	1	1	1
McRae (Subaru)	-	-	-	-	3	11

Finish Lines

Renault demolished all opposition in 'Formula 2', **Jean Ragnotti** finishing a comfortable eighth on the first appearance of the two-litre Clio Williams, backed up by his Diac team-mate, Alain Oreille...Remarkably, the French firm came very close to winning **Group N** as well, **Serge Jordan** leading the turbos most of the way, only to break a gearbox mount three stages from the end and drop to second...The Italian, **Giovanni Manfrinato**, gratefully seized the production award instead in his private **Escort Cosworth** ...A catastrophic clutch change cost **Miki Biasion** 11 minutes in road penalties at the end of the first leg, restricting the works **Escort** driver to seventh at the finish...**Colin McRae** produced a calculated drive, bringing the lone 555 **Legacy** home in fifth place on his first attempt at the rally; a small off on the third stage provided the only untoward moment...**Yves Loubet** had a disappointing run on home ground, crashing his Gema **Celica** when he hit a damp patch on the Col de Verde while running on slicks.

Results

1	François Delecour/ Daniel Grataloup	Ford Escort Cosworth 6h 14m 41s	Gr A
2	Didier Auriol/ Bernard Occelli	Toyota Celica Turbo 4WD 6h 15m 43s	Gr A
3	François Chatriot/ Denis Giraudet	Toyota Celica Turbo 4WD 6h 17m 23s	Gr A
4	Carlos Sainz/ Luis Moya	Lancia Delta HF Integrale 6h 18m 29s	Gr A
5	Colin McRae/ Derek Ringer	Subaru Legacy RS 6h 23m 44s	Gr A
6	Bernard Béguin/ Jean-Paul Chiaroni	Ford Escort Cosworth 6h 31m 12s	Gr A
7	Miki Biasion/ Tizianc Siviero	Ford Escort Cosworth 6h 33m 39s	Gr A
8	Jean Ragnotti/ Gilles Thimonier	Renault Clio Williams 6h 36m 11s	Gr A
9	Alain Oreille/ Jean-Marc André	Renault Clio Williams 6h 38m 48s	Gr A
10	Giovanni Manfrinato/ Claudio Condotta	Ford Escort Cosworth 6h 55m 30s	Gr N

85 starters, 44 finishers

Previous Winners

1960	Walter Strahle/Herbert Linge	Porsche SC90
1961	René Trautmann/Jean-Claude Ogier	Citroën DS19
1962	Pierre Orsini/Jean-Baptiste Canonici	Renault Dauphine
1963	René Trautmann/Alexis Chabert	Citroën DS19
1964	Jean Vinatier/Roger Masson	Renault 8 Gordini
1965	Pierre Orsini/Jean-Baptiste Canonici	Renault 8 Gordini
1966	Jean-François Piot/Jean-François Jacob	Renault 8 Gordini
1967	Sandro Munari/Luciano Lombardini	Lancia Fulvia HF
1968	Jean-Claude Andruet/Maurice Gelin	Alpine Renault A110
1969	Gérard Larrousse/Maurice Gelin	Porsche 911R
1970	Bernard Darniche/Guy Demage	Alpine Renault A110
1972	Jean-Claude Andruet/'Biche'	Alpine Renault A110
1973	Jean-Pierre Nicolas/Michel Vial	Alpine Renault A110
1974	Jean-Claude Andruet/'Biche'	Lancia Stratos
1975	Bernard Darniche/Alain Mahé	Lancia Stratos
1976	Sandro Munari/Silvio Maiga	Lancia Stratos
1977	Bernard Darniche/Alain Mahé	Fiat 131 Abarth
1978	Bernard Darniche/Alain Mahé	Fiat 131 Abarth
1979	Bernard Darniche/Alain Mahé	Lancia Stratos
1980	Jean-Luc Thérier/Michel Vial	Porsche 911SC
1981	Bernard Darniche/Alain Mahé	Lancia Stratos
1982	Jean Ragnotti/Jean-Marc Andrié	Renault 5 Turbo
1983	Markku Alén/Ilkka Kivimäki	Lancia Rally 037
1984	Markku Alén/Ilkka Kivimäki	Lancia Rally 037
1985	Jean Ragnotti/Pierre Thimonier	Renault 5 Maxi Turbo
1986	Bruno Saby/Jean-François Fauchille	Peugeot 205 Turbo 16
1987	Bernard Béguin/Jean-Jacques Lenne	BMW M3
1988	Didier Auriol/Bernard Occelli	Ford Sierra Cosworth
1989	Didier Auriol/Bernard Occelli	Lancia Delta HF Integrale
1990	Didier Auriol/Bernard Occelli	Lancia Delta HF Integrale
1991	Carlos Sainz/Luis Moya	Toyota Celica GT4
1992	Didier Auriol/Bernard Occelli	Lancia Delta HF Integrale

Bruno Thiry failed to dominate Formula 2 for once, wrenching his wrist and then crashing the Astra.

Acropolis Rally, 30 May-1 June, FIA World Rally Championship Round 6

Leading Entries

1	Didier Auriol/ Bernard Occelli	Toyota Celica Turbo 4WD Gr A
2	François Delecour/ Daniel Grataloup	Ford Escort Cosworth Gr A
3	Carlos Sainz/ Luis Moya	Lancia Delta HF Integrale Gr A
4	Kenneth Eriksson/ Staffan Parmander	Mitsubishi Lancer RS-E Gr A
5	Colin McRae/ Derek Ringer	Subaru Legacy RS Gr A
6	Juha Kankkunen/ Juha Piironen	Toyota Celica Turbo 4WD Gr A
7	Miki Biasion/ Tiziano Siviero	Ford Escort Cosworth Gr A
8	Andrea Aghini/ Sauro Farnocchia	Lancia Delta HF Integrale Gr A
9	Armin Schwarz/ Nicky Grist	Mitsubishi Lancer RS-E Gr A
10	Ari Vatanen/ Bruno Berglund	Subaru Legacy RS Gr A
11	Gustavo Trelles/ Jorge Del Buono	Lancia Delta HF Integrale Gr A
12	Alessandro Fiorio/ Vittorio Brambilla	Lancia Delta HF Integrale Gr A
14	Jorge Recalde/ Martin Christie	Lancia Delta HF Integrale Gr N
15	Hiroshi Nishiyama/ Rocky Sugura	Nissan Sunny GTI-R Gr N
16	Bruno Thiry/ Stéphane Prévot	Opel Astra GSi Gr A
17	Christine Driano/ Marie-Christine Lallement	Citroën AX Sport Gr A
18	Tommi Mäkinen/ Seppo Harjanne	Lancia Delta HF Integrale Gr A
19	Rudi Stohl/ Peter Diekmann	Audi Coupé S2 Gr A
20	Mohammed Bin Sulayem/ Ronan Morgan	Ford Escort Cosworth Gr N
21	Alessandro Fassina/ Luigi Pirollo	Mazda 323 Turbo GT-R Gr N

Special Stage Times

SS1 Mandra (10.84 km)
1 A.Vatanen/B.Berglund (Subaru Legacy RS) 8m 24s; **2** C.McRae/D.Ringer (Subaru Legacy RS), J.Kankkunen/J.Piironen (Toyota Celica Turbo 4WD) 8m 25s; **4** D.Auriol/B.Occelli (Toyota Celica Turbo 4WD) 8m 29s; **5** C.Sainz/L.Moya (Lancia Delta HF Integrale) 8m 31s; **6** A.Schwarz/N.Grist (Mitsubishi Lancer RS-E) 8m 32s

SS2 Kineta (25.49 km)
1 Vatanen/Berglund (Subaru) 17m 48s; **2** Auriol/Occelli (Toyota) 17m 53s; **3** McRae/Ringer (Subaru), M.Biasion/T.Siviero (Ford Escort Cosworth) 18m 02s; **5** F.Delecour/D.Grataloup (Ford Escort Cosworth) 18m 03s; **6** Kankkunen/Piironen (Toyota) 18m 05s

SS3 Harvati (12.58 km)
1 Vatanen/Berglund (Subaru) 10m 15s; **2** Biasion/Siviero (Ford) 10m 17s; **3** Auriol/Occelli (Toyota), McRae/Ringer (Subaru) 10m 20s; **5** Sainz/Moya (Lancia) 10m 21s; **6** Kankkunen/Piironen (Toyota), Schwarz/Grist (Mitsubishi) 10m 23s

SS4 Kitheronas (10.75 km)
1 Vatanen/Berglund (Subaru) 7m 02s; **2** Auriol/Occelli (Toyota), Kankkunen/Piironen (Toyota) 7m 05s; **4** McRae/Ringer (Subaru) 7m 06s; **5** Schwarz/Grist (Mitsubishi) 7m 08s; **6** Delecour/Grataloup (Ford), A.Fiorio/V.Brambilla (Lancia Delta HF Integrale) 7m 09s

SS5 Stiri (20.86 km)
1 Vatanen/Berglund (Subaru) 13m 55s; **2** Delecour/Grataloup (Ford) 13m 57s; **3** McRae/Ringer (Subaru) 14m 00s; **4** Schwarz/Grist (Mitsubishi) 14m 01s; **5** Auriol/Occelli (Toyota), Biasion/Siviero (Ford) 14m 05s

SS6 Tsoukalades (8.56 km)
1 Biasion/Siviero (Ford) 6m 30s; **2** Auriol/Occelli (Toyota) 6m 31s; **3** Delecour/Grataloup (Ford), Vatanen/Berglund (Subaru) 6m 34s; **5** Sainz/Moya (Lancia), Kankkunen/Piironen (Toyota) 6m 35s

SS7 Elatia (15.06 km)
1 Vatanen/Berglund (Subaru) 10m 34s; **2** McRae/Ringer (Subaru) 10m 44s; **3** Biasion/Siviero (Ford) 10m 46s; **4** Kankkunen/Piironen (Toyota) 10m 48s; **5** Sainz/Moya 10m 51s; **6** A.Aghini/S.Farnocchia (Lancia Delta HF Integrale) 10m 57s

SS8 Eleftherohori (18.41 km)
1 Delecour/Grataloup (Ford) 12m 41s; **2** Vatanen/Berglund (Subaru) 12m 44s; **3** McRae/Ringer (Subaru) 12m 53s; **4** Schwarz/Grist (Mitsubishi) 12m 54s; **5** Sainz/Moya (Lancia) 12m 55s; **6** Biasion/Siviero (Ford) 12m 56s

SS9 Inohori (6.91 km)
1 Biasion/Siviero (Ford) 5m 18s; **2** Schwarz/Grist (Mitsubishi),Vatanen/Berglund (Subaru), Fiorio/Brambilla (Lancia) 5m 19s; **5** Delecour/Grataloup (Ford), McRae/Ringer (Subaru) 5m 20s

SS10 Kaloskopi (14.45 km)
1 Vatanen/Berglund (Subaru) 12m 13s; **2** Delecour/Grataloup (Ford), Sainz/Moya (Lancia) 12m 18s; **4** Biasion/Siviero (Ford) 12m 20s; **5** Schwarz/Grist (Mitsubishi) 12m 25s; **6** McRae/Ringer (Subaru) 12m 27s

SS11 Karoutes 1 (19.50 km)
1 Vatanen/Berglund (Subaru) 13m 02s; **2** Biasion/Siviero (Ford) 13m 05s; **3** McRae/Ringer (Subaru) 13m 08s; **4** Schwarz/Grist (Mitsubishi) 13m 11s; **5** Delecour/Grataloup (Ford) 13m 14s; **6** Sainz/Moya (Lancia) 13m 19s

SS12 Bauxite 1 (8.68 km)
1 Sainz/Moya (Lancia) 4m 55s; **2** Delecour/Grataloup (Ford) 4m 56s; **3** Kankkunen/Piironen (Toyota) 4m 57s; **4** McRae/Ringer (Subaru), Biasion/Siviero (Ford) 4m 58s; **6** Schwarz/Grist (Mitsubishi) 5m 00s

SS13 Agia Efthimia 1 (19.09 km)
1 Biasion/Siviero (Ford) 12m 06s; **2** Kankkunen/Piironen (Toyota) 12m 08s; **3** Delecour/Grataloup (Ford) 12m 09s; **4** Vatanen/Berglund (Subaru) 12m 10s; **5** Sainz/Moya (Lancia) 12m 12s; **6** Schwarz/Grist (Mitsubishi) 12m 17s

SS14 Prossilio 1 (9.30 km)
1 Sainz/Moya (Lancia) 6m 07s; **2** Kankkunen/Piironen (Toyota) 6m 11s; **3** Biasion/Siviero (Ford), Delecour/ Grataloup (Ford) 6m 12s; **5** Aghini/Farnocchia (Lancia), Fiorio/Brambilla (Lancia) 6m 17s

SS15 Pavliani (14.86 km)
1 Delecour/Grataloup (Ford) 12m 40s; **2** Sainz/Moya (Lancia) 12m 45s; **3** Biasion/Siviero (Ford) 12m 49s; **4** Vatanen/Berglund (Subaru) 12m 50s; **5** Kankkunen/Piironen (Toyota) 12m 51s; **6** Fiorio/Brambilla (Lancia) 12m 51s

SS16 Arhani-Asvestis (20.43 km)
1 Delecour/Grataloup (Ford) 14m 27s; **2** Sainz/Moya (Lancia) 14m 28s; **3** Kankkunen/Piironen (Toyota) 14m 29s; **4** Schwarz/Grist (Mitsubishi) 14m 30s; **5** Biasion/Siviero (Ford) 14m 32s; **6** Fiorio/Brambilla (Lancia) 14m 38s

SS17 Makrirahi (13.55 km)
1 Delecour/Grataloup (Ford) 7m 38s; **2** Kankkunen/Piironen (Toyota), Biasion/Siviero (Ford) 7m 43s; **4** Sainz/Moya (Lancia) 7m 44s; **5** Schwarz/Grist (Mitsubishi) 7m 45s; **6** Vatanen/Berglund (Subaru) 7m 49s

SS18 Anavra (13.23 km)
1 Sainz/Moya (Lancia) 8m 11s; **2** Schwarz/Grist (Mitsubishi) 8m 12s; **3** Delecour/Grataloup (Ford) 8m 16s; **4** Kankkunen/Piironen (Toyota) 8m 17s; **5** Aghini/Farnocchia (Lancia) 8m 20s; **6** Fiorio/Brambilla (Lancia) 8m 22s

SS19 Loutra Smokovou (8.99 km)
1 Schwarz/Grist (Mitsubishi) 5m 20s; **2** Sainz/Moya (Lancia) 5m 21s; **3** Delecour/Grataloup (Ford) 5m 24s; **4** Kankkunen/Piironen (Toyota) 5m 25s; **5** Fiorio/Brambilla (Lancia) 5m 36s; **6** Biasion/Siviero (Ford), Aghini/Farnocchia (Lancia) 5m 27s

SS20 Tarzan (27.31 km)
1 Vatanen/Berglund (Subaru) 23m 10s; **2** Kankkunen/Piironen (Toyota) 23m 18s; **3** Delecour/Grataloup (Ford), Biasion/Siviero (Ford) 23m 20s; **5** Sainz/Moya (Lancia) 23m 22s; **6** Aghini/Farnocchia (Lancia) 23m 30s

SS21 Dipotamia (11.07 km)
1 Delecour/Grataloup (Ford) 9m 09s; **2** Biasion/Siviero (Ford) 9m 12s; **3** Schwarz/Grist (Mitsubishi) 9m 16s; **4** Fiorio/Brambilla (Lancia) 9m 19s; **5** Aghini/Farnocchia (Lancia) 9m 20s; **6** G.Trelles/J.Del Buono (Lancia Delta HF Integrale) 9m 24s

SS22 Domnista (15.45 km)
1 Delecour/Grataloup (Ford) 14m 09s; **2** Sainz/Moya (Lancia) 14m 13s; **3** Biasion/Siviero (Ford) 14m 17s; **4** Schwarz/Grist (Mitsubishi) 14m 26s; **5** T.Mäkinen/S.Harjanne (Lancia Delta HF Integrale) 14m 27s; **6** Aghini/Farnocchia (Lancia) 14m 30s

SS23 Krioneria (14.88 km)
1 Sainz/Moya (Lancia) 14m 24s; **2** Biasion/Siviero (Ford), Aghini/Farnocchia (Lancia) 14m 42s; **4** Schwarz/Grist (Mitsubishi) 14m 45s; **5** Mäkinen/Harjanne (Lancia) 14m 45s; **6** Trelles/Del Buono (Lancia) 14m 48s

SS24 Ano Hora (13.18 km)
1 Sainz/Moya (Lancia) 10m 01s; **2** Schwarz/Grist (Mitsubishi) 10m 02s; **3** Biasion/Siviero (Ford), Aghini/ Farnocchia (Lancia) 10m 03s; **5** Trelles/Del Buono (Lancia) 10m 10s; **6** Mäkinen/Harjanne (Lancia) 10m 16s

SS25 Bauxite 2 (8.68 km)
1 Delecour/Grataloup (Ford), Biasion/Siviero (Ford) 4m 59s; **3** Sainz/Moya (Lancia), Schwarz/Grist (Mitsubishi) 5m 00s; **5** Fiorio/Brambilla (Lancia) 5m 01s; **6** Aghini/Farnocchia (Lancia) 5m 04s

SS26 Agia Efthimia 2 (19.09 km)
1 Sainz/Moya (Lancia) 12m 14s; **2** Biasion/Siviero (Ford), Schwarz/Grist (Mitsubishi) 12m 18s; **4** Delecour/Grataloup (Ford) 12m 19s; **5** Fiorio/Brambilla (Lancia) 12m 20s; **6** Mäkinen/Harjanne (Lancia) 12m 28s

SS27 Prossilio 2 (9.30 km)
1 Delecour/Grataloup (Ford) 6m 02s; **2** Sainz/Moya (Lancia) 6m 05s; **3** Biasion/Siviero (Ford), Schwarz/Grist (Mitsubishi) 6m 07s; **5** Mäkinen/Harjanne (Lancia) 6m 10s; **6** Fiorio/Brambilla (Lancia) 6m 17s

SS28 Mavrolithari (24.49 km)
1 Delecour/Grataloup (Ford) 21m 25s; **2** Sainz/Moya (Lancia) 21m 28s; **3** Biasion/Siviero (Ford) 21m 38s; **4** Mäkinen/Harjanne (Lancia) 21m 44s; **5** Fiorio/Brambilla (Lancia) 21m 46s; **6** Schwarz/Grist (Mitsubishi) 21m 47s

SS29 Anatoli (9.29 km)
1 Delecour/Grataloup (Ford) 8m 23s; **2** Sainz/Moya (Lancia), Aghini/Farnocchia (Lancia) 8m 26s; **4** Mäkinen/Harjanne (Lancia) 8m 28s; **5** Biasion/Siviero (Ford) 8m 30s; **6** Fiorio/Brambilla (Lancia) 8m 31s

SS30 Perivoli (12.72 km)
1 Delecour/Grataloup (Ford) 11m 08s; **2** Sainz/Moya (Lancia) 11m 13s; **3** Aghini/Farnocchia (Lancia), Mäkinen/Harjanne (Lancia) 11m 14s; **5** Trelles/Del Buono (Lancia) 11m 18s; **6** Schwarz/Grist (Mitsubishi) 11m 23s

SS31 Gardiki (22.87 km)
1 Sainz/Moya (Lancia) 19m 38s; **2** Aghini/Farnocchia (Lancia) 19m 39s; **3** Mäkinen/Harjanne (Lancia) 19m 42s; **4** Delecour/Grataloup (Ford) 19m 43s; **5** Biasion/Siviero (Ford) 19m 51s; **6** Schwarz/Grist (Mitsubishi) 20m 01s

SS32 Grammeni Oxia (11.46 km)
1 Sainz/Moya (Lancia) 9m 45s; **2** Aghini/Farnocchia (Lancia) 9m 48s; **3** Mäkinen/Harjanne (Lancia) 9m 54s; **4** Trelles/Del Buono (Lancia) 10m 04s; **5** Biasion/Siviero (Ford) 10m 05s; **6** Schwarz/Grist (Mitsubishi) 10m 07s

SS33 Pendagi (10.90 km)
1 Sainz/Moya (Lancia) 10m 04s; **2** Aghini/Farnocchia (Lancia) 10m 09s; **3** Schwarz/Grist (Mitsubishi), Trelles/Del Buono (Lancia) 10m 12s; **5** Biasion/Siviero (Ford), Mäkinen/Harjanne (Lancia) 10m 15s

SS34 Diakopi (14.97 km)
1 Sainz/Moya (Lancia) 13m 32s; **2** Aghini/Farnocchia (Lancia) 13m 40s; **3** Trelles/Del Buono (Lancia) 13m 43s; **4** Schwarz/Grist (Mitsubishi) 13m 47s; **5** Mäkinen/Harjanne (Lancia) 13m 51s; **6** Biasion/Siviero (Ford) 13m 53s

SS35 Karoutes 2 (19.50 km)
1 Sainz/Moya (Lancia) 13m 07s; **2** Trelles/Del Buono (Lancia) 13m 16s; **3** Aghini/Farnocchia (Lancia) 13m 18s; **4** Schwarz/Grist (Mitsubishi) 13m 19s; **5** Mäkinen/Harjanne (Lancia) 13m 20s; **6** Biasion/Siviero (Ford) 13m 29s

SS36 Karakolithos (28.69 km)
1 Aghini/Farnocchia (Lancia) 19m 04s; **2** Schwarz/Grist (Mitsubishi) 19m 12s; **3** Biasion/Siviero (Ford) 19m 13s; **4** Trelles/Del Buono (Lancia) 19m 18s; **5** Sainz/Moya (Lancia) 19m 22s; **6** Mäkinen/Harjanne (Lancia) 20m 10s

Major Retirements

1	Auriol/Occelli	Toyota Celica Turbo 4WD	
	Engine	SS8	Gr A
2	Delecour/Grataloup	Ford Escort Cosworth	
	Engine	SS32	Gr A
4	Eriksson/Parmander	Mitsubishi Lancer RS-E	
	Suspension	SS2	Gr A
5	McRae/Ringer	Subaru Legacy RS	
	Accident	SS13	Gr A
6	Kankkunen/Piironen	Toyota Celica Turbo 4WD	
	Engine	SS21	Gr A
10	Vatanen/Berglund	Subaru Legacy RS	
	Accident	SS21	Gr A
14	Recalde/Christie	Lancia Delta HF Integrale	
	Mechanical	SS22	Gr N
15	Nishiyama/Sugura	Nissan Sunny GTI-R	
	Accident	SS28	Gr N
16	Thiry/Prévot	Opel Astra GSi	
	Accident	SS8	Gr A
19	Stohl/Diekmann	Audi Coupé S2	
	Engine	SS1	Gr A
20	Bin Sulayem/Morgan	Ford Escort Cosworth	
	Gearbox	SS23	Gr N

FIA Class Winners

A8 Over 2000 cc	Biasion/Siviero
	Ford Escort Cosworth
A7 1600-2000 cc	'Leonidas'/Korre
	Renault Clio Williams
A6 1300-1600 cc	Aliasov/Levitan
	Lada Samara
A5 Up to 1300 cc	Triner/Klima
	Skoda Favorit 136L
N4 Over 2000 cc	Fassina/Pirollo
	Mazda 323 Turbo GT-R
N3 1600-2000 cc	Briffa/Rousset
	Citroën AX GTI
N2 1300-1600 cc	Lambropoulos/Galanakis
	Toyota Corolla
N1 Up to 1300 cc	Sagnard/Muller
	Peugeot 205 Rallye

Rally Leaders

Vatanen **SS1-20;** Delecour **SS21-23;** Biasion **SS24-36**

World Championship Points

Drivers
1 Delecour 55; **2** Biasion 51; **3** Kankkunen 43; **4** Auriol 35; **5** Alén, Sainz 25; **7** McRae 24; **8** Aghini 22; **9** Jonsson 20; **10** Eriksson, Schwarz 18, etc.

Manufacturers
1 Toyota, Ford 77; **3** Mitsubishi 47; **4** Lancia 43; **5** Subaru 36

FIA Cup for Production Car Drivers
1 Fassina 26; **2** Coutinho 14; **3** Spiliotis, Bäcklund, Shamji, Manfrinato 13, etc.

FIA Cup for Manufacturers
1 GME 36; **2** Skoda 29; **3** Peugeot 22; **4** Citroën 20; **5** Renault 16, etc.

Route Details

Leg 1
Sunday 30 May, Athens-Delphi. 11 special stages (166.71 km) in a total route of 535.59 km
Leg 2
Monday 31 May, Delphi-Delphi. 13 special stages (199.69 km) in a total route of 541.68 km
Leg 3
Tuesday 1 June, Delphi-Athens. 12 special stages (191.96 km) in a total route of 580.08 km

Weather

Hot and dry

Special Stage Analysis

	1	2	3	4	5	6
Sainz (Lancia)	11	9	1	1	8	1
Delecour (Ford)	11	3	6	2	3	1
Vatanen (Subaru)	9	2	1	2	-	1
Biasion (Ford)	4	6	10	2	6	4
Aghini (Lancia)	1	6	3	-	3	5
Schwarz (Mitsubishi)	1	5	4	8	3	8
Kankkunen (Toyota)	-	6	2	3	2	2
Auriol (Toyota)	-	3	1	1	1	-
McRae (Subaru)	-	2	5	2	1	1
Trelles (Lancia)	-	1	2	2	2	2
Fiorio (Lancia)	-	1	-	1	5	6
Mäkinen	-	-	3	2	6	3

Finish Lines

Both **Ari Vatanen** and **Colin McRae** crashed, while lying first and second respectively, when **Subaru** looked highly likely to take its first victory at World Championship level...**Toyota** had a disastrous rally: **Didier Auriol** survived cracking the sump on a road section, but retired towards the end of the first leg with dire engine problems, while **Juha Kankkunen** stopped during the second when his **Celica**'s electrics failed... **Kenneth Eriksson** was the first major retirement, his **Lancer**'s front suspension collapsing on SS2...**Bruno Thiry** wrenched his hand when the steering snatched and, finding it difficult to control the **Astra,** crashed near the end of the first leg...**Emil Triner** was the top two-wheel drive finisher in his **Skoda**... Reliability paid off once more for **Alessandro Fassina** as well, the Italian winning **Group N** in his Mazda after both **Mohammed Bin Sulayem**'s Escort and **Jorge Recalde**'s Delta succumbed to mechanical problems.

Results

1	Miki Biasion/	Ford Escort Cosworth	
	Tiziano Siviero	6h 54m 35s	Gr A
2	Carlos Sainz/	Lancia Delta HF Integrale	
	Luis Moya	6h 55m 48s	Gr A
3	Armin Schwarz/	Mitsubishi Lancer RS-E	
	Nicky Grist	6h 57m 19s	Gr A
4	Andrea Aghini/	Lancia Delta HF Integrale	
	Sauro Farnocchia	7h 00m 15s	Gr A
5	Gustavo Trelles/	Lancia Delta HF Integrale	
	Jorge Del Buono	7h 02m 39s	Gr A
6	Tommi Mäkinen/	Lancia Delta HF Integrale	
	Seppo Harjanne	7h 02m 44s	Gr A
7	Alessandro Fiorio/	Lancia Delta HF Integrale	
	Vittorio Brambilla	7h 23m 44s	Gr A
8	Costas Apostolou/	Lancia Delta HF Integrale	
	Mihali Kriadis	7h 39m 00s	Gr A
9	Nikos Tsadaris/	Lancia Delta HF Integrale	
	Elias Kafaoglou	7h 39m 45s	Gr A
10	Alessandro Fassina/	Mazda 323 Turbo GT-R	
	Luigi Pirollo	8h 08m 04s	Gr N

93 starters, 48 finishers

Previous Winners

1960	Walter Schock/Rolf Moll	Mercedes-Benz 220SE
1961	Erik Carlsson/Walter Carlsson	Saab 96
1962	Eugen Bohringer/Peter Lang	Mercedes-Benz 220SE
1963	Eugen Bohringer/Rolf Moll	Mercedes-Benz 300SE
1964	Tom Trana/Gunnar Thermenius	Volvo PV544
1965	Carl-Magnus Skogh/'Tandlakare'	Volvo 122S
1966	Bengt Söderstrom/Gunnar Palm	Ford Lotus Cortina
1967	Paddy Hopkirk/Ron Crellin	Mini-Cooper S
1968	Roger Clark/Jim Porter	Ford Escort TC
1969	Pauli Toivonen/Matti Kolari	Porsche 911S
1970	Jean-Luc Thérier/Marcel Callewaert	Alpine Renault A110
1971	Ove Andersson/Arne Hertz	Alpine Renault A110
1972	Håkan Lindberg/Helmut Eisendle	Fiat 124 Spyder
1973	Jean-Luc Thérier/Christian Delferrier	Alpine Renault A110
1975	Walter Röhrl/Jochen Berger	Opel Ascona
1976	Harry Kallström/Claes-Goran Andersson	Datsun 160J
1977	Björn Waldegård/Hans Thorszelius	Ford Escort RS1800
1978	Walter Röhrl/Christian Geistdörfer	Fiat 131 Abarth
1979	Björn Waldegård/Hans Thorszelius	Ford RS1800
1980	Ari Vatanen/David Richards	Ford Escort RS
1981	Ari Vatanen/David Richards	Ford Escort RS
1982	Michèle Mouton/Fabrizia Pons	Audi Quattro
1983	Walter Röhrl/Christian Geistdörfer	Lancia Rallye 037
1984	Stig Blomqvist/Björn Cederberg	Audi Quattro
1985	Timo Salonen/Seppo Harjanne	Peugeot 205 Turbo 16
1986	Juha Kankkunen/Juha Piironen	Peugeot 205 Turbo 16
1987	Markku Alén/Ilkka Kivimäki	Lancia Delta HF 4x4
1988	Miki Biasion/Tiziano Siviero	Lancia Delta HF Integrale
1989	Miki Biasion/Tiziano Siviero	Lancia Delta HF Integrale
1990	Carlos Sainz/Luis Moya	Toyota Celica GT4
1991	Juha Kankkunen/Juha Piironen	Lancia Delta HF Integrale
1992	Didier Auriol/Bernard Occelli	Lancia Delta HF Integrale

Once a little development had been carried out, Rudi Stohl's Quattro S2 proved capable of finishing well inside the top ten.

Rally of Argentina, 14-17 July, FIA World Rally Championship Round 7

Leading Entries

1	Didier Auriol/ Bernard Occelli	Toyota Celica Turbo 4WD Gr A
2	Carlos Sainz/ Luis Moya	Lancia Delta HF Integrale Gr A
3	Miki Biasion/ Tiziano Siviero	Ford Escort Cosworth Gr A
4	Juha Kankkunen/ Nicky Grist	Toyota Celica Turbo 4WD Gr A
5	Gustavo Trelles/ Jorge Del Buono	Lancia Delta HF Integrale Gr A
6	Carlos Menem jnr/ Victor Zucchini	Ford Escort Cosworth Gr A
7	Jorge Recalde/ Martin Christie	Lancia Delta HF Integrale Gr N
8	Christine Driano/ Marie-Christine Lallement	Citroën AX Sport Gr A
9	Rudi Stohl/ Peter Diekmann	Audi Coupe S2 Gr A
10	Gabriel Raies/ José-Marie Volta	Renault 18 GTX Gr A
11	Mohammed Bin Sulayem/ Ronan Morgan	Ford Escort Cosworth Gr N
12	Manfred Stohl/ Kay Gerlach	Audi Coupe S2 Gr A
14	Jorge Bescham/ José-Alberto Garcia	Fiat Regatta 2000 Gr A
15	Carlos Malarczuk/ Jorge Gonzales	Fiat Regatta 2000 Gr A
16	Juan Raies/ Rodolfo Ortiz	Renault 18 GTX Gr A
17	Marcelo Foche/ Jorge Ferro	Renault 18 GTX Gr A
18	Miguel Torras/ Luis Maciel	Renault 18 GTX Gr A
20	Antonio Coutinho/ Paulo Brandao	Ford Escort Cosworth Gr N
21	Stefan Reininger/ Simon Young	Subaru Legacy RS Gr N

Special Stage Times

SS1 Hipodromo (4.07 km)
1 J.Kankkunen/N.Grist (Toyota Celica Turbo) 2m 56s; 2 D.Auriol/B.Occelli (Toyota Celica Turbo), M.Biasion/T.Siviero (Ford Escort Cosworth) 2m 59s; 4 C.Sainz/L.Moya (Lancia Delta HF Integrale), G.Trelles/J.Del Buono (Lancia Delta HF Integrale) 3m 00s; 6 C.Menem/V.Zucchini (Ford Escort Cosworth) 3m 05s

SS2 Sauce Punco-Empalme Ruta (6.25 km)
1 Auriol/Occelli (Toyota) 4m 28s; 2 Biasion/Siviero (Ford) 4m 29s; 3 Kankkunen/Grist (Toyota) 4m 30s; 4 Trelles/Del Buono (Lancia) 4m 35s; 5 J.Recalde/ M.Christie (Lancia Delta HF Integrale) 4m 51s; 6 Menem/Zucchini (Ford), R.Stohl/P.Diekmann (Audi Coupé S2) 4m 53s

SS3 Museo Fader-Canada de Rio Pinto (44.13 km)
1 Kankkunen/Grist (Toyota) 24m 05s; 2 Auriol/Occelli (Toyota) 24m 07s; 3 Biasion/Siviero (Ford) 24m 20s; 4 Trelles/Del Buono (Lancia) 25m 02s; 5 Menem/ Zucchini (Ford) 26m 11s; 6 M.Bin Sulayem/R. Morgan (Ford Escort Cosworth) 26m 57s

SS4 Canada de Rio Pinto (31.92 km)
1 Kankkunen/Grist (Toyota) 19m 23s; 2 Biasion/ Siviero (Ford) 19m 29s; 3 Auriol/Occelli (Toyota) 19m 42s; 4 Trelles/Del Buono (Lancia) 20m 04s; 5 Menem/Zucchini (Ford) 21m 00s; 6 Bin Sulayem/ Morgan (Ford) 21m 20s

SS5 La Pampa (31.41 km)
1 Kankkunen/Grist (Toyota) 20m 14s; 2 Biasion/ Siviero (Ford) 20m 20s; 3 Trelles/Del Buono (Lancia) 21m 02s; 4 Auriol/Occelli (Toyota) 21m 09s; 5 Menem/Zucchini (Ford) 21m 32s; 6 Bin Sulayem/ Morgan (Ford) 21m 54s

SS6 Ascochinga-La Cumbre Estancia El Rosario (31.80 km)
1 Kankkunen/Grist (Toyota) 21m 52s; 2 Biasion/ Siviero (Ford) 22m 06s; 3 Trelles/Del Buono (Lancia) 22m 24s; 4 Menem/Zucchini (Ford) 22m 55s; 5 Bin Sulayem/Morgan (Ford) 23m 14s; 6 G.Raies/J.M. Volta (Renault 18 GTX) 24m 13s

SS7 Cosquin-Villa Allende (22.43 km)
1 Biasion/Siviero (Ford) 16m 04s; 2 Kankkunen/Grist (Toyota) 16m 06s; 3 Trelles/Del Buono (Lancia) 16m 22s; 4 Menem/Zucchini (Ford) 16m 49s; 5 Bin Sulayem/Morgan (Ford) 17m 23s; 6 Auriol/Occelli (Toyota) 17m 56s

SS8 Camping Gral San Martin (3.10 km)
1 Biasion/Siviero (Ford) 2m 36s; 2 Trelles/Del Buono (Lancia) 2m 39s; 3 Kankkunen/Grist (Toyota) 2m 40s; 4 Stohl/Diekmann (Audi) 2m 45s; 5 Auriol/ Occelli (Toyota) 2m 47s; 6 Bin Sulayem/Morgan (Ford) 2m 49s

SS9 El Mirador-Taninga (44.45 km)
1 Kankkunen/Grist (Toyota) 26m 17s; 2 Biasion/ Siviero (Ford) 26m 18s; 3 Auriol/Occelli (Toyota) 26m 55s; 4 Trelles/Del Buono (Lancia) 27m 12s; 5 Menem/Zucchini (Ford) 28m 19s; 6 Bin Sulayem/ Morgan (Ford) 28m 35s

SS10 Chamico-Ambul (22.50 km)
1 Kankkunen/Grist (Toyota) 19m 48s; 2 Biasion/ Siviero (Ford) 20m 19s; 3 Trelles/Del Buono (Lancia) 20m 42s; 4 Menem/Zucchini (Ford) 21m 45s; 5 Auriol/Occelli (Toyota) 22m 10s; 6 Bin Sulayem/ Morgan (Ford) 22m 43s

SS11 El Azul-Las Maravillas (14.14 km)
1 Kankkunen/Grist (Toyota) 8m 49s; 2 Auriol/Occelli (Toyota) 8m 50s; 3 Biasion/Siviero (Ford) 8m 52s; 4 Trelles/Del Buono (Lancia) 9m 07s; 5 Menem/ Zucchini (Ford) 9m 25s; 6 Bin Sulayem/Morgan (Ford) 9m 45s

SS12 Cura Brochero-Nono (19.75 km)
1 Kankkunen/Grist (Toyota) 10m 59s; 2 Biasion/ Siviero (Ford) 11m 01s; 3 Trelles/Del Buono (Lancia) 11m 31s; 4 Auriol/Occelli (Toyota) 11m 43s; 5 Menem/Zucchini (Ford) 12m 19s; 6 Bin Sulayem/ Morgan (Ford) 12m 24s

SS13 Mina Clavero-Giulio Cesare (2.26 km)
1 Kankkunen/Grist (Toyota) 19m 07s; **2** Biasion/Siviero (Ford) 19m 09s; **3** Trelles/Del Buono (Lancia) 19m 30s; **4** Menem/Zucchini (Ford) 20m 10s; **5** Auriol/Occelli (Toyota) 20m 16s; **6** Bin Sulayem/Morgan (Ford) 21m 03s

SS14 El Condor-Copina (16.87 km)
1 Biasion/Siviero (Ford) 14m 25s; **2** Auriol/Occelli (Toyota), Kankkunen/Grist (Toyota) 14m 36s; **4** Trelles/Del Buono (Lancia) 14m 42s; **5** Menem/Zucchini (Ford) 15m 06s; **6** Bin Sulayem/Morgan (Ford) 15m 31s

SS15 Villa Carlos Paz-El Pantanillo-Villa Garcia (16.14 km)
1 Kankkunen/Grist (Toyota) 11m 32s; **2** Biasion/Siviero (Ford) 11m 37s; **3** Auriol/Occelli (Toyota) 11m 55s; **4** Trelles/Del Buono (Lancia) 12m 00s; **5** Menem/Zucchini (Ford) 12m 09s; **6** Bin Sulayem/Morgan (Ford) 12m 58s

SS16 Tanti-Cosquin (21.18 km)
1 Biasion/Siviero (Ford) 11m 31s; **2** Kankkunen/Grist (Toyota) 11m 33s; **3** Auriol/Occelli (Toyota) 11m 39s; **4** Trelles/Del Buono (Lancia) 11m 46s; **5** Menem/Zucchini (Ford) 12m 05s; **6** Bin Sulayem/Morgan (Ford) 12m 36s

SS17 La Falda Rio Ceballos (12.56 km)
1 Kankkunen/Grist (Toyota) 10m 43s; **2** Auriol/Occelli (Toyota), Biasion/Siviero (Ford) 10m 50s; **4** Trelles/Del Buono (Lancia) 11m 01s; **5** Menem/Zucchini (Ford) 11m 20s; **6** Stohl/Diekmann (Audi) 12m 07s

SS18 Camping Gral San Martin (3.10 km)
1 Biasion/Siviero (Ford) 2m 31s; **2** Auriol/Occelli (Toyota) 2m 32s; **3** Kankkunen/Grist (Toyota), Trelles/Del Buono (Lancia) 2m 33s; **5** Menem/Zucchini (Ford) 2m 35s; **6** Stohl/Diekmann (Audi) 2m 40s

SS19 Rosa de Calamuchita-San Agustin (27.62 km)
1 Kankkunen/Grist (Toyota) 17m 01s; **2** Biasion/Siviero (Ford) 17m 29s; **3** Auriol/Occelli (Toyota) 17m 59s; **4** Trelles/Del Buono (Lancia) 18m 06s; **5** Menem/Zucchini (Ford) 19m 04s; **6** M.Stohl/K.Gerlach (Audi Coupe S2) 20m 10s

SS20 Las Bajadas-Villa Del Dique (19.64 km)
1 Kankkunen/Grist (Toyota) 11m 12s; **2** Biasion/Siviero (Ford) 11m 27s; **3** Auriol/Occelli (Toyota) 11m 56s; **4** Trelles/Del Buono (Lancia) 11m 59s; **5** Menem/Zucchini (Ford) 12m 26s; **6** Bin Sulayem/Morgan (Ford) 12m 53s

SS21 Amboy-Rosa de Calamuchita (21.37 km)
1 Kankkunen/Grist (Toyota) 11m 45s; **2** Biasion/Siviero (Ford) 12m 00s; **3** Trelles/Del Buono (Lancia) 12m 25s; **4** Auriol/Occelli (Toyota) 12m 42s; **5** Menem/Zucchini (Ford) 13m 16s; **6** Stohl/Gerlach (Audi) 13m 33s

SS22 Villa Ciudad de America-Jose de la Quintana (11.36 km)
1 Kankkunen/Grist (Toyota) 8m 33s; **2** Auriol/Occelli (Toyota), Biasion/Siviero (Ford) 8m 36s; **4** Trelles/Del Buono (Lancia) 8m 44s; **5** Menem/Zucchini (Ford) 9m 10s; **6** Stohl/Diekmann (Audi), Bin Sulayem/Morgan (Ford) 9m 36s

SS23 Camping Gral San Martin (3.10 km)
1 Auriol/Occelli (Toyota) 2m 30s; **2** Biasion/Siviero (Ford), Kankkunen/Grist (Toyota), Trelles/Del Buono (Lancia) 2m 32s; **5** Menem/Zucchini (Ford) 2m 35s; **6** Stohl/Diekmann (Audi) 2m 39s

SS24 Ascochinga-La Cumbre Estancio El Rosario (31.80 km)
1 Biasion/Siviero (Ford) 21m 42s; **2** Auriol/Occelli (Toyota) 21m 49s; **3** Kankkunen/Grist (Toyota) 21m 55s; **4** Stohl/Gerlach (Audi) 23m 32s; **5** Bin Sulayem/Morgan (Ford) 24m 23s; **6** Stohl/Diekmann (Audi) 24m 32s

SS25 Tanti-Cosquin (21.18 km)
1 Biasion/Siviero (Ford) 11m 33s; **2** Auriol/Occelli (Toyota); Kankkunen/Grist (Toyota) 11m 40s; **4** Menem/Zucchini (Ford) 12m 11s; **5** Trelles/Del Buono (Lancia) 12m 25s; **6** Bin Sulayem/Morgan (Ford) 12m 49s

Major Retirements

2	Sainz/Moya	Lancia Delta HF Integrale	
	Engine	SS1	Gr A
7	Recalde/Christie	Lancia Delta HF Integrale	
	Suspension	SS6	Gr N
14	Bescham/Garcia	Fiat Regatta 2000	
	Clutch	SS16	Gr A
21	Reininger/Young	Subaru Legacy RS	
	Electrics	SS10	Gr N

FIA Class Winners

A8 Over 2000 cc	Kankkunen/Grist Toyota Celica Turbo 4WD
A7 1600-2000 cc	Raies/Volta Renault 18 GTX
A6 1300-1600 cc	Manzanares/Manzanares VW Golf 1.6
A5 Up to 1300 cc	Driano/Lallement Citroën AX Sport
N4 Over 2000cc	Bin Sulayem/Morgan Ford Escort Cosworth
N3 1600-2000 cc	No starters
N2 1300-1600 cc	No starters
N1 Up to 1300 cc	No finishers

Rally Leaders

SS1-25 Kankkunen

World Championship Points

Drivers
1 Biasion 66; **2** Kankkunen 63; **3** Delecour 55; **4** Auriol 47; **5** Alén, Sainz 25; **7** McRae 24; **8** Aghini 22; **9** Jonsson 20; **10** Eriksson, Schwarz, Trelles 18, etc.

Manufacturers
1 Toyota 97; **2** Ford 94; **3** Lancia 55; **4** Mitsubishi 47; **5** Subaru 36

FIA Cup for Production Car Drivers
1 Fassina 26; **2** Coutinho 24; **3** Spiliotis, Bäcklund, Shamji, Manfrinato, Bin Sulayem 13

FIA Cup for Manufacturers
1 GM 36; **2** Skoda 29; **3** Peugeot 22; **4** Citroën 20; **5** Renault (F) 16; **6** Renault (RA) 10, etc.

Route Details

Leg 1
Wednesday-Thursday, 14-15 July, Tucuman-Cordoba. 8 special stages (175.11 km) in a total route of 797.52 km
Leg 2
Friday, 16 July, Cordoba-Cordoba. 10 special stages (213.48 km) in a total route of 484.93 km
Leg 3
Saturday, 17 July, Cordoba-Cordoba. 7 special stages (136.07 km) in a total route of 553.81 km

Weather

Cool and dry

Special Stage Analysis

	1	2	3	4	5	6
Kankkunen (Toyota)	16	4	5	-	-	-
Biasion (Ford)	7	16	2	-	-	-
Auriol (Toyota)	2	9	6	3	3	1
Trelles (Lancia)	-	2	9	12	1	-
Menem (Ford)	-	-	-	5	16	2
R.Stohl (Audi)	-	-	-	1	-	5
M.Stohl (Audi)	-	-	-	1	-	2
Sainz (Lancia)	-	-	-	1	-	-
Bin Sulayem (Ford)	-	-	-	-	3	15
Recalde (Lancia)	-	-	-	-	1	-
Raies (Renault)	-	-	-	-	-	1

Finish Lines

Carlos Menem Junior invariably got the kind of reception normally reserved for a pop star and survived a last-minute suspension breakage to finish a good fifth in his MLP **Escort Cosworth**...**Gustavo Trelles** shot off the road near the end but, while he brought the surviving Jolly Club **Delta** to the finish anyway, he injured his wrist in the process... **Mohammed Bin Sulayem** finally achieved his first finish since changing from a Sierra to an **Escort** and won Group N into the bargain...**Christine Driano** set out to drive the rally as slowly as she could, since she had to finish a certain number of rallies to take the world Ladies' title. Ironically, she nearly brought her **Citroën** into the top 20 and a points-scoring position anyway.

Results

1	Juha Kankkunen/ Nicky Grist	Toyota Celica Turbo 5h 32m 31s	Gr A
2	Miki Biasion/ Tiziano Siviero	Ford Escort Cosworth 5h 34m 25s	Gr A
3	Didier Auriol/ Bernard Occelli	Toyota Celica Turbo 5h 49m 29s	Gr A
4	Gustavo Trelles/ Jorge Del Buono	Lancia Delta HF Integrale 6h 00m 36s	Gr A
5	Carlos Menem jnr/ Victor Zucchini	Ford Escort Cosworth 6h 04m 05s	Gr A
6	Mohammed Bin Sulayem/ Ronan Morgan	Ford Escort Cosworth 6h 09m 42s	Gr N
7	Rudi Stohl/ Peter Diekmann	Audi Coupé S2 6h 21m 53s	Gr A
8	Antonio Coutinho/ Paulo Brandao	Ford Escort Cosworth 6h 30m 53s	Gr N
9	Gabriel Raies/ José Maria Volta	Renault 18 GTX 6h 33m 01s	Gr A
10	José Ceccheto/ Justo Carrera	Fiat Regatta 2000 6h 43m 37s	Gr A
12	Manfred Stohl/ Kay Gerlach	Audi Coupé S2 6h 46m 47s	Gr A

86 starters, 30 finishers

Previous Winners

1979	Jean Guichet/Jean Todt	Peugeot 504
1980	Walter Röhrl/Christian Geistdörfer	Fiat 131 Abarth
1981	Guy Fréquelin/Jean Todt	Talbot Sunbeam Lotus
1983	Hannu Mikkola/Arne Hertz	Audi Quattro A1
1984	Stig Blomqvist/Björn Cederberg	Audi Quattro A2
1985	Timo Salonen/Seppo Harjanne	Peugeot 205 Turbo 16
1986	Miki Biasion/Tiziano Siviero	Lancia Delta S4
1987	Miki Biasion/Tiziano Siviero	Lancia Delta HF 4x4
1988	Jorge Recalde/Jorge Del Buono	Lancia Delta HF Integrale
1989	Mikael Ericsson/Claes Billstam	Lancia Delta HF Integrale
1990	Miki Biasion/Tiziano Siviero	Lancia Delta HF Integrale
1991	Carlos Sainz/Luis Moya	Toyota Celica GT4
1992	Didier Auriol/Bernard Occelli	Lancia Delta HF Integrale

8
Rothmans
RALLY NEW ZEALAND
23RD ANNIVERSARY 1993

Rally of New Zealand, 5-8 August, FIA World Rally Championship Round 8

Leading Entries

1	Carlos Sainz/ Luis Moya	Lancia Delta HF Integrale Gr A
2	Didier Auriol/ Bernard Occelli	Toyota Celica Turbo 4WD Gr A
3	François Delecour/ Daniel Grataloup	Ford Escort Cosworth Gr A
4	Ari Vatanen/ Bruno Berglund	Subaru Legacy RS Gr A
5	Juha Kankkunen/ Nicky Grist	Toyota Celica Turbo 4WD Gr A
6	Miki Biasion/ Tiziano Siviero	Ford Escort Cosworth Gr A
7	Colin McRae / Derek Ringer	Subaru Legacy RS Gr A
8	Gustavo Trelles/ Jorge Del Buono	Lancia Delta HF Integrale Gr A
9	Ross Dunkerton/ Fred Gocentas	Mitsubishi Lancer RS-E Gr A
10	'Possum' Bourne/ Rodger Freeth	Subaru Legacy RS Gr A
11	Jorge Recalde/ Martin Christie	Lancia Delta HF Integrale Gr A
12	Christine Driano Marie-Christine Lallement	Citroën AX Sport Gr A
14	Alessandro Fassina/ Luigi Pirollo	Mazda 323 Turbo GT-R Gr N
15	Sepp Haider/ Klaus Wendel	Audi Coupé S2 Gr A
16	Yoshio Fujimoto/ Hakaru Ichino	Mitsubishi Lancer RS-E Gr N
17	Kurt Gottlicher/ Kris Rosenberger	Ford Sierra Cosworth 4x4 Gr N
18	Neil Allport/ Jim Robb	Mazda 323 Turbo GT-R Gr A
19	Joe McAndrew/ Bob Haldane	Subaru Legacy RS Gr A
20	Brian Stokes/ Jeff Judd	Ford Escort Cosworth Gr A
21	Barry Sexton/ Leo Bult	Subaru Legacy RS Gr A

Special Stage Times

SS1 Totara Park 1 (2.07 km)
1 C.Sainz/L.Moya (Lancia Delta HF Integrale), D.Auriol/B.Occelli (Toyota Celica Turbo), J.Kankkunen/N.Grist (Toyota Celica Turbo) 1m 13s; **4** C.McRae/D.Ringer (Subaru Legacy RS) 1m 14s; **5** F.Delecour/D.Grataloup (Ford Escort Cosworth), M.Biasion/T.Siviero (Ford Escort Cosworth), A.Vatanen/B.Berglund (Subaru Legacy RS), P.Bourne/R.Freeth (Subaru Legacy RS), N.Allport/J.Robb (Mazda 323 GT-R) 1m 15s

SS2 Springhill (5.73 km)
1 McRae/Ringer (Subaru), Bourne/Freeth (Subaru) 2m 51s; **3** Kankkunen/Grist (Toyota) 2m 52s; **4** Auriol/Occelli (Toyota), Vatanen/Berglund (Subaru) 2m 53s; **6** Delecour/Grataloup (Ford), Biasion/Siviero (Ford) 2m 54s

SS3 Waitetuna Valley (16.35 km)
1 Vatanen/Berglund (Subaru) 8m 13s; **2** Delecour/Grataloup (Ford) 8m 15s; **3** Biasion/Siviero (Ford), McRae/Ringer (Subaru) 8m 17s; **5** Allport/Robb 8m 18s; **6** Auriol/Occelli (Toyota), Bourne/Freeth (Subaru), Sainz/Moya (Lancia) 8m 19s

SS4 Whaanga Coast (29.59 km)
1 Delecour/Grataloup (Ford) 22m 22s; **2** Sainz/Moya (Lancia), Vatanen/Berglund (Subaru) 22m 23s; **4** McRae/Ringer (Subaru) 22m 28s; **5** Auriol/Occelli (Toyota) 22m 29s; **6** Kankkunen/Grist (Toyota) 22m 43s

SS5 Bridal Veil (24.14 km)
1 Sainz/Moya (Lancia) 18m 09s; **2** Auriol/Occelli (Toyota) 18m 10s; **3** Delecour/Grataloup (Ford) 18m 14s; **4** Vatanen/Berglund (Subaru) 18m 19s; **5** McRae/Ringer (Subaru) 18m 25s; **6** Kankkunen/Grist (Toyota) 18m 26s

SS6 Okupata (15.81 km)
1 Vatanen/Berglund (Subaru) 9m 36s; **2** Kankkunen/Grist (Toyota) 9m 37s; **3** Delecour/Grataloup (Ford) 9m 38s; **4** Auriol/Occelli (Toyota), McRae/Ringer (Subaru) 9m 39s; **6** Sainz/Moya (Lancia) 9m 40s

SS7 Hautaru North (17.53 km)
1 Auriol/Occelli (Toyota) 14m 02s; **2** Delecour/Grataloup (Ford) 14m 03s; 3 Vatanen/Berglund (Subaru) 14m 07s; **4** Sainz/Moya (Lancia) 14m 08s; **5** McRae/Ringer (Subaru) 14m 14s; **6** Kankkunen/Grist (Toyota) 14m 15s

SS8 Taupaki 1 (17.26 km)
1 Delecour/Grataloup (Ford) 11m 54s; **2** McRae/Ringer (Subaru), Vatanen/Berglund (Subaru) 11m 59s; **4** Sainz/Moya (Lancia) 12m 01s; **5** Kankkunen/Grist (Toyota) 12m 04s; **6** Auriol/Occelli (Toyota) 12m 09s

SS9 Hurimu 1 (5.95 km)
1 Delecour/Grataloup (Ford) 2m 57s; **2** Kankkunen/Grist (Toyota) 2m 59s; **3** McRae/Ringer (Subaru) 3m 00s; **4** Vatanen/Berglund (Subaru), Sainz/Moya (Lancia) 3m 01s; **6** Auriol/Occelli (Toyota) 3m 04s

SS10 Manawahe (24.10 km)
1 Vatanen/Berglund (Subaru) 17m 05s; **2** McRae/Ringer (Subaru) 17m 13s; **3** Delecour/Grataloup (Ford) 17m 14s; **4** Auriol/Occelli (Toyota) 17m 16s; **5** Kankkunen/Grist (Toyota) 17m 22s; **6** Sainz/Moya (Lancia) 17m 31s

SS11 Stanley (15.03 km)
1 Delecour/Grataloup (Ford) 10m 24s; **2** Kankkunen/Grist (Toyota), McRae/Ringer (Subaru) 10m 32s; **4** Auriol/Occelli (Toyota) 10m 36s; **5** Sainz/Moya (Lancia), Vatanen/Berglund (Subaru) 10m 37s

SS12 Motu (44.80 km)
1 McRae/Ringer (Subaru) 37m 57s; **2** Auriol/Occelli (Toyota) 38m 04s; **3** Sainz/Moya (Lancia) 38m 12s; **4** Delecour/Grataloup (Ford) 38m 39s; **5** Kankkunen/Grist (Toyota) 38m 50s; **6** G.Trelles/J.Del Buono (Lancia Delta HF Integrale) 38m 55s

SS13 Whakarau (32.80 km)
1 Auriol/Occelli (Toyota) 23m 32s; **2** McRae/Ringer (Subaru) 23m 36s; **3** Delecour/Grataloup (Ford) 23m 41s; **4** Sainz/Moya (Lancia) 23m 49s; **5** Kankkunen/Grist (Toyota) 23m 55s; **6** Trelles/Del Buono (Lancia) 24m 06s

SS14 Parikanapa (25.24 km)
1 Auriol /Occelli (Toyota) 18m 31s; **2** McRae/Ringer (Subaru) 18m 33s; **3** Delecour/Grataloup (Ford) 18m 35s; **4** Kankkunen/Grist (Toyota) 18m 36s; **5** Bourne/Freeth (Subaru) 18m 53s; **6** Sainz/Moya (Lancia) 18m 54s

SS15 Ruakaka (18.30 km)
1 McRae/Ringer (Subaru) 12m 36s; **2** Delecour/Grataloup (Ford) 12m 37s; **3** Auriol/Occelli (Toyota) 12m 38s; **4** Kankkunen/Grist (Toyota) 12m 44s; **5** Trelles/Del Buono (Lancia) 13m 01s; **6** Bourne/Freeth (Subaru) 13m 02s

SS16 Pehiri (29.48 km)
1 Delecour/Grataloup (Ford) 16m 38s; **2** Auriol/Occelli (Toyota) 16m 42s; **3** Sainz/Moya (Lancia), McRae/Ringer (Subaru) 16m 49s; **5** Kankkunen/Grist (Toyota) 16m 56s; **6** Trelles/Del Buono (Lancia) 17m 07s

SS17 Wharekopae (28.51 km)
1 Delecour/Grataloup (Ford) 17m 13s; **2** Auriol/Occelli (Toyota) 17m 15s; **3** McRae/Ringer (Subaru) 17m 16s; **4** Sainz/Moya (Lancia) 17m 25s; **5** Kankkunen/Grist (Toyota) 17m 26s; **6** Trelles/Del Buono (Lancia) 17m 33s

SS18 Old Creamery (8.15 km)
1 Kankkunen/Grist (Toyota) 4m 57s; **2** McRae/Ringer (Subaru) 4m 59s; **3** Delecour/Grataloup (Ford) 5m 00s; **4** Sainz/Moya (Lancia), Auriol/Occelli (Toyota) 5m 03s; **6** Bourne/Freeth (Subaru) 5m 07s

SS19 Manawahe-Rotoehu (20.95 km)
1 Delecour/Grataloup (Ford) 11m 12s; **2** McRae/Ringer (Subaru) 11m 24s; **3** Auriol/Occelli (Toyota) 11m 25s; **4** Kankkunen/Grist (Toyota) 11m 26s; **5** Sainz/Moya (Lancia) 11m 47s; **6** Bourne/Freeth (Subaru) 11m 48s

SS20 Taupaki 2 (17.26 km)
1 McRae/Ringer (Subaru) 11m 42s; **2** Sainz/Moya (Lancia), Auriol/Occelli (Toyota), Delecour/Grataloup (Ford) 11m 44s; **5** Kankkunen/Grist (Toyota) 11m 47s; **6** Bourne/Freeth (Subaru) 11m 51s

SS21 Hurimu 2 (5.95 km)
1 Kankkunen/Grist (Toyota) 2m 54s; **2** Sainz/Moya (Lancia), Delecour/Grataloup (Ford), McRae/Ringer (Subaru) 2m 55s; **5** Auriol/Occelli (Toyota) 2m 57s; **6** Bourne/Freeth (Subaru) 2m 58s

SS22 Hoddle Valley (10.04 km)
1 Sainz/Moya (Lancia) 6m 26s; **2** Kankkunen/Grist (Toyota) 6m 28s; **3** Bourne/Freeth (Subaru) 6m 29s; **4** McRae/Ringer (Subaru) 6m 30s; **5** Delecour/Grataloup (Ford) 6m 31s; **6** Auriol/Occelli (Toyota) 6m 33s

SS23 Tahaia (17.27 km)
1 Sainz/Moya (Lancia) 9m 58s; **2** Auriol/Occelli (Toyota), McRae/Ringer (Subaru) 10m 00s; **4** Kankkunen/Grist (Toyota) 10m 02s; **5** Delecour/Grataloup (Ford) 10m 06s; **6** Bourne/Freeth (Subaru) 10m 08s

SS24 Boddies (9.37 km)
1 Sainz/Moya (Lancia) 6m 11s; **2** Delecour/Grataloup (Ford), Kankkunen/Grist (Toyota) 6m 17s; **4** McRae/Ringer (Subaru) 6m 20s; **5** Trelles/Del Buono (Lancia) 6m 23s; **6** Auriol/Occelli (Toyota) 6m 24s

SS25 Mystery Creek (5.48 km)
1 McRae/Ringer (Subaru) 4m 13s; **2** Auriol/Occelli (Toyota), Kankkunen/Grist (Toyota) 4m 14s; **4** Delecour/Grataloup (Ford), Bourne/Freeth (Subaru) 4m 19s; **6** Sainz/Moya (Lancia) 4m 21s

SS26 Maungakawa (7.94 km)
1 Sainz/Moya (Lancia) 5m 04s; **2** Delecour/Grataloup (Ford) 5m 05s; **3** McRae/Ringer (Subaru) 5m 06s; **4** Kankkunen/Grist (Toyota) 5m 07s; **5** Bourne/Freeth (Subaru) 5m 09s; **6** Allport/Robb (Mazda) 5m 10s

SS27 Piakonui Loop (9.43 km)
1 Sainz/Moya (Lancia) 6m 43s; **2** Delecour/Grataloup (Ford) 6m 48s; **3** Kankkunen/Grist (Toyota) 6m 49s; **4** Bourne/Freeth (Subaru) 6m 51s; **5** McRae/Ringer (Subaru) 6m 52s; **6** Trelles/Del Buono (Lancia) 6m 56s

SS28 Maramarua Forest West (12.95 km)
1 Sainz/Moya (Lancia) 7m 03s; **2** Kankkunen/Grist (Toyota), McRae/Ringer (Subaru) 7m 04s; **4** Bourne/Freeth (Subaru) 7m 08s; **5** Auriol/Occelli (Toyota) 7m 09s; **6** Delecour/Grataloup (Ford) 7m 12s

SS29 Maramarua HQ (10.54 km)
1 Sainz/Moya (Lancia) 5m 58s; **2** Delecour/Grataloup (Ford) 6m 02s; **3** McRae/Ringer (Subaru) 6m 05s; **4** Kankkunen/Grist (Toyota) 6m 07s; **5** Auriol/Occelli (Toyota) 6m 10s; **6** Bourne/Freeth (Subaru) 6m 13s

SS30 Totara Park 2 (2.07 km)
1 Kankkunen/Grist (Toyota) 1m 13s; **2** Sainz/Moya (Lancia), Delecour/Grataloup (Ford), McRae/Ringer (Subaru) 1m 14s; **5** Auriol/Occelli (Toyota) 1m 15s; **6** Bourne/Freeth (Subaru) 1m 16s

SS31 Ellerslie Racecourse (2.87 km)
1 Kankkunen/Grist (Toyota) 1m 54s; **2** Auriol/Occelli (Toyota), McRae/Ringer (Subaru), Bourne/Freeth (Subaru) 1m 55s; **5** Sainz/Moya (Lancia), Delecour/Grataloup (Ford) 1m 56s

SS32 Riverhead 1 (11.30 km)
1 Auriol/Occelli (Toyota) 5m 31s; **2** Sainz/Moya (Lancia) 5m 32s; **3** Delecour/Grataloup (Ford) 5m 33s; **4** McRae/Ringer (Subaru) 5m 34s; **5** Kankkunen/Grist (Toyota) 5m 35s; **6** Bourne/Freeth (Subaru) 5m 37s

SS33 Kiwitahi (14.33 km)
1 Delecour/Grataloup (Ford) 7m 23s; **2** Auriol/Occelli (Toyota) 7m 24s; **3** Sainz/Moya (Lancia) 7m 28s; **4** Kankkunen/Grist (Toyota) 7m 30s; **5** McRae/Ringer (Subaru) 7m 31s; **6** Bourne/Freeth (Subaru) 7m 35s

SS34 Burnside (16.66 km)
1 McRae/Ringer (Subaru) 9m 58s; **2** Delecour/Grataloup (Ford) 10m 02s; **3** Auriol/Occelli (Toyota) 10m 04s; **4** Kankkunen/Grist (Toyota) 10m 11s; **5** Sainz/Moya (Lancia) 10m 19s; **6** Bourne/Freeth (Subaru) 10m 23s

SS35 Kaipara Hills (16.19 km)
1 McRae/Ringer (Subaru) 10m 54s; **2** Auriol/Occelli (Toyota) 11m 00s; **3** Sainz/Moya (Lancia) 11m 06s; **4** Delecour/Grataloup (Ford) 11m 08s; **5** Kankkunen/Grist (Toyota) 11m 20s; **6** Bourne/Freeth (Subaru) 11m 21s

SS36 Riverhead 2 (11.30 km)
1 Auriol/Occelli (Toyota) 5m 29s; **2** McRae/Ringer (Subaru) 5m 36s; **3** Delecour/Grataloup (Ford) 5m 38s; **4** Sainz/Moya (Lancia) 5m 39s; **5** Kankkunen/Grist (Toyota), Bourne/Freeth (Subaru) 5m 40s

Major Retirements

4	Vatanen/Berglund Accident	Subaru Legacy RS SS12	Gr A
6	Biasion/Siviero Accident	Ford Escort Cosworth SS4	Gr A
9	Dunkerton/Gocentas Engine	Mitsubishi Lancer RS-E SS4	Gr A
11	Recalde/Christie Engine	Lancia Delta HF Integrale SS4	Gr N
15	Haider/Wendel Gearbox	Audi Coupé S2 SS16	Gr A
17	Gottlicher/Rosenberger	Ford Sierra Cosworth SS11	Gr N
20	Stokes/Judd	Ford Escort Cosworth SS6	Gr A

FIA Class Winners

A8 Over 2000 cc	McRae/Ringer Subaru Legacy RS
A7 1600-2000 cc	No starters
A6 1300-1600 cc	Artemenko/Timkovsky Lada Samara
A5 Up to 1300 cc	Slee/de Leeuwe Subaru Vivio
N4 Over 2000 cc	Fujimoto/Ichino Mitsubishi Lancer RS-E
N3 1600-2000 cc	No finishers
N2 1300-1600 cc	Shiragami/Moriya Mitsubishi Mirage
N1 Up to 1300 cc	No starters

Rally Leaders

SS1 Sainz, Auriol, Kankkunen; **SS2** McRae, Kankkunen; **SS3-4** Vatanen; **SS5** Delecour, Sainz; **SS6-8** Delecour; **SS9-11** Vatanen; **SS12-13** McRae; **SS14** Auriol; **SS15** McRae; **SS16-19** Auriol; **SS20** McRae, Auriol; **SS21-36** McRae

World Championship Points

Drivers
1 Kankkunen 71; **2** Delecour 70; **3** Biasion 66; **4** Auriol 59; **5** McRae 44; **6** Sainz 35; **7** Alén 25; **8** Aghini, Trelles; **10** Jonsson 20, etc.

Manufacturers
1 Toyota, Ford 111; **3** Lancia 57; **4** Subaru 56; **5** Mitsubishi 47

FIA Cup for Production Car Drivers
1 Fassina 36; **2** Coutinho 24; **3** Spiliotis, Bäcklund, Shamji, Manfrinato, Bin Sulayem, Fujimoto 13, etc.

FIA Cup for Manufacturers
1 GME 36; **2** Skoda 29; **3** Citroën 24; **4** Peugeot 22; **5** Lada 18, etc.

Route Details

Leg 1
Thursday, 5 August, Manukau-Rotorua. 9 special stages (132.74 km) in a total route of 483.74 km
Leg 2
Friday, 6 August, Rotorua-Rotorua. 10 special stages (247.36 km) in a total route of 690.33 km
Leg 3
Saturday, 7 August, Rotorua-Auckland. 11 special stages (108.30 km) in a total route of 585.06 km
Leg 4
Sunday, 8 August, Auckland-Auckland. 6 special stages (85.25 km) in a total route of 273.04 km

Weather

Mainly dry, but wet in the fourth leg

Special Stage Analysis

	1	2	3	4	5	6
Sainz (Lancia)	9	5	4	7	4	5
Delecour (Ford)	8	11	8	3	4	2
McRae (Subaru)	7	13	6	6	4	-
Auriol (Toyota)	6	10	3	5	5	5
Kankkunen (Toyota)	5	7	2	7	11	3
Vatanen (Subaru)	3	2	1	3	2	-
Bourne (Subaru)	1	1	1	3	4	12
Biasion (Ford)	-	-	1	-	1	1
Trelles (Lancia)	-	-	-	-	2	5
Allport (Mazda)	-	-	-	-	2	1

Easy does it: Christine Driano had to finish in New Zealand no matter what, and drove her Citroën accordingly.

Finish Lines

Carlos Sainz endured a frustrating event, finishing fourth after setting more fastest times than anyone else. Electrical problems during the third leg scuppered any chance of a **Lancia** victory...**Yoshio Fujimoto** won Group N by a convincing margin in his **Lancer Evolution**... **'Possum' Bourne** was the top New Zealander. He finished a steady sixth in the third 555 **Subaru,** making sure of Pacific-Asian Championship points... **Gustavo Trelles** drove the entire rally with a broken wrist following his accident in Argentina. He still came seventh...**Ari Vatanen** was very much in contention for victory until he clouted a rock and tore a front wheel off his **Legacy**...**Neil Allport** ripped a front wheel off his **Mazda** as well, but survived...**Christine Driano** cruised round yet another World Championship event in her **Citroën AX,** but a finish brought her a step closer to the Ladies' title.

Results

1	Colin McRae/ Derek Ringer	Subaru Legacy RS 6h 12m 31s	Gr A
2	François Delecour/ Daniel Grataloup	Ford Escort Cosworth 6h 12m 58s	Gr A
3	Didier Auriol/ Bernard Occelli	Toyota Celica Turbo 4WD 6h 13m 00s	Gr A
4	Carlos Sainz/ Luis Moya	Lancia Delta HF Integrale 6h 14m 38s	Gr A
5	Juha Kankkunen/ Nicky Grist	Toyota Celica Turbo 4WD 6h 15m 26s	Gr A
6	'Possum' Bourne/ Rodger Freeth	Subaru Legacy RS 6h 20m 46s	Gr A
7	Gustavo Trelles/ Jorge Del Buono	Lancia Delta HF Integrale 6h 23m 48s	Gr A
8	Neil Allport/ Jim Robb	Mazda 323 Turbo GT-R 6h 36m 58s	Gr A
9	Joe McAndrew/ Bob Haldane	Subaru Legacy RS 6h 43m 29s	Gr A
10	Yoshio Fujimoto/ Hakaru Ichino	Mitsubishi Lancer RS-E 6h 43m 58s	Gr N

75 starters, 46 finishers

Previous Winners

1969	Grady Thompson/Rick Rimmer	Holden Monaro
1970	Paul Adams/Don Fenwick	BMW 2002
1971	Bruce Hodgson/Mike Mitchell	Ford Lotus Cortina
1972	Andrew Cowan/Jim Scott	Mini 1275GT
1973	Hannu Mikkola/Jim Porter	Ford Escort RS1600
1975	Mike Marshall/Arthur McWatt	Ford Escort RS1600
1976	Andrew Cowan/Jim Scott	Hillman Avenger
1977	Fulvio Bacchelli/Francesco Rosetti	Fiat 131 Abarth
1978	Russell Brookes/Chris Porter	Ford Escort RS
1979	Hannu Mikkola/Arne Hertz	Ford Escort RS
1980	Timo Salonen/Seppo Harjanne	Datsun 160J
1981	Jim Donald/Kevin Lancaster	Ford Escort RS
1982	Björn Waldegård/Hans Thorszelius	Toyota Celica Turbo
1983	Walter Röhrl/Christian Geistdörfer	Lancia Rally 037
1984	Stig Blomqvist/Björn Cederberg	Audi Quattro A2
1985	Timo Salonen/Seppo Harjanne	Peugeot 205 Turbo 16
1986	Juha Kankkunen/Juha Piironen	Peugeot 205 Turbo 16
1987	Franz Wittmann/Jorg Pettermann	Lancia Delta HF 4x4
1988	Josef Haider/Ferdinand Hinterleitner	Opel Kadett GSi
1989	Ingvar Carlsson/Per Carlsson	Mazda 323 Turbo 4x4
1990	Carlos Sainz/Luis Moya	Toyota Celica GT4
1991	Carlos Sainz/Luis Moya	Toyota Celica GT4
1992	Carlos Sainz/Luis Moya	Toyota Celica Turbo 4WD

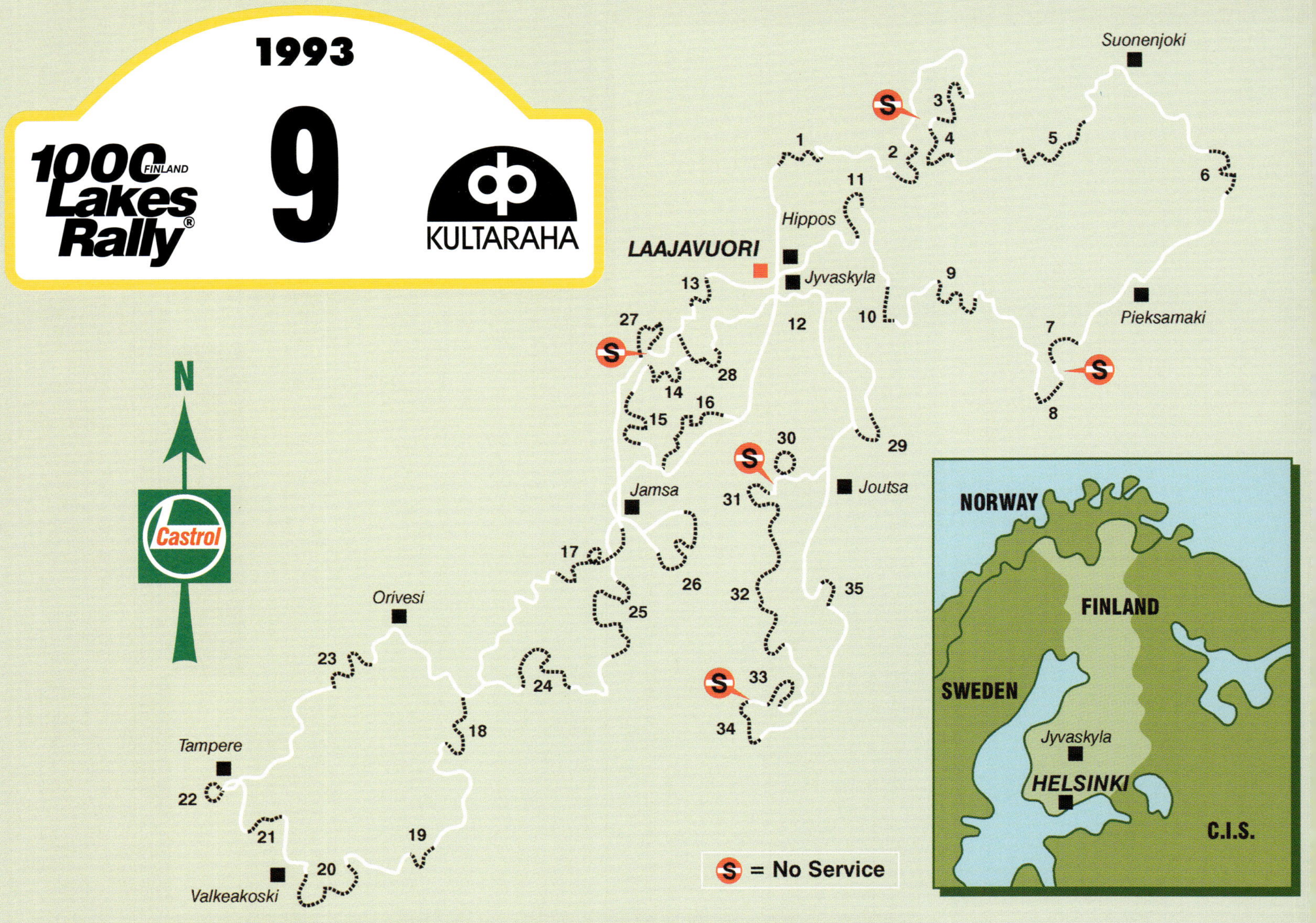

1000 Lakes Rally, 27-29 August, FIA World Rally Championship Round 9

Leading Entries

1	Didier Auriol/ Bernard Occelli	Toyota Celica Turbo 4WD Gr A
2	Ari Vatanen/ Bruno Berglund	Subaru Impreza 555 Gr A
3	Kenneth Eriksson/ Staffan Parmander	Mitsubishi Lancer RS-E Gr A
4	Juha Kankkunen/ Denis Giraudet	Toyota Celica Turbo 4WD Gr A
5	Markku Alén/ Ilkka Kivimäki	Subaru Impreza 555 Gr A
6	Armin Schwarz/ Nicky Grist	Mitsubishi Lancer RS-E Gr A
7	Malcolm Wilson/ Bryan Thomas	Ford Escort Cosworth Gr A
8	Hannu Mikkola/ Arne Hertz	Toyota Celica Turbo 4WD Gr A
9	Sebastian Lindholm/ Timo Hantunen	Ford Escort Cosworth Gr A
10	Bruno Thiry/ Stéphane Prévot	Opel Astra GSi Gr A
11	Jarmo Kytölehto/ Arto Kapanen	Mitsubishi Galant VR-4 Gr N
12	Lasse Lampi/ Pentii Kuukkala	Mitsubishi Galant VR-4 Gr A
13	Tommi Mäkinen/ Seppo Harjanne	Lancia Delta HF Integrale Gr A
15	Esa Saarenpaa/ Lasse Hirvijarvi	Audi Coupé S2 Gr A
16	Marcus Grönholm/ Voitto Silander	Toyota Celica Turbo 4WD Gr A
17	Mika Sohlberg/ Risto Mannisenmaki	Mitsubishi Galant VR-4 Gr A
18	Tomas Radström/ Anders Dawidson	Toyota Celica Turbo Gr A
19	Joukko Puhakka/ Keijo Eerola	Mitsubishi Galant VR-4 Gr N
20	Juha Hellman/ Tapio Jarvi	Mitsubishi Galant VR-4 Gr N
21	Kari Kivenne/ Juha Oksa	Mitsubishi Galant VR-4 Gr N

Special Stage Times

SS1 Valkola (8.46 km)
1 J.Kankkunen/D.Giraudet (Toyota Celica Turbo 4WD) 4m 47s; **2** D.Auriol/B.Occelli (Toyota Celica Turbo 4WD) 4m 48s; **3** A.Vatanen/B.Berglund (Subaru Impreza 555) 4m 53s; **4** T.Mäkinen/ S.Harjanne (Lancia Delta HF Integrale) 4m 57s; **5** K.Eriksson/ S.Parmander (Mitsubishi Lancer RS-E) 4m 58s; **6** M.Grönholm/V.Silander (Toyota Celica Turbo 4WD) 4m 59s

SS2 Lankamaa (14.99 km)
1 Kankkunen/Giraudet (Toyota) 7m 18s; **2** Auriol/ Occelli (Toyota), Vatanen/Berglund (Subaru) 7m 21s; **4** M.Wilson/B.Thomas (Ford Escort Cosworth) 7m 28s; **5** Mäkinen/Harjanne (Lancia) 7m 29s; **6** Eriksson/Parmander (Mitsubishi) 7m 30s

SS3 Kalliokoski (16.85 km)
1 Vatanen/Berglund (Subaru) 7m 58s; **2** Auriol/ Occelli (Toyota) 7m 59s; **3** Kankkunen/Giraudet (Toyota) 8m 00s; **4** Mäkinen/Harjanne (Lancia) 8m 05s; **5** Wilson/Thomas (Ford), Grönholm/Silander (Toyota) 8m 07s

SS4 Hannula (12.31 km)
1 Auriol/Occelli (Toyota) 7m 02s; **2** Kankkunen/ Giraudet (Toyota) 7m 03s; **3** Vatanen/Berglund (Subaru) 7m 05s; **4** Eriksson/Parmander (Mitsubishi), Wilson/Thomas (Ford), Mäkinen/Harjanne (Lancia) 7m 10s

SS5 Myhinpää (15.28 km)
1 Vatanen/Berglund (Subaru), Kankkunen/Giraudet (Toyota) 7m 18s; **3** Auriol/Occelli (Toyota) 7m 26s; **4** Mäkinen/Harjanne (Lancia), Grönholm/Silander (Toyota) 7m 29s; **6** Eriksson/Parmander (Mitsubishi), S.Lindholm/T.Hantunen (Ford Escort Cosworth) 7m 30s

SS6 Jappila (17.70 km)
1 Auriol/Occelli (Toyota) 8m 27s; **2** Vatanen/Berglund (Subaru), Kankkunen/Giraudet (Toyota) 8m 30s; **4** Mäkinen/Harjanne (Lancia) 8m 38s; **5** Eriksson/ Parmander (Mitsubishi) 8m 40s; **6** Wilson/Thomas (Ford) 8m 41s

SS7 Tolkkala (9.53 km)
1 Vatanen/Berglund (Subaru) 5m 06s; **2** Auriol/ Occelli (Toyota) 5m 07s; **3** Kankkunen/Giraudet (Toyota) 5m 08s; **4** Wilson/Thomas (Ford) 5m 13s; **5** Mäkinen/Harjanne (Lancia) 5m 14s; **6** Lindholm/ Hantunen (Ford) 5m 15s

SS8 Kutemajärvi (6.67 km)
1 Vatanen/Berglund (Subaru) 3m 33s; **2** Auriol/ Occelli (Toyota), Kankkunen/Giraudet (Toyota) 3m 35s; **4** Mäkinen/Harjanne (Lancia) 3m 38s; **5** Eriksson/Parmander (Mitsubishi), Wilson/Thomas (Ford), A.Schwarz/N.Grist (Mitsubishi Lancer RS-E) 3m 41s

SS9 Haltulla (7.82 km)
1 Kankkunen/Giraudet (Toyota) 4m 05s; **2** Auriol/ Occelli (Toyota), Vatanen/Berglund (Subaru) 4m 07s; **4** Mäkinen/Harjanne (Lancia) 4m 08s; **5** Schwarz/ Grist (Mitsubishi) 4m 11s; **6** Eriksson/Parmander (Mitsubishi), Grönholm/Silander (Toyota), L.Lampi/ P.Kuukkala (Mitsubishi Galant VR-4) 4m 12s

SS10 Ruuhimäki (7.28 km)
1 Auriol/Occelli (Toyota) 4m 00s; **2** Vatanen/Berglund (Subaru), Kankkunen/Giraudet (Toyota) 4m 03s; **4** Eriksson/Parmander (Mitsubishi) 4m 07s; **5** Schwarz/ Grist (Mitsubishi), Mäkinen/Harjanne (Lancia) 4m 08s

SS11 Laukaa (12.33 km)
1 Kankkunen/Giraudet (Toyota) 6m 29s; **2** Auriol/ Occelli (Toyota), Vatanen/Berglund (Subaru) 6m 31s; **4** Wilson/Thomas (Ford), Mäkinen/Harjanne (Lancia) 6m 37s; **6** Eriksson/Parmander (Mitsubishi), Lampi/ Kuukkala (Mitsubishi), Grönholm/Silander (Toyota) 6m 40s

SS12 Harju (2.57 km)
1 Kankkunen/Giraudet (Toyota) 1m 52s; **2** Vatanen/ Berglund (Subaru) 1m 53s; **3** Auriol/Occelli (Toyota), Eriksson/Parmander (Mitsubishi), Wilson/Thomas (Ford) 1m 54s; **6** Schwarz/Grist (Mitsubishi), Mäkinen/Harjanne (Lancia), H.Mikkola/A.Hertz (Toyota Celica Turbo 4WD) 1m 55s

SS13 Kuoho (7.74 km)
1 Vatanen/Berglund (Subaru), Kankkunen/Giraudet (Toyota) 3m 52s; **3** Auriol/Occelli (Toyota) 3m 54s; **4** Mäkinen/Harjanne (Lancia) 3m 57s; **5** Lindholm/ Hantunen (Ford) 3m 58s; **6** Wilson/Thomas (Ford) 4m 00s

SS14 Parkkola (22.48 km)
1 Vatanen/Berglund (Subaru) 11m 33s; **2** Auriol/ Occelli (Toyota), Kankkunen/Giraudet (Toyota) 11m 36s; **4** Wilson/Thomas (Ford) 11m 52s; **5** Lindholm/ Hantunen (Ford) 11m 56s; **6** Mäkinen/Harjanne (Lancia) 12m 00s

SS15 Ehikki (17.01 km)
1 Auriol/Occelli (Toyota), Vatanen/Berglund (Subaru), Kankkunen/Giraudet (Toyota) 8m 25s; **4** Lindholm/Hantunen (Ford) 8m 41s; **5** Eriksson/Parmander (Mitsubishi) 8m 42s; **6** Mäkinen/Harjanne (Lancia) 8m 57s

SS16 Leustu (23.61 km)
1 Vatanen/Berglund (Subaru) 12m 13s; **2** Kankkunen/Giraudet (Toyota) 12m 15s; **3** Auriol/Occelli (Toyota) 12m 18s; **4** Mäkinen/Harjanne (Lancia) 12m 30s; **5** Lindholm/Hantunen (Ford) 12m 38s; **6** Eriksson/Parmander (Mitsubishi) 12m 39s

SS17 Ouninpohja (30.54 km)
1 Kankkunen/Giraudet (Toyota) 15m 05s; **2** Vatanen/Berglund (Subaru) 15m 09s; **3** Mäkinen/Harjanne (Lancia) 15m 14s; **4** Auriol/Occelli (Toyota) 15m 17s; **5** Eriksson/Parmander (Mitsubishi) 15m 24s; **6** Lampi/Kuukkala (Mitsubishi) 15m 35s

SS18 Västilä (17.17 km)
1 Auriol/Occelli (Toyota), Vatanen/Berglund (Subaru), Kankkunen/Giraudet (Toyota) 8m 30s; **4** Mäkinen/Harjanne (Lancia) 8m 34s; **5** Eriksson/Parmander (Mitsubishi) 8m 36s; **6** Schwarz/Grist (Mitsubishi) 8m 38s

SS19 Koivulahti (9.62 km)
1 Vatanen/Berglund (Subaru), Kankkunen/Giraudet (Toyota) 4m 53s; **3** Auriol/Occelli (Toyota), Mäkinen/Harjanne (Lancia) 4m 56s; **5** Lindholm/Hantunen (Ford) 4m 58s; **6** Eriksson/Parmander (Mitsubishi), Schwarz/Grist (Mitsubishi) 5m 00s

SS20 Uskila (22.48 km)
1 Auriol/Occelli (Toyota) 10m 58s; **2** Kankkunen/Giraudet (Mitsubishi) 11m 01s; **3** Vatanen/Berglund (Subaru) 11m 04s; **4**Mäkinen/Harjanne (Lancia) 11m 09s; **5** Eriksson/Parmander (Mitsubishi) 11m 11s; **6** Schwarz/Grist (Mitsubishi) 11m 12s

SS21 Savo (8.64 km)
1 Vatanen/Berglund (Subaru) 4m 39s; **2** Auriol/Occelli (Toyota) 4m 40s; **3** Eriksson/Parmander (Mitsubishi), Kankkunen/Giraudet (Toyota) 4m 41s; **5** Mäkinen/Harjanne (Lancia), Grönholm/Silander (Toyota) 4m 43s

SS22 Tampere (2.60 km)
1 Auriol/Occelli (Toyota) 1m 54s; **2** Kankkunen/Giraudet (Toyota) 1m 56s; **3** Eriksson/Parmander (Mitsubishi), Schwarz/Grist (Mitsubishi) 1m 57s; **5** Vatanen/Berglund (Subaru) 1m 58s; **6** Lampi/Kuukkala (Mitsubishi) 2m 00s

SS23 Siitima (14.70 km)
1 Auriol/Occelli (Toyota), Kankkunen/Giraudet (Toyota) 7m 38s; **3** Vatanen/Berglund (Subaru) 7m 42s; **4** Mäkinen/Harjanne (Lancia) 7m 45s; **5** Eriksson/Parmander (Mitsubishi) 7m 49s; **6** Mikkola/Hertz (Toyota), Grönholm/Silander (Toyota) 7m 52s

SS24 Päijälä (23.29 km)
1 Vatanen/Berglund (Subaru) 12m 37s; **2** Kankkunen/Giraudet (Toyota) 12m 41s; **3** Auriol/Occelli (Toyota), Mäkinen/Harjanne (Lancia) 12m 47s; **5** Mikkola/Hertz (Toyota) 12m 57s; **6** Eriksson/Parmander (Mitsubishi) 12m 59s

SS25 Hassi (36.27 km)
1 Vatanen/Berglund (Subaru) 19m 23s; **2** Kankkunen/Giraudet (Toyota) 19m 27s; **3** Mäkinen/Harjanne (Lancia) 19m 34s; **4** Eriksson/Parmander (Mitsubishi) 19m 42s; **5** Auriol/Occelli (Toyota) 19m 44s; **6** Mikkola/Hertz (Toyota) 19m 51s

SS26 Vaheri (20.94 km)
1 Vatanen/Berglund (Subaru) 10m 38s; **2** Auriol/Occelli (Toyota) 10m 48s; **3** Kankkunen/Giraudet (Toyota) 10m 49s; **4** Mäkinen/Harjanne (Lancia) 10m 57s; **5** Mikkola/Hertz (Toyota) 10m 59s; **6** Lindholm/Hantunen (Ford), Lampi/Kuukkala (Mitsubishi) 11m 03s

SS27 Sahloinen (12.32 km)
1 Kankkunen/Giraudet (Toyota) 6m 38s; **2** Vatanen/Berglund (Subaru) 6m 43s; **3** Auriol/Occelli (Toyota) 6m 46s; **4** Mäkinen/Harjanne (Lancia) 6m 52s; **5** Schwarz/Grist (Mitsubishi), Lindholm/Hantunen (Ford) 6m 54s

SS28 Surkee (21.29 km)
1 Kankkunen/Giraudet (Toyota) 11m 17s; **2** Vatanen/Berglund (Subaru) 11m 32s; **3** Eriksson/Parmander (Mitsubishi) 11m 34s; **4** Mäkinen/Harjanne (Lancia) 11m 40s; **5** Auriol/Occelli (Toyota) 11m 43s; **6** Lindholm/Hantunen (Ford) 11m 44s

SS29 Soimaharju (8.11 km)
1 Mäkinen/Harjanne (Lancia) 4m 25s; **2** Vatanen/Berglund (Subaru) 4m 26s; **3** Kankkunen/Giraudet (Toyota) 4m 27s; **4** Eriksson/Parmander (Mitsubishi) 4m 32s; **5** Lampi/Kuukkala (Mitsubishi) 4m 33s; **6** Auriol/Occelli (Toyota) 4m 34s

SS30 Mutanen (13.33 km)
1 Kankkunen/Giraudet (Toyota) 6m 46s; **2** Vatanen/Berglund (Subaru) 6m 49s; **3** Eriksson/Parmander (Mitsubishi) 6m 51s; **4** Mikkola/Hertz (Toyota) 6m 59s; **5** Auriol/Occelli (Toyota) 7m 01s; **6** Lampi/Kuukkala (Mitsubishi) 7m 02s

SS31 Topposphoja (7.04 km)
1 Kankkunen/Giraudet (Toyota) 4m 04s; **2** Eriksson/Parmander (Mitsubishi) 4m 09s; **3** Lindholm/Hantunen (Ford), Lampi/Kuukkala (Mitsubishi), Mäkinen/Harjanne (Lancia) 4m 12s; **6** Auriol/Occelli (Toyota), Vatanen/Berglund (Subaru), Schwarz/Grist (Mitsubishi), Mikkola/Hertz (Toyota) 4m 14s

SS32 Lempää (28.40 km)
1 Kankkunen/Giraudet (Toyota) 14m 14s; **2** Vatanen/Berglund (Subaru) 14m 24s; **3** Mäkinen/Harjanne (Lancia) 14m 25s; **4** Eriksson/Parmander (Mitsubishi) 14m 26s; **5** Auriol/Occelli (Toyota) 14m 32s; **6** Lindholm/Hantunen (Ford) 14m 33s

SS33 Yiemmainen (11.61 km)
1 Mäkinen/Harjanne (Lancia) 6m 33s; **2** Vatanen/Berglund (Subaru) 6m 35s; **3** Eriksson/Parmander (Mitsubishi), Kankkunen/Giraudet (Toyota) 6m 37s; **5** Auriol/Occelli (Toyota), Mikkola/Hertz (Toyota) 6m 41s

SS34 Mynnilä (8.36 km)
1 Vatanen/Berglund (Subaru), Eriksson/Parmander (Mitsubishi) 4m 18s; **3** Auriol/Occelli (Toyota), Mäkinen/Harjanne (Lancia) 4m 19s; **5** Kankkunen/Giraudet (Toyota), Grönholm/Silander (Toyota) 4m 21s

SS35 Vartiamäki (8.20 km)
1 Mäkinen/Harjanne (Lancia) 4m 26s; **2** Grönholm/Silander (Toyota) 4m 27s; **3** Schwarz/Grist (Mitsubishi), Lindholm/Hantunen (Ford) 4m 28s; **5** Auriol/Occelli (Toyota), Eriksson/Parmander (Mitsubishi), Kankkunen/Giraudet (Toyota) 4m 29s

A major rally team is like an army on the move. A small TTE detachment services the three Celicas.

Major Retirements

5	Alén/Kivimäki Accident	Subaru Impreza 555 SS1	Gr A
7	Wilson/Thomas Accident	Ford Escort Cosworth SS17	Gr A
17	Sohlberg/Mannisenmaki Transmission	Mitsubishi Galant VR-4 SS20	Gr A
18	Radström/Dawidson Fuel system	Toyota Celica Turbo 4WD SS19	Gr A
21	Kivenne/Oksa Mechanical	Mitsubishi Galant VR-4 SS32	Gr N

FIA Class Winners

A8 Over 2000 cc	Kankkunen/Giraudet Toyota Celica Turbo 4WD
A7 1600-2000 cc	Thiry/Prévot Opel Astra GSI
A6 1300-1600 cc	Heikkila/Liljama Alfa Romeo 33 4x4
A5 Up to 1300 cc	Sibera/Gross Skoda Favorit 136L
N4 Over 2000 cc	Kytölehto/Kapanen Mitsubishi Galant VR-4
N3 1600-2000 cc	Laakso/Niemi VW Golf GTI-16v
N2 1300-1600 cc	Jokinen/Peltonen Toyota Corolla 1600 GT
N1 Up to 1300 cc	Sundman/Sandstrom Suzuki Swift 1300

Rally Leaders

SS1-25 Kankkunen; **SS26** Vatanen; **SS27-35** Kankkunen

World Championship Points

Drivers
1 Kankkunen 91; **2** Auriol 71; **3** Delecour 70; **4** Biasion 66; **5** McRae 44; **6** Sainz 35; **7** Mäkinen, Eriksson 26; **9** Alén 25; **10** Aghini, Trelles 22

Manufacturers
1 Toyota 131; **2** Ford 111; **3** Subaru 73; **4** Lancia 67; **5** Mitsubishi 57

FIA Cup for Production Car Drivers
1 Fassina 36; **2** Coutinho 24; **3** Kytölehto 23, etc.

FIA Cup for Manufacturers
1 GME 46; **2** Skoda 37; **3** Peugeot, Citroën, Lada 24, etc.

Route Details

Leg 1
Friday, 27 August, Jyvaskyla-Jyvaskyla. 15 stages (179.17km) in a total route of 179.17 km
Leg 2
Saturday, 28 August, Jyvaskyla-Jyvaskyla. 13 stages (243.48 km) in a total route of 243.47 km
Leg 3
Sunday, 29 August, Jyvaskyla-Jyvaskyla. 7 stages (85.05 km) in a total route of 85.05 km

Weather

Dry and cool

Special Stage Analysis

	1	2	3	4	5	6
Kankkunen (Toyota)	17	10	6	-	2	-
Vatanen (Subaru)	15	13	4	-	1	1
Auriol (Toyota)	8	10	8	1	6	2
Mäkinen (Lancia)	3	-	6	17	4	3
Eriksson (Mitsubishi)	1	1	6	5	9	7
Grönholm (Toyota)	-	1	-	1	3	4
Lindholm (Ford)	-	-	2	1	5	5
Schwarz (Mitsubishi)	-	-	2	-	4	5
Wilson (Ford)	-	-	1	5	2	2
Lampi (Mitsubishi)	-	-	1	-	2	6
Mikkola (Toyota)	-	-	-	1	3	4

Finish Lines

Lancia was officially absent, but still picked up fourth place thanks to a strong performance from **Tommi Mäkinen** in an Astra-prepared Integrale...**Markku Alén** became the first notable retirement when he crashed his **Impreza** halfway through the first stage...**Jarmo Kytölehto** took Group N for the second year running and 11th overall in his **Galant** VR-4...He did rather better than the official Ralliart Europe **Lancers**: badly outgunned, **Kenneth Eriksson** and **Armin Schwarz** could do no better than fifth and ninth respectively. **Mitsubishi**'s suspect transmission hampered the latter, who did much of the first leg with a faulty front differential...**Toyota** conducted a transmission experiment of a different kind, fitting a prototype traction control system to **Hannu Mikkola**'s Celica; 30 years after he first entered the 1000 Lakes, he came seventh...**Bruno Thiry** demolished slender two-wheel drive opposition to give **Opel** maximum F2 points and 18th overall on his first 1000 Lakes...**Sebastian Lindholm** took a disappointed sixth in his **Escort**, having lost time through a misfire and steering trouble in the first leg...**Malcolm Wilson** cracked his shoulder in the second of two massive accidents in his **Escort;** he had held fifth in the early stages...**Tomas Radström** retired his **Celica** with fuel feed trouble.

Results

1	Juha Kankkunen/ Denis Giraudet	Toyota Celica Turbo 4WD 4h 23m 51s	Gr A
2	Ari Vatanen/ Bruno Berglund	Subaru Impreza 555 4h 24m 38s	Gr A
3	Didier Auriol/ Bernard Occelli	Toyota Celica Turbo 4WD 4h 26m 01s	Gr A
4	Tommi Mäkinen/ Seppo Harjanne	Lancia Delta HF Integrale 4h 28m 26s	Gr A
5	Kenneth Eriksson/ Staffan Parmander	Mitsubishi Lancer RS-E 4h 29m 32s	Gr A
6	Sebastian Lindholm/ Timo Hantunen	Ford Escort Cosworth 4h 31m 34s	Gr A
7	Hannu Mikkola/ Arne Hertz	Toyota Celica Turbo 4WD 4h 32m 33s	Gr A
8	Lasse Lampi/ Pentii Kuukkala	Mitsubishi Galant VR-4 4h 33m 18s	Gr A
9	Armin Schwarz/ Nicky Grist	Mitsubishi Lancer RS-E 4h 34m 06s	Gr A
10	Marcus Grönholm/ Voitto Silander	Toyota Celica Turbo 4WD 4h 40m 20s	Gr A

113 starters, 61 finishers

Previous Winners (since 1965)

1965	Timo Mäkinen/Pekka Keskitalo	Mini-Cooper S
1966	Timo Mäkinen/Pekka Keskitalo	Mini-Cooper S
1967	Timo Mäkinen/Pekka Keskitalo	Mini-Cooper S
1968	Hannu Mikkola/Anssi Jarvi	Ford Escort TC
1969	Hannu Mikkola/Anssi Jarvi	Ford Escort TC
1970	Hannu Mikkola/Gunnar Palm	Ford Escort TC
1971	Stig Blomqvist/Arne Hertz	Saab 96 V4
1972	Simo Lampinen/Klaus Sohlberg	Saab 96 V4
1973	Timo Mäkinen/Henry Liddon	Ford Escort RS1600
1974	Hannu Mikkola/John Davenport	Ford Escort RS1600
1975	Hannu Mikkola/Atso Aho	Toyota Corolla
1976	Markku Alén/Ilkka Kivimäki	Fiat Abarth 131
1977	Kyosti Hamalainen/Marti Tiukkanen	Ford Escort RS
1978	Markku Alén/Ilkka Kivimäki	Fiat Abarth 131
1979	Markku Alén/Ilkka Kivimäki	Fiat Abarth 131
1980	Markku Alén/Ilkka Kivimäki	Fiat Abarth 131
1981	Ari Vatanen/David Richards	Ford Escort RS
1982	Hannu Mikkola/Arne Hertz	Audi Quattro
1983	Hannu Mikkola/Arne Hertz	Audi Quattro
1984	Ari Vatanen/Terry Harryman	Peugeot 205 Turbo 16
1985	Timo Salonen/Seppo Harjanne	Peugeot 205 Turbo 16
1986	Juha Kankkunen/Juha Piironen	Peugeot 205 Turbo 16
1987	Markku Alén/Ilkka Kivimäki	Lancia Delta HF 4x4
1988	Markku Alén/Ilkka Kivimäki	Lancia Delta HF Integrale
1989	Mikael Ericsson/Claes Billstam	Mitsubishi Galant VR-4
1990	Carlos Sainz/Luis Moya	Toyota Celica GT4
1991	Juha Kankkunen/Juha Piironen	Lancia Delta HF Integrale
1992	Didier Auriol/Bernard Occelli	Lancia Delta HF Integrale

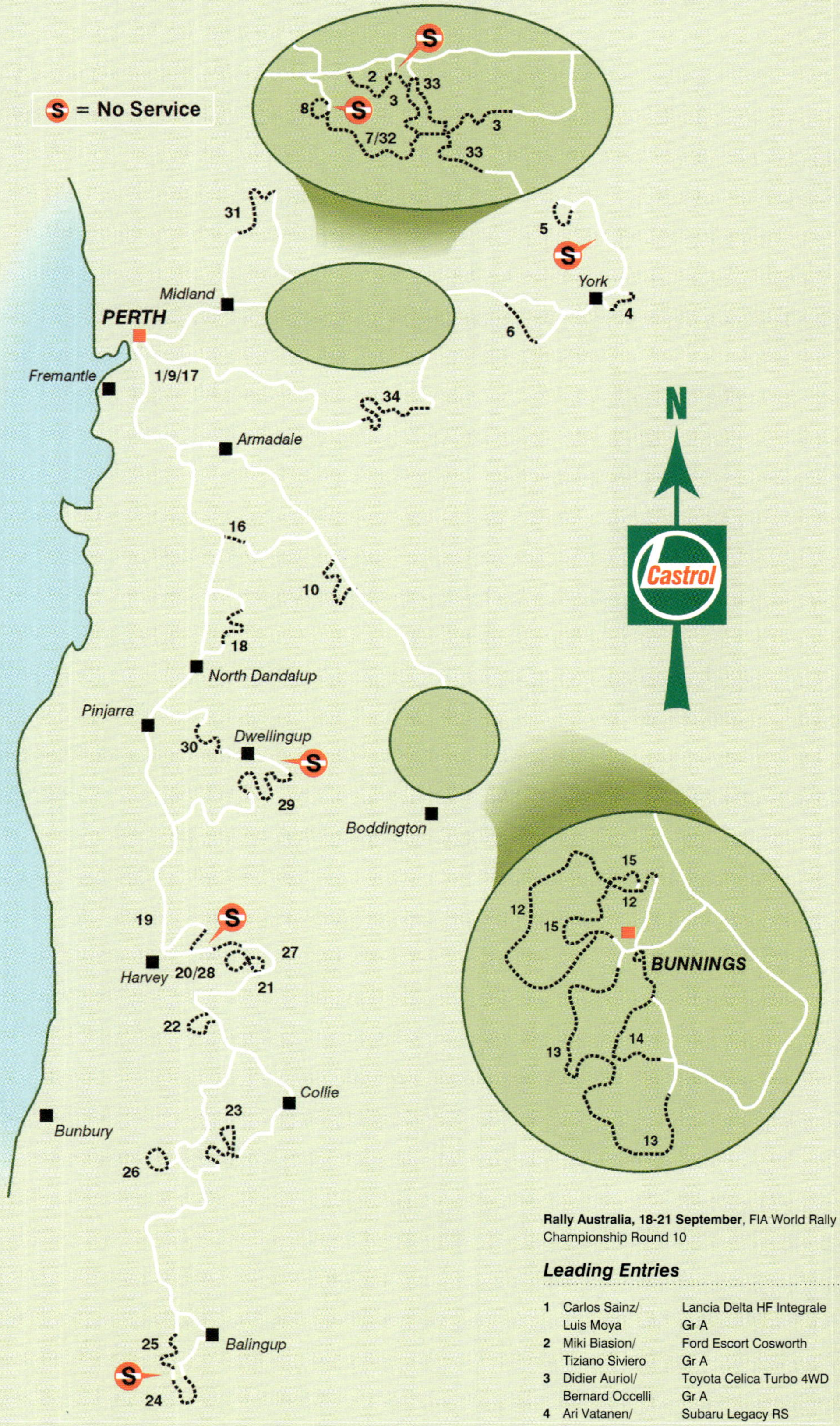

Rally Australia, 18-21 September, FIA World Rally Championship Round 10

Leading Entries

1	Carlos Sainz/ Luis Moya	Lancia Delta HF Integrale Gr A
2	Miki Biasion/ Tiziano Siviero	Ford Escort Cosworth Gr A
3	Didier Auriol/ Bernard Occelli	Toyota Celica Turbo 4WD Gr A
4	Ari Vatanen/ Bruno Berglund	Subaru Legacy RS Gr A
5	François Delecour/ Daniel Grataloup	Ford Escort Cosworth Gr A
6	Juha Kankkunen/ Nicky Grist	Toyota Celica Turbo 4WD Gr A
7	Colin McRae/ Derek Ringer	Subaru Legacy RS Gr A
8	Ross Dunkerton/ Fred Gocentas	Mitsubishi Lancer RS-E Gr A
9	'Possum' Bourne/ Rodger Freeth	Subaru Legacy RS Gr A
11	Jorge Recalde/ Martin Christie	Lancia Delta HF Integrale Gr N
12	Sepp Haider/ Klaus Wendel	Audi Coupé S2 Gr A
13	Ed Ordynski/ Mark Stacey	Mitsubishi Lancer RS-E Gr N
14	Yoshio Fujimoto/ Hakaru Ichino	Mitsubishi Lancer RS-E Gr N
15	Rob Herridge/ Rod Horsely	Subaru Legacy RS Gr N
16	John Buffum/ Tom Grimshaw	Honda Civic Gr A
17	Tolley Challis/ Rod Van Der Straaten	Ford Escort Cosworth Gr N
18	Neal Bates/ Coral Taylor	Toyota Celica Turbo Gr A
19	Wayne Hoy/ Murry Coote	Nissan Sunny GTI-R Gr A
20	Graham Alexander/ Jim Gleeson	Mitsubishi Galant VR-4 Gr A

Special Stage Times

SS1 Langley Park 1 (2.33 km)
1 J.Kankkunen/N.Grist (Toyota Celica Turbo 4WD) 1m 39s; **2** C.Sainz/L.Moya (Lancia Delta HF Integrale), D.Auriol/B.Occelli (Toyota Celica Turbo 4WD) 1m 41s; **4** M.Biasion/T.Siviero (Ford Escort Cosworth) 1m 42s; **5** R.Dunkerton/F.Gocentas (Mitsubishi Lancer RS-E) 1m 43s; **6** F.Delecour/ D.Grataloup (Ford Escort Cosworth) 1m 44s

SS2 Kev's (7.67 km)
1 Auriol/Occelli (Toyota), Kankkunen/Grist (Toyota) 4m 25s; **3** Sainz/Moya (Lancia) 4m 31s; **4** C.McRae/ D.Ringer (Subaru Legacy RS) 4m 32s; **5** A.Vatanen/ B.Berglund (Subaru Legacy RS) 4m 34s; **6** P.Bourne/R.Freeth (Subaru Legacy RS), Delecour/ Grataloup (Ford) 4m 37s

SS3 Flynns (32.20 km)
1 Auriol/Occelli (Toyota), Kankkunen/Grist (Toyota) 19m 44s; **3** McRae/Ringer (Subaru) 19m 59s; **4** Vatanen/Berglund (Subaru) 20m 06s; **5** Delecour/ Grataloup (Ford) 20m 36s; **6** Biasion/Siviero (Ford) 20m 40s

SS4 York Railway (5.30 km)
1 Auriol/Occelli (Toyota), Kankkunen/Grist (Toyota) 2m 33s; **3** McRae/Ringer (Subaru) 2m 36s; **4** Vatanen/Berglund (Subaru) 2m 37s; **5** Delecour/ Grataloup (Ford) 2m 40s; **6** Biasion/Siviero (Ford) 2m 45s

SS5 Muresk (6.81 km)
1 Kankkunen/Grist (Toyota) 3m 31s; **2** Auriol/Occelli (Toyota) 3m 32s; **3** Vatanen/Berglund (Subaru) 3m 35s; **4** McRae/Ringer (Subaru) 3m 36s; **5** Delecour/ Grataloup (Ford) 3m 39s; **6** Biasion/Siviero (Ford) 3m 46s

SS6 Mount Observation (11.69 km)
1 Kankkunen/Grist (Toyota) 6m 23s; **2** Auriol/Occelli (Toyota) 6m 26s; **3** Vatanen/Berglund (Subaru) 6m 29s; **4** McRae/Ringer (Subaru) 6m 33s; **5** Delecour/ Grataloup (Ford) 6m 35s; **6** Biasion/Siviero (Ford) 6m 47s

SS7 Helena 1 (30.05 km)
1 Kankkunen/Grist (Toyota) 17m 02s; **2** McRae/ Ringer (Subaru) 17m 29s; **3** Delecour/Grataloup (Ford) 17m 36s; **4** Biasion/Siviero (Ford) 17m 47s; **5** Vatanen/Berglund (Subaru) 18m 32s; **6** Dunkerton/ Gocentas (Mitsubishi) 18m 33s

SS8 Atkins (4.42 km)
1 Kankkunen/Grist (Toyota) 3m 14s; **2** Vatanen/ Berglund (Subaru) 3m 16s; **3** McRae/Ringer (Subaru) 3m 18s; **4** Delecour/Grataloup (Ford) 3m 23s; **5** Dunkerton/Gocentas (Mitsubishi) 3m 31s; **6** Biasion/Siviero (Ford), N.Bates/C.Taylor (Toyota Celica Turbo) 3m 32s

SS9 Langley Park 2 (2.33 km)
1 Kankkunen/Grist (Toyota), McRae/Ringer (Subaru) 1m 38s; **3** Biasion/Siviero (Ford), Delecour/Grataloup (Ford) 1m 39s; **5** Vatanen/Berglund (Subaru) 1m 40s; **6** Dunkerton/Gocentas (Mitsubishi) 1m 41s

SS10 TOS (15.67 km)
1 Kankkunen/Grist (Toyota) 8m 18s; **2** Vatanen/ Berglund (Subaru) 8m 23s; **3** McRae/Ringer (Subaru) 8m 24s; **4** Delecour/Grataloup (Ford) 8m 33s; **5** Biasion/Siviero (Ford) 8m 45s; **6** S.Haider/ K.Wendel (Audi Coupé S2), Bates/Taylor (Toyota) 9m 09s

SS11 Bunnings Central (6.96 km)
1 McRae/Ringer (Subaru) 4m 36s; **2** Vatanen/ Berglund (Subaru) 4m 38s; 3 Kankkunen/Grist (Toyota) 4m 41s; **4** Delecour/Grataloup (Ford) 4m 42s; **5** Biasion/Siviero (Ford) 4m 45s; **6** Dunkerton/ Gocentas (Mitsubishi) 4m 53s

SS12 Bunnings North (29.27 km)
1 Kankkunen/Grist (Toyota) 15m 15s; **2** McRae/ Ringer (Subaru) 15m 20s; **3** Vatanen/Berglund (Subaru) 15m 40s; **4** Delecour/Grataloup (Ford) 15m 44s; **5** Biasion/Siviero (Ford) 15m 52s; **6** Dunkerton/ Gocentas (Mitsubishi) 16m 26s

SS13 Bunnings West (36.67 km)
1 McRae/Ringer (Subaru) 20m 32s; **2** Vatanen/ Berglund (Subaru), Kankkunen/Grist (Toyota) 20m 38s; **4** Delecour/Grataloup (Ford) 21m 11s; **5** Biasion/Siviero (Ford) 21m 25s; **6** Dunkerton/ Gocentas (Mitsubishi) 21m 53s

SS14 Bunnings South (16.08 km)
1 McRae/Ringer (Subaru) 9m 20s; **2** Kankkunen/Grist (Toyota) 9m 28s; **3** Vatanen/Berglund (Subaru), Delecour/Grataloup (Ford) 9m 34s; **5** Biasion/Siviero (Ford) 9m 47s; **6** Dunkerton/ Gocentas (Mitsubishi) 10m 07s

SS15 Bunnings East (17.76 km)
1 Kankkunen/Grist (Toyota) 10m 11s; 2 McRae/Ringer (Subaru) 10m 13s; **3** Vatanen/Berglund (Subaru) 10m 26s; **4** Biasion/Siviero (Ford), Delecour/Grataloup (Ford) 10m 38s; **6** Haider/Wendel (Audi) 10m 53s

SS16 Roller Coaster (5.61 km)
1 Kankkunen/Grist (Toyota) 3m 00s; **2** McRae/Ringer (Subaru) 3m 07s; **3** Vatanen/Berglund (Subaru) 3m 09s; **4** Biasion/Siviero (Ford) 3m 12s; **5** Delecour/Grataloup (Ford) 3m 13s; **6** Haider/Wendel (Audi) 3m 18s

SS17 Langley Park 3 (2.44 km)
1 Kankkunen/Grist (Toyota) 1m 35s; **2** McRae/Ringer (Subaru) 1m 36s; **3** Biasion/Siviero (Ford), Vatanen/Berglund (Subaru), Delecour/Grataloup (Ford) 1m 37s; **6** Dunkerton/Gocentas (Mitsubishi) 1m 38s

SS18 Myara (10.81 km)
1 Kankkunen/Grist (Toyota) 6m 07s; **2** McRae/Ringer (Subaru) 6m 08s; **3** Vatanen/Berglund (Subaru) 6m 14s; **4** Delecour/Grataloup (Ford) 6m 27s; **5** Biasion/Siviero (Ford) 6m 28s; **6** Dunkerton/Gocentas (Mitsubishi) 6m 37s

SS19 Harvey Weir (8.19 km)
1 Kankkunen/Grist (Toyota) 4m 57s; 2 McRae/Ringer (Subaru) 5m 00s; 3 Vatanen/Berglund (Subaru) 5m 03s; **4** Delecour/Grataloup (Ford) 5m 13s; **5** Biasion/Siviero (Ford) 5m 18s; **6** Haider/Wendel (Audi) 5m 21s

SS20 Stirling West 1 (15.89 km)
1 Kankkunen/Grist (Toyota) 9m 45s; **2** Vatanen/Berglund (Subaru) 9m 50s; **3** McRae/Ringer (Subaru) 9m 51s; **4** Delecour/Grataloup (Ford) 10m 01s; **5** Biasion/Siviero (Ford) 10m 08s; **6** Haider/Wendel (Audi) 10m 22s

SS21 Stirling East (29.23 km)
1 Kankkunen/Grist (Toyota) 16m 39s; **2** McRae/Ringer (Subaru) 16m 49s; **3** Vatanen/Berglund (Subaru) 16m 58s; **4** Delecour/Grataloup (Ford) 17m 09s; **5** Biasion/Siviero (Ford) 17m 30s; **6** Dunkerton/Gocentas (Mitsubishi) 17m 47s

SS22 Brunswick (16.63 km)
1 Kankkunen/Grist (Toyota) 9m 35s; **2** McRae/Ringer (Subaru) 9m 42s; **3** Delecour/Grataloup (Ford) 9m 47s; **4** Vatanen/Berglund (Subaru) 9m 58s; **5** Biasion/Siviero (Ford) 10m 08s; **6** Dunkerton/Gocentas (Mitsubishi), Haider/Wendel (Audi) 10m 17s

SS23 Wellington Dam (45.00 km)
1 McRae/Ringer (Toyota) 26m 43s; **2** Kankkunen/Grist (Toyota) 26m 48s; **3** Vatanen/Berglund (Subaru) 27m 46s; **4** Biasion/Siviero (Ford) 27m 59s; **5** Haider/Wendel (Audi) 28m 36s; **6** Dunkerton/Gocentas (Mitsubishi) 28m 52s

SS24 Lewana (21.80 km)
1 McRae/Ringer (Subaru) 7m 42s; **2** Kankkunen/Grist (Toyota) 7m 46s; 3 Biasion/Siviero (Ford) 7m 58s; **4** Delecour/Grataloup (Ford) 8m 01s; **5** Vatanen/Berglund (Subaru) 8m 05s; **6** Haider/Wendel (Audi) 8m 09s

SS25 Ferndale (19.16 km)
1 Kankkunen/Grist (Toyota) 11m 26s; **2** McRae/Ringer (Subaru) 11m 34s; **3** Vatanen/Berglund (Subaru) 11m 49s; **4** Biasion/Siviero (Ford) 11m 59s; **5** Delecour/Grataloup (Ford) 12m 01s; **6** Dunkerton/Gocentas (Mitsubishi) 12m 19s

SS26 Dongara Ridge (11.86 km)
1 Kankkunen/Grist (Toyota) 6m 43s; **2** McRae/Ringer (Subaru) 6m 45s; 3 Vatanen/Berglund (Subaru) 6m 49s; **4** Delecour/Grataloup (Ford) 6m 56s; **5** Biasion/Siviero (Ford) 7m 01s; **6** Haider/Wendel (Audi) 7m 15s

SS27 Stirling North (15.65 km)
1 Kankkunen/Grist (Toyota) 8m 41s; **2** McRae/Ringer (Subaru) 8m 46s; **3** Vatanen/Berglund (Subaru) 8m 47s; **4** Delecour/Grataloup (Ford) 9m 03s; **5** Biasion/Siviero (Ford) 9m 21s; **6** Dunkerton/Gocentas (Mitsubishi) 9m 30s

SS28 Stirling West 2 (15.89 km)
1 Kankkunen/Grist (Toyota) 9m 41s; **2** McRae/Ringer (Subaru) 9m 43s; **3** Vatanen/Berglund (Subaru) 9m 45s; **4** Delecour/Grataloup (Ford) 10m 00s; **5** Biasion/Siviero (Ford) 10m 05s; **6** Dunkerton/Gocentas (Mitsubishi) 10m 23s

SS29 Murray Pines (20.35 km)
1 Kankkunen/Grist (Toyota) 13m 08s; **2** McRae/Ringer (Subaru) 13m 15s; **3** Vatanen/Berglund (Subaru) 13m 16s; **4** Delecour/Grataloup (Ford) 13m 38s; **5** Biasion/Siviero (Ford) 13m 48s; **6** Dunkerton/Gocentas (Mitsubishi) 13m 58s

SS30 Marrinup (10.49 km)
1 Kankkunen/Grist (Toyota) 5m 51s; **2** Vatanen/Berglund (Subaru) 5m 54s; **3** McRae/Ringer (Subaru) 5m 59s; **4** Biasion/Siviero (Ford) 6m 08s; **5** Dunkerton/Gocentas (Mitsubishi) 6m 21s; **6** Haider/Wendel (Audi) 6m 22s

SS31 Swan Valley (11.69 km)
1 Kankkunen/Grist (Toyota) 6m 50s; **2** McRae/Ringer (Subaru) 6m 54s; **3** Vatanen/Berglund (Subaru) 6m 59s; **4** Delecour/Grataloup (Ford) 7m 02s; **5** Biasion/Siviero (Ford) 7m 10s; **6** Haider/Wendel (Audi) 7m 12s

SS32 Helena 2 (30.05 km)
1 Vatanen/Berglund (Subaru) 16m 54s; **2** Kankkunen/Grist (Toyota) 17m 14s; **3** Delecour/Grataloup (Ford) 17m 29s; **4** Dunkerton/Gocentas (Mitsubishi), Haider/Wendel (Audi) 17m 43s; **6** Biasion/Siviero (Ford) 17m 50s

SS33 Wellbucket (15.44 km)
1 Vatanen/Berglund (Subaru) 9m 27s; **2** Kankkunen/Grist (Toyota) 9m 31s; **3** McRae/Ringer (Subaru) 9m 40s; **4** Dunkerton/Gocentas (Mitsubishi) 9m 46s; **5** Haider/Wendel (Audi) 9m 59s; **6** Delecour/Grataloup (Ford) 10m 29s

SS34 Beraking (30.34 km)
1 Vatanen/Berglund (Subaru) 15m 52s; **2** McRae/Ringer (Subaru) 15m 57s; **3** Kankkunen/Grist (Toyota) 16m 01s; **4** Dunkerton/Gocentas (Mitsubishi) 16m 36s; **5** Delecour/Grataloup (Ford) 16m 43s; **6** Haider/Wendel (Audi) 17m 13s

Major Retirements

1	Sainz/Moya Accident	Lancia Delta HF Integrale SS3	Gr A
2	Biasion/Siviero Electrics/OTL	Ford Escort Cosworth SS33	Gr A
3	Auriol/Occelli Engine	Toyota Celica Turbo 4WD SS7	Gr A
9	Bourne/Freeth Accident	Subaru Legacy RS SS3	Gr A
11	Recalde/Christie Suspension	Lancia Delta HF Integrale SS2	Gr N
14	Fujimoto/Ichino Transmission	Mitsubishi Lancer RS-E SS9	Gr N
15	Herridge/Horsely Withdrawn	Subaru Legacy RS SS7	Gr N

FIA Class Winners

A8 Over 2000 cc	Kankkunen/Grist Toyota Celica Turbo 4WD
A7 1600-2000 cc	No starters
A6 1300-1600 cc	No finishers
A5 Up to 1300 cc	Middleton/Middleton Daihatsu Charade 1.3i
N4 Over 2000 cc	Ordynski/Stacey Mitsubishi Lancer RS-E
N3 1600-2000 cc	Hynes/MacNeall Daihatsu Charade GTti
N2 1300-1600 cc	No finishers
N1 Up to 1300 cc	West/Best Suzuki Swift

Rally Leaders

SS1-34 Kankkunen

World Championship Points

Drivers
1 Kankkunen 111; **2** Delecour 82; **3** Auriol 71; **4** Biasion 66; **5** McRae 50; **6** Sainz 35; **7** Vatanen 30; **8** Mäkinen, Eriksson 26; **10** Alén 25, etc.

Manufacturers
1 Toyota 151; **2** Ford 125; **3** Subaru 90; **4** Mitsubishi 69; **5** Lancia 67

FIA Cup for Production Car Drivers
1 Fassina 36; **2** Coutinho 24; **3** Kytölehto 23

FIA Cup for Manufacturers
1 GME 46; **2** Skoda 37; **3** Peugeot, Citroën, Lada 24, etc.

Route Details

Leg 1
Saturday, 18 September, 9 stages (102.80 km) in a total route of 356.83 km
Leg 2
Sunday, 19 September, 8 stages (130.35 km) in a total route of 411.99 km
Leg 3
Monday, 20 September, 13 stages (240.95 km) in a total route of 882.89 km
Leg 4
Tuesday, 21 September, 4 stages (87.52 km) in a total route of 266.30 km

Weather

Cold, wet at first

Special Stage Analysis

	1	2	3	4	5	6
Kankkunen (Toyota)	26	6	2	-	-	-
McRae (Subaru)	6	16	7	3	-	-
Vatanen (Subaru)	3	6	17	3	4	-
Auriol (Toyota)	3	3	-	-	-	-
Sainz (Lancia)	-	1	1	-	-	-
Delecour (Ford)	-	-	5	17	7	3
Biasion (Ford)	-	-	3	7	15	6
Dunkerton (Mitsubishi)	-	-	-	3	3	15
Haider (Mitsubishi)	-	-	-	1	2	11
Bates (Toyota)	-	-	-	-	-	2

Ed Ordynski demolished the opposition in Group N, which was dominated by the latest Mitsubishi.

Finish Lines

Ford had a thoroughly disappointing rally, but **Miki Biasio**n definitely had the worst of it: he had moved up to a secure third place when his **Escort** was halted by a mysterious electronic problem two stages from the finish. As a result, his team-mate, **François Delecour**, collected third instead. The Frenchman had been delayed for 12 minutes by a similar electronic fault the day before...**Ross Dunkerton** drove sensibly to make sure of fourth in the Ralliart Australia **Lancer,** despite intercom trouble during the first leg and a road penalty...**Mitsubishi** also won Group N thanks to **Ed Ordynski**, who was hardly opposed once **Yoshio Fujimoto** crashed...**Ari Vatanen** went off on two of the first three stages, but it was an electronic problem with his re-shelled **Legacy** on the seventh stage that knocked him out of the running for good...**Sepp Haider** scored an encouraging result in the **Konrad Schmidt Quattro** S2, despite tackling around half of the rally with low boost, thanks to an air leak....**Neal Bates** might have brought Toyota Australia's **Celica** into the top six if it hadn't been for a broken propshaft on SS25.

Results

1	Juha Kankkunen/ Nicky Grist	Toyota Celica Turbo 4WD 5h 19m 58s	Gr A
2	Ari Vatanen/ Bruno Berglund	Subaru Legacy RS 5h 25m 50s	Gr A
3	François Delecour/ Daniel Grataloup	Ford Escort Cosworth 5h 43m 42s	Gr A
4	Ross Dunkerton/ Fred Gocentas	Mitsubishi Lancer RS-E 5h 46m 18s	Gr A
5	Sepp Haider/ Klaus Wendel	Audi Coupé S2 5h 48m 48s	Gr A
6	Colin McRae/ Derek Ringer	Subaru Legacy RS 5h 56m 33s	Gr A
7	Ed Ordynski/ Mark Stacey	Mitsubishi Lancer RS-E 5h 58m 42s	Gr N
8	Neal Bates/ Coral Taylor	Toyota Celica Turbo 6h 04m 50s	Gr A
9	Kiyoshi Inoue/ Satoshi Hayashi	Mitsubishi Lancer RS-E 6h 09m 04s	Gr N
10	David Officer/ Kate Officer	Mitsubishi Lancer RS-E 6h 11m 43s	Gr N

84 starters, 44 finishers

Previous Winners

1989 Juha Kankkunen/Juha Piironen Toyota Celica GT4
1990 Juha Kankkunen/Juha Piironen Lancia Delta HF Integrale
1991 Juha Kankkunen/Juha Piironen Lancia Delta HF Integrale
1992 Didier Auriol/Bernard Occelli Lancia Delta HF Integrale

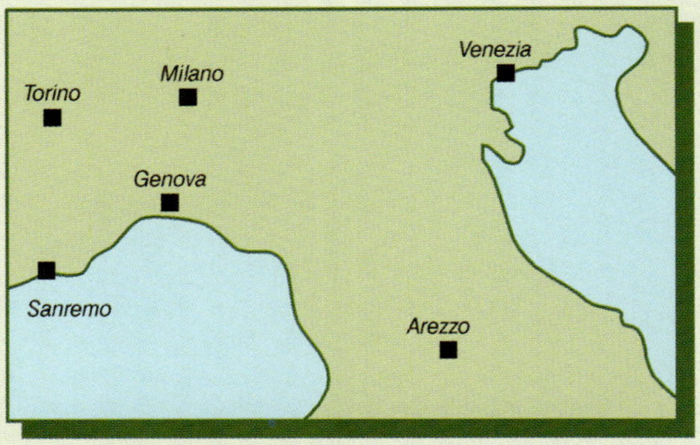

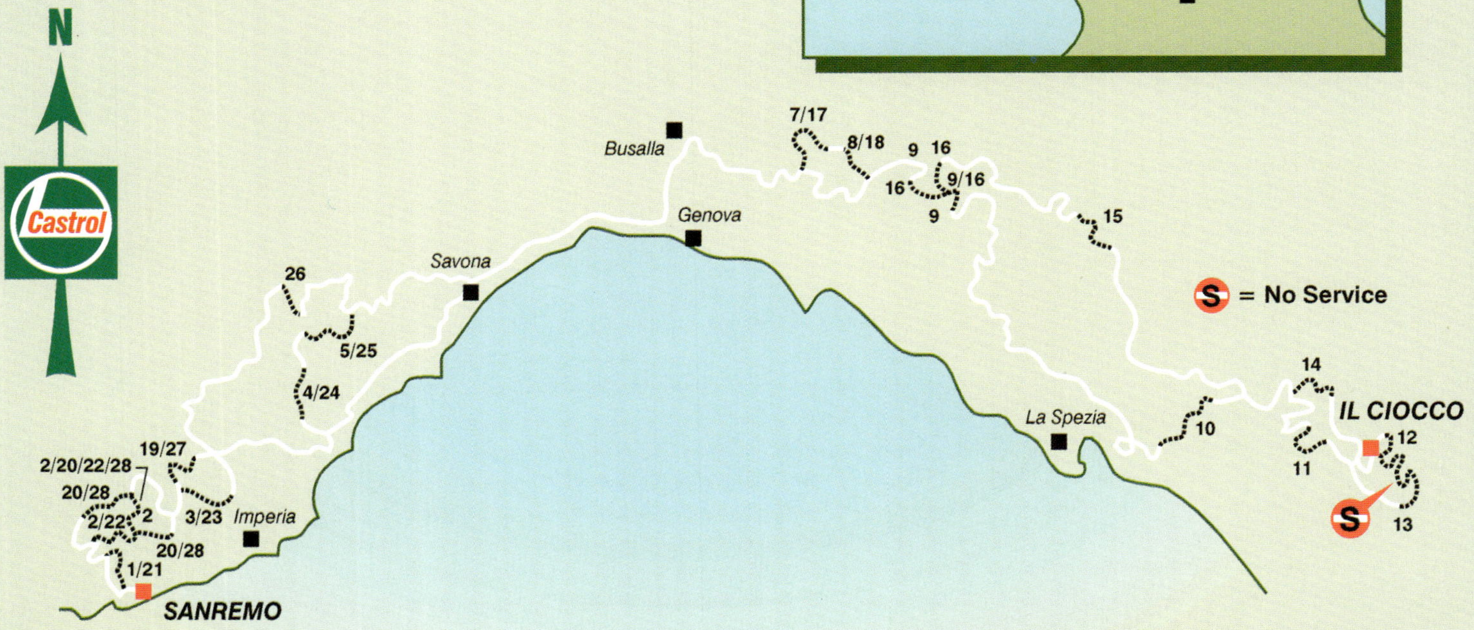

Sanremo Rally, 11-13 October, FIA World Rally Championship Round 11

Leading Entries

1	Andrea Aghini/ Sauro Farnocchia	Lancia Delta HF Integrale Gr A
2	François Delecour/ Daniel Grataloup	Ford Escort Cosworth Gr A
3	Piero Liatti/ Alessandro Alessandrini	Subaru Legacy RS Gr A
4	Carlos Sainz/ Luis Moya	Lancia Delta HF Integrale Gr A
5	Miki Biasion/ Tiziano Siviero	Ford Escort Cosworth Gr A
6	Alessandro Fiorio/ Vittorio Brambilla	Lancia Delta HF Integrale Gr A
7	Franco Cunico/ Steve Evangelisti	Ford Escort Cosworth Gr A
8	Bruno Thiry/ Stéphane Prévot	Opel Astra GSi Gr A
9	Piero Longhi/ Maurizio Imerito	Lancia Delta HF Integrale Gr A
10	Dario Cerrato/ Lucio Guizzardi	Lancia Delta HF Integrale Gr A
11	Patrick Snijers/ Dany Colebunders	Ford Escort Cosworth Gr A
12	Gilberto Pianezzola/ Loris Roggia	Lancia Delta HF Integrale Gr A
14	Pavel Sibera/ Petr Gross	Skoda Favorit 136L Gr A
15	Mohammed Bin Sulayem/ Ronan Morgan	Ford Escort Cosworth Gr N
16	Christine Driano/ Marie-Christine Lallement	Citroën AX GTI Gr A
18	Ladislav Krecek/ Jan Krecman	Lancia Delta HF Integrale Gr A
19	Alessandro Fassina/ Luigi Pirollo	Mazda 323 Turbo GT-R Gr N
20	Emil Triner/ Jiri Klima	Skoda Favorit 136L Gr A
21	Christophe Spiliotis/ Hervé Thibaud	Ford Escort Cosworth Gr N
22	Giovanni Manfrinato/ Claudio Condotta	Ford Escort Cosworth Gr N

Special Stage Times

SS1 Coldirodi 1 (12.35 km)
1 F.Delecour/D.Grataloup (Ford Escort Cosworth) 8m 25s; **2** P.Liatti/A.Alessandrini (Subaru Legacy RS) 8m 35s; **3** C.Sainz/L.Moya (Lancia Delta HF Integrale) 8m 39s; **4** M.Biasion/T.Siviero (Ford Escort Cosworth) 8m 41s; **5** A.Aghini/S.Farnocchia (Lancia Delta HF Integrale) 8m 48s; **6** P.Snijers/D.Colebunders (Ford Escort Cosworth) 8m 50s

SS2 Apricale-Molini di Trioria (36.35 km)
1 Delecour/Grataloup (Ford) 25m 36s; **2** Biasion/Siviero (Ford) 25m 47s; **3** Aghini/Farnocchia (Lancia) 25m 48s; **4** Liatti/Alessandrini (Subaru) 25m 58s; **5** D.Cerrato/L.Guizzardi (Lancia Delta HF Integrale) 26m 15s; **6** F.Cunico/S.Evangelisti (Ford Escort Cosworth) 26m 16s

SS3 Colle d'Oggia 1 (15.66 km)
1 Delecour/Grataloup (Ford) 11m 10s; **2** Liatti/Alessandrini (Subaru) 11m 15s; **3** Snijers/Colebunders (Ford) 11m 19s; **4** Biasion/Siviero (Ford) 11m 22s; **5** Cunico/Evangelisti (Ford) 11m 24s; **6** Cerrato/Guizzardi (Lancia) 11m 27s

SS4 Castelvecchio 1 (10.12 km)
1 Delecour/Grataloup (Ford) 6m 22s; **2** Cunico/Evangelisti (Ford) 6m 28s; **3** Liatti/Alessandrini (Subaru) 6m 30s; **4** Biasion/Siviero (Ford), Snijers/Colebunders (Ford) 6m 32s; **6** Aghini/Farnocchia (Lancia) 6m 34s

SS5 Colle Melogno 1 (12.98 km)
1 Delecour/Grataloup (Ford) 8m 25s; **2** Cunico/Evangelisti (Ford) 8m 36s; **3** Liatti/Alessandrini (Subaru) 8m 39s; **4** Aghini/Farnocchia (Lancia) 8m 41s; **5** Biasion/Siviero (Ford) 8m 43s; **6** Sainz/Moya (Lancia),Snijers/Colebunders (Ford) 8m 45s

SS6 Campoligure Cancelled

SS7 Cassingheno 1 (28.20 km)
1 Cunico/Evangelisti (Ford) 20m 39s; **2** Sainz/Moya (Lancia) 20m 41s; **3** Cerrato/Guizzardi (Lancia) 20m 59s; **4** Biasion/Siviero (Ford) 21m 21s; **5** A.Fiorio/V.Brambilla (Lancia Delta HF Integrale) 21m 26s; **6** G.Pianezzola/L.Roggia (Lancia Delta HF Integrale) 21m 43s

SS8 Cabanne 1 (15.81 km)
1 Sainz/Moya (Lancia) 12m 03s; **2** Cunico/Evangelisti (Ford) 12m 11s; **3** Liatti/Alessandrini (Subaru) 12m 14s; **4** Cerrato/Guizzardi (Lancia) 12m 18s; **5** Fiorio/Brambilla (Lancia) 12m 23s; **6** Snijers/Colebunders (Ford) 12m 37s

SS9 Monte Penna (18.09 km)
1 Sainz/Moya (Lancia) 14m 39s; **2** Cunico/Evangelisti (Ford) 14m 42s; **3** Fiorio/Brambilla (Lancia) 15m 02s; **4** B.Thiry/S.Prévot (Opel Astra GSI) 15m 53s; **5** Liatti/Alessandrini (Subaru) 16m 02s; **6** Snijers/Colebunders (Lancia) 17m 01s

SS10 Castelnuovo Magra (21.79 km)
1 Cunico/Evangelisti (Ford) 16m 30s; **2** Liatti/Alessandrini (Subaru) 16m 49s; 3 Sainz/Moya (Lancia) 16m 58s; **4** Fiorio/Brambilla (Lancia) 17m 15s; **5** Snijers/Colebunders (Ford) 17m 25s; **6** Pianezzola/Roggia (Lancia) 17m 28s

SS11 Carregine (19.17 km)
1 Cunico/Evangelisti (Ford) 13m 41s; **2** Liatti/Alessandrini (Subaru) 13m 48s; **3** Fiorio/Brambilla (Lancia) 14m 09s; **4** Sainz/Moya (Lancia) 14m 11s; **5** Snijers/Colebunders (Ford) 14m 28s; **6** Pianezzola/Roggia (Lancia) 14m 30s

SS12 Renaio (22.42 km)
1 Cunico/Evangelisti (Ford) 17m 54s; **2** Liatti/Alessandrini (Subaru) 18m 08s; **3** Sainz/Moya (Lancia) 18m 21s; **4** Snijers/Colebunders (Ford) 18m 30s; **5** Fiorio/Brambilla (Lancia) 18m 36s; **6** Pianezzola/Roggia (Lancia) 18m 52s

SS13 Coreglia (16.87 km)
1 Cunico/Evangelisti (Ford) 12m 34s; **2** Snijers/Colebunders (Ford) 12m 38s; **3** Sainz/Moya (Lancia) 13m 00s; **4** G.Vita/M.Cesaretti (Toyota Celica GT4) 13m 01s; **5** Pianezzola/Roggia (Lancia) 13m 02s; **6** Fiorio/Brambilla (Lancia) 13m 10s

SS14 Corfino (15.30 km)
1 Sainz/Moya (Lancia) 11m 14s; **2** Cunico/Evangelisti (Ford) 11m 21s; **3** Snijers/Colebunders (Ford) 11m 23s; **4** Liatti/Alessandrini (Subaru) 11m 24s; **5** Pianezzola/Roggia (Lancia) 11m 37s; **6** Fiorio/Brambilla (Lancia) 11m 42s

SS15 Pontremoli (16.97 km)
1 Snijers/Colebunders (Ford) 10m 48s; **2** Cunico/Evangelisti (Ford) 10m 57s; **3** Liatti/Alessandrini (Subaru) 10m 59s; **4** Sainz/Moya (Lancia) 11m 05s; **5** Fiorio/Brambilla (Lancia) 11m 08s; 6 Pianezzola/Roggia (Lancia), Vita/Cesaretti (Toyota) 11m 21s

SS16 Monte Tomarlo (14.07 km)
1 Liatti/Alessandrini (Subaru), Snijers/Colebunders (Ford) 10m 36s; **3** Sainz/Moya (Lancia) 10m 42s; **4** Cunico/Evangelisti (Ford) 10m 52s; **5** Fiorio/Brambilla (Lancia) 10m 53s; 6 Pianezzola/Roggia (Lancia) 11m 09s

SS17 Cassingheno 2 (28.20 km)
1 Cunico/Evangelisti (Ford) 20m 37s; **2** Sainz/Moya (Lancia) 20m 53s; **3** Snijers/Colebunders (Ford) 20m 54s; **4** Liatti/Alessandrini (Subaru) 21m 24s; **5** Pianezzola/Roggia (Lancia) 21m 45s; **6** Vita/Cesaretti (Toyota) 22m 11s

SS18 Cabanne 2 (15.81 km)
1 Cunico/Evangelisti (Ford) 11m 55s; **2** Sainz/Moya (Lancia) 12m 01s; **3** Liatti/Alessandrini (Subaru) 12m 13s; **4** Snijers/Colebunders (Ford) 12m 16s; **5** Pianezzola/Roggia (Lancia) 12m 36s; **6** A.Dallavilla/D.Fappani (Ford Escort Cosworth) 12m 00s

SS19 Rezzo-Col le d'Oggia 1 (15.24 km)
1 Sainz/Moya (Lancia) 11m 06s; **2** Liatti/Alessandrini (Subaru) 11m 09s; **3** Cunico/Evangelisti (Ford) 11m 12s; **4** Snijers/Colebunders (Ford) 11m 32s; **5** Pianezzola/Roggia (Lancia) 11m 45s; **6** Thiry/Prévot (Opel), Dallavilla/Fappani (Ford) 11m 57s

SS20 Vignai 1 (40.49 km)
1 Cunico/Evangelisti (Ford) 30m 48s; **2** Sainz/Moya (Lancia) 31m 15s; **3** Liatti/Alessandrini (Subaru) 32m 16s; **4** Thiry/Prévot (Opel) 33m 10s; **5** Pianezzola/

Roggia (Lancia) 33m 19s; **6** Dallavilla/Fappini (Ford) 34m 01s

SS21 Coldirodi 2 (12.35 km)
1 Liatti/Alessandrini (Subaru) 8m 40s; **2** Sainz/Moya (Lancia), Cunico/Evangelisti (Ford) 8m 44s; **4** Snijers/Colebunders (Ford) 9m 04s; **5** Pianezzola/Roggia (Lancia) 9m 08s; **6** Vita/Cesaretti (Toyota) 9m 11s

SS22 Apricale-Colle Langan (29.25 km)
1 Cunico/Evangelisti (Ford) 20m 49s; **2** Liatti/Alessandrini (Subaru) 20m 51s; **3** Sainz/Moya (Lancia) 21m 09s; **4** Snijers/Colebunders (Ford) 21m 28s; **5** Pianezzola/Roggia (Lancia) 21m 42s; **6** Dallavilla/Fappani (Ford) 22m 17s

SS23 Colle d'Oggia 2 (15.66 km)
1 Liatti/Alessandrini (Subaru) 11m 03s; **2** Cunico/Evangelisti (Ford) 11m 08s; **3** Snijers/Colebunders (Ford) 11m 14s; **4** Sainz/Moya (Lancia) 11m 17s; **5** Pianezzola/Roggia (Lancia) 11m 33s; **6** Dallavilla/Fappani (Ford) 11m 39s

SS24 Castelvecchio 2 (10.13 km)
1 Liatti/Alessandrini (Subaru) 6m 18s; **2** Snijers/Colebunders (Ford) 6m 21s; **3** Cunico/Evangelisti (Ford) 6m 22s; **4** Sainz/Moya (Lancia) 6m 24s; **5** Dallavilla/Fappani (Ford) 6m 27s; **6** Pianezzola/Roggia (Lancia) 6m 30s

SS25 Colle Melogno 2 (12.98 km)
1 Liatti/Alessandrini (Subaru) 7m 55s; **2** Snijers/Colebunders (Ford) 7m 57s; **3** Sainz/Moya (Lancia) 8m 02s; **4** Pianezzola/Roggia (Lancia) 8m 06s; **5** Cunico/Evangelisti (Ford) 8m 09s; **6** Dallavilla/Fappani (Ford) 8m 17s

SS26 Colle del Giovetti (8.70 km)
1 Liatti/Alessandrini (Subaru) 5m 16s; **2** Sainz/Moya (Lancia), Snijers/Colebunders (Ford) 5m 18s; **4** Cunico/Evangelisti (Ford) 5m 23s; **5** Pianezzola/Roggia (Lancia) 5m 30s; **6** Dallavilla/Fappani (Ford) 5m 32s

SS27 Rezzo-Colle d'Oggia 2 (15.24 km)
1 Liatti/Alessandrini (Subaru) 10m 28s; **2** Snijers/Colebunders (Ford) 10m 42s; **3** Cunico/Evangelisti (Ford) 10m 45s; **4** Sainz/Moya (Lancia) 10m 47s; **5** Pianezzola/Roggia (Lancia) 10m 50s; **6** Dallavilla/Fappani (Ford) 11m 12s

SS28 Vignai 2 (40.49 km)
1 Liatti/Alessandrini (Subaru) 29m 23s; **2** Sainz/Moya (Lancia) 29m 32s; **3** Snijers/Colebunders (Ford) 30m 01s; **4** Pianezzola/Roggia (Lancia) 30m 11s; **5** Cunico/Evangelisti (Ford) 30m 24s; **6** Dallavilla/Fappani (Ford) 30m 40s

Major Retirements

1	Aghini/Farnocchia	Lancia Delta HF Integrale	
	Accident	SS7	Gr A
2	Delecour/Grataloup	Ford Escort Cosworth	
	Accident	SS7	Gr A
5	Biasion/Siviero	Ford Escort Cosworth	
	Engine	SS7	Gr A
6	Fiorio/Brambilla	Lancia Delta HF Integrale	
	Engine	SS18	Gr A
9	Longhi/Imerito	Lancia Delta HF Integrale	
	Accident	SS2	Gr A
10	Cerrato/Guizzardi	Lancia Delta HF Integrale	
	Electrical	SS10	Gr A
18	Krecek/Krecman	Lancia Delta HF Integrale	
		SS14	Gr A
21	Spiliotis/Thibaud	Ford Escort Cosworth	
	Mechanical	SS11	Gr N
22	Manfrinato/Condotta	Ford Escort Cosworth	
		SS20	Gr N

FIA Class Winners

A8 Over 2000 cc	Cunico/Evangelisti Ford Escort Cosworth
A7 1600-2000 cc	Thiry/Prévot Opel Astra GSi
A6 1300-1600 cc	Medeghini/Cecchini Peugeot 106 XSi
A5 Up to 1300 cc	Triner/Klima Skoda Favorit 136L
N4 Over 2000 cc	Travaglia/Alessandro Ford Escort Cosworth
N3 1600-2000 cc	Castore/Grua Opèl Astra GSi
N2 1300-1600 cc	Molinaris/Molinaris Opel Corsa GSi
N1 Up to 1300 cc	Duterte/Vielle Peugeot 205 Rallye

Rally Leaders

SS1-5 Delecour; **SS7** Biasion; **SS8-9** Sainz; **SS10-28** Cunico

World Championship Points

Drivers
1 Kankkunen 111; **2** Delecour 82; **3** Auriol 71; **4** Biasion 66; **5** McRae, Sainz 50; **7** Vatanen 30; **8** Mäkinen, Eriksson 26; **10** Alén 25, etc.

Manufacturers
1 Toyota 151; **2** Ford 125; **3** Subaru 100; **4** Lancia 84; **5** Mitsubishi 69

FIA Cup for Production Car Drivers
1 Fassina 43; **2** Coutinho 28; **3** Kytölehto 23; **4** Bin Sulayem 15, etc.

FIA Cup for Manufacturers
1 GME 56; **2** Skoda 42; **3** Peugeot 32; **4** Citroën, Lada 24, etc.

Route Details

Leg 1
Monday, 11 October, Sanremo-Il Ciocco. 10 asphalt stages (190.53 km) (1 cancelled) in a total route of 639.75 km
Leg 2
Tuesday, 12 October, Il Ciocco-Sanremo. 9 asphalt stages (184.79 km) in a total route of 672.71 km
Leg 3
Wednesday, 13 October, Sanremo-Sanremo. 8 asphalt stages (144.22 km) in a total route of 414.18 km

Weather

Mainly wet, dry in Leg 3

Special Stage Analysis

	1	2	3	4	5	6
Cunico (Ford)	9	8	3	2	3	1
Liatti (Subaru)	8	7	6	3	1	-
Delecour (Ford)	5	-	-	-	-	-
Sainz (Lancia)	4	7	7	5	-	1
Snijers (Ford)	2	5	5	6	2	4
Biasion (Ford)	-	1	-	4	1	-
Fiorio (Lancia)	-	-	2	1	5	2
Aghini (Lancia)	-	-	1	1	1	1
Cerrato (Lancia)	-	-	1	1	1	1
Pianezzola (Lancia)	-	-	-	2	11	7
Thiry (Opel)	-	-	-	2	-	1
Vita (Toyota)	-	-	-	1	-	3
Dallavilla (Ford)	-	-	-	-	1	9

Gilberto Pianezzola recovered well from a lethargic start, taking fourth place in his Grifone Delta.

Finish Lines

The foul weather conditions during the first leg brought the front-wheel drive cars to the fore: **Bruno Thiry** put up an outstanding performance in the Marlboro/**Opel** Belgium Astra to finish sixth; he was only deprived of fifth by **Piero Liatti**'s **Legacy** on the final stage...**Angelo Medeghini** was the other star in the rain, catching and passing Group N cars galore in his 140 bhp **Peugeot** 106. He eventually finished ninth as the roads dried...**Piero Longhi** crashed his Esso **Delta** on the second stage, but still won the Italian Championship by 1.25 points, since his team-mate, **Gilberto Pianezzola**, could do no better than fourth after a cautious drive during the first leg...**Dario Cerrato** had been in with a chance of his sixth Italian crown – despite driving for nearly 30 miles in darkness with no lights – until his Martini **Integrale** succumbed to a catalogue of electrical problems...**Patrick Snijers** scored his best-ever World Championship result, taking third in the Bastos **Escort**, despite a major turbo problem on SS7...**Paolo Andreucci** was lying second in F2 when he crashed his 106 on the fifth stage...**Piero Liatti**'s trials included two accidents and broken power steering; his road penalty total was equivalent to an extra stage...**Freddy Loix** drove very sensibly on his first World Championship appearance, finishing tenth in the second **Opel** Belgium Astra.

Results

1	Franco Cunico/	Ford Escort Cosworth	
	Steve Evangelisti	6h 19m 40s	Gr A
2	Carlos Sainz/	Lancia Delta HF Integrale	
	Luis Moya	6h 21m 18s	Gr A
3	Patrick Snijers/	Ford Escort Cosworth	
	Dany Colebunders	6h 30m 08s	Gr A
4	Gilberto Pianezzola/	Lancia Delta HF Integrale	
	Loris Roggia	6h 38m 03s	Gr A
5	Piero Liatti/	Subaru Legacy RS	
	Alessandro Alessandrini	6h 44m 47s	Gr A
6	Bruno Thiry/	Opel Astra GSi	
	Stéphane Prévot	6h 46m 27s	Gr A
7	Renato Travaglia/	Ford Escort Cosworth	
	Mari Alessandro	6h 58m 21s	Gr N
8	Andrea Dallavilla/	Ford Escort Cosworth	
	Danilo Fappani	6h 58m 31s	Gr N
9	Angelo Medeghini/	Peugeot 106 XSi	
	Paulo Cecchini	6h 58m 38s	Gr A
10	Freddy Loix/	Opel Astra GSi	
	Johnny Vranken	7h 04m 55s	Gr A

120 starters, 57 finishers

Previous Winners (since 1970)

1970 Jean-Luc Thérier/Marcel Callewaert — Alpine Renault A110
1971 Ove Andersson/Tony Nash — Alpine Renault A110
1972 Amilcare Ballestrieri/Arnaldo Bernacchini — Lancia Fulvia
1973 Jean-Luc Thérier/Jacques Jaubert — Alpine Renault A110
1974 Sandro Munari/Mario Mannucci — Lancia Stratos
1975 Björn Waldegård/Hans Thorszelius — Lancia Stratos
1976 Björn Waldegård/Hans Thorszelius — Lancia Stratos
1977 Jean-Claude Andruet/Christian Delferrier — Fiat 131 Abarth
1978 Markku Alén/Ilkka Kivimäki — Lancia Stratos
1979 Tony Fassina/Mauro Mannini — Lancia Stratos
1980 Walter Röhrl/Christian Geistdörfer — Fiat 131 Abarth
1981 Michèle Mouton/Fabrizia Pons — Audi Quattro A1
1982 Stig Blomqvist/Björn Cederberg — Audi Quattro A2
1983 Markku Alén/Ilkka Kivimäki — Lancia 037 Rallye
1984 Ari Vatanen/Terry Harryman — Peugeot 205 Turbo 16
1985 Walter Röhrl/Christian Geistdörfer — Audi Quattro Sport S1
1986 Markku Alén/Ilkka Kivimäki — Lancia Delta S4
1987 Massimo Biasion/Tiziano Siviero — Lancia Delta HF Turbo
1988 Massimo Biasion/Tiziano Siviero — Lancia Delta HF Integrale
1989 Massimo Biasion/Tiziano Siviero — Lancia Delta HF Integrale
1990 Didier Auriol/Bernard Occelli — Lancia Delta HF Integrale
1991 Didier Auriol/Bernard Occelli — Lancia Delta HF Integrale
1992 Andrea Aghini/Sauro Farnocchia — Lancia Delta HF Integrale

CATALONIA RALLY/Statistics

Catalonia Rally, 2-4 November, FIA World Rally Championship Round 12

Leading Entries

1	Carlos Sainz/ Luis Moya	Lancia Delta HF Integrale Gr A
2	Juha Kankkunen/ Nicky Grist	Toyota Celica Turbo 4WD Gr A
3	François Delecour/ Daniel Grataloup	Ford Escort Cosworth Gr A
4	Didier Auriol/ Bernard Occelli	Toyota Celica Turbo 4WD Gr A
5	Miki Biasion/ Tiziano Siviero	Ford Escort Cosworth Gr A
6	Gustavo Trelles/ Jorge Del Buono	Lancia Delta HF Integrale Gr A
7	Alessandro Fiorio/ Vittorio Brambilla	Lancia Delta HF Integrale Gr A
8	Bruno Thiry/ Stéphane Prévot	Opel Astra GSi Gr A
9	Alessandro Fassina/ Luigi Pirollo	Mazda 323 Turbo GT-R Gr N
10	Pavel Sibera/ Petr Gross	Skoda Favorit 136L Gr A
11	Mohammed Bin Sulayem/ Ronan Morgan	Ford Escort Cosworth Gr N
12	Kenny McKinstry/ Robbie Philipott	Subaru Legacy RS Gr A
14	Emil Triner/ Jiri Klima	Skoda Favorit 136L Gr A
15	Pier-Giorgio Bedini/ Andrea Bettini	Ford Escort Cosworth Gr N
16	Antonio Coutinho/ Antonio Lisboa	Ford Escort Cosworth Gr N
17	Mia Bardolet/ Joaquim Muntada	Opel Astra GSi Gr A
18	Daniel Alonso/ Salvador Belzunces	Ford Escort Cosworth Gr N
19	Borja Moratal/ Alfredo Rodriguez	Peugeot 309 GTI 16v Gr A
20	Luis Climent/ Jose-Antonio Munoz	Opel Astra GSi Gr A
21	Kiko Clima/ Jacinto Martinez	Renault Clio Williams Gr A
22	Erwin Doctor/ Theo Badenberg	Opel Calibra Turbo Gr A

Special Stage Times

SS1 Tossa 1 (18.70 km)
1 C.Sainz/L.Moya (Lancia Delta HF Integrale), F.Delecour/D.Grataloup (Ford Escort Cosworth) 13m 16s; **3** M.Biasion/T.Siviero (Ford Escort Cosworth) 13m 26s; **4** J.Kankkunen/N.Grist (Toyota Celica Turbo), A.Fiorio/V.Brambilla (Lancia Delta HF Integrale) 13m 27s; **6** D.Auriol/B.Occelli (Toyota Celica Turbo) 13m 32s

SS2 Els Angels 1 (15.00 km)
1 Delecour/Grataloup (Ford) 9m 47s; **2** Kankkunen/Grist (Toyota) 9m 55s; **3** Biasion/Siviero (Ford) 9m 56s; **4** Auriol/Occelli (Toyota) 10m 00s; **5** Sainz/Moya (Lancia) 10m 04s; **6** Fiorio/Brambilla (Lancia) 10m 19s

SS3 Coll de Bracons 1 (19.89 km)
1 Auriol/Occelli (Toyota) 13m 45s; **2** Delecour/Grataloup (Ford), G.Trelles/J.Del Buono (Lancia Delta HF Integrale) 13m 56s; **4** Fiorio/Brambilla (Lancia) 13m 57s; **5** Biasion/Siviero (Ford) 13m 59s; **6** Kankkunen/Grist (Toyota) 14m 07s

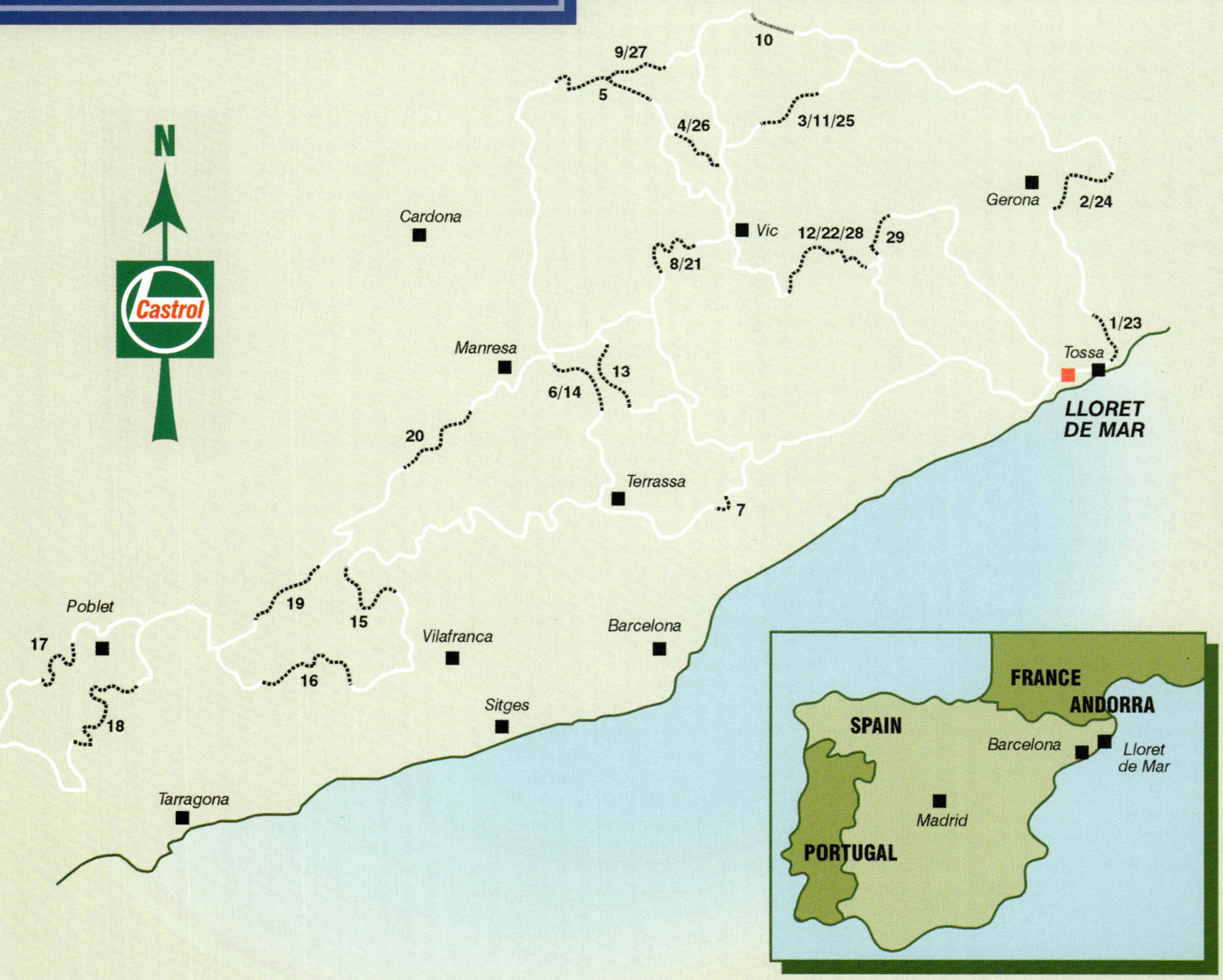

You've seen the car, now buy the T-shirt. Spanish fans wear their colours on their sleeves.

SS4 La Trona 1 (12.85 km)
1 Biasion/Siviero (Ford) 8m 49s; 2 Delecour/Grataloup (Ford) 8m 51s; 3 Auriol/Occelli (Toyota) 8m 53s; 4 Sainz/Moya (Lancia) 8m 54s; 5 Fiorio/Brambilla (Lancia), Trelles/Del Buono (Lancia) 8m 58s

SS5 Alpens-Vilada (21.23 km)
1 Delecour/Grataloup (Ford) 13m 47s; 2 Auriol/Occelli (Toyota) 13m 55s; 3 Sainz/Moya (Lancia) 13m 58s; 4 Biasion/Siviero (Ford), Kankkunen/Grist (Toyota), Trelles/Del Buono (Lancia) 14m 02s

SS6 Talamanca 1 (14.47 km)
1 Delecour/Grataloup (Ford) 8m 48s; 2 Auriol/Occelli (Toyota) 8m 50s; 3 Kankkunen/Grist (Toyota) 8m 53s; 4 Biasion/Siviero (Ford) 8m 56s; 5 Sainz/Moya (Lancia) 8m 57s; 6 Trelles/Del Buono (Lancia) 9m 00s

SS7 Circuit de Catalunya (3.65 km)
1 Delecour/Grataloup (Ford) 2m 22s; 2 Sainz/Moya (Lancia), Kankkunen/Grist (Toyota), Auriol/Occelli (Toyota) 2m 23s; 5 Biasion/Siviero (Ford) 2m 24s; 6 Trelles/Del Buono (Lancia) 2m 26s

SS8 Santa Eulalia 1 (12.60 km)
1 Auriol/Occelli (Toyota), Delecour/Grataloup (Ford) 7m 23s; 3 Biasion/Siviero (Ford) 7m 24s; 4 Kankkunen/Grist (Toyota) 7m 25s; 5 Sainz/Moya (Lancia) 7m 28s; 6 Trelles/Del Buono (Lancia) 7m 30s

SS9 Alpens-Les Lloses 1 (21.91 km)
1 Auriol/Occelli (Toyota) 15m 03s; 2 Delecour/Grataloup (Ford), Trelles/Del Buono (Lancia) 15m 12s; 4 Kankkunen/Grist (Toyota) 15m 18s; 5 Sainz/Moya (Lancia) 15m 20s; 6 Biasion/Siviero (Ford) 15m 24s

SS10 Coll de Santigosa (10.60 km)
1 Trelles/Del Buono (Lancia) 7m 30s; 2 Kankkunen/Grist (Toyota) 7m 31s; 3 Fiorio/Brambilla (Lancia) 7m 36s; 4 Delecour/Grataloup (Ford) 7m 37s; 5 Biasion/Siviero (Ford) 7m 41s; 6 Auriol/Occelli (Toyota) 7m 52s

SS11 Coll de Bracons 2 (19.89 km)
1 Auriol/Occelli (Toyota) 13m 38s; 2 Delecour/Grataloup (Ford) 13m 42s; 3 Kankkunen/Grist (Toyota) 13m 46s; 4 Biasion/Siviero (Ford) 13m 51s; 5 Fiorio/Brambilla (Lancia) 13m 54s; 6 Trelles/Del Buono (Lancia) 13m 57s

SS12 L'Enclusa-Sant Hilari 1 (27.44 km)
1 Delecour/Grataloup (Ford) 18m 36s; 2 Biasion/Siviero (Ford) 18m 39s; 3 Kankkunen/Grist (Toyota) 18m 41s; 4 Auriol/Occelli (Toyota) 18m 42s; 5 Fiorio/Brambilla (Lancia) 18m 54s; 6 Trelles/Del Buono (Lancia) 19m 05s

SS13 Les Solanes (11.83 km)
1 Delecour/Grataloup (Ford) 7m 19s; 2 Auriol/Occelli (Toyota) 7m 22s; 3 Kankkunen/Grist (Toyota) 7m 24s; 4 Biasion/Siviero (Ford) 7m 27s; 5 Trelles/Del Buono (Lancia), Fiorio/Brambilla (Lancia) 7m 33s

SS14 Talamanca 2 (14.47 km)
1 Auriol/Occelli (Toyota) 8m 44s; 2 Delecour/Grataloup (Ford) 8m 45s; 3 Biasion/Siviero (Ford) 8m 51s; 4 Fiorio/Brambilla (Lancia) 9m 00s; 5 Trelles/Del Buono (Lancia) 9m 06s; 6 B.Thiry/S.Prévot (Opel Astra GSI) 9m 28s

SS15 La Llacuna (20.05 km)
1 Kankkunen/Grist (Toyota) 11m 26s; 2 Auriol/Occelli (Toyota) 11m 29s; 3 Delecour/Grataloup (Ford) 11m 32s; 4 Biasion/Siviero (Ford) 11m 33s; 5 Fiorio/Brambilla (Lancia) 11m 39s; 6 Trelles/Del Buono (Lancia) 11m 46s

SS16 Can Ferrer (23.82 km)
1 Kankkunen/Grist (Toyota) 13m 14s; 2 Delecour/Grataloup (Ford) 13m 16s; 3 Auriol/Occelli (Toyota) 13m 19s; 4 Biasion/Siviero (Ford) 13m 25s; 5 Fiorio/Brambilla (Lancia) 13m 32s; 6 Trelles/Del Buono (Lancia) 13m 48s

SS17 Prades (16.25 km)
1 Delecour/Grataloup (Ford) 9m 48s; 2 Kankkunen/Grist (Toyota), Auriol/Occelli (Toyota) 9m 51s; 4 Biasion/Siviero (Ford) 9m 55s; 5 Fiorio/Brambilla (Lancia) 10m 04s; 6 Trelles/Del Buono (Lancia) 10m 10s

SS18 La Riba (32.45 km)
1 Auriol/Occelli (Toyota) 20m 33s; 2 Kankkunen/Grist (Toyota) 20m 34s; 3 Delecour/Grataloup (Ford) 20m 50s; 4 Biasion/Siviero (Ford) 20m 53s; 5 Fiorio/Brambilla (Lancia) 21m 02s; 6 Trelles/Del Buono (Lancia) 21m 18s

SS19 Pont d'Armentera (13.06 km)
1 Delecour/Grataloup (Ford) 7m 35s; 2 Auriol/Occelli (Toyota) 7m 36s; 3 Kankkunen/Grist (Toyota) 7m 40s; 4 Biasion/Siviero (Ford) 7m 44s; 5 Trelles/Del Buono (Lancia) 7m 53s; 6 Fiorio/Brambilla (Lancia) 7m 57s

SS20 Castelfollit del Boix (14.42 km)
1 Delecour/Grataloup (Ford) 8m 42s; 2 Auriol/Occelli (Toyota) 8m 44s; 3 Kankkunen/Grist (Toyota) 8m 48s; 4 Biasion/Siviero (Ford) 8m 50s; 5 Trelles/Del Buono (Lancia) 8m 59s; 6 Fiorio/Brambilla (Lancia) 9m 02s

SS21 Santa Eulalia 2 (12.60 km)
1 Delecour/Grataloup (Ford) 7m 25s; 2 Kankkunen/Grist (Toyota), Auriol/Occelli (Toyota) 7m 26s; 4 Biasion/Siviero (Ford) 7m 33s; 5 Fiorio/Brambilla (Lancia) 7m 40s; 6 Trelles/Del Buono (Lancia) 7m 52s

SS22 L'Enclusa-Sant Hilari 2 (27.44 km)
1 Delecour/Grataloup (Ford) 18m 13s; 2 Auriol/Occelli (Toyota) 18m 17s; 3 Kankkunen/Grist (Toyota); 4 Fiorio/Brambilla (Lancia) 18m 32s; 5 Trelles/Del Buono (Lancia) 18m 51s; 6 J.Bardolet/J.Muntada (Opel Astra GSI) 19m 34s

SS23 Tossa 2 (18.70 km)
1 Delecour/Grataloup (Ford) 13m 29s; 2 Auriol/Occelli (Toyota) 13m 44s; 3 Kankkunen/Grist (Toyota) 13m 53s; 4 Fiorio/Brambilla (Lancia) 14m 01s; 5 Trelles/Del Buono (Lancia) 14m 03s; 6 Biasion/Siviero (Ford) 14m 12s

SS24 Els Angels 2 (15.00 km)
1 Kankkunen/Grist (Toyota) 10m 24s; 2 Delecour/Grataloup (Ford) 10m 31s; 3 Auriol/Occelli (Toyota) 10m 35s; 4 Biasion/Siviero (Ford) 10m 38s; 5 Trelles/Del Buono (Lancia) 10m 49s; 6 Fiorio/Brambilla (Lancia) 10m 58s

SS25 Coll de Bracons 3 (19.89 km)
1 Auriol/Occelli (Toyota) 13m 42s; 2 Delecour/Grataloup (Ford) 13m 47s; 3 Biasion/Siviero (Ford) 13m 56s; 4 Kankkunen/Grist (Toyota) 13m 58s; 5 Fiorio/Brambilla (Lancia) 14m 01s; 6 Trelles/Del Buono (Lancia) 14m 15s

SS26 La Trona 2 (12.85 km)
1 Auriol/Occelli (Toyota) 8m 37s; 2 Delecour/Grataloup (Ford) 8m 38s; 3 Biasion/Siviero (Ford) 8m 40s; 4 Kankkunen/Grist (Toyota) 8m 42s; 5 Fiorio/Brambilla (Lancia) 8m 44s; 6 Trelles/Del Buono (Lancia) 8m 51s

SS27 Alpens-Les Lloses 2 (21.91 km)
1 Auriol/Occelli (Toyota) 14m 45s; 2 Delecour/Grataloup (Ford) 14m 46s; 3 Kankkunen/Grist (Toyota) 14m 55s; 4 Fiorio/Brambilla (Lancia) 14m 58s; 5 Trelles/Del Buono (Lancia) 14m 59s; 6 Biasion/Siviero (Ford) 16m 00s

SS28 L'Enclusa-Sant Hilari 3 (27.44 km)
1 Delecour/Grataloup (Ford) 18m 53s; 2 Auriol/Occelli (Toyota) 18m 58s; 3 Biasion/Siviero (Ford) 19m 06s; 4 Kankkunen/Grist (Toyota), Trelles/Del Buono (Lancia) 19m 19s; 6 Fiorio/Brambilla (Lancia) 19m 21s

SS29 Sant Hilari-Osor (13.19 km)
1 Biasion/Siviero (Ford) 9m 32s; 2 Delecour/Grataloup (Ford) 9m 33s; 3 Auriol/Occelli (Toyota) 9m 41s; 4 Kankkunen/Grist (Toyota) 9m 43s; 5 Trelles/Del Buono (Lancia) 10m 05s; 6 Fiorio/Brambilla (Lancia) 10m 06s

Major Retirements

1	Sainz/Moya Electronics	Lancia Delta HF Integrale SS10	Gr A
11	Bin Sulayem/Morgan Transmission	Ford Escort Cosworth SS10	Gr N
12	McKinstry/Philipott Withdrawn	Subaru Legacy RS SS7	Gr A
15	Bedini/Bettini Withdrawn	Ford Escort Cosworth SS2	Gr N
16	Coutinho/Lisboa Excluded	Ford Escort Cosworth SS29	Gr N
18	Alonso/Belzunces Gearbox	Ford Escort Cosworth SS15	Gr N
19	Moratal/Rodriguez Lost Wheel	Peugeot 309 GTI 16v SS13	Gr A
21	Clima/Martinez Engine	Renault Clio Williams SS8	Gr A
22	Doctor/Badenberg Engine	Opel Calibra Turbo SS22	Gr A

FIA Class Winners

A8 Over 2000 cc	Delecour/Grataloup Ford Escort Cosworth
A7 1600-2000 cc	Thiry/Prévot Opel Astra GSi
A6 1300-1600 cc	Gomez/Marti Peugeot 106 XSi
A5 Up to 1300 cc	Sibera/Gross Skoda Favorit 136L
N4 Over 2000 cc	Fassina/Pirollo Mazda 323 Turbo GT-R
N3 1600-2000 cc	Serracanta/Serracanta Peugeot 309 GTI
N2 1300-1600 cc	Casasayas/Dalmases Honda Civic Vti
N1 Up to 1300 cc	Margenat/Guilera Peugeot 205 Rallye

Rally Leaders

SS1 Delecour, Sainz; **SS2-29** Delecour

World Championship Points

Drivers
1 Kankkunen 123; 2 Delecour 102; 3 Auriol 86; 4 Biasion 76; 5 McRae, Sainz 50; 7 Vatanen 30; 8 Trelles 28; 9 Mäkinen, Eriksson 26, etc.

Manufacturers
1 Toyota 151; 2 Ford 145; 3 Subaru 100; 4 Lancia 92; 5 Mitsubishi 69

FIA Cup for Production Car Drivers
1 Fassina 56; Coutinho 28; 3 Kytölehto 23; 4 Bin Sulayem 15, etc.

FIA Cup for Manufacturers
1 GME 66; 2 Skoda 46; 3 Peugeot 36; 4 Citroën 26; 5 Lada 23; 6 Renault (F) 19, etc.

Route Details

Leg 1
Tuesday, 2 November, Lloret de Mar-Lloret de Mar. 12 asphalt stages (198.23 km) in a total route of 674.02 km.
Leg 2
Wednesday, 3 November, Lloret de Mar-Lloret de Mar. 10 asphalt stages (186.39 km) in a total route of 701.09 km
Leg 3
Thursday, 4 November, Lloret de Mar-Lloret de Mar. 7 asphalt stages (128.98 km) in a total route of 375.74 km

Weather

Wet in Leg 1, dry later

Special Stage Analysis

	1	2	3	4	5	6
Delecour (Ford)	15	11	2	1	-	-
Auriol (Toyota)	9	12	4	2	-	2
Kankkunen (Toyota)	3	6	9	8	-	1
Biasion (Ford)	2	1	7	12	3	3
Trelles (Lancia)	1	2	-	2	10	12
Sainz (Lancia)	1	1	1	1	4	-
Fiorio (Lancia)	-	-	1	6	11	6
Thiry (Opel)	-	-	-	-	-	1
Bardolet (Opel)	-	-	-	-	-	1

Finish Lines

The Jolly Club bowed out quietly. **Carlos Sainz** shared the lead after the first stage, but got a puncture and later retired with electronic problems...The top **Lancia** was eventually **Alex Fiorio**'s Astra machine, which came close to beating **Miki Biasion**'s **Escort** thanks to the latter's turbo problems and a poor tyre choice on the last day...**Gustavo Trelles** led Fiorio initially, but finished sixth after a brush with a spectator ...**Bruno Thiry** was the Formula 2 star once again, beating the **Opel** Spain Astras of **Luis Climent** and **Mia Bardolet** by a handsome margin...Group N ended in turmoil: **Antonio Coutinho** won on the road, but his **Escort** was excluded for using an undersize front anti-roll bar. **David Guixeras** inherited victory in his **309 GTI,** but the Spaniard was thrown out when a fellow Peugeot driver protested that the rear seat was underweight. Victory and the Group N world title therefore went to a surprised **Alessandro Fassina**, driving his usual **Mazda.** He had lost more than a quarter of an hour thanks to a loose intercooler pipe... **Mohammed Bin Sulayem** retired the Marlboro **Escort** after cracking the rear differential...**Borja Moratal** was the Opels' closest challenger until his 309's wheel studs sheared...**Kenny McKinstry** was holding a top ten place when an electrical connection worked loose on SS3 and cost him 17 minutes. He retired the Kaliber **Subaru** soon afterwards. GM's four-wheel drive **Calibra** Turbo made a rare appearance, **Erwin Doctor** holding a top ten place when the oil pump broke.

Results

1	François Delecour/ Daniel Grataloup	Ford Escort Cosworth 5h 36m 19s	Gr A
2	Didier Auriol/ Bernard Occelli	Toyota Celica Turbo 4WD 5h 37m 19s	Gr A
3	Juha Kankkunen/ Nicky Grist	Toyota Celica Turbo 4WD 5h 40m 28s	Gr A
4	Miki Biasion/ Tiziano Siviero	Ford Escort Cosworth 5h 42m 57s	Gr A
5	Alessandro Fiorio/ Vittorio Brambilla	Lancia Delta HF Integrale 5h 44m 07s	Gr A
6	Gustavo Trelles/ Jorge Del Buono	Lancia Delta HF Integrale 5h 46m 27s	Gr A
7	Bruno Thiry/ Stéphane Prévot	Opel Astra GSI 6h 03m 47s	Gr A
8	Luis Climent/ José-Antonio Munoz	Opel Astra GSI 6h 07m 37s	Gr A
9	José-Marie Bardolet/ Joaquim Muntada	Opel Astra GSI 6h 08m 02s	Gr A
10	Oriol Gomez/ Marc Marti	Peugeot 106 XSi 6h 18m 19s	Gr A

95 starters, 39 finishers

Previous Winners (since 1980)

1980 Antonio Zanini/Jordi Sabater Porsche 911SC
1981 Eugenio Ortiz/Guillermo Barreras Renault 5 Turbo
1982 Antonio Zanini/Victor Sabater Talbot Sunbeam Lotus
1983 Adartico Vudafieri/Tiziano Siviero Lancia 037 Rallye
1984 Salvador Servia/Jordi Sabater Opel Manta 400
1985 Fabrizio Tabaton/Luciano Tedeschini Lancia 037 Rally
1986 Fabrizio Tabaton/Luciano Tedeschini Lancia Delta S4
1987 Dario Cerrato/Giuseppe Cerri Lancia Delta HF
1988 Bruno Saby/Jean-François Fauchille Lancia Delta HF
1989 Yves Loubet/Jean-Marc André Lancia Delta HF Integrale
1990 Dario Cerrato/Giuseppe Cerri Lancia Delta HF Integrale
1991 Armin Schwarz/Arne Hertz Toyota Celica GT4
1992 Carlos Sainz/Luis Moya Toyota Celica Turbo 4WD

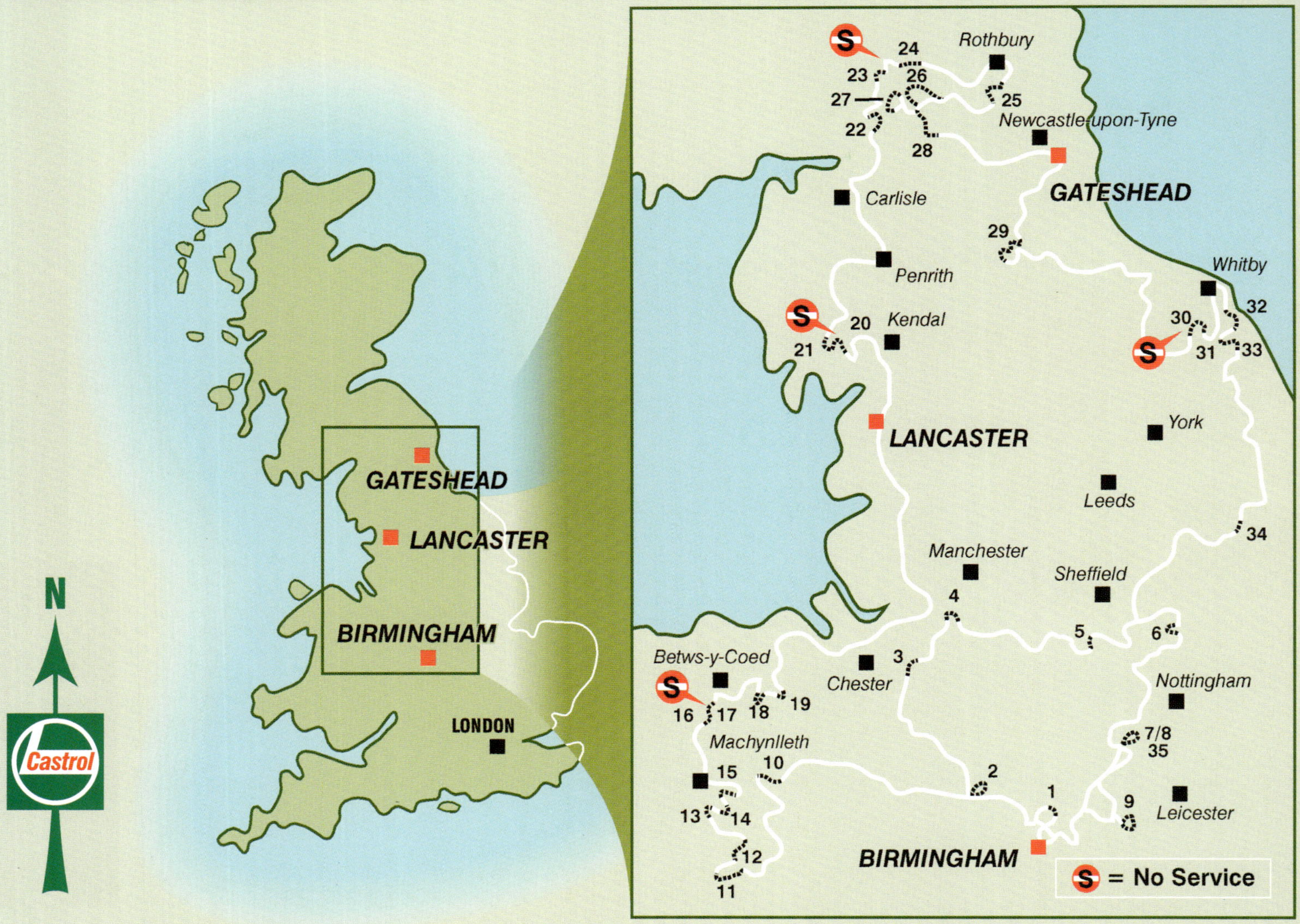

NETWORK Q RAC RALLY 1993 Birmingham 13 FIA WORLD RALLY CHAMPIONSHIP

RAC Rally, 21-24 November, FIA World Rally Championship Round 13

Leading Entries

1	Juha Kankkunen/ Nicky Grist	Toyota Celica Turbo 4WD Gr A
2	Colin McRae/ Derek Ringer	Subaru Impreza 555 Gr A
3	François Delecour/ Daniel Grataloup	Ford Escort Cosworth Gr A
4	Kenneth Eriksson/ Staffan Parmander	Mitsubishi Lancer RS-E Gr A
5	Ari Vatanen/ Bruno Berglund	Subaru Impreza 555 Gr A
6	Didier Auriol/ Bernard Occelli	Toyota Celica Turbo 4WD Gr A
7	Armin Schwarz/ Peter Thul	Mitsubishi Lancer RS-E Gr A
8	Malcolm Wilson/ Bryan Thomas	Ford Escort Cosworth Gr A
9	Mats Jonsson/ Lars Bäckman	Toyota Celica Turbo 4WD Gr A
10	Richard Burns/ Robert Reid	Subaru Legacy RS Gr A
11	Sebastian Lindholm/ Timo Hakala	Ford Escort Cosworth Gr A
12	Alister McRae/ David Senior	Subaru Legacy RS Gr A
15	David Llewellin/ Ian Grindrod	Vauxhall Astra GSi Gr A
16	Grégoire de Mevius/ Willy Lux	Nissan Sunny GTi Gr A
17	Pavel Sibera/ Petr Gross	Skoda Favorit 136L Gr A
18	Emil Triner/ Jiri Klima	Skoda Favorit 136L Gr A
19	Gilberto Pianezzola/ Loris Roggia	Lancia Delta HF Integrale Gr A
22	Robbie Head/ Campbell Roy	Ford Escort Cosworth Gr A
25	Gwyndaf Evans/ Howard Davies	Ford Escort Cosworth Gr N
27	Ari Mokkonen/ Risto Mannisenmaki	Audi Coupé S2 Gr N

Special Stage Times

SS1 Sutton Park (4.77 km)
1 J.Kankkunen/N.Grist (Toyota Celica Turbo 4WD) 2m 54s; **2** A.Schwarz/P.Thul (Mitsubishi Lancer RS-E) 2m 55s; **3** K.Eriksson/S.Parmander (Mitsubishi Lancer RS-E) 2m 56s; **4** C.McRae/D.Ringer (Subaru Impreza 555) 2m 57s; **5** A.Vatanen/B.Berglund (Subaru Impreza 555) 2m 59s; **6** F.Delecour/ D.Grataloup (Ford Escort Cosworth) 3m 00s

SS2 Weston Park (4.10 km)
1 Schwarz/Thul (Mitsubishi), G.Evans/H.Davies (Ford Escort Cosworth N) 3m 13s; **3** Delecour/Grataloup (Ford) 3m 14s; **4** M.Wilson/B.Thomas (Ford Escort Cosworth), A.McRae/D.Senior (Subaru Legacy RS) 3m 15s; **6** Eriksson/Parmander (Mitsubishi), M.Jonsson/L.Bäckman (Toyota Celica Turbo) 3m 16s

SS3 Oulton Park (4.40 km)
1 Kankkunen/Grist (Toyota), Schwarz/Thul (Mitsubishi), Delecour/Grataloup (Ford) 2m 40s; **4** McRae/ Ringer (Subaru), D.Auriol/B.Occelli (Toyota Celica Turbo 4WD), Vatanen/Berglund (Subaru) 2m 43s

SS4 Tatton Park (6.88 km)
1 Schwarz/Thul (Mitsubishi) 4m 53s; **2** Vatanen/ Berglund (Subaru) 4m 55s; **3** Kankkunen/Grist (Toyota) 4m 56s; **4** McRae/Ringer (Subaru) 4m 58s; **5** Eriksson/Parmander (Mitsubishi), Auriol/Occelli (Toyota) 4m 59s

SS5 Chatsworth (10.52 km)
1 McRae/Ringer (Subaru) 8m 11s; **2** Kankkunen/Grist (Toyota) 8m 12s; **3** Eriksson/Parmander (Mitsubishi) 8m 13s; **4** Vatanen/Berglund (Subaru) 8m 17s; **5** Schwarz/Thul (Mitsubishi), Jonsson/Bäckman (Toyota) 8m 18s

SS6 Clumber Park (5.14 km)
1 Kankkunen/Grist (Toyota), McRae/Ringer (Subaru), Eriksson/Parmander (Mitsubishi) 2m 58s; **4** Delecour/Grataloup (Ford), Vatanen/Berglund (Subaru), R.Burns/R.Reid (Subaru Legacy RS) 2m 59s

SS7 Donington 1 (7.67 km)
1 McRae/Ringer (Subaru) 4m 34s; **2** Kankkunen/Grist (Toyota), Eriksson/Parmander (Mitsubishi) 4m 36s; **4** Vatanen/Berglund (Subaru) 4m 37s; **5** Delecour/ Grataloup (Ford), Auriol/Occelli (Toyota) 4m 38s

SS8 Donington 2 (7.67 km)
1 Auriol/Occelli (Toyota) 4m 32s; **2** Delecour/ Grataloup (Ford), Vatanen/Berglund (Subaru) 4m 34s; **4** Kankkunen/Grist (Toyota) 4m 35s; **5** Eriksson/ Parmander (Mitsubishi), Schwarz/Grist (Mitsubishi), Wilson/Thomas (Ford), Burns/Reid (Subaru) 4m 36s

SS9 MIRA (7.51 km)
1 Kankkunen/Grist (Toyota) 4m 26s; **2** McRae/Ringer (Subaru) 4m 27s; **3** Delecour/Grataloup (Ford) 4m 28s; 4 Eriksson/Parmander (Mitsubishi), Auriol/ Occelli (Toyota), Schwarz/Grist (Mitsubishi) 4m 31s

SS10 Dyfnant (20.55 km)
1 Kankkunen/Grist (Toyota) 16m 32s; **2** Wilson/ Thomas (Ford) 16m 45s; **3** Vatanen/Berglund (Subaru) 16m 53s; **4** Auriol/Occelli (Toyota) 16m 54s; **5** Burns/Reid (Subaru) 17m 15s; **6** S.Lindholm/ T.Hakala (Ford Escort Cosworth) 17m 16s

SS11 Myherin (33.64 km)
1 Eriksson/Parmander (Mitsubishi) 20m 45s; **2** Delecour/Grataloup (Ford) 20m 47s; **3** McRae/Ringer (Subaru) 20m 48s; **4** Kankkunen/Grist (Toyota), Burns/Reid (Subaru) 21m 04s; **6** Vatanen/Berglund (Subaru) 21m 06s

SS12 Hafren (24.40 km)
1 Eriksson/Parmander (Mitsubishi) 17m 43s; **2** Wilson/Thomas (Ford) 17m 57s; **3** Schwarz/Thul (Mitsubishi) 18m 05s; **4** McRae/Ringer (Subaru) 18m 12s; **5** Kankkunen/Grist (Toyota), Delecour/Grataloup (Ford) 18m 13s

SS13 Pantperthog (15.17 km)
1 McRae/Ringer (Subaru) 9m 44s; **2** Eriksson/ Parmander (Mitsubishi) 9m 48s; **3** Delecour/ Grataloup (Ford) 9m 49s; **4** Kankkunen/Grist

(Toyota) 9m 50s; **5** Vatanen/Berglund (Subaru), Schwarz/Thul (Mitsubishi) 9m 54s

SS14 Dyfi Main (23.48 km)
1 McRae/Ringer (Subaru) 15m 28s; **2** Eriksson/Parmander (Mitsubishi) 15m 33s; **3** Schwarz/Thul (Mitsubishi) 15m 40s; **4** Delecour/Grataloup (Ford) 15m 41s; **5** Kankkunen/Grist (Toyota) 15m 45s; **6** Wilson/Thomas (Ford) 15m 50s

SS15 Gartheiniog (23.40 km)
1 McRae/Ringer (Subaru) 14m 36s; **2** Eriksson/Parmander (Mitsubishi), Kankkunen/Grist (Toyota) 14m 47s; **4** Burns/Reid (Subaru) 14m 50s; **5** Delecour/Grataloup (Ford) 14m 55s; **6** Wilson/Thomas (Ford) 15m 04s

SS16 Penmachno South (13.40 km)
1 McRae/Ringer (Subaru) 7m 46s; **2** Kankkunen/Grist (Toyota) 7m 49s; **3** Eriksson/Parmander (Mitsubishi) 7m 57s; **4** Wilson/Thomas (Ford) 7m 58s; **5** Schwarz/Thul (Mitsubishi) 8m 02s; **6** Delecour/Grataloup (Ford) 8m 05s

SS17 Penmachno North (10.07 km)
1 McRae/Ringer (Subaru) 6m 05s; **2** Kankkunen/Grist (Toyota), Eriksson/Parmander (Mitsubishi) 6m 08s; **4** Vatanen/Berglund (Subaru) 6m 10s; **5** Delecour/Grataloup (Ford) 6m 11s; **6** Schwarz/Thul (Mitsubishi) 6m 12s

SS18 Brenig (9.19 km)
1 McRae/Ringer (Subaru), Kankkunen/Grist (Toyota) 6m 46s; **3** Eriksson/Parmander (Mitsubishi) 6m 49s; **4** Schwarz/Thul (Mitsubishi) 6m 52s; **5** Wilson/Thomas (Ford) 6m 54s; **6** Vatanen/Berglund (Subaru) 6m 55s

SS19 Clocaenog (19.28 km)
1 McRae/Ringer (Subaru) 12m 49s; **2** Delecour/Grataloup (Ford) 12m 54s; **3** Eriksson/Parmander (Mitsubishi) 12m 56s; **4** Vatanen/Berglund (Subaru) 12m 58s; **5** Schwarz/Grist (Mitsubishi) 13m 06s; **6** Wilson/Thomas (Ford) 13m 14s

SS20 Grizedale East (7.20 km)
1 Vatanen/Berglund (Subaru) 4m 59s; **2** McRae/Ringer (Subaru) 5m 00s; **3** Kankkunen/Grist (Toyota), Delecour/Grataloup (Ford), Auriol/Occelli (Toyota) 5m 02s; **6** Eriksson/Parmander (Mitsubishi), Schwarz/Thul (Mitsubishi) 5m 04s

SS21 Grizedale West (27.90 km)
1 Delecour/Grataloup (Ford) 19m 06s; **2** Eriksson/Parmander (Mitsubishi) 19m 07s; **3** Auriol/Occelli (Toyota) 19m 08s; **4** Kankkunen/Grist (Toyota) 19m 09s; **5** McRae/Ringer (Subaru) 19m 14s; **6** Schwarz/Thul (Mitsubishi) 19m 19s

SS22 Kershope (39.78 km)
1 Kankkunen/Grist (Toyota) 30m 47s; **2** Eriksson/Parmander (Mitsubishi) 31m 10s; **3** Delecour/Grataloup (Ford), Auriol/Occelli (Toyota) 31m 16s; **5** Vatanen/Berglund (Subaru), Schwarz/Thul (Mitsubishi) 31m 28s

SS23 Wauchope West (11.44 km)
1 Vatanen/Berglund (Subaru) 8m 09s; **2** Eriksson/Parmander (Mitsubishi) 8m 12s; **3** Kankkunen/Grist (Toyota) 8m 16s; **4** Jonsson/Bäckman (Toyota) 8m 33s; **5** Burns/Reid (Subaru) 8m 41s; **6** McRae/Senior (Subaru) 8m 49s

SS24 Wauchope East (11.07 km)
1 Vatanen/Berglund (Subaru) 8m 52s; **2** Eriksson/Parmander (Mitsubishi) 8m 54s; **3** Kankkunen/Grist (Toyota) 8m 56s; **4** McRae/Senior (Subaru) 9m 16s; **5** Burns/Reid (Subaru) 9m 29s; **6** Delecour/Grataloup (Ford), Wilson/Thomas (Ford) 9m 55s

SS25 Harwood (21.34 km)
1 Wilson/Thomas (Ford) 15m 37s; **2** Kankkunen/Grist (Toyota) 15m 58s; **3** Auriol/Occelli (Toyota), Vatanen/Berglund (Subaru) 16m 01s; **5** Eriksson/Parmander (Mitsubishi) 16m 22s; **6** Schwarz/Thul (Mitsubishi) 16m 23s

SS26 Falstone (29.90 km)
1 Wilson/Thomas (Ford) 21m 39s; **2** Delecour/Grataloup (Ford) 22m 21s; **3** Eriksson/Parmander (Mitsubishi) 22m 25s; **4** Auriol/Occelli (Toyota) 22m 26s; **5** Vatanen/Berglund (Subaru) 22m 37s; **6** Schwarz/Thul (Mitsubishi) 23m 31s

SS27 Broomylinn (17.86 km)
1 Eriksson/Parmander (Mitsubishi) 13m 54s; **2** Wilson/Thomas (Ford) 14m 05s; **3** Auriol/Occelli (Toyota) 14m 08s; **4** Delecour/Grataloup (Ford), Vatanen/Berglund (Subaru) 14m 13s; **6** Kankkunen/Grist (Toyota) 14m 24s

SS28 Pundershaw (30.26 km)
1 Kankkunen/Grist (Toyota) 20m 30s; **2** Wilson/Thomas (Ford) 20m 47s; **3** Vatanen/Berglund (Subaru) 20m 54s; **4** Delecour/Grataloup (Ford) 21m 11s; **5** Eriksson/Parmander (Mitsubishi) 21m 19s; **6** Auriol/Occelli (Toyota) 21m 32s

SS29 Hamsterley (18.45 km)
1 Kankkunen/Grist (Toyota) 12m 39s; **2** Eriksson/Parmander (Mitsubishi) 12m 51s; **3** Vatanen/Berglund (Subaru) 13m 07s; **4** Wilson/Thomas (Ford) 13m 23s; **5** Delecour/Grataloup (Ford) 13m 31s; **6** Burns/Reid (Subaru) 13m 51s

SS30 Cropton (13.00 km)
1 Eriksson/Parmander (Mitsubishi) 8m 53s; **2** Kankkunen/Grist (Toyota) 9m 06s; **3** Vatanen/Berglund (Subaru) 9m 19s; **4** Wilson/Thomas (Ford), Burns/Reid (Subaru) 9m 33s; **6** Schwarz/Thul (Mitsubishi) 9m 42s

SS31 Gale Rigg (8.35 km)
1 Kankkunen/Grist (Toyota) 6m 14s; **2** Eriksson/Parmander (Mitsubishi) 6m 23s; **3** Delecour/Grataloup (Ford) 6m 28s; **4** Vatanen/Berglund (Subaru) 6m 30s; **5** Wilson/Thomas (Ford) 6m 34s; **6** Schwarz/Thul (Mitsubishi) 6m 40s

SS32 Langdale (16.29 km)
1 Kankkunen/Grist (Toyota) 11m 25s; **2** Eriksson/Parmander (Mitsubishi) 11m 34s; **3** Delecour/Grataloup (Ford) 11m 51s; **4** Vatanen/Berglund (Subaru) 12m 13s; **5** Schwarz/Thul (Mitsubishi) 12m 15s; **6** Wilson/Thomas (Ford) 12m 17s

SS33 Dalby (32.16 km)
1 Kankkunen/Grist (Toyota) 21m 55s; **2** Eriksson/Parmander (Mitsubishi) 22m 09s; **3** Wilson/Thomas (Ford) 22m 13s; **4** Delecour/Grataloup (Ford) 22m 46s; **5** Schwarz/Thul (Mitsubishi) 22m 58s; **6** Vatanen/Berglund (Subaru) 23m 21s

SS34 Scunthorpe (7.17 km)
1 Schwarz/Thul (Mitsubishi) 4m 38s; **2** Vatanen/Berglund (Subaru), McRae/Senior (Subaru) 4m 48s; **4** Wilson/Thomas (Ford) 4m 52s; **5** Eriksson/Parmander (Mitsubishi) 4m 56s; **6** Jonsson/Bäckman (Toyota) 5m 01s

SS35 Donington 3 (4.53 km)
1 Schwarz/Thul (Mitsubishi) 3m 20s; **2** Kankkunen/Grist (Toyota), Eriksson/Parmander (Mitsubishi) 3m 21s; **4** Vatanen/Berglund (Subaru) 3m 22s; **5** Jonsson/Bäckman (Toyota) 3m 24s; **6** Evans/Davies (Ford) 3m 37s

Major Retirements

2	McRae/Ringer Engine	Subaru Impreza 555 SS22	Gr A
11	Lindholm/Hakala Accident	Ford Escort Cosworth SS21	Gr A
16	de Mevius/Lux Engine	Nissan Sunny GTI SS10	Gr A
19	Pianezzola/Roggia Accident	Lancia Delta HF Integrale SS5	Gr A
22	Head/Roy Accident	Ford Escort Cosworth SS27	Gr A
27	Mokkonen/Mannisenmaki Engine	Audi Coupé S2 SS11	Gr N

FIA Class Winners

A8 Over 2000 cc	Kankkunen/Grist	Toyota Celica Turbo 4WD
A7 1600-2000 cc	Llewellin/Grindrod	Vauxhall Astra GSi
A6 1300-1600 cc	Deville/Lhuguenot	Peugeot 106 XSi
A5 Up to 1300 cc	Triner/Klima	Skoda Favorit 136L
N4 Over 2000 cc	Evans/Davies	Ford Escort Cosworth
N3 1600-2000 cc	Green/Foy	Vauxhall Astra GSi
N2 1300-1600 cc	Crealey/Jones	Honda Civic Vti
N1 Up to 1300 cc	Yamada/Tashiro	Subaru Vivio

Rally Leaders

SS1 Kankkunen; **SS2-4** Schwarz; **SS5** Kankkunen, Schwarz; **SS6-18** Kankkunen; **SS19-21** McRae; **SS22-35** Kankkunen

World Championship Points

Drivers
1 Kankkunen 135; **2** Delecour 112; **3** Auriol 92; **4** Biasion 76; **5** Sainz, McRae 50; **7** Eriksson 41; **8** Vatanen 38; **9** Trelles 28; **10** Mäkinen 26, etc.

Manufacturers
1 Toyota 157; **2** Ford 145; **3** Subaru 110; **4** Lancia 92; **5** Mitsubishi 86

FIA Cup for Production Car Drivers
1 Fassina 56; **2** Coutinho 28; **3** Kytölehto 23; **4** Bin Sulayem 15; **5** Shamji, Fujimoto, Ordynski 13, etc.

FIA Cup for Manufacturers
1 GME 76; **2** Skoda 54; **3** Peugeot 39; **4** Citroën 26; **5** Lada 23, etc.

Route Details

Leg 1
Sunday 21 November, Birmingham-Birmingham. 9 special stages totalling 58.66 km
Leg 2
Monday 22 November, Birmingham-Lancaster.10 special stages totalling 192.58 km
Leg 3
Tuesday 23 November, Lancaster-Gateshead. 9 special stages totalling 196.75 km
Leg 4
Wednesday 24 November,Gateshead-Birmingham. 7 special stages totalling 99.95 km

Weather

Mainly dry and frosty with lying snow and ice

Special Stage Analysis

	1	2	3	4	5	6
Kankkunen (Toyota)	12	8	4	4	2	1
C.McRae (Subaru)	9	3	1	4	1	-
Eriksson (Mitsubishi)	5	14	6	1	5	2
Schwarz (Mitsubishi)	5	1	2	2	8	7
Vatanen (Subaru)	3	3	5	10	4	3
Delecour (Ford)	2	4	7	5	5	3
Wilson (Ford)	2	4	1	5	3	5
Auriol (Toyota)	1	-	5	4	2	1
Evans (Ford)	1	-	-	-	-	1
A.McRae (Subaru)	-	1	-	2	-	1
Burns (Subaru)	-	-	-	4	4	1
Jonsson (Toyota)	-	-	-	1	2	2
Lindholm (Ford)	-	-	-	-	-	1

The RAC epitomised Subaru's season. The Imprezas underlined their promise, but the result didn't quite live up to expectations, although Ari Vatanen did bring his to the finish.

Finish Lines

Malcolm Wilson's third place was his best World Championship result in Europe. He might have done better still if he had used snow tyres in Scotland and a rock hadn't jammed the Michelin **Escort**'s brakes in Hamsterley...**François Delecour** survived major gearbox problems near the finish to come fourth in the 'full' works **Escort**...There were precious few major retirements. Aside from **Colin McRae**, **Sebastian Lindholm** rolled his **Escort** in Grizedale and **Robbie Head** crashed his in Kielder ...**Armin Schwarz** plunged to 77th after going off the road for 15 minutes in Dyfnant, fighting back to eighth by the finish...**Gwyndaf Evans** dominated Group N in the Shell Helix **Escort**, but the low retirement rate kept him just outside the top 10...The Formula 2 category fell quite easily to **David Llewellin**, despite electronic problems and a road accident that broke his **Astra**'s front suspension...**Emil Triner** drove brilliantly in the snow to give **Skoda** a top 15 result...**Grégoire de Mevius** retired the works **Sunny** GTi with engine trouble.

Results

1	Juha Kankkunen/ Nicky Grist	Toyota Celica Turbo 4WD 6h 25m 48s	Gr A
2	Kenneth Eriksson/ Staffan Parmander	Mitsubishi Lancer RS-E 6h 27m 32s	Gr A
3	Malcolm Wilson/ Bryan Thomas	Ford Escort Cosworth 6h 31m 26s	Gr A
4	François Delecour/ Daniel Grataloup	Ford Escort Cosworth 6h 32m 57s	Gr A
5	Ari Vatanen/ Bruno Berglund	Subaru Impreza 555 6h 33m 59s	Gr A
6	Didier Auriol/ Bernard Occelli	Toyota Celica Turbo 4WD 6h 39m 59s	Gr A
7	Richard Burns/ Robert Reid	Subaru Legacy RS 6h 47m 25s	Gr A
8	Armin Schwarz/ Peter Thul	Mitsubishi Lancer RS-E 6h 51m 02s	Gr A
9	Mats Jonsson/ Lars Bäckman	Toyota Celica Turbo 4WD 7h 00m 48s	Gr A
10	Alister McRae/ David Senior	Subaru Legacy RS 7h 02m 12s	Gr A

165 starters, 94 finishers

Previous Winners (since 1960)

1960	Erik Carlsson/Stuart Turner	Saab 96
1961	Erik Carlsson/John Brown	Saab 96
1962	Erik Carlsson/David Stone	Saab 96
1963	Tom Trana/Sven Lindström	Volvo P544
1964	Tom Trana/Gunnar Thermenius	Volvo P544
1965	Rauno Aaltonen/Tony Ambrose	Mini-Cooper S
1967	Bengt Soderström/Gunnar Palm	Ford Lotus Cortina
1968	Simo Lampinen/John Davenport	Saab 96 V4
1969	Harry Kallström/Gunnar Haggbom	Lancia Fulvia HF
1970	Harry Kallström/Gunnar Haggbom	Lancia Fulvia HF
1971	Stig Blomqvist/Arne Hertz	Saab 96 V4
1972	Roger Clark/Tony Mason	Ford Escort RS1600
1973	Timo Mäkinen/Henry Liddon	Ford Escort RS1600
1974	Timo Mäkinen/Henry Liddon	Ford Escort RS1600
1975	Timo Mäkinen/Henry Liddon	Ford Escort RS1800
1976	Roger Clark/Stuart Pegg	Ford Escort RS1800
1977	Björn Waldegård/Hans Thorszelius	Ford Escort RS
1978	Hannu Mikkola/Arne Hertz	Ford Escort RS
1979	Hannu Mikkola/Arne Hertz	Ford Escort RS
1980	Henri Toivonen/Paul White	Talbot Sunbeam Lotus
1981	Hannu Mikkola/Arne Hertz	Audi Quattro A1
1982	Hannu Mikkola/Arne Hertz	Audi Quattro A1
1983	Stig Blomqvist/Björn Cederberg	Audi Quattro A2
1984	Ari Vatanen/Terry Harryman	Peugeot 205 Turbo 16
1985	Henri Toivonen/Neil Wilson	Lancia Delta S4
1986	Timo Salonen/Seppo Harjanne	Peugeot 205 Turbo 16
1987	Juha Kankkunen/Juha Piironen	Lancia Delta HF Turbo
1988	Markku Alén/Ilkka Kivimäki	Lancia Delta HF Integrale
1989	Pentti Airikkala/Ronan McNamee	Mitsubishi Galant VR-4
1990	Carlos Sainz/Luis Moya	Toyota Celica GT4
1991	Juha Kankkunen/Juha Piironen	Lancia Delta HF Integrale
1992	Carlos Sainz/Luis Moya	Toyota Celica Turbo 4WD

1993

RESULTS

FIA WORLD RALLY CHAMPIONSHIP FOR DRIVERS

Round		1	2	3	4	5	6	7	8	9	10	11	12	13	Total
1	Juha Kankkunen	8	15	-	20	-	R	20	(8)	20	20	-	12	20	**135 (143)**
2	François Delecour	15	-	20	-	20	R	-	15	-	12	R	20	10	**112**
3	Didier Auriol	20	R	-	-	15	R	12	12	12	R	-	15	6	**92**
4	Massimo Biasion	12	-	15	-	4	20	15	R	-	R	R	10	-	**76**
5 =	Colin McRae	-	12	4	R	8	R	-	20	-	6	-	-	R	**50**
5 =	Carlos Sainz	-	-	R	-	10	15	R	10	-	R	15	R	-	**50**
7	Kenneth Eriksson	10	-	8	-	-	R	-	-	8	-	-	-	15	**41**
8	Ari Vatanen	-	-	-	-	-	R	-	R	15	15	-	-	8	**38**
9	Gustavo Trelles	-	-	-	-	-	8	10	4	-	-	-	6	-	**28**
10	Tommi Mäkinen	-	10	-	-	-	6	-	-	10	-	-	-	-	**26**
11	Markku Alén	-	-	10	15	-	-	-	-	R	-	-	-	-	**25**
12	Armin Schwarz	6	-	R	-	-	12	-	-	2	-	-	-	3	**23**
13 =	Mats Jonsson	-	20	-	-	-	-	-	-	-	-	-	-	2	**22**
13 =	Andrea Aghini	R	-	12	-	R	10	-	-	-	-	R	-	-	**22**
15	Gianfranco Cunico	-	-	-	-	-	-	-	-	-	-	20	-	-	**20**
16	Alessandro Fiorio	-	-	6	-	-	4	-	-	-	-	R	8	-	**18**
17	Bruno Thiry	3	-	1	-	R	R	-	-	0	-	6	4	-	**14**
18 =	Ian Duncan	-	-	-	12	-	-	-	-	-	-	-	-	-	**12**
18 =	François Chatriot	-	-	-	-	12	-	-	-	-	-	-	-	-	**12**
18 =	Patrick Snijers	-	-	-	-	-	-	-	-	-	-	12	-	-	**12**
18 =	Malcolm Wilson	-	R	-	-	-	-	-	-	R	-	-	-	12	**12**
18 =	Sepp Haider	-	4	-	-	-	-	-	R	-	8	-	-	-	**12**
23 =	Yasuhiro Iwase	-	-	-	10	-	-	-	-	-	-	-	-	-	**10**
23 =	Ross Dunkerton	-	-	-	-	-	-	-	R	-	10	-	-	-	**10**
23 =	Gilberto Pianezzola	-	-	-	-	-	-	-	-	-	-	10	-	R	**10**
26 =	Björn Johansson	-	8	-	-	-	-	-	-	-	-	-	-	-	**8**
26 =	Guy Jack	-	-	-	8	-	-	-	-	-	-	-	-	-	**8**
26 =	Carlos Menem Jnr	-	-	R	-	-	-	8	-	-	-	-	-	-	**8**
26 =	Piero Liatti	-	-	-	-	-	-	-	-	-	-	8	-	-	**8**
30	Rudi Stohl	-	-	-	3	-	R	4	-	-	-	-	-	-	**7**

FIA CUP FOR PRODUCTION CAR DRIVERS

Round		1	2	3	4	5	6	7	8	9	10	11	12	13	Total
1	Alessandro Fassina	-	-	13	-	-	13	-	10	-	-	7	13		**56**
2	Antonio Coutinho	-	-	10	-	4	-	10	-	-	-	4	Ex		**28**
3	Jarmo Kytölehto	-	10	-	-	-	-	-	-	13	-	-	-	-	**23**
4	Mohammed Bin Sulayem	-	R	R	-	-	R	13	-	-	-	2	R	-	**15**
5 =	Christophe Spiliotis	13	-	-	-	-	-	-	-	-	-	-	-	-	**13**
5 =	Kenneth Bäcklund	-	13	-	-	-	-	-	-	-	-	-	-	-	**13**
5 =	Hasmat Shamji	-	-	-	13	-	-	-	-	-	-	-	-	-	**13**
5 =	Giovanni Manfrinato	-	-	-	-	13	-	-	-	-	-	R	-	-	**13**
5 =	Yoshio Fujimoto	-	-	-	-	-	-	-	13	-	R	-	-	-	**13**
5 =	Ed Ordynski	-	-	-	-	-	-	-	-	-	13	-	-	-	**13**
5 =	Renato Travaglia	-	-	-	-	-	-	-	-	-	-	13	-	-	**13**
5 =	Gwyndaf Evans	-	-	-	-	-	-	-	-	-	-	-	-	13	**13**

Whitewash: Juha Kankkunen piled success on success with a brilliant display on the RAC Rally, taking a convincing victory for Toyota.

FIA WORLD RALLY CHAMPIONSHIP FOR MANUFACTURERS

Round		1	2	3	4	5	6	7	8	9	10	11	12	13	Total
1	**Toyota**	20	20	-	20	17	0	20	(14)	20	20	-	-	20	**157 (171)**
2	**Ford**	17	0	20	-	20	20	17	17	-	14	0	20	-	**145**
3	**Subaru**	-	14	12	0	10	0	-	20	17	17	10	-	10	**110**
4	**Lancia**	0	-	14	-	12	17	12	12	-	0	17	8	-	**92**
5	**Mitsubishi**	12	11	10	0	-	14	-	0	10	12	-	-	17	**86**

Key to rounds: 1 Monte Carlo; **2** Swedish; **3** Portugal; **4** Safari; **5** Corsica; **6** Acropolis; **7** Argentina; **8** New Zealand; **9** 1000 Lakes; **10** Australia; **11** Sanremo; **12** Catalonia; **13** RAC.

1993

RALLY CAR SPECIFICATIONS

Opel/Vauxhall Astra GSi

Opel Calibra Turbo

Toyota Celica Turbo 4WD

Photo Pascal Huit

Car	Opel/Vauxhall Astra GSi	Opel Calibra Turbo	Toyota Celica Turbo 4WD
Team Manager	Alain Lopes	Mike Broad	Ove Andersson
Chief Engineer	David Whitehead/Tim Ashton	David Whitehead	Dieter Bulling
Sponsor/s	–	–	Castrol, Marlboro
Engine			
Cylinders	4 in-line	4 in-line	4 in-line
Mounts	Transverse/front	Transverse/front	Transverse/front
Capacity	1998 cc	1998 cc	1988 cc
Bore & stroke	86 x 86 mm	86 x 86 mm	86 x 86 mm
Compression ratio	11.8:1	8:1	8.5:1
Valves/camshafts	16/DOHC	16/DOHC	16/4
Fuel system	MBE electronic injection	MBE electronic injection	Nippondenso electronic injection
Turbocharger	–	KKK	Toyota CT26
Max. power	225 bhp @ 7500 rpm	300 bhp @ 6500 rpm	299 bhp @ 5600 rpm
Max. torque	230 Nm @ 5500 rpm	420 Nm @ 4500 rpm	460 Nm @ 4000 rpm
Oil contract	–	–	Castrol
Transmission			
Gearbox	GM/Xtrac 6-speed	GM/Xtrac 6-speed	Xtrac 6-speed
Drive type	2WD (front)	4WD	4WD
Clutch/differentials	AP twin-plate/Xtrac clutch and ramp diff.	AP single-plate carbon/electronic-hydraulic centre diff.	Xtrac diffs with hydraulic control/FF Developments viscous coupling
Chassis			
Steering	Rack and pinion (power assisted)	Rack and pinion (power assisted)	Rack and pinion (assisted)
Front suspension	McPherson strut	McPherson strut	McPherson strut with Bilstein shock absorbers
Rear suspension	Compound crank beam with coil springs	Independent trailing arms	McPherson strut with Bilstein shock absorbers
Wheel rim widths	6 x 15 in./7.5 x 15 in. OZ Racing	7 x 15 in./8 x 17 in. OZ Racing	6–8 x 15–17 in.
Tyres	Michelin	Michelin	Michelin
Front brakes	295 x 28 mm (6 pot calipers)	310 x 28mm (4 pot) 355 x 28mm (6 pot)	Ventilated discs
Rear brakes	254 x 21 mm (6 pot calipers)	254 x 21 mm (4 pot)	Ventilated discs
Dimensions			
Overall length	4086 mm	4492 mm	4410 mm
Overall width	1688 mm	1688 mm	1745 mm
Height	1520 mm	1520 mm	1300 mm
Wheelbase	2517 mm	2600 mm	2545 mm
Weight	950 kg	1200 kg	1200 kg
Front track	1426 mm	1426 mm	1510 mm
Rear track	1446 mm	1446 mm	1510 mm
Body	3-door unitary steel	3-door steel	3-door steel

Photo Pascal Huit

Photo Pascal Huit

Car	Renault Clio Williams	Ford Escort RS Cosworth	Lancia Delta HF Integrale
Team Manager	Patrick Landon	Colin Dobinson	Claudio Bortoletto
Chief Engineer	Gilles Lallement	John Wheeler	Franco Antoniazzi
Sponsor/s	Elf, Michelin, Diac, Philips Car Stereo	Mobil	Repsol, Totip
Engine			
Cylinders	4 in-line	4 in-line	4 in-line
Mounts	Transverse/front	Front, north-south	Transverse/front
Capacity	1998 cc	1998 cc	1995 cc
Bore & stroke	82.7 x 99 mm	90.8 x 77 mm	84 x 90 mm
Compression ratio	12:1	7.2:1	–
Valves/camshafts	16/DOHC	16/DOHC	16/DOHC
Fuel system	Sodemo Sytel electronic injection	Weber/Marelli electronic injection and ignition	Digital IAW-Weber electronic injection
Turbocharger	–	Garrett TB03	Garrett T3, air to air intercooler
Max. power	220 bhp @ 6900 rpm	300 bhp @ 6250 rpm	295 bhp @ 7000 rpm
Max. torque	23 kg/m @ 6000 rpm	450 Nm @ 4000 rpm	43 kg/m @ 4500 rpm
Oil contract	Elf	Mobil	Repsol
Transmission			
Gearbox	6-speed	Ford MS93 7-speed, non-synchromesh	6-speed
Drive type	2WD (front)	4WD	4WD, central self-locking torque split
Clutch/differentials	Tilton single-plate, ZF limited slip differential	AP 7.25 twin-plate/VC	2-plate, ZF plate-type front and rear differentials
Chassis			
Steering	Rack and pinion (assisted)	Rack and pinion (assisted)	Rack and pinion (assisted)
Front suspension	McPherson strut aluminium hub carriers, Bilstein dampers	McPherson compression/ strut with TCA	McPherson strut, lower wishbone, anti–roll bar
Rear suspension	Trailing arms, torsion bars, extra anti-roll bar, Bilstein dampers	Semi-trailing arm with coil over springs and dampers	McPherson strut, transverse link, anti-roll bar
Wheel rim widths	7.25 x 16 in. Speedline	6–8 x 16–17 in.	9 x 16/17 in. (asp), 5.5/7 x 15 in. (grav)
Tyres	Michelin	Michelin	Michelin/Pirelli
Front brakes	323 mm ventilated discs, 4 pot caliper	315-355 x 28 mm with 6 pot AP caliper	282/313/332 mm ventilated discs
Rear brakes	254 mm ventilated discs, 2 pot caliper	285 x 28 mm with 4 pot AP caliper	282 mm ventilated discs
Dimensions			
Overall length	3728 mm	4211 mm	3900 mm
Overall width	1645 mm	1734 mm	1770 mm
Height	1365 mm	1425 mm	1360 mm
Wheelbase	2472 mm	2551 mm	2480 mm
Weight	930 kg	1200 kg	1200 kg
Front track	1406 mm	1490 mm	1566 mm
Rear track	1351 mm	1490 mm	1526 mm
Body	3-door steel	Unitary 3-door steel	5-door steel

Subaru Impreza 555

Subaru Legacy RS

Mitsubishi Lancer E

Photo Pascal Huit

Car	Mitsubishi Lancer E	Subaru Impreza 555	Subaru Legacy RS
Team Manager	Andrew Cowan	David Richards	David Richards
Chief Engineer	Roland Lloyd	David Lapworth	David Lapworth
Sponsor/s	Mitsubishi Oil, Michelin, PIAA, Sabelt, Bilstein	555	555
Engine			
Cylinders	4 in-line	Flat-4	Flat-4
Mounts	Transverse/front	Front, in-line	Front, in-line
Capacity	1997 cc	1994 cc	1994 cc
Bore & stroke	85 x 88 mm	92.6 x 75 mm	92.6 x 75 mm
Compression ratio	8.5:1	8:1	8:1
Valves/camshafts	16/DOHC	16/4	16/4
Fuel system	Electronic injection	Subaru sequential injection	Subaru
Turbocharger	Mitsubishi	IHI	IHI
Max. power	298 bhp @ 6000rpm	295 bhp	295 bhp @ 6400 rpm
Max. torque	42.9 kg/m @ 4000 rpm	45 kg/m @ 4000 rpm	320 Nm
Oil contract	Mitsubishi Oil	–	–
Transmission			
Gearbox	6-speed	6-speed	6-speed
Drive type	4WD	4WD	4WD
Clutch/differentials	Single-plate/VC and hydraulic/plate diff. options	AP carbon, Prodrive mechanical diffs with hydraulic control	AP carbon, Prodrive diffs with hydraulic control
Chassis			
Steering	Rack and pinion (assisted)	Rack and pinion	Rack and pinion
Front suspension	McPherson strut	Struts with TCA	Struts with TCA
Rear suspension	Independent multi-link with trailing arms, coil springs, Showa dampers	Struts with lateral and triangle links	Struts with lateral and triangle links
Wheel rim widths	5/6/7/8 x 16 in. 9 x 17 in.	7 x 16 in. (grav) 8 x 17 in. (asp)	7 x 16 in. (grav) 8 x 17 in. (asp)
Tyres	Michelin	Michelin	Michelin/Pirelli
Front brakes	6 pot caliper, ventilated discs	AP 330–355 x 32 mm ventilated discs	AP 330–355 x 32 mm ventilated discs
Rear brakes	6 pot caliper, ventilated discs	AP 304 x 28 mm ventilated discs	AP 304 x 28 mm ventilated discs
Dimensions			
Overall length	4310 mm	4340 mm	4150 mm
Overall width	1695 mm	1690 mm	1705 mm
Height	1440 mm	1390 mm	1325 mm
Wheelbase	2500 mm	2520 mm	2580 mm
Weight	1200 kg	1200 kg	1200 kg
Front track	1450 mm	1490 mm	1450 mm
Rear track	1460 mm	1490 mm	1450 mm
Body	4-door steel	4-door steel	4-door steel

555
MICHELIN
SUBARU TECNICA INTERNATIONAL
prodrive

European Championship Review

A TRADITION LOST IN THE MISTS OF TIME

by David Williams

Every now and then, one encounters an act of childlike faith that shines out like a good deed in a naughty world. Renault Italy's actions in late 1993 were a case in point. Gianni Fiora/Max Sghedoni had already clinched the two-wheel drive category in the Italian Rally Championship and, rather than enter their home round of the World Championship, possibly earning Renault some Touring Car Cup points and offering a real challenge to the dominant Opel Belgium team, they chose to contest the ELPA and San Marino Rallies, making sure that they won the new two-wheel drive award within the European Championship. Without wishing to sound rude, most observers would have considered them to be out of their minds. What good will the two-wheel drive title do? Why pass up the chance of World Championship publicity that might go down well with influential people in Renault's Paris offices? It is true that there were a few sightings of Sghedoni lounging on the sofas in the Royal Hotel prior to the start, but that was as close as Renault came to exploiting the World Championship possibilities on the Sanremo Rally.

It would be inconsistent to stop at the two-wheel drive contest. Come to that, what good will the overall title do its recipient? In all probability, Pierre-César Baroni's new crown will not be his ticket to fame and fortune. Yet to ask is to beg the question. In Italy, at least, the European Championship is an enduring and valuable tradition. It has been won by most of the country's leading rally drivers, from Sandro Munari to Miki Biasion, from Maurizio Verini to Dario Cerrato. The fact that few of them have progressed much further is beside the point. To picture a comparable state of affairs in Britain, imagine that Colin McRae, Jim McRae, David Llewellin, Tony Pond, Roger Clark, Russell Brookes and Chris Sclater had all at some point been European Champions – and then try dismissing it as an irrelevance. It is precisely this tradition of Italian success that led Fiora/Sghedoni to skip the largest and most prestigious rally in their homeland.

While the European Championship has always been a driver's contest, the real winner in 1993 was a man who hasn't made his living from driving rally cars for six or seven years: Mauro Pregliasco. A works driver for Lancia and Alfa Romeo in the 1970s and early 1980s, he built up a good working relationship with Abarth through his own preparation company, Astra, based in Cuneo in north-western Italy; a certain amount of prototype work was entrusted to him and the 'Deltona' was in part his creation. Astra has now grown to the extent that it employs 22 mechanics, which is more than RED did in its heyday and more than Boreham had only four or five years ago. Pregliasco then broadened the scope of his operations dramatically by acquiring RAS, the Belgian tuner best known for its Sierra Cosworths, driven with conspicuous success by the likes of Robert Droogmans and Patrick Snijers.

At a stroke, he gave himself an avenue for future expansion as Lancia's power waned and made himself the arbiter of the European series. In the tradition of the Jolly Club, Grifone, or Tre Gazzelle, he ran a Delta in the 1993 championship, choosing the Sanremo-born Frenchman, Baroni, to drive it. Meanwhile, RAS was running an Escort Cosworth for that ever-present thorn in the Italians' side, Snijers. The Ford was not a success at first: it would have been easier to extract teeth than 'proper' Group A parts from the factory and Snijers had a job to beat Grégoire de Mevius's Pirelli-shod Sunny GTi-R on home ground. By the summer, all that had changed and, hitting winning form with a vengeance, the Ford man took the 24 Hours of Ieper, the Deutschland and the Madeira Rally in the space of six weeks. On the latter, he trounced Andrea Aghini's Jolly Club Integrale before the Italian crashed, while Baroni struggled home in fourth. Suddenly, the Lancia man's European title didn't look so secure and the decision to pursue French Championship points at Rouergue rather than tackle the Deutschland looked ill-advised, to say the least.

At that point, Pregliasco called off the fight. Baroni and his sponsors had been promised the European crown, not Snijers. A tense, thrilling struggle that might in other circumstances have taken the pair to the dusty heat of northern Greece and Cyprus, interspersed with the dauntingly quick tarmac lanes of the Isle of Man fizzled out on the spot. Neither man took part in any of the last three co-efficient 20 rounds of the series, leaving Baroni free to swap to an RAS Escort and make a last-ditch bid for the French title, while Snijers picked off the lesser Belgian rallies and was offered a run at Sanremo as a consolation prize. It must be said that the gangling Belgian had the better of the deal.

Instead, the little-known Italian, Vanio Pasquali, overcame slender opposition to win the ELPA in a private Escort, the British were left to their own devices on the Isle of Man and Astra won in Cyprus anyway, since Alex Fiorio collected his second successive victory on the island in one of the team's Deltas. If he broke into a sweat, it was only because of the heat.

Lovers of a pure sporting contest may decry this lacklustre finale, but Pregliasco would have been foolish to permit anything else. One of his drivers would win no matter what and there was no point in spending money twice over. In practice, a win for either of the two would have suited him very well. He views the European Championship as a practical demonstration of his team's expertise. It may not carry much significance in the outside world, but it is not lost on his clients. 'It's good publicity for Astra,' he declared, when the dust had settled. He had been in an agreeable situation in which he could not lose and it must be said that Astra/RAS cars dominated the championship, winning six of the top-scoring co-efficient 20 rallies.

It remains to be seen whether Pregliasco can exploit this feast of riches, but it's a fair bet that he will get more out of it than the official winner, Baroni. Certainly this was the greatest success of a career begun in the late 1970s, but it wasn't exactly a resounding triumph. He won just two co-efficient 20 qualifiers, demolishing slender opposition in Bulgaria and then putting up a far more convincing performance to beat the pick of his fellow countrymen at Antibes, underlining a good impression made when he won the Grasse-Alpin some weeks earlier; whatever trials he faced with Escorts later in the year, he didn't have much trouble with the French Champion, Bernard Béguin, at this point and in Grasse he also beat a troubled François Delecour in the factory car. These two events were of course on very familiar territory – good drives, but no different to Snijers winning at Ieper or, say, Erwin Weber on the Deutschland –

All Photos Hugh Bishop

Lancia was rudely shoved aside on the world stage, but the likes of César Baroni (far left) and Gilberto Pianezzola kept the faith in the European Championship, the former earning his first major title.

and he never looked like winning abroad thereafter. Moreover, he didn't so much as start a loose surface rally. As team managers aren't exactly glued to the results of the European Championship, it may be argued that this is mere hairsplitting and that the manner of Baroni's success didn't carry much significance in any event.

In his defence, it must be said that he coped well with a constant stream of co-driver changes, variously employing Denis Giraudet, Hervé Sauvage and Didier Breton, and faced an increasingly difficult task by retaining a Lancia. Quite apart from Snijers' mid-season burst, the development of the Escort as the tarmac car to beat was confirmed by Robert Droogmans's Polish victory in mid-June. In spite of persistent suggestions that Baroni would swap cars, it seems that Astra never seriously intended to do so until the championship was secured: the Delta was a known quantity, there are still plenty of Lancia spares in Cuneo and Pregliasco thinks the Italian machine is capable of winning the 1994 series too. He may well be right, but the driver is apt to be made to look like a plodder – a points hoarder rather than a sprinter – just as Baroni was in 1993. Given his extremely mixed experiences when he did change to an Escort for the last few rounds of the French series, the winner has some grounds for being grateful that he was usually confined to yesterday's car.

Although Prodrive and Ralliart scoured Europe for 'tarmac experts' in the latter months of 1993, Baroni's name was somehow never mentioned, but then he has some consolation for this oblique insult: he has a guaranteed job for next year, when Astra – or RAS – will retain him to tackle the French Championship and perhaps three tarmac World Championship rallies. It isn't exactly the equivalent of rocketing from F3000 to Formula One after winning what is theoretically the second-most prestigious title that rallying can offer, but the promise of stable employment for a driver who is over 40 is not to be turned down lightly.

That apart, Baroni's fate corresponds all too well with that of countless other Lancia-driving European Champions, such as Fabrizio Tabaton and Yves Loubet. Winning the crown is an end in itself rather than a springboard to greater things. If anything, the European title signals the onset of a driver's twilight years.

It is a rare thing to have as many as half a dozen drivers making any attempt at winning the European Championship, but the past year has been notable for a conspicuous lack of interest, since Baroni and Snijers were the only drivers to pursue the championship trail with any real enthusiasm – apart from Fiora. In part, this no doubt reflected the crippling cost of good Group A machinery, in part the recession afflicting the Continent, which naturally limits the scope for an expensive undertaking of this kind, particularly when the benefits won't be immediately obvious to a sponsor. The benefits to the competitors were brought into question this year as well. As soon as the FIA hinted that it would not award A- and B- seedings for European Championship results, the value of, say, winning Group N against sketchy opposition on the ELPA Rally diminished markedly. Truly, 1993 was a season in which overstretched budgets were better spent at home.

Belgians traditionally figure prominently in the European Championship, because their domestic series not only permits, but encourages them to score points abroad. It is indicative of how little support there was for European campaigning in 1993 that Robert Droogmans got as high as third in the points table with minimal effort. The highlight of the 1990 champion's season was his victory in Poland in the Gordon Spooner Escort but, in general, he was overshadowed by Snijers and he wasn't able to offer much of a challenge even at Ieper, a rally he has won more often than anyone. There has long been a question mark over the affable Droogmans's grasp of four-wheel drive and the fact that he has gone into semi-retirement suggests that his motivation is no longer what it was either.

Mentioning the likes of Richard Burns and Piero Liatti, the British and Italian Champions respectively, implies that they were in some way pursuing the championship. They were not, but domestic sucess got them a long way up the points table in a year like 1993, the same applying to Longhi's Grifone team-mate, Gilberto Pianezzola.

There were drivers who turned up on a number of co-efficient 20 rounds, such as Ramon Ferreyros, who deployed a Grifone Delta to spectacular effect at Ieper and in Madeira, both rallies he knows intimately. Yet it wasn't so much a European Championship bid as the linking together of a programme on a number of prestigious, well-financed rallies able to dangle financial inducements in front of talented drivers. It is this technique just as much as its elevated European status that draws a good entry to Ieper every June. The funds that lured Ferreyros also brought Alister McRae, for example, who made a one-off appearance in a Mike Taylor-prepared Group A Escort sponsored by the Belgian furniture company, Crack. Jim McRae's second son also attempted the Manx as part of his British Championship programme and, through another local sponsor, the Cyprus Rally, driving yet another car. In this case, it was a locally prepared Group N Legacy that wouldn't have passed an MOT and didn't survive the first road section. In the end, the 22-year-old Scot tackled more top European rounds than any of his fellow countrymen, but he no more had designs on the European title than Juha Kankkunen did. It remains one of the paradoxes of the European series that it includes a number of magnificent rallies, but that the whole adds up to something less than the sum of its parts.

Even the championship's most stalwart defenders agree that it needs to change. Given that the Formula 2 bandwagon has started to gather speed (Fiora faced a challenge of a kind from the Dane, Tim Svanholt, and the Russian, Evgeni Vasin) and that most of the top qualifying rounds are on tarmac, it seems sensible to turn the series and perhaps

The perennial runner-up, Patrick Snijers actually won more rallies in his Escort than the Champion in 1993, including the Madeira Rally. No matter what the result, Mauro Pregliasco (right) was onto a winner.

the rallies themselves over to two-wheel drive cars. In doing so, costs would be reduced dramatically and the title might at last become a rung on the way up, not down the ladder. Transforming the series into a sort of rallying equivalent of F3000 could also impose some kind of structure on an amorphous sport that outsiders have trouble understanding.

It will not be easy. The new two-wheel drive title apart, the European Championship has remained exceptionally resistant to the changes sweeping the sport at international level. While World, French and British Championship organisers, to name but three, slash the length of their events and attempt, however reluctantly, to cut costs, the top European organisers plough their own furrow, oblivious to anyone else. The European calendar takes no account of clashes with World Championship events, nor even the plight of the competitor: it is next to impossible to use the same vans for the ELPA, Manx and Cyprus Rallies, considering the intervals between the three and their locations at opposite ends of Europe. Moreover, this state of affairs has prevailed for time out of mind. Were it not for the compulsory changes inflicted on international rallying in the wake of the Group B catastrophes in 1986, there would be events in the series that hadn't changed materially in 15 or 20 years. While other organisers have reduced the number of stages and restricted servicing, or the number of tyres to be used, there are European Championship events such as the Manx and Ieper that include almost 40 stages (half as many again as the Monte or the Rally of Argentina, despite running less than three-quarters of the stage distance) and allow crews to service wherever they please. It is true to say that the compact nature of both Ieper and the Manx means that the minimum level of service cover can be provided with two vehicles on either, but Paris rarely takes account of such niceties in framing the rules. The point is that no one, either in FISA's offices or elsewhere, seems to have considered the economic question so far as the European series is concerned. Indeed, when Max Mosley was asked a question about the European Championship at his press conference on the eve of the 1000 Lakes, most of the assembled journalists were as surprised as he was. Whether one chooses to treat this as evidence of FISA inertia, that the championship is stuck in a time warp, or of its fundamental irrelevance is a matter of taste.

A change to Formula 2 would be greeted by widespread and powerful opposition. After all, three-quarters of the top 20 points scorers benefitted from four-wheel drive. A rally such as Ieper is staged in large part as a spectator attraction and the prospect of losing the turbocharged big bangers might not appeal, while team owners such as Pregliasco would also be hostile. He feels that the series needs the 'Formula 1' cars to inject some glamour and points out that the expense of running two different types of car for a team such as his, which also contests the World Championship, would be a major deterrent. How this accords with running two types of car as it is, the Delta Integrale and the Escort Cosworth, is a matter of conjecture.

Yet Pregliasco whole heartedly agrees that something needs to be done about costs. He would welcome a reduction in the size of the championship. The fact that it has no fewer than 50 rounds is an irrelevance, as serious teams concentrate exclusively on the co-efficient 20 rallies, with perhaps the occasional co-efficient ten qualifier thrown in. In effect, it is a ten-round series, but even that is too many in Pregliasco's eyes. He finds it ludicrous that the second division championship should have more qualifying events than the first division series and regards six to seven rounds as being about right. Cutting the number of high-scoring rallies would not only reduce costs significantly, but it might also entice a few more contestants into the open. From a competitor's point of view, it is hard to see a drawback.

There is of course a very obvious snag. The European Championship is pre-eminently a system of patronage, whereby individual countries are kept in the FISA fold by being awarded a major event. There is little prospect of an important race being run in, say, Bulgaria, but the awarding of co-efficient 20 status to the Zlatni Piassatzi Rally confers prestige of a kind. Given the mess FISA has got itself into by attempting to thin down the World Championship, it is barely conceivable that anything similar might be tried, far less achieved, at European level.

Curiously enough, though, the European Championship edifice may be under threat from a most unexpected source: the European Commission. To avoid breaching laws freeing trade and movement within the European Community, the RACMSA has declared that the holder of any national competition licence issued by a country within the European Community may take part in any national rally in Britain in 1994, thus extending a privilege only available to Irish competitors in the past. This development can only expand. In due course, the organisers of smaller internationals may wonder if the expense of FISA observers and mountains of paperwork are worth the effort, if they can attract foreign competitors when running under a national permit. This will apply with added force to clubs running lowly co-efficient two and five rounds of the European Championship. Provided money can still be prised from the tourist board and the chamber of commerce, why bother?

Photo LAT

EUROPEAN CHAMPIONSHIP RESULTS

PIANCAVALLO RALLY, 22-25 April, Italy.

1	P. Longhi/ M. Imerito	Lancia Delta HF Integrale	3h 50m 41s.
2	G. Pianezzola/ L. Roggia	Lancia Delta HF Integrale	3h 51m 18s.
3	G. Cunico/ S. Evangelisti	Ford Escort RS Cosworth	3h 53m 40s.
4	D. Cerrato/ L. Guizzardi	Lancia Delta HF Integrale	3h 59m 41s.
5	C. Baroni/ H. Sauvage	Lancia Delta HF Integrale	4h 03m 04s.
6	G. Fiora/ M. Sghedoni	Renault Clio 16S	4h 06m 20s.
7	R. Cimolai/ N. Vazzoler	Lancia Delta HF Integrale	4h 06m 59s.
8	G. Manfrinato/ C. Condotta	Ford Sierra RS Cosworth	4h 08m 09s.
9	R. Travaglia/ M. Mari	Ford Escort RS Cosworth	4h 08m 54s.
10	B. Bentivogli/ C. Hedinger	Ford Escort RS Cosworth	4h 10m 28s.

ZLATNI PIASSATZI RALLY, 8-9 May, Bulgaria.

1	C. Baroni/ H. Sauvage	Lancia Delta HF Integrale	3h 20m 17s.
2	G. Petrov/ I. Tonev	Volkswagen Golf GTI 16V	3h 32m 49s.
3	H. Gassner/ H. Brock	Mitsubishi Galant VR-4	3h 35m 21s.
4	P. Jekov/ S. Tcholakov	Mazda 323 Turbo 4x4	3h 36m 43s.
5	E. Vasin/ E. Kalachev	Opel Corsa GSi	3h 40m 57s.
6	G. Capre/ J. Jannalfo	Nissan Sunny GTi-R	3h 44m 11s.
7	A. Potapov/ S. Lotko	Lada Samara	3h 53m 07s.
8	S. Radkov/ V. Bonev	Lada Samara	3h 56m 03s.
9	D. Ivanov/ I. Boyadjiev	Lada Samara	3h 56m 14s.
10	A. Markov/ K. Milanov	Lada Samara	3h 58m 36s.

ANTIBES RALLY, 27-29 May, France.

1	C. Baroni/ D. Giraudet	Lancia Delta HF Integrale	4h 25m 07s.
2	D. De Meyer/ O. Solut	BMW M3	4h 26m 54s.
3	B. Béguin/ J. P. Chiaroni	Ford Escort RS Cosworth	4h 27m 33s.
4	J. Ragnotti/ G. Thimonier	Renault Clio Williams	4h 29m 03s.
5	A. Oreille/ J. M. André	Renault Clio Williams	4h 32m 29s.
6	J. M. Beuzelin/ J. Bourgoin	Lancia Delta HF Integrale	4h 33m 48s.
7	P. Magaud/ G. Brun	Citroën ZX 16V	4h 36m 26s.
8	S. Polo/ S. Chapuis	Ford Escort RS Cosworth	4h 41m 52s.
9	P. Orsucci/ D. Savignoni	Renault Clio 16S	4h 44m 11s.
10	J. H. Hazard/ Y. Roussel	Ford Escort RS Cosworth	4h 44m 33s.

POLISH RALLY, 10-13 June, Poland.

1	R. Droogmans/ R. Joosten	Ford Escort RS Cosworth	3h 36m 33s.
2	C. Baroni/ D. Giraudet	Lancia Delta HF Integrale	3h 39m 17s.
3	P. Przybylski/ K. Geborys	Toyota Celica Turbo 4WD	3h 45m 37s.
4	M. Gieruszczak/ M. Skrobot	Toyota Celica Turbo 4WD	3h 48m 42s.
5	N. Min/ J. Lambert	Mitsubishi Galant VR-4	3h 57m 06s.
6	W. Stec/ M. Maciejewski	Mitsubishi Galant VR-4	4h 00m 31s.
7	K. Göttlicher/ W. Jahrbacher	Ford Sierra RS Cosworth	4h 03m 11s.
8	S. Girdauskas/ Z. Sakalauskas	Lada Samara	4h 06m 25s.
9	A. Simashka/ L. Bachiliunas	Nissan Sunny GTi-R	4h 07m 24s.
10	K. Holowczyc/ R. Burchard	Toyota Celica Turbo 4WD	4h 10m 24s.

24 HOURS OF IEPER, 25-27 June, Belgium.

1	P. Snijers/ D. Colebunders	Ford Escort RS Cosworth	3h 33m 13s.
2	R. Droogmans/ R. Joosten	Ford Escort RS Cosworth	3h 39m 35s.
3	R. Ferreyros/ G. Van Oosten	Lancia Delta HF Integrale	3h 42m 41s.
4	P. Lietaer/ H. De Maegd	Ford Escort RS Cosworth	3h 45m 41s.
5	C. Baroni/ D. Giraudet	Lancia Delta HF Integrale	3h 47m 16s.
6	G. de Mevius/ W. Lux	Nissan Sunny GTi-R	3h 48m 54s.
7	P. Dumoulin/ J. Termote	Lancia Delta HF Integrale	3h 51m 14s.
8	D. Bruyneel/ J. Debeaussaert	Lancia Delta HF Integrale	3h 52m 17s.
9	B. Thiry/ S. Prévot	Opel Astra GSi	3h 55m 35s.
10	F. Loix/ J. Vranken	Opel Astra GSi	3h 56m 14s.

DEUTSCHLAND RALLY, 8-11 July, Germany.

1	P. Snijers/ D. Colebunders	Ford Escort RS Cosworth	3h 07m 29s.
2	E. Weber/ M. Hiemer	Mitsubishi Galant VR-4	3h 08m 50s.
3	D. Depping/ P. Thul	Ford Escort RS Cosworth	3h 11m 05s.
4	G. de Mevius/ W. Lux	Nissan Sunny GTi-R	3h 12m 51s.
5	J. Mulvad/ F. Pedersen	Toyota Celica Turbo 4WD	3h 18m 17s.
6	P. Van Merksteijn/ H. Van Beek	Ford Escort RS Cosworth	3h 20m 03s.
7	M. Moosleitner/ M. Eckhardt	Mitsubishi Galant VR-4	3h 22m 57s.
8	J. Mortensen/ F. Mogensen	Ford Escort RS Cosworth	3h 25m 35s.
9	G. Senge/ D. Schneppenheim	Toyota Celica Turbo 4WD	3h 25m 42s.
10	H. Vossen/ A. Luteijn	Mitsubishi Galant VR-4	3h 26m 02s.

RALLYE VINHO MADEIRA, 6-7 August, Portugal.

1	P. Snijers/ D. Colebunders	Ford Escort RS Cosworth	3h 10m 22s.
2	R. Ferreyros/ G. Van Oosten	Lancia Delta HF Integrale	3h 11m 20s.
3	F. Peres/ R. Caldeira	Ford Escort RS Cosworth	3h 11m 51s.
4	C. Baroni/ D. Breton	Lancia Delta HF Integrale	3h 15m 35s.
5	S. Pianezzola/ D. Zanatta	Lancia Delta HF Integrale	3h 18m 20s.
6	J. Bica/ J. Capelo	Lancia Delta HF Integrale	3h 21m 44s.
7	D. Bruyneel/ J. Debeaussaert	Lancia Delta HF Integrale	3h 22m 54s.
8	A. Campos/ J. Camacho	Volkswagen Golf GTI 16V	3h 29m 33s.
9	A. Abel/ J. Ferreira	Ford Escort RS Cosworth	3h 31m 07s.
10	L. Gomes/ R. Fernando	Ford Sierra RS Cosworth	3h 33m 36s.

RALLYE ELPA, 28-30 August, Greece.

1	V. Pasquali/ L. Tedeschini	Ford Escort RS Cosworth	4h 02m 19s.
2	C. Apostolou/ M. Kriadis	Lancia Delta HF Integrale	4h 12m 47s.
3	'Stratissino'/ T. Pavli	Nissan Sunny GTi-R	4h 15m 13s.
4	G. Fiora/ M. Sghedoni	Renault Clio Williams	4h 19m 41s.
5	M. Klimatsakis/ V. Tsouvaltsis	Lancia Delta HF Integrale	4h 23m 11s.
6	P. Giagnissis/ G. Kerantzakis	Mazda 323GT-R	4h 25m 21s.
7	G. Aggelidis/ A. Goussetis	Mercedes-Benz 190E 16	4h 32m 02s.
8	P. Jekov/ S. Tcholakov	Mazda 323GT-X	4h 33m 57s.
9	S. Kokkinis/ S. Mokkas	Peugeot 205 Rallye	4h 36m 26s.
10	A. Koloithas/ G. Karavaggelis	Mazda 323GT-X	4h 38m 05s.

MANX INTERNATIONAL RALLY, 15-17 September, Britain.
(See British Championship review.)

ROTHMANS CYPRUS RALLY, 1-3 October, Cyprus.

1	A. Fiorio/ V. Brambilla	Lancia Delta HF Integrale	5h 44m 38s.
2	A. Jeropoulos/ M. Michael	Mitsubishi Galant VR-4	5h 48m 47s.
3	'Bagheera'/ N. Stephan	Lancia Delta HF Integrale	5h 56m 47s.
4	V. Terzian/ G. Sergides	Toyota Celica Turbo 4WD	6h 07m 33s.
5	D. Mavropoulos/ N. Antoniades	Ford Escort RS Cosworth	6h 12m 04s.
6	S. Hadjisavvas/ C. Hadjisavvas	Mitsubishi Galant VR-4	6h 23m 06s.
7	C. Georgallis/ A. Kollitiris	Nissan Sunny GTi-R	6h 25m 19s.
8	E. Antypas/ Z. Richa	Audi 90 Quattro	6h 31m 22s.
9	N. Chrysanthou/ D. Demetriou	Ford Escort RS Cosworth	6h 36m 42s.
10	Z. Prastides/ G. Demetriades	Honda Civic Si	6h 39m 03s.

EUROPEAN CHAMPIONSHIP STANDINGS:
1 Baroni 1760; **2** Snijers 1350; **3** Droogmans 760; **4** G. Pianezzola 630; **5** Longhi 624; **6** Burns 600; **7** Weber 600; **8** Petrov 580; **9** Ferreyros 540; **10** Depping 540.

MOBIL 1/Top Gear British Championship Review

YOUTH TRIUMPHS OVER EXPERIENCE

by David Campbell, Editor, Top Race & Rally

Richard Burns climbed from his Subaru Legacy RS at St John's on the Isle of Man and hugged his father. The final service after the last stage of the Manx International Rally was the scene of much jubilation among the Prodrive team as the Elonex machine slipped into the car park. An ecstatic Burns was even moved to offer a kiss to the Team Manager, Andy Moss!

Burns had every right to celebrate. At only 22 years of age, he had just become the youngest-ever British Rally Champion, beating the previous title-holder, Colin McRae, by one year. Commentators were quick to draw comparisons.

On the face of it, one might suppose that it was a fairly easy victory. The cool, lanky redhead had just won the Manx, his fourth win of the season, but in fact he had only needed to finish 15th. After just three rounds, the threat posed by Malcolm Wilson's Michelin Pilot Ford Escort Cosworth had all but vanished. One has to ask just how difficult it was, but only because the Checkendon hotshoe had done such a fine job of making success look easy. His British Championship triumph was in no sense the empty honour that Colin McRae had pocketed the previous season. Potentially, Burns did have a battle on his hands: from the outset, Wilson posed a formidable threat and Richard's own team-mate, Alister McRae – Colin's 22-year-old brother – was widely believed to be the faster driver. Any bookie would have given you longish odds on Burns winning and Wilson was a clear favourite. The fact that Wilson and McRae ended the season bemoaning their luck, and reflecting on severe punishment for minute errors is very much to Burns's credit; like most top drivers, he has a gift for staying out of trouble.

As Colin McRae said before the start of the season: 'If you look at Malcolm Wilson's times on the 1992 RAC Rally, he was right up there with the best in the world. And this year is Alister's and Richard's learning year, so you can't expect them to beat Malcolm straight away.'

But they did beat him, and Burns started a winning streak that lasted until the Ulster Rally and a mistake that landed the Subaru the wrong side of a hedge. While the gods seemed to favour the younger driver, Wilson endured one of the most miserable seasons of his career. The television pictures from the Scottish Rally told the whole story – there was Wilson, sitting beside his service barge with his head in his hands, mumbling: 'What do I have to do?'

That was after his third mechanical failure in as many rounds. On the Vauxhall Rally of Wales, an indifferent performance was attributed to teething problems. After all, it was the first time Malcolm's Escort had turned a wheel in anger and electrical trouble, culminating in an infuriating windscreen wiper failure in heavy rain, combined with a lack of power to allow Burns to storm into a comfortable lead, while the more experienced Cumbrian struggled home in a disappointing fifth place. Wilson promised that next time, things would be different. They were not.

The two-day Pirelli International Rally – essentially, the old one-day national event, upgraded and spread over the weekend through some ingenious logistical engineering from the Clerk of the Course, Andrew Kellitt – was really Wilson's last chance to put his stamp on the series. With only five rounds in the new 'revamped' British Championship, there was no room for error.

His pace was astonishing. Any question marks raised over his performance in Wales were soon wiped from the mind as he proved that his Escort had been down on power on the first round and he was, in fact, quicker than Burns. His vile luck had not deserted him, though, and the alternator practically fell off the car when the opposition was trailing in his wake. After winning seven of the eight stages, Wilson scraped through to finish second and that was after a comedy of errors as Ford tried to engineer a result.

Perhaps the biggest blow to the British Championship's credibility was dealt on the Pirelli as Ford fumbled its team orders. Gwyndaf Evans was lying second going into the last stage of the event, Wilson third. Representatives of Ford denied that any instructions had been issued, but orders indeed came through that Evans was to let Wilson past into second place. The Welshman was driving the Vecta Group N Escort and his overall position made little difference to his title hopes. It made all the difference in the world to Wilson and certainly the decision was a good one in tactical terms. However, a very public exercise in 'fixing' the result became a farce. With the BBC Top Gear in-car camera switched on, Evans pulled to the side of the road close to the end of the stage. Clearly recorded discussions took place between Evans and co-driver Howard Davies as to how long they should wait. Wilson blasted past, a quick calculation was made, and Evans took off again for the stage finish. However, they had miscalculated: Wilson was still third.

Eventually, Evans had to book in to the final control one minute late to achieve the desired result. No one had missed a thing and yet Ford continued to deny that there had been even a hint of interference! The company's man-on-the-spot, Nick Palmer, caught the brunt of an unprecedented attack from the motoring press, irritated by his patronising denial rather than the team orders themselves, while, to complete Ford's humiliation, several million Top Gear viewers witnessed the full story unfold from Evans's cockpit the following week.

The incident had all the elements of the Russell Brookes and Mark Lovell

All Photos LAT

Photo Gavin Lodge

débâcle on the 1989 Manx, when the latter was ordered to stand aside and let his team-mate through. There wasn't the same drama this time. No one was hurt by the exercise, Evans was just as happy in third place and the Subaru squad simply shrugged its shoulders. Everyone agreed that it was bad luck that Malcolm didn't win anyway and that he deserved to be promoted to second after a scintillating performance in the Escort. Yet it was a messy affair – sad rather than funny – and it didn't win any new fans for a sport which is difficult to understand in the first place.

The championship lurched onward. With just five rounds it was hard to build up any momentum in excitement or drama. Wilson's problems on the first two rallies had put Burns a long way in front and only a victory on the third round, the Scottish, would salvage much more than a mathematical hope of the Ford man winning his first British International title, or rescue the championship itself from the doom that was widely predicted after the 1992 nadir. Wilson's never-ending catalogue of disasters continued in Scotland when a gearbox mainshaft gave way on the fourth stage, McRae got a puncture at the critical moment and Burns cruised home to another victory.

The Manx typified the championship as a whole: Richard Burns (far left) drove coolly to a decisive victory, while the spectacular Kenny McKinstry added to Subaru's success with second place. Malcolm Wilson led every round of the series, but the Ford driver's luck didn't so much run out as desert him entirely; his only win came on the Ulster.

At this point, after just three rounds, the championship had virtually run its course. The national newspapers gave a nodding acknowledgement to Burns's achievement in becoming the youngest-ever driver to score a hat-trick of wins and bade farewell. There wasn't enough left to keep them interested. In their eyes, the series had gone the same way as in the previous four years, with one driver and car dominating and no contest worthy of the name.

Those close to the sport hoped for better. There was a slim chance that Wilson could still challenge the youngster and suddenly, after one small slip-up by Burns on the Ulster, the championship contest twitched with life once more. On the fifth stage the newcomer overlooked a patch of polished, slippery tarmac – an infamous trap in Ireland – and slid off the road. Meanwhile, Wilson was in irresistible form and powered his, by now reliable, Escort into the lead for his first victory. The national press cocked an ear once more but, as the mathematicians got to work on possible outcomes, it became clear that Burns's chances were hardly impaired. Before the Ulster, he had had a 24-point advantage; prior to the Manx, this had slipped to a six-point deficit. Since only four scores counted, he needed to finish no lower than fourth; if he did, even victory wouldn't be enough for Wilson.

All the mathematical wizardry in the world could not compensate for Wilson's and McRae's dismal performance during the season. The Championship Manager, John Horton, had devised a points-scoring scheme that he felt was sure to take the championship through to the final round. Increased points were awarded for the Ulster and Manx Rallies, and there was a ten-point bonus for starting all five events. While this made it harder for anyone to win the championship before the final round, it also made it harder to explain to the non-specialist media, who eventually gave up trying to comprehend it altogether.

Wilson's dramatic exit from the championship on the eighth stage of the Manx when he rolled his Escort and aggravated the shoulder injury sustained on the 1000 Lakes was the last straw for the pre-season favourite. His declared intention of winning the British series and then making one last attempt at breaking into the World Championship before he was 40 was shattered. To tell the truth, he had been on a hiding to nothing: if he had won, it would have been no more than what was expected; if he lost, he was over the hill. Just as damagingly, his personal failure did nothing to enhance the sport's standing within Britain. McRae didn't even get as far as stage eight, putting his Legacy off the road as early as the second stage of the Manx and finishing the year behind the Group N and 'Formula 2' category winners, Gwyndaf Evans and David Llewellin. One non-finish too many had cost him dear. Like Wilson, he found that a host of good stage times was not enough.

Yet the 'green shoots' of recovery were evident. The national media, though confused at times, even despairing, took a greater interest than in recent years. The potential for a battle was there and it was blunted largely by the mechanical unreliability of Wilson's car on the first three rounds. The complex scoring system achieved its aim in prolonging the outcome to the final round and ensured that the top runners appeared on each of the five rallies.

Running just five events (compared with up to eight in recent years) cut the costs of competing and, with one rally in each country of the United Kingdom, it should have made it easier to package. Fine on paper, the idea seemed to miss its target. With just five events, Wilson's and McRae's demise was all the more rapid. They were not allowed the luxury afforded in previous years of recovering from early-season problems. Burns complained that the long gaps between events left him short of 'match practice' and, from a promotional point of view, it was difficult to maintain interest. As a package, the series failed to sell itself because, in part, of the reluctance or inability of each event's organisers to play an integrated role in the championship – and even the basic premise of each country hosting a round fell down when the English event insisted on calling itself the 'Pirelli International Rally' without the word 'England' or 'English' mentioned in the title.

The lack of co-ordination between the championship organisers and the event organisers reverberated through the whole series. Promotional efforts to attract spectators and media interest collapsed thanks to poor communications, although this hardly reflects on the individual organisers. It has to be said that Horton attempted to resuscitate what was essentially a moribund championship, and through sheer force of will and energy succeeded to some extent. However, budgets were ridiculously low and many, much-needed innovations were deemed impossible through lack of funding. The individual motor clubs and organising teams should nevertheless be applauded for their efforts, often running events on the lower limits of financial viability with stretched resources.

But the qualified success of the British series threw up a number of serious issues that need to be addressed if the championship is to continue its upward climb. It became quite clear that the system of individual event organisers working separately from the championship organisers is no longer viable, especially when competitors continue to be thin on the ground. The risk of cancellation was real and on a number of events, especially the Pirelli International, the credibility of the whole series was in jeopardy. What would have happened to the British Championship's chances of survival if the Pirelli had been cancelled, as it so nearly was?

Just two weeks before the event, Kellitt was warned by his committee that the level of entries was too low and the

K200FMC

event should be scrapped. A quietly determined organiser, he refused to be thwarted, for he was only too aware that the future of professional British rallying hung for a moment on his decision. Had he given up, there is little doubt that the sport would have been relegated to amateur status. After a heavy session on pocket calculators and a route modification to reduce the cost of running the event, Kellitt was finally able to give the green light, and the Pirelli International Rally – and British international rallying as a whole – survived by the skin of its financial teeth.

Reducing the championship to five rounds and retaining events that ran as one-day rallies in the old National Championship helped to reduce the cost of contesting the series, but it also had the damaging effect of reducing the glamour and appeal of the championship, and it did little to lower the cost of competing on individual events. Entry fees continued to rise (even a tarmac event such as the Ulster now costs £500 to enter) and, given such a high financial threshold, privateers remained scarce. The works teams were in a somewhat different position. Unsubstantiated rumours put Prodrive's costs for running Richard Burns alone at over £200,000, which is 20 per cent less than a typical late-1980s Group A budget – albeit for fewer rallies.

Horton has a gift for attracting the clubmen, honed on his revival of the Mintex National Series. His salesman's patter drew in the one-make championships, including the Metro GTi Cup and the Skoda Trophy, and he managed to assemble a package of prize money, bonuses and other benefits which, along with manufacturers' incentives such as the Vauxhall Bonus scheme, amounted to £70,000. Nevertheless, amateur competitors were hard pushed to find the money to compete. The indisputable fact remains that the fortunes of the British Rally Championship are closely tied to the state of the economy. The drive to reduce costs is, perhaps, leading the organisers down a blind alley. It would be better, according to many commentators, to increase the value of the product to make it worth the vast sums required to take part – although this isn't easy to balance with the needs of the clubman. Certainly, the value to sponsors is low. Worryingly, one team member, holding a very senior position, sniffed: 'The British Championship? Don't talk to me about that. What a waste of time and money!'

Others would have one believe that the British Championship has now established itself as a real breeding ground for young British talent. 'Look at Colin McRae,' they say. 'He won the championship twice and now he's doing tremendously well in the World Championship!' Certainly, there is every reason to believe that Burns will now follow a similar path, but that belief is not based on the fact that he has won the British Championship. Rather he has, as Colin McRae did, demonstrated to Prodrive that he can control his urge to drive fast and channel his energy into winning championships. In practice, Prodrive is the breeding ground for young British stars, not the championship itself, which is used as little more than a laboratory to test its new products (the drivers) under realistic conditions. Burns's probable absence from the British scene next year will emphasise the point. Prodrive's new star will be taken to a different laboratory.

It is easy to be too dismissive of Britain's premier rally championship. For the sponsor, Mobil, valuable exposure was gained on Top Gear and elsewhere. Michelin, too, felt that its association with Wilson and Robbie Head was sufficiently worthwhile to justify a similar level in 1994. Vecta, the car immobiliser manufacturer, strengthened links with Ford through its involvement with Gwyndaf Evans in the Group N car, and Evans's performance in winning the Group N Championship did a great deal to sell the average Ford buyer the merits of the catalytic converter. Prior to Gwyndaf's victory, it suffered from a negative image with anyone remotely interested in performance.

The benefits to Elonex, the computer company that backed Burns and McRae, were less clear-cut but, judging by the mass of column inches devoted to rallying in computer trade magazines, the company must be pleased. Richard Burns is almost as familiar a name with Information Technology managers as motorsport fans these days!

For those less fortunate in the sponsorship stakes, the year was a struggle. Chris Birkbeck made fleeting appearances in a privately-run Vauxhall Astra GTE, but stood little chance in taking on David Llewellin and the official Vauxhall Sport entry in the race for the new Formula 2 crown. For Llewellin, the Formula 2 title came to him as easily as his double British Championship victories in 1989 and 1990.

Throughout the year, there was a great deal of talk about turning the British series into a Formula 2-only affair. While Formula 2 cars made up many of the entries, the basic flaw remained that they were decidedly unspectacular, although Llewellin often did a fine job of proving otherwise. The ease with which the Welshman won pointed to an amplification of the problems that already exist at the top level. Paul Frankland's unsavoury brush with the Central Television entertainment programme, The Cook Report, and allegations of organised car

Escorts proliferated, but Ford was thwarted at nearly every turn, Gwyndaf Evans's Group N success (top right) being a notable exception. Robbie Head (previous page) and Chris Birkbeck did their reputations no harm with good results on the Manx, though. Once he discovered that he could make a front-wheel drive car oversteer, David Llewellin was very much at home in the Astra, his efforts ensuring that Vauxhall dominated the Formula 2 category (left).

Photo Gavin Lodge

Photo Gavin Lodge

crime didn't help when Peugeot pulled the plug on his Formula 2 programme, but neither did the fact that the eventual Lombard Finance Junior Champion, Brendan Crealey, led the Formula 2 category after the Pirelli International in a Group N Honda Civic 1600!

Ford and Subaru have both made their opposition to Formula 2 clear and Vauxhall is easily the most vociferous advocate of two-wheel drive, calling for new regulations to outlaw the 'big bangers', with Peugeot offering comparatively muted support. The Formula 2 question indicates a major flaw in the thinking of those responsible for promoting and organising the British Rally Championship, that is, preventing solutions from being developed for other problems facing the sport. Rallying is quite clearly contemplating its own navel when considering the move to Formula 2, or any of the other cost-reducing innovations. No one has asked those that pay either directly or indirectly for the sport what they want to see! Spectators, television viewers, magazine and newspaper readers all want spectacle and drama. These are the people who pay to see the competitors in one way or another and who buy the products that team and event sponsors are trying to sell. Being generous, one could argue that great strides were made in improving a championship being counted out on its feet. These improvements did much to attract competitors and bring the series back to life, even to enthuse the non-specialist press. But little or nothing was done to improve the commercial value of the package. While in pure marketing terms, the product was cut to the bone with cost-cutting measures to make it cheaper, no effort was made to sell it to anyone that counted. The costs to amateurs were reduced from extortionately high to plain too expensive, but then mechanisms to help them afford it were never put in place. These mechanisms would have allowed for greater sponsorship.

Richard Burns achieved an amazing feat by becoming the youngest-ever British Champion. He set himself on a path that could easily lead to World Championship stardom, but not enough people know about it and fewer still care.

BRITISH CHAMPIONSHIP RESULTS

Vauxhall Rally of Wales, Mobil 1/Top Gear Round 1, 20-21 March.

1 Richard Burns/ Subaru Legacy RS
Robert Reid 2h 25m 23s.
2 Alister McRae/ Subaru Legacy RS
David Senior 2h 29m 00s.
3 Stephen Finlay/ Ford Sierra RS Cosworth 4x4
Dessie Wilson 2h 31m 35s.
4 Gwyndaf Evans/ Ford Escort RS Cosworth
Howard Davies 2h 34m 03s.
5 Malcolm Wilson/ Ford escort RS Cosworth
Bryan Thomas 2h 35m 32s.
6 David Llewellin/ Vauxhall Astra GSi
Ian Grindrod 2h 37m 53s.
7 Mark Higgins/ Vauxhall Astra GSi
Mike Corner 2h 43m 05s.
8 Steve Bennett/ Peugeot 205GTI 1.9
Michael Park 2h 44m 55s.
9 Kevin Curran/ Ford Sierra RS Cosworth 4x4
Simon Warner 2h 48m 11s.
10 Brendan Crealey/ Honda Civic VTi
Nicky Beech 2h 52m 57s.

Championship points. Drivers (overall): **1** Burns 25; **2** McRae 21; **3** Finlay 18. Formula 2: **1** Llewellin 25; **2** Higgins 21; **3** Bennett 18.

Pirelli International Rally, Mobil 1/Top Gear Round 2, 17-18 April.

1 Richard Burns/ Subaru Legacy RS
Robert Reid 1h 55m 42s.
2 Malcolm Wilson/ Ford Escort RS Cosworth
Bryan Thomas 2h 01m 34s.
3 Gwyndaf Evans/ Ford Escort RS Cosworth
Howard Davies 2h 01m 48s.
4 Dougie Watson-Clark/ Ford Escort RS Cosworth
Ian Connelly 2h 03m 24s.
5 Jonny Milner/ Audi Quattro S2
Mike Corner 2h 06m 26s.
6 Rob Barry/ Ford Escort RS Cosworth
Allan Whittaker 2h 08m 57s.
7 Chris Birkbeck/ Vauxhall Astra GTE
Mike Kidd 2h 09m 20s.
8 Peter Stephenson/ Ford Sierra RS Cosworth 4x4
James Burns 2h 10m 26s.
9 Brian Bell/ Ford Escort RS Cosworth
Philip Mills 2h 11m 00s.
10 Kevin Curran/ Ford Sierra RS Cosworth 4x4
Simon Warner 2h 12m 04s.

Championship points. Drivers (overall): **1** Burns 50; **2** Wilson 36; **3** Evans 34; Formula 2: **1** Crealey 37; **2** Ruck 30; **3** Wedgbury 28.

Perth & Kinross Scottish Rally, Mobil 1/Top Gear Round 3, 4-6 June.

1 Richard Burns/ Subaru Legacy RS
Robert Reid 2h 32m 04s.
2 Alister McRae/ Subaru Legacy RS
David Senior 2h 35m 10s.
3 Robbie Head/ Ford Escort RS Cosworth
Campbell Roy 2h 41m 10s.
4 David Llewellin/ Vauxhall Astra GSi
Ian Grindrod 2h 41m 58s.
5 Malcolm Wilson/ Ford Escort RS Cosworth
Bryan Thomas 2h 42m 41s.
6 Paul Frankland/ Peugeot 205GTI 1.9
Keith Chipchase 2h 46m 20s.
7 Paul Dyas/ Ford Sierra RS Cosworth 4x4
Stuart Derry 2h 47m 01s.
8 Kevin Curran/ Ford Sierra RS Cosworth 4x4
Simon Warner 2h 47m 15s.
9 Jonny Milner/ Audi Quattro S2
Dave Orrick 2h 51m 37s.
10 Peter Stephenson/ Ford Sierra RS Cosworth 4x4
Chris Patterson 2h 53m 03s.

Championship points. Drivers (overall): **1** Burns 75; **2** Wilson 51; **3** McRae 42. Formula 2: **1** Crealey 51; **2** Llewellin 50; **3** Ruck 48.

Village Homes Ulster Rally, Mobil 1/Top Gear Round 4, 30-31 July.

1 Malcolm Wilson/ Ford Escort RS Cosworth
Bryan Thomas 2h 55m 16s.
2 Bertie Fisher/ Subaru Legacy RS
Rory Kennedy 2h 58m 29s.
3 Alister McRae/ Subaru Legacy RS
David Senior 2h 59m 09s.
4 Kenny McKinstry/ Subaru Legacy RS
Robbie Philpott 3h 01m 25s.
5 David Llewellin/ Vauxhall Astra GSi
Ian Grindrod 3h 07m 22s.
6 Gwyndaf Evans/ Ford Escort RS Cosworth
Howard Davies 3h 09m 43s.
7 Paul Frankland/ Peugeot 205GTI 1.9
Mary Fullerton 3h 12m 57s.
8 Robin Phillips/ Ford Escort RS Cosworth
George Millar 3h 15m 25s.
9 Campbell Adams/ Ford Sierra RS Cosworth 4x4
Michael Reid3h 17m 13s.
10 Tony Pond/ Rover Metro GTi
Peter Joy 3h 22m 52s.

Championship points. Drivers (overall): **1** Wilson 81; **2** Burns 75; **3** McRae 68. Formula 2: **1** Llewellin 80; **2** Crealey 51; **3** Ruck 48.

Manx International Rally, Mobil 1/Top Gear Round 5, 15-17 September.

1 R. Burns/ Subaru Legacy RS
R. Reid 3h 36m 54s.
2 K. McKinstry/ Subaru Legacy RS
R. Philpott 3h 37m 51s.
3 R. Head/ Ford Escort RS Cosworth
C. Roy 3h 42m 21s.
4 F. Meagher/ Ford Sierra RS Cosworth 4x4
M. Maher 3h 44m 36s.
5 C. Birkbeck/ Ford Escort RS Cosworth
S. Turvey 3h 47m 04s.
6 J. Cullen/ Ford Escort RS Cosworth
E. Morgan 3h 50m 14s.
7 D. Llewellin/ Vauxhall Astra GSi
I. Grindrod 3h 50m 30s.
8 G. Evans/ Ford Escort RS Cosworth
H. Davies 3h 52m 36s.
9 D. Greer/ Ford Escort RS Cosworth
M. Reid 3h 54m 55s.
10 S. Fenwick/ Ford Sierra RS Cosworth 4x4
P. Bayes 4h 01m 34s.

1 R. Burns 120 points; **2** M. Wilson 91 points; **3** G. Evans 90 points; **4** D. Llewellin 89 points; **5** A. McRae 78 points; **6** J. Milner 61 points.

Mintex National Series Review

OLD VALUES DIE HARD

by Paul Evans, Assistant Rallies Editor, Motoring News

Dougie Watson-Clark hadn't even booked a hotel room for the night after the finish. He had entered the Artemis Rally to collect his ten-point bonus for contesting every round of the Mintex Series. The very idea of winning it outright was ridiculous.

It wasn't the first time the final round of the Mintex National Series had threatened to cause a major upset, but Murray Grierson can rightly feel aggrieved that he was on the receiving end when threat became reality. Already crowned Scottish Champion, he ventured into the North Yorkshire forests only needing to finish in the top 12 of the Artemis Equipment Rally to gain a second title and, when his main rival, Chris Mellors, retired his Sierra on the first stage, the odds improved considerably: a top 17 finish would suffice. Murray was the first to admit he wasn't driving particularly well, but nevertheless he had stolen a one-second lead after the third stage and extended it to 21 seconds after the next. The situation was a familiar one. He had neither stretched himself nor strained the Metro in taking the lead, and a British championship double looked inevitable. Then, quite unexpectedly, the 6R4 refused to fire up at the start of the longest stage of the rally, Langdale. A bad connection inside the fuel tank had isolated the primary pump and, in such situations, the secondary pump won't draw petrol out on its own. After 11 frantic minutes of tugging wires and checking fuses, the engine sparked into life, although the connection was so weak that the vibration soon severed it completely. Spinning backwards into Mike Horne's abandoned Sierra three corners into the stage didn't help matters, but it just added salt to the wounds when the car eventually stopped halfway through the test.

Dougie Watson-Clark had started the stage well before Grierson, and had no idea that he held a 35-second lead when he reached the end of it. Nor did he realise that he was now locked in a head-to-head fight with David Mann for the championship. Quite simply, whoever won the event, won the title. The Group N Escort man's end of season treat had abruptly turned into a high-pressure struggle for supremacy. Mann, driving the Darell Staniforth-prepared Artemis Celica, couldn't make any inroads into Dougie's lead and a calculated run ensured the title went to the Cumbrian.

Watson-Clark's victory was much more than a *Boy's Own* tale of the underdog beating the favourite. It was a significant one for the National Series, as it laid to rest the controversy surrounding the ethics of pitting homologated cars directly against non-homologated cars in a series which is just one step down from the British Championship. The Association of National Championship Rally Organisers has weathered the prolonged storm that has accompanied the debate with dignity. While new formats have been widely proposed and, in some cases, adopted, the National Series has stuck to its 'anti-apartheid' policy. Four Group A, four Group N and four Group B classes encompass a wide variety of vehicles, extending an open invitation to almost anyone with a rally car and a National A competition licence. The series may not have escaped the recession, but it has fared significantly better than most and, while the British Championship considers whether spending £220,000 on a Formula 2 programme (as Vauxhall did in 1993) would be financially more attractive than the prospect of spending at least the same amount on a Group A four-wheel drive project, the National Series has benefitted from its steadfast philosophy. It was by no means a foregone conclusion that Group N would vanquish Group B this year, but it had remained a possibility throughout. Indeed, the impact of familiar Group B cars is steadily declining for two clear reasons. Firstly, second-hand homologated cars and parts are becoming easier and cheaper to obtain; secondly, the outdated Escorts and Mantas are no match for the latest Group N machines, never mind Group A – a state of affairs highlighted by the fact that a 'showroom category' car won the title for the second year in succession.

'When you see the support the National Series has had in 1993, it's the best out of all the British championships,' claimed its new Champion. 'It proves that a Group N car can still be competitive, as Richard Burns showed in '92 and I suppose I have now. It's all down to commitment and reliability, which is basically what rallying is all about. Our car has proved to be as quick as a clubmans Group A car and the old Group B cars.'

Increasingly, however, even the 'Group B' entries are beginning to look like modern road cars, for wide-arched hybrid specials are being replaced by machinery with a contemporary look, even though it is often fitted with alien parts. The sight of a well-turned-out Escort Cosworth helps to raise the image of the National Series and it scarcely matters if it's fitted with a five-speed gearbox or a Pinto engine. These new age clubmans cars need a home, and the series provides an ideal compromise between regional championships and spending thousands of pounds more for a vehicle to contest internationals. They're competitive too, as Neil Hiorns illustrated when he led the opening stages of the Artemis Forest Rally. The most controversial car of all, the Metro 6R4, which once threatened to suffocate the series even in 2.5-litre guise, has all but disappeared. Grierson has been the sole conservationist to keep the species alive at Mintex level, but even he is giving up the fight to save rallying's albatross from extinction. He argues that outdated cars (his Metro is eight years old, for instance) should neither be banned nor penalised, as they are at a disadvantage against sophisticated modern machines anyway. In addition, he believes that a championship shouldn't restrict itself to just one type of car, be it Group A, Group N or Formula 2. In 1994, the Scottish Champion plans to contest both the National Series and the British Championship in a four-wheel drive Group A machine, and he wouldn't even consider entering either series if the destiny of the title were restricted to drivers of Group N or F2 cars.

After he saw Vauxhall's Formula 2 budget to run an Astra GSi in one five-round series was 'at least ten times' the cost of running a 6R4 in two championships (consisting of a total of 12 rallies, of which Grierson did all but two), convincing Murray that Formula 2 is the cheaper option is difficult. 'I think a lot of people forget that rallying was made for the competitor,' he said. 'People now talk that it has to be entertaining for the spectators, but as far as I'm concerned they get a free day's entertainment anyway and they shouldn't dictate what we're allowed to use. Manufacturers seem to have an awful lot to say about what should be run, but if a manufacturer can't produce a car that can beat a Mk2 Escort, the way around it is not to ban the Mk2 Escort but to produce a car that is capable of beating it. I don't think banning a car, nor handicapping it, is the way to go. I think Group A and Group B cars are exciting and that's the whole idea of being in the sport.'

ANCRO agrees and plans no major changes to the rules in the foreseeable future. 'Business as usual sounds very boring, but if you've got a successful format, why change it?' argues its Chairman, Rod Parkin. Of course, innovations conceived in the National Series (like bonus points for starting all rounds and a prize draw after each rally, awarding free entries on the next) have been copied by other championships. If imitation is the sincerest form of flattery, then ANCRO could be excused for feeling a little smug. However, it is also aware of the fine line that separates standing still from sliding backwards, and it continues to listen to competitors and plan for the future. It is commendable that a band of volunteers can organise the series to such a professional standard. The mere fact that all six Clerks of the Course, including the Chairman and Manager, are on the Committee has contributed to its stability. Politics and personal interests rarely mix, but that combination is currently its greatest strength. Although instigating change for change's sake is a dangerous gamble, one wonders if replacing an event would be the ultimate test of strength, or the equivalent of giving

Stephen Finlay (top left) was the quickest, but generally the unluckiest man in the championship, but Murray Grierson ran him close, a fuel problem with the Metro robbing him of victory when the national crown looked to be his for the taking.

Samson a crewcut. Furthermore, if a rally currently in the series failed to meet the desired standard and competitors urged for its replacement, who on the Committee would make the initial proposal? At the moment all six rallies merit National Series status, and, like the individuals who organise them, they all have their own personalities. They also have their own press relations representatives and the public's awareness varies greatly from rally to rally. The Mazda Car-Line Winter is the best publicised, with its Bournemouth start and the traditional first stage through the town's Lower Gardens Park and along the promenade to Boscombe Pier. It puts the start of all British international rallies to shame, and local enthusiasm contributes to Tudor Publications selling three times as many rally programmes as on any other round of the championship. In some respects, then, the organisers are free to do as they please and standards vary accordingly.

Like any other championship, the Mintex Series has suffered from a lack of money. The new marketing lady at Mintex Don has brought with her new demands and ideas and, while the brake specialist has confirmed its support for a fourth season, the renewed sense of urgency to get the Mintex National Series into non-specialist publications is long overdue.

Despite the costs, the fierce competition and the prestige of becoming National Champion, it remains a friendly championship. It is a widespread view, shared by Watson-Clark among others. Back in 1986, he remembers things were a lot more cut-throat and less sociable in

consequence. When he couldn't find the budget to run a new Group A Sierra Cosworth for the 1987 season, he shed few tears on selling the car to Malcolm Wilson Motorsport and retiring from the sport.

Four seasons elapsed before he returned to competition, driving an Escort on selected events. It was immediately obvious that he had lost none of his speed and, enthusiasm renewed, he contested the 1992 Mintex Series in a Sierra Cosworth 4x4, eventually finishing runner-up in Group N to Burns. The car was sold after he had taken it to eighth on the final event and Dennis Osborne was asked to build an Escort Cosworth for the following year. The target was the Group N title and, after running the machine in while driving it to the south coast for the opening round, he and Ian Connelly finished sixth on the Mazda Winter. However, although he maintains reliability has been a major factor in his success, he was lucky as well. For instance, he ripped wheels off twice – once on the Manx while challenging for the lead and again on the Kayel Graphics while fighting for second – but managed to get to the finish both times, and Osborne reckoned his rally was run when the engine started to overheat on just the second stage of the Kerridge National, yet he eventually finished third.

Nevertheless, having won the series, Watson-Clark would like to progress into the British Championship, although he wants to continue supporting the National Series as much as possible too.

Grierson holds a similar affection for the Mintex contest, even though the title has always eluded him. Despite winning three events and finishing second once, his two non-scores (on the Manx, when he broke a driveshaft and then the final round disappointment) cost him dearly and he could only finish fourth in the final points table.

Chris Mellors eventually finished second to Watson-Clark, after enjoying his most successful season in the Mellors Elliot-prepared Sierra Cosworth. Second overall on the Kayel Graphics was his best result but, even though he and Mann were at times difficult to separate, the new tyre rules which were introduced at the beginning of the season prevented them from battling for the Group A title and prevented Mellors from challenging for the free entry on the RAC Rally. The gentle giant from Chesterfield was one of several drivers running 1992 tyres, which are now too big for Group A. He was therefore placed in the top Group B category. When Group A cars were required to use forestry tyres with a slightly reduced height, the Sierras also had to change from 16-inch to 15-inch rims. However, the smaller wheels wouldn't fit over the brake calipers and no Sierra driver had found a solution by the time the first round started. Mann's Toyota, meanwhile, ran on 15-inch wheels anyway and, as Yokohama already had a suitable tyre, David didn't have a problem.

However, his award was no good to him, since Mann could not afford to contest the RAC Rally despite the free entry. Neither could Watson-Clark, nor Julian Reynolds, who also gained a free ticket to the final round of the World Championship for winning his Group N class and the Formula 2 title. Unless the RACMSA ensures any such awards can be honoured in the future, they will continue to be worthless.

There is little doubt that the National Series is an integral part of the structure of British rallying, filling the void between the BTRDA and the British Championship. ANCRO is not pleased that the latter series has introduced a 'Stepping Stone' category of its own, which has been approved by the RACMSA despite being in contradiction of the basic guidelines set by the MSA's Rally Steering Committee.

Nonetheless, the Mintex organisers can rely on the continued support of the high-profile Shell Scholarship team. Its involvement in the 1994 series will be nothing short of a works Audi UK programme, running a Quattro S2 for its latest protégé, Ashley Blenkhorn. In the past season, the Mintex Series has been largely instrumental in furthering the career of another Shell-supported driver, Martin Rowe. Winning the Manx National (and becoming the first Manxman to do so) was obviously the high point, but the way in which he developed a blistering pace on stage and confident grace off it suggests greater things to come. To leap directly from a Peugeot 205GTI, straight into one of the hottest Group N Escort Cosworths and drive with such maturity is a credit to a 22-year-old. To finish every event without so much as scratching the paintwork is sensational. A bright future awaits him, and he has the personality and intelligence to become one of the sport's great ambassadors. And just think, he didn't even win the Shell Scholarship!

Stephen Finlay dominated the series for much of the year, but there is no trace of his name on the leaderboard. At 26, he must be one of the youngest drivers ever to make a comeback, even though at times he rather wished he hadn't. Almost immediately, it looked as though the year would develop into a two-horse race between Finlay and Grierson, even though the former was, bar four stages, generally quicker on the opening round. However, Finlay's season was to be a frustrating one. A timing error by Dessie Wilson on the Granite City Rally started the rot, dropping them from first to last. Even though the Manx National was his first all-tarmac event for three years, the Ballygawley man led until his Malcolm Wilson Motorsport-prepared Sierra broke its gearbox. With only one score to drop, the Ulsterman's championship aspirations didn't look good and he gave up the chase after finishing second to Grierson on the Kayel Graphics.

Penny Mallory's fortunes could not have provided a stronger contrast and she ultimately denied Finlay even a top ten place in the points table. After a nervous start in her Hendy Ford Motorsport/ Wash & Go Escort Cosworth, the 27-year-old public relations expert from St Albans gradually got to grips with her immaculate Group N machine. It was a frightening beast to control, unfamiliarity with the car not helped by a lack of testing between events but, with considerable guts and determination, Mallory ignored the male taunts that the car was wasted on her and made her critics eat their words with 11th on the final round. Many couldn't understand why the car had not been given to Trevor Smith, who had finished second in the previous year's British Championship in a Hendy Sierra, but Penny proved remarkably adept at gaining media coverage in a championship intended primarily for the moderately financed amateur. It was sheer persistence that landed her the sponsorship deal with Vidal Sasson in the first place. Furthermore, the media attention she has generated, not just for the National Series but for the sport in general, is remarkable. A feature in *The Sun*, another in the cookery section of *The Times*, the cover story in May's issue of *Aerobics & Fitness World* – the list is endless. She has probably gained more publicity than all the other registered contenders put together, which is a great credit to her and a disgrace to others, particularly the perennial whingers who believe finishing third in class merits a BBC documentary.

However, behind all the articles and interviews is an extremely serious rally driver, totally dedicated to the sport and determined to make it to the top. Given the opposition, becoming Ladies National Champion wasn't difficult, but it should boost her confidence nonetheless. Her record was further proof that the

Dougie Watson-Clark (above) and Martin Rowe underlined the worth of a Group N Escort Cosworth at this level, both scoring outright victories, while David Higgins was one of the leading two-wheel drive contenders in the Genesis Sport 205GTI.

Mintex Series can appeal on very different levels.

As in every other championship, more emphasis is being placed on Formula 2. ANCRO approached the new fad cautiously, preferring to study its development in other championships before declaring it to be rallying's only salvation. As it happened, the Formula 2 challenge provided an exciting battle between two British youngsters who have taken unconventional routes in an attempt to get to the top, although a third driver had a chance to steal the title after both failed to finish two rounds. Like most of the awards, the F2 trophy wasn't decided until the final event and, by virtue of scoring more points on the opening round, Julian Reynolds just managed to pip Richard Forster on a tie-break. Although the former is well known for his exploits at the wheel of his Skip Brown-prepared 205GTI, he has never seriously contested the Peugeot Challenge, while Forster has never driven a Peugeot at all, preferring Vauxhalls instead and winning the Nova GSi Super Challenge. Both have subsequently missed out on the headlines, with several good results overshadowed by the impressive Peugeot Challenge press steamroller. Reynolds is a particularly aggressive driver, but has managed to control and direct his enthusiasm into getting results when it matters. Forster soon got to grips with his new Astra GSi, particularly after Tim Ashton Motorsport introduced a new engine management system for the Granite City. Even having the Astra stolen and recovered among the shopping trolleys behind a supermarket before the start of the Kayel Graphics failed to unsettle him, yet a strong end to the season could not deny Reynolds the title.

Nigel Cannell, as expected, scored maximum points on the Manx, but his Toyota Corolla struggled to overcome its age deficit on 'foreign' territory. Nevertheless, consistency also paid dividends, for if Reynolds and Forster had failed to finish the final round, the F2 title would have been his. It remains to be seen whether the new category will catch on at this level. When so much of the championship takes place in the forests, the temptation for the ambitious driver to lay his hands on a four-wheel-drive car is overwhelming.

The Mintex National Series continues to grow from strength to strength, not because of any particularly aggressive marketing or a huge prize fund, but because it offers good events at a sensible price. It should be heartening for other championship organisers to note that offering value for money is still the best way to gain popularity.

The old and the new: Brian Bell was one of the first amateurs to use an Escort (left), while David Mann was always a threat in his trusty Celica.

MINTEX NATIONAL RALLY SERIES RESULTS

MAZDA CAR-LINE WINTER RALLY

Pos	Crew	Car	Time
1	S. Finlay/ D. Wilson	Ford Sierra RS Cosworth 4x4	1h 06m 33s;
2	M. Grierson/ S. Merry	MG Metro 6R4	1h 07m 17s;
3	C. Mellors/ R. Smith	Ford Sierra RS Cosworth 4x4	1h 07m 54s;
4	D. Appleby/ B. Hardie	TPR 4100	1h 08m 10s;
5	D. Mann/ I. Wray	Toyota Celica GT4	1h 08m 34s;
6	D. Watson-Clark/ I. Connelly	Ford Escort RS Cosworth	1h 08m 49s;
7	B. Barton/ D. George	MG Metro 6R4	1h 09m 07s;
8	M. Dodd/ S. McAuley	Ford Sierra RS Cosworth	1h 09m 23s;
9	S. Smith/ B. Hughes	Lancia Delta Integrale	1h 10m 13s;
10	D. J. Williams/ M. Park	Ford Sierra RS Cosworth	1h 11m 19s.

GRANITE CITY RALLY

Pos	Crew	Car	Time
1	M. Grierson/ S. Merry	MG Metro 6R4	1h 06m 48s;
2	D. Gillanders/ C. Roy	Ford Escort RS Cosworth	1h 07m 21s;
3	C. Mellors/ R. Smith	Ford Sierra RS Cosworth 4x4	1h 08m 25s;
4	D. Watson-Clark/ I. Connelly	Ford Escort RS Cosworth	1h 08m 34s;
5	J. McRae/ B. Wilson	Ford Sierra RS Cosworth 4x4	1h 09m 12s;
6	J. Gray/ F. Loudon	Ford Sierra RS Cosworth 4x4	1h 09m 55s;
7	A. Hudson/ N. Hudson	Ford Sierra XR4i	1h 10m 14s;
8	S. Petch/ G. Tindall	Ford Escort RS Cosworth	1h 10m 39s;
9	J. Leckey/ D. Orrick	Ford Escort RS Cosworth	1h 10m 40s;
10	D.J. Williams/ M. Park	Ford Sierra RS Cosworth	1h 10m 43s.

COY-Y-CAT MANX NATIONAL RALLY

Pos	Crew	Car	Time
1	M. Rowe/ C. Wood	Ford Escort RS Cosworth	1h 49m 35s;
2	D. Mann/ I. Wray	Toyota Celica GT4	1h 49m 54s;
3	D. Watson-Clark/ I. Connelly	Ford Escort RS Cosworth	1h 51m 42s;
4	P. Doughty/ J. Freeman	Ford Sierra RS Cosworth 4x4	1h 52m 43s;
5	C. Mellors/ R. Smith	Ford Sierra RS Cosworth 4x4	1h 53m 10s;
6	N. Worswick/ K. Savage	Ford Sierra RS Cosworth 4x4	1h 55m 54s;
7	S. Price/ N. Orr	MG Metro 6R4	1h 56m 03s;
8	S. Petch/ G. Tindall	Ford Escort RS Cosworth	1h 56m 59s;
9	J. Dalton/ A. Davies	Darrian T9	1h 57m 43s,
10	P. Christian/ P. Briggs	Ford Sierra RS Cosworth 4x4	1h 58m 53s.

KERRIDGE NATIONAL RALLY

Pos	Crew	Car	Time
1	M. Grierson/ S. Merry	MG Metro 6R4	1h 19m 31s;
2	S. Finlay/ D. Wilson	Ford Sierra RS Cosworth 4x4	1h 21m 55s;
3	D. Watson-Clark/ I. Connelly	Ford Escort RS Cosworth	1h 22m 11s;,
4	D. Mann/ I. Wray	Toyota Celica GT4	1h 23m 13s;
5	C. Mellors/ R. Smith	Ford Sierra RS Cosworth 4x4	1h 23m 47s;
6	S. Petch/ G. Tindall	Ford Escort RS Cosworth	1h 23m 52s;
7	M. Jones/ A. Morgan	Mitsubishi Galant VR4	1h 24m 23s;
8	T. Ellis-Jones/ H. Lewis	Ford Sierra RS Cosworth 4x4	1h 25m 25s;
9	A. Struthers/ A. Sankey	Ford Escort RS	1h 25m 30s;
10	M. Rowe/ C. Wood	Ford Escort RS Cosworth	1h 25m 41s.

KAYEL GRAPHICS NATIONAL RALLY

Pos	Crew	Car	Time
1	M. Grierson/ S. Merry	MG Metro 6R4	1h 14m 45s;
2	C. Mellors/ B. Goff	Ford Sierra RS Cosworth 4x4	1h 16m 08s;
3	D. Mann/ I. Wray	Toyota Celica GT4	1h 16m 56s;
4	M. Rowe/ C. Wood	Ford Escort RS Cosworth	1h 16m 58s;
5	S. Petch/ G. Tindall	Ford Escort RS Cosworth	1h 17m 19s;
6	V. Wetton/ H. Edwards	VW Golf Rallye	1h 18m 25s;
7	B. Fowden/ P. Morgan	Ford Escort RS Cosworth	1h 18m 40s;
8	S. Smith/ B. Hughes	Lancia Delta Integrale	1h 18m 41s;
9	M. Dodd/ S. McAuley	Ford Escort RS Cosworth	1h 18m 53s;
10	P. Squires/ M. Squires	Ford Escort RS	1h 18m 58s.

ARTEMIS FOREST STAGES RALLY

Pos	Crew	Car	Time
1	D.Watson-Clark/ I. Connelly	Ford Escort RS Cosworth	1h 06m 58s;
2	D. Mann/ I.`Wray	Toyota Celica GT4	1h 07m 31s;
3	M. Rowe/ C. Wood	Ford Escort RS Cosworth	1h 08m 16s;
4	S. Petch/ J. Richardson	Ford Escort RS Cosworth	1h 08m 55s;
5	B. Bell/ P. Mills	Ford Escort RS Cosworth	1h 09m 43s;
6	T. Davies/ R. James	MG Metro 6R4	1h 10m 44s;
7	M. Dodd/ S. McAuley	Ford Escort RS Cosworth	1h 10m 53s;
8	G. Smith/ I. MacIvor	Ford Sierra RS Cosworth 4x4	1h 12m 32s;
9	M. Pollard/ A. Cathers	Ford Sierra RS Cosworth 4x4	1h 12m 49s;
10	A. Tough/ A. Bland	Opel Manta GT/E	1h 13m 16s.

Drivers (overall) T=Total

POSN		1	2	3	4	5	6	7	T
1	Watson-Clark,Douglas	17	20	20	20	12	25	10	112
2	Mellors, Christopher	20	22	19	18	22	0	10	111
3	Mann, David	18	0	22	19	20	22	10	111
4	Grierson, Murray	22	25	0	25	25	0	10	107
5	Rowe, Martin	6	15	25	16	19	20	10	105
6	Petch, Steve	0	18	18	17	18	19	10	100
7	Smith, Gordon	8	11	17	13	9	16	10	76
8	Smith, Steve	14	0	14	15	16	0	10	69
9	Dodd, Marcus	15	0	0	0	15	17	10	57
10	Mallory, Penny	0	6	8	7	11	14	10	56
11	Finlay, Stephen	25	0	0	22	-	-	-	47
12	Forster, Richard	0	5	0	10	8	13	10	46
13	Reynolds, Julian	0	9	0	14	0	11	10	44
14	Bradshaw, Scott	0	0	16	2	3	12	10	43
15	Vassallo, Peter	7	10	-	8	14	0	-	39
16	Bell, Brian	0	2	-	0	13	18	-	33
17	Cannell, Nigel	0	3	15	0	0	5	10	33
18	Pollard, Mark	3	1	0	3	0	15	10	32
19	Wetton, Vince	0	13	-	0	17	0	-	30
20	Williams, David	13	16	-	-	-	-	-	29
21	Hiorns, Neil	10	12	0	-	-	7	-	29
22	Porter, Julian	0	0	7	0	2	8	10	27
23	Shering, David	9	0	10	6	-	-	-	25
24	Moore, Richard	0	-	13	0	10	0	-	23
25	Rocke, John	0	-	4	1	6	10	-	21
26	Jones, Ken	0	8	-	12	-	-	-	20
27	Bennett, Rodney	0	0	1	0	0	9	10	20
28	Appleby, David	19	0	-	-	-	-	-	19
29	Hudson, Andy	0	19	0	-	-	-	-	19
30	Bird, Jason	12	7	0	0	-	-	-	19
31	Bird, Keith	0	14	-	4	-	-	-	18
32	Cossey, Derek	0	-	11	0	7	-	-	18
33	Lockey, James	0	17	-	-	-	-	-	17
34	Young, Philip	5	0	12	0	0	-	-	17
35	Gunningham, Jane	0	0	5	0	0	2	10	17
36	Barton, William	16	-	-	-	-	-	-	16
37	Meadows, Martin	0	0	2	0	0	4	10	16
38	Griffiths, Paul	0	4	-	5	5	-	-	14

Drivers (Group N)

POSN		1	2	3	4	5	6	7	T
1	Watson-Clark, Douglas	25	25	22	25	19	25	10	132
2	Rowe, Martin	16	19	25	20	25	22	10	121
3	Petch, Steve	0	22	20	22	22	20	10	116
4	Smith, Gordon	7	18	19	19	18	18	10	102
5	Bradshaw, Scott	11	14	18	14	15	16	10	87
6	Cannell, Nigel	10	16	17	5	10	14	10	77
7	Dodd, Marcus	22	0	0	0	20	19	10	71
8	Pollard, Mark	13	15	0	15	0	17	10	70
9	Meadows, Martin	8	0	12	12	13	13	10	68
10	Brazier, John	1	12	13	11	14	0	10	61
11	Rocke, John	9	-	14	13	17	0	-	53
12	Shering, David	18	0	15	16	-	-	-	49
13	Bird, Jason	20	17	0	9	-	-	-	46
14	Tate, Dennis	-	-	9	8	11	11	-	39
15	Hammond, Doug	3	10	-	7	9	9	-	38
16	Robertson, Leslie	6	9	11	10	-	-	-	36
17	Gunningham, Jane	0	0	0	0	12	12	10	34
18	Young, Philip	15	0	16	0	0	-	-	31